PATERNOSTER THEOLOGICAL MONOGRAPHS

Methods in the Madness

Diversity in Twentieth-Century Christian Social Ethics

PATERNOSTER THEOLOGICAL MONOGRAPHS

A complete listing of all titles in this series and Paternoster Biblical
Monographs will be found at the close of this book.

PATERNOSTER THEOLOGICAL MONOGRAPHS

Methods in the Madness

Diversity in Twentieth-Century Christian Social Ethics

Anna M. Robbins

Foreword by Alan P. F. Sell

Paternoster:
thinking faith

Paternoster is an imprint of Authentic Media
9 Holdom Avenue, Bletchley, Milton Keynes, MK1 1QR, UK
and
P.O. Box 1047, Waynesboro, GA 30830–2047, USA

10 09 08 07 06 05 04 7 6 5 4 3 2 1

British Library Cataloguing in Publication Data
A catalogue record for this book is available from the British Library

ISBN-10 1–84227–211–X
ISBN-13 978–1–84227–211–4

Printed and bound in Great Britain
for Paternoster
by Nottingham Alpha Graphics

Series Preface

In the West the churches may be declining, but theology—serious, academic (mostly doctoral level) and mainstream orthodox in evaluative commitment—shows no sign of withering on the vine. This series of *Paternoster Theological Monographs* extends the expertise of the Press especially to first-time authors whose work stands broadly within the parameters created by fidelity to Scripture and has satisfied the critical scrutiny of respected assessors in the academy. Such theology may come in several distinct intellectual disciplines—historical, dogmatic, pastoral, apologetic, missional, aesthetic and no doubt others also. The series will be particularly hospitable to promising constructive theology within an evangelical frame, for it is of this that the church's need seems to be greatest. Quality writing will be published across the confessions—Anabaptist, Episcopalian, Reformed, Arminian and Orthodox—across the ages—patristic, medieval, reformation, modern and counter-modern—and across the continents. The aim of the series is theology written in the twofold conviction that the church needs theology and theology needs the church—which in reality means theology done for the glory of God.

Series Editors

For Peter
Fellow pilgrim beyond the madness

Contents

FOREWORD

I have much pleasure in introducing the Reverend Dr Anna Robbins and her book. A native of New Brunswick, Canada, Anna Robbins took a degree in political science at Carleton University, Ottawa, and then proceeded to the Divinity College of Acadia University, Nova Scotia, where she gained masters degrees in religious education and arts (theology). By now she and her husband, Peter, had been ordained, and were jointly serving the Baptist pastorate at Clementsvale, NS. From there they removed to Wales, where Peter became minister of Newtown Baptist Church, and Anna pursued the doctoral studies of which this book is the fruit. Peter is now minister of the historic Beechen Grove Baptist church, Watford, while Anna lectures in theology and contemporary culture at the London School of Theology, an affiliated college of Brunel University, which offers courses from diploma to doctorate.

In recent years there has been a veritable explosion of writings in the field of Christian ethics. In view of the numerous, frequently complex, moral challenges posed to individuals and societies at the present time it is not surprising that many of these studies fall within the category of *applied* Christian social ethics. Their authors are concerned with specific issues such as genetic engineering and economic policy, and they seek to view these in the light of a Christian view of the world. In the last resort, such studies, illuminating and provocative though many of them are, are only as sound as the methodological foundations upon which they are built. Indeed, in some studies the foundations are not clearly exposed or their strength tested. For this reason it is important that some writers are willing and able to devote themselves to methodological questions, standing back from specific pressing issues and reflecting upon the nature and appropriate procedures of Christian social ethics.

Anna Robbins is one such writer. She here compares and contrasts three significant twentieth-century approaches in Christian social ethics, namely, those of Walter Rauschenbusch, Reinhold Niebuhr and the World Council of Churches. In choosing two individuals and one prominent corporate body for consideration she acknowledges that increasingly over the past seventy-five years many ethical publications (no less, incidentally, than theological and ecclesiological ones) have resulted from collaborative study and discussion, much of it trans-confessional in nature. It seems especially appropriate that an analysis of such activity should feature in this book, one of whose prominent themes is the nature and relations of individual and collective responsibility.

In order successfully to bring theologico-philosophical considerations to bear upon Christian socio-ethical method as practised over a century, a number of things are required: a solid grounding in biblical thought, sound historical judgment, competence in philosophical analysis, a firm grasp of ethical theory and knowledge of contemporary theological trends. These features are clearly displayed here, and they lend authority to the author's argument and recommendations. Dr Robbins's book will serve as a major resource to all who are wise enough to ponder the methods of Christian social ethics *before* they dive headlong into the 'issues'. May their tribe increase!

Alan P. F. Sell
Milton Keynes

PREFACE

It was out of a need for answers to some very practical ethical questions that I first came to study theology. Working in the field of international development education for a well-known secular organization, I became frustrated with an anthropology which believed in the goodness of humanity but which could not adequately address the tension between such idealism and the facts of conflict, suffering, and oppression. After several years of reflecting upon issues of social ethics from a theological perspective, I became similarly perplexed by the apparent inability of participants in Christian organizations to do much better. In fact, it seemed that for many Christian groups involved in social ethics, there was far less cohesion, common outlook, and agreement about methods, than for many secular organizations whose membership at least shared a common ideology. Although some work was being accomplished, and occasional grassroots movements were finding means of local empowerment, it appeared that broader ecumenical efforts to achieve consensus or agreement on doing ethics together were faltering. If such appearances were real, then it was essential to try and discover at least some of the reasons for the problems, and to make some tentative suggestions for possible ways forward.

I have come to the present task with commitment and conviction, and also with much fear and trembling. I recognize that my own view is conditioned by my contemporary western culture, and that I have not been a participant in ecumenical ethics gatherings. For some, those facts alone would mitigate against the validity of my voice. Nevertheless, as this study will suggest, such contextual factors should not automatically exclude me from the discussion. If, as will become clear through the argument of the book, methodological issues lie at the heart of the problem, then a theoretical, theological study is both an appropriate and necessary means of addressing some of the issues. Moreover, it will be demonstrated that the social-ethical scene is especially vulnerable to the influences 'in the air' in western philosophy – a situation exacerbated in a globalized world. Only as these issues are examined and addressed from a theological point of view may some of the roadblocks to wide and effective participation in social-ethical discussions be removed. It is to that end that I offer the fruits of the opportunities I have had for study and reflection.

This book represents the culmination of many years of formal theological study, much of which was focused on issues of social ethics. In many ways I am left with more questions than I had at the outset. And yet I find myself with a strengthened conviction that if life is to be lived to the full by an increasing number of people in this world, it will be made possible only as the rich resources of faith and theology are brought to bear on the injustice that too often prevails. It is my sincere desire that what is discussed here in a theoretical capacity will have obvious implications for ethical practice in real situations, for the real church - in the richness of diversity and yet one in Christ.

Anna M. Robbins
London School of Theology
May 2004

Acknowledgements

Thankfully, a commitment to the theological task is not a lonely one. I am grateful to those who made library and archive resources available, including Mr Pierre Beffa at the WCC in Geneva, Mrs Susan Hughes at the United Theological College in Aberystwyth, and others at libraries and archives in Aberystwyth, London, Oxford, Wolfville, and Rochester.

I am further indebted to my teachers at Acadia Divinity College who nurtured my first of many steps in the study of theology; to my students at the London School of Theology, who not only encourage me to keep asking tough questions, but who wrestle with the possible answers along with me; and to my colleagues who, through their own commitments, provide a constant motivation towards excellence in teaching, research, and Christian service. Professor Alan P. F. Sell made this project possible in many ways, as supervisor and mentor. His eirenical spirit constantly challenges my prejudices, and his reasoned eclecticism invites continuing work on theological and ethical method in a varied philosophical climate.

The congregations of several churches followed the progress of this work, particularly those in Clementsvale, Newtown, and Beechen Grove Baptist Churches. Throughout, I have depended on their fellowship and prayers. The Welsh Presbyterians offered the practical encouragements of providing both a scholarship and regular preaching venues, which helped to keep potentially cerebral work anchored in the stuff of real life.

In recent days, I have become deeply appreciative of friends at the Evangelical Alliance, particularly Rev. Joel Edwards and Dr. David Hilborn, who have either drawn on the latter fruit of this work, or facilitated its continuation and dissemination. They offer great encouragement that the time and effort spent on academic research is of some practical use to the church.

Many thanks are due to Mr Jeremy Mudditt at Paternoster Press for his good-natured assistance, and unobtrusive but persistent prodding, and to Dr Anthony Cross for offering careful attention to the manuscript. I am similarly grateful to those who read the manuscript and offered constructive comments, and to Ms Annette Glaw for her help in formatting the work, and compiling lists for the indexes.

Friends and family in Canada may sometimes wonder what all of this is about, but they have surrendered me to two Kingdoms, and I thank them for their understanding. My husband Peter offers true companionship and joy in the journey. His confidence in me, and unwavering support of all my work, means more than the dedication of this book is able to express.

Abbreviations

AJT	*American Journal of Theology*
AJTP	*American Journal of Theology and Philosophy*
BJT	*British Journal of Theology*
C&C	*Christianity and Crisis*
CC	*Christian Century*
CQ	*Congregational Quarterly*
CT	*Christianity Today*
CTJ	*Christian Theological Journal*
EpRev	*Epworth Review*
ER	*Ecumenical Review*
ERT	*Evangelical Review of Theology*
EvQ	*Evangelical Quarterly*
ExpTim	*Expository Times*
Int	*Interpretation*
IRM	*International Review of Mission*
JChSt	*Journal of Church and State*
JCTR	*Journal of Theological Research*
JES	*Journal of Ecumenical Studies*
JRE	*Journal of Religious Ethics*
JREd	*Journal of Religious Education*
JRelS	*Journal of Religious Studies*
JSP	*Journal of Social Philosophy*
MC	*Modern Churchman*
MQR	*Mennonite Quarterly Review*
MS	*Mid-stream*
MT	*Modern Theology*
OW	*One World*

Phil   *Philosophy*
PSB   *Princeton Seminary Bulletin*
PSC   *Philosophical and Sociological Criticism*
RL   *Religion in Life*
SCE   *Studies in Christian Ethics*
SJRS   *Scottish Journal of Religious Studies*
SJT   *Scottish Journal of Theology*
TToday *Theology Today*
USQR Union Seminary Quarterly Review

CHAPTER 1

The Way of the Philosopher or the Fool?

The danger threatening the institution is that outward observance will be substituted for inward surrender. But the besetting sin of the fellowship is that harmony will be preferred to holiness, popularity to principle, and unanimous resolutions to obedience to the word of God.

H. F. Lovell Cocks

There is inexhaustible meaning in the statement that God has chosen the foolish things of the world to put to shame them that are wise, and the weak things to confound those that are strong, but there is all the difference in the world between believing that and supposing that God takes delight in immaturity, incompetence, wishy-washiness and muddle.

J. H. Oldham

The Nature of the Problem

At a time when contextual factors loom large in ethical interpretation, the expression of Christian unity on social issues may seem like a dream from a by-gone era. For many, epistemological foundations have crumbled, ethics have become a relativistic matter of culture, and reaching consensus is seen to be not only impossible, but undesirable. In the midst of our fragmentation, we comfort ourselves by telling stories in the dark.

Each of our stories describes an experience of the world that is uniquely ours. The stories relate our feelings to others, and in the midst of the telling, we hope we communicate something of truth. We may nod together in agreement that the stories are true. They may make us who we are, as we are made in the telling. But they do not, necessarily, tell us what to do. When we meet together with other Christians locally, or in a wider scale, it becomes enormously difficult to determine a course of action to which everyone may subscribe. Moreover, appeals to the Christian narrative seem insufficient to overcome the divisions between us, as we succumb to the pressure to admit a plurality of Christian narratives, which represent our various experiences of the world. We end up with a situation that complicates rather than clarifies our potential action on issues of deep concern.

Often times, the best that can happen is for all delegates at a given meeting to agree on a generally-worded statement that is interpreted in whatever way its members desire when they have returned to their own churches. On other occasions, we may not be able to get even that far. Take, for example, the case of a local ecumenical group that meets to discuss how Christians might build bridges to their community, and minister to its needs. They all agree that this is an important and significant thing to do. But some interpret the task as one of social action, and others as one of evangelism. Some want to improve the public image of the church in community, and others to get more warm bodies in pews. Their differences are not simply a matter of interpretation of what it means to build bridges to the community. Their differences reflect varied presuppositions about the very nature of approaching ethics, embracing philosophy, theology and practical factors. When Christians show up at such meetings, they each represent an entire web of understanding, which weaves together their doctrines of God, sin, and salvation; philosophical understandings of what we can know and how we know it; practical ideas about how these things relate to the world of experience. Why is it so difficult for them to decide together how to engage the task? Why do their meetings often end up in dissension and disagreement? We are vulnerable to the philosophical forces in the air: In a world of fragmentation, and philosophical ambiguity, Christians often find it difficult to swim against the tide.

The fable is recounted of a Philosopher who saw a Fool beating his donkey. He implored the Fool to abstain from such cruel behaviour, exhorting that, 'those who resort to violence shall suffer from violence.' The Fool assured him that was the very thing he was trying to teach the beast which had kicked him. "Doubtless," said the Philosopher to himself, as he walked away, "the wisdom of Fools is no deeper nor truer than ours, but they really do seem to have a more impressive way of imparting it".[1]

The parable highlights the significance of method for our ethical dialogue as Christians from varying traditions. Social ethics cannot be simply a matter of assenting to the same words and principles if the methods – the practical representation of the presuppositions of doctrine and philosophy - that lie behind them and work themselves out in wisdom or madness are categorically opposed. We may find ourselves agreeing in word, but when we try to implement our understanding of those agreements, our unity suddenly collapses into fragmented reflections of our social concern. It is not surprising when little is accomplished.

Whether in local church organisations or global meetings, a lack of consideration for the importance of method, and for the diversity of methods that find expression around the meeting table, and in practical application, can lead discussions and good intentions into dead-end alleyways. On the other hand, an awareness of methodological factors, though representative of more

---

[1]Ambrose Bierce, *A Matter of Method,* taken from the website: http://www.pacificnet.net/~johnr/cgi?ab&AmatterofMethod

pain-staking and time-consuming labour, may lead to agreements that are more comprehensive and enduring. The practical result may be dramatically more significant. In a world of stories, we still need to know what to do, and how to decide what to do, as individuals, and communities of faith.

If any sense is to be made of the contemporary ethical task, clarification of meta-ethical methodology must be seen as a crucial issue. In the past two decades, it became abundantly clear to many, if not most, participants in ecumenical Christian social ethics that the field of social ethics was in rough shape.[2] At the end of the Conciliar Process of Mutual Commitment to Justice, Peace and the Integrity of Creation in 1990, many recognised that serious methodological issues needed to be confronted if ecumenical ethics in organizations such as the World Council of Churches were to have a future at all. The key motives for the present study arise from the confused state of Christian social ethics at the cusp of transition to a new era, fraught with anxiety, uncertainty, triviality, complacency, and suspicion.[3] A comparative study of different ways of 'doing' ethics together may help to highlight some of the strengths and weaknesses of each, and suggest some signposts for a way through the confusion.

Identifying the Madness

The challenge to address ethical methodology has been issued from many quarters. Several scholars closely engaged in ecumenical ethics have recognized the present crisis, admitting to the inadequacies of recent approaches, and their inability to move in any concrete direction.[4] Some have attempted to offer helpful paradigms as a way forward, but have found themselves often overlooked, if not disregarded.[5] The need for a study of methodologies in Christian social ethics begins to emerge as essential, if Christians are to understand not only their own theological presuppositions, but also their complex relationships with other approaches within Christendom.

---

[2] The documentary evidence of a critique by a group of predominant, and largely retired, ecumenists confirms this. For example, see *The Future of Ecumenical Social Thought*, Report of an informal discussion of church leaders, theologians, social ethicists and laity, Berlin, May 29-June 3, 1992. The critique of 'the Berlin Group' will be covered in more depth in Chapter 10.

[3] Similar tendencies were observed by P. T. Forsyth nearly a century ago. See Peter Taylor Forsyth, *Positive Preaching and the Modern Mind* (London: Hodder and Stoughton, 1917), 169ff.

[4] See Emilio Castro's editorial, and the accompanying articles in *ER* 43 (July 1991). Cf. Shin Chiba *et. al.* eds., *Christian Ethics in Ecumenical Context: Theology, Culture, and Politics in Dialogue* (Grand Rapids, MI: Eerdmans, 1995).

[5] Members in the group mentioned previously do not receive as much attention as they ought, considering their vast experience and degree of expertise. Indeed, documents and letters suggest they have been sometimes summarily and angrily dismissed.

Such work is desperately needed if the church is to engage effectively with any of the deep social concerns that cry out for justice in the contemporary world.

This study seeks to take up at least a small part of the methodological challenge presented by several scholars and ecumenical participants. In *Confusions in Christian Social Ethics,* Ronald Preston suggests that the state of social ethics in the World Council of Churches is nearly beyond repair, and that theology and practice must be held together if any recovery is to be made.[6] His concern for the state of Christian social ethics is echoed through a group of ecumenists who have met several times in the past decade to discuss how the present crisis might be addressed. There is an important suggestion in their work that any new approach must take into consideration those methods of the past which were effective and helpful, but which have since been neglected - a conviction which will be affirmed at various stages of the present study.[7]

Further, Alan Sell has elaborated the challenge to social ethics as including questions of philosophical method, as Christians encounter pluralism both within and without the faith. Christians must understand, he argues, from whence their moral arguments and statements come, and their implications, if progress is to be made at all.[8] A stronger ethical theology and an understanding of its relationship to moral philosophy will provide helpful building blocks for a practical ethic which is able to withstand challenges, and yet is flexible enough to demonstrate its relevance to society's needs, in an age where change seems to be the only enduring concept.

Similar thoughts pervade the work of other direct observers. Douglas John Hall, in his reflection on one process of the World Council of Churches, expressed his concern for the state of ecumenical ethical methodology. Expressing ideas in sympathy with Lovell Cocks's concern registered at the opening of this chapter, Hall stated with courage that, 'the very *first* requirement for ecumenical Christian dialogue today is that all participants must learn to distinguish between genuine solidarity with the oppressed on the one hand, and the sort of passive public agreement that is born, not of Christian love, but of a combination of diplomacy, guilt and fear of conflict.'[9] Fragmentation and rugged contextualisation mean that, as the church, 'we are fast becoming incapable of *knowing* what we think, let alone articulating it in public.'[10] Concerned that the pressure for the church to pursue ever new approaches and contextualized methods means that the lessons of the past and the unity of the present might be lost, Hall queries, 'What if, while enthusiastically discovering the pertinence of the Evangel for the problems and

---

[6]Ronald Preston, *Confusions in Christian Social Ethics* (London: SCM Press, 1994).
[7]Roger Shinn cited in ibid., 178.
[8]Alan P. F. Sell, 'A Renewed Plea for Impractical Divinity,' *SCE* 8 (1995): 68-91.
[9]Douglas John Hall, 'The State of the Ark: Lessons from Seoul,' *Between the Flood and the Rainbow,* compiled by D. Preman Niles (Geneva: WCC, 1992), 37.
[10]Ibid.

possibilities of our immediate situation, we were to lose touch with the larger historical tradition as well as with other provinces of the oikoumene?'[11] We need to remember that the church does not approach the contemporary situation in a vacuum of time, and with a singularity of belief.

Another long-time ecumenist decries the loss of ecumenical memory, and the consequent state of ecumenical ethical reflection.[12] Thirty years ago, Paul Abrecht highlighted the difficulty of understanding how much theological agreement was needed before an authentic word could be spoken or action taken.[13] He further pointed to the tension that was developing between an ethic based on principles and one that sought to be more contextual.[14] Prophetically, he stated that 'as the pressures for rapid change in society increase, the polarization of opinion in our Churches on basic social questions will undoubtedly become greater rather than diminish. The continuing division of the Churches on basic issues of theology and ecclesiology also weakens the possibility of a more substantial Christian witness.' This was all that could be hoped for, considering that up to that time 'ecumenical consensus on Christian social responsibility (had) been limited, experimental, and provisional, and with relatively slight impact on the action of the Churches in society.' Abrecht possessed 'no doubt' that 'the ecumenical witness will become more difficult in the future.'[15] He was able to confirm the accuracy of this prediction by the early and mid 1990s.

By this time, the confusion in Christian social ethics reached new proportions of 'madness'. In response, some offered an ethic based on a theology that responded to the most recent post-modern philosophical challenge by focusing on the church as a morally formative community, but one which finds it undesirable - indeed impossible - to say anything meaningful in the public realm. The need for clarification of how they reached this conclusion, and an assessment of how they piece together their approach is crucial to an understanding of the contemporary situation.[16]

---

[11]Ibid.

[12]In various articles, documents and letters, this is the consistent critique of long-time ecumenist, Paul Abrecht. Abrecht's critique will be considered in Chapter 10.

[13]Paul Abrecht, 'The Development of Ecumenical Social Thought and Action,' *A History of the Ecumenical Movement, 1948-1968,* ed. Harold E. Fey, 3rd ed., Geneva: WCC, 1993.

[14]Ibid., 258.

[15]Ibid., 259.

[16]Former WCC librarian Ans van der Bent expressed the conviction that ecumenical ethics was often guilty of neglecting methodological concerns, suggesting that the WCC has the problem of making lots of contextual proclamations, and doing neither the background work to support them, nor the practical work to see them applied in an effective way. See Ans van der Bent, *Commitment to God's World: A Concise Critical Survey of Ecumenical Social Thought* (Geneva: WCC, 1995). The need for methodological work is also confirmed by Robin Lovin, *Reinhold Niebuhr and*

As these and other theologians, philosophers and practitioners have implied either directly or indirectly, a study of methodology offers the potential to understand how philosophy and theology have contributed to the formation of various ethical approaches, and how theoretical aspects work out in, and are influenced by, various contexts - a crucial practical concern in an increasingly pluralistic world. In the contemporary situation, there is no agreement that there must be a Christian voice, let alone how that voice should be defined, what it should say, and how it should be said. The danger in the midst of such a crisis is that mutually contradicting ecclesial pronouncements on socio-ethical matters will be made, each of which claims to speak for 'the church' and actually speaks for a less than truly representative group. The tragedy would be if the church withdrew from ethical reflection on public issues, risking disengagement, irrelevance, and the denial of its responsibility for public witness.

While complete agreement on ethical issues may be impossible, a study in methodology will encourage Christians with various backgrounds and approaches to at least seek to understand the importance of discussing their diverse theological and philosophical presuppositions in a more constructive manner. This may pave the way for an interaction with society that is truly prophetic, maintaining the centre of common faith in the Cross of Christ, and allowing the church to speak from and to the needs of this generation. In this study I shall attempt to explore some of these issues through an examination of theological, philosophical, and practical method in Christian social ethics.

It should be immediately obvious that this challenge comprises not only a 'precarious enterprise' but also an immense task.[17] The need to narrow the scope and define an approach that will help to identify the main methods, and analyse their differences is evident. In this study, I will seek to uncover several methods of ecumenical ethics from the past century as 'gifts to the church', very much connected to the intellectual and practical influences of their time.[18] The contention is that the various philosophical and theological impulses, which were 'in the air' and informed the culture of a particular historical period, largely determined the method that dominated ecumenical ethics for that time, finding expression in various documents and statements. In other words, the content of statements issued by ecumenical bodies do not tell the

---

Christian Realism (Cambridge: Cambridge University Press, 1995); and by Donald Hay, 'What Does the Lord Require? Three Statements on Christian Faith and Economic Life,' *Transformation* (January 1993): 10-15.

[17]Abrecht describes the pursuit of Christian social ethics as 'a precarious enterprise.' 'The Development of Ecumenical Social Thought and Action', 259.

[18]I borrow this phrase from Stanley Hauerwas, despite disagreement with some aspects of his method. The concept of studying the contributions of individuals as 'gifts to the Church' is highlighted in Samuel Wells, *Transforming Fate into Destiny: The Theological Ethics of Stanley Hauerwas* (Carlisle: Paternoster Press, 1998).

whole story, though they may point to it, or confirm assumptions about it. Such documents need to be seen in their broader context, as expressions of the balance struck between various participants, and generally expressing the dominant philosophical and theological influences of the day, or at least of that meeting.

If it is the case that ethical methods reflect their contemporary philosophical climates, then, when we consider the intellectual climate of contemporary culture, we should not be surprised to find ecumenical ethics in a state of 'madness'. And we may be reasonably confident that the situation need not remain this way forever. Nevertheless, the task facing the church is an urgent one. Is it possible that as we explore the gifts of ethical methods from the past that we may be provided with clues as to what direction social ethics might take from here? Could it be that if we retrace our steps to a place where social ethics were most effective that we might learn something of how to beat a clearer path through the present disarray? Is it possible for the church in all of its diversity to agree on ways of addressing social issues so that as much is done as is said, maintaining an active witness that reflects both justice and unity?

Seeking a Method

In an attempt to answer these questions, an examination of several methods in twentieth-century Christian social ethics will be undertaken. First of all, the social gospel approach of Walter Rauschenbusch will be explored, considering some philosophical impulses in chapter two, and theological impulses in chapter three. Along the way, reflection will focus on the relationship between philosophy and theology, and the degree to which one or the other took precedence in his method. The next 'sounding' will be taken from several years later, analysing the realist method of Reinhold Niebuhr. I shall explore some philosophical influences in chapter four, and highlight some elements of Niebuhr's theology in relation to his ethical approach in chapter five.

In chapter six, I intend to consider how Rauschenbusch's social gospel and Niebuhr's realism worked out in ecumenical social ethical method. This will demonstrate further that not only are these two methods reflective of various influences of their day, but that they in turn influenced the approach to ethics taken by an ecumenical body, namely the World Council of Churches. In chapter seven, I shall explore how these methods work out in ecumenical discourse, confirming that even the method of ethical discourse presupposes a host of philosophical and theological interactions, which are largely dependent on the dominant ethical method of any particular historical period. Through this discussion, three particular methods of social ethics within the WCC are identified, including the study-dialogue approach of the realist period; the action-reflection model of the revolutionary period; and the moral formation method of the contemporary period. Some suggestions are made as to how the benefits of each might be understood in relation to one another in order for a method of integrity to be developed.

The philosophical and theological climate that gave rise to the action-reflection model is examined critically in chapter eight, while in chapter nine the moral formation approach is explored. Then, in chapter ten, I shall outline some practical concerns of recent critics of ecumenical social ethics and seek to address those concerns in light of conclusions drawn from previous chapters. An adaptation is made of the middle axiom approach, in order to suggest a practical method of ethical dialogical integrity which incorporates the best insights of twentieth-century ethical theory, and which addresses some of the concerns of the contemporary post-modern climate. In this concluding chapter, I shall argue for a necessary but critical retrieval of important aspects of the ecumenical memory - particularly those of the realist period - in order for Christian social ethics to be able to be effective in a fragmented world in need of reconciliation and renewal.

In order to define and clarify further the task at hand, these various methods will be examined primarily on the basis of their portrayal and understanding of the nature and interaction of individual and collective moral agency. In some ways, it may seem that this is too obvious a path to take. After all, Ronald Preston has suggested that issues between the person and the collective 'are perennial in discussions of political philosophy and political institutions.'[19] However, making the bald statement that 'neither should be pursued without reference to the other,' is not the same as saying that their aspects or relationships are clearly identified and addressed in Christian social ethical methods.[20] To the contrary, it may be argued that a confusion of their aspects and relationships, and disagreement over the nature of each is a large part of the source of that disarray which plagues Christian social ethics today. At very least, clarifying the way in which both aspects are understood by various methods offers a means of assessing the similarities and differences between the methods themselves.

And yet, it may well be far more significant as an issue of ethical method than at first it seems. For while this individual-community dynamic may seem evident to some thinkers, others believe it is a crucial and central aspect that requires clarification. Even when social ethics seemed less confused than they do at present, at least one thinker recognised the importance of clarifying individual and collective aspects of moral agency. In *The Divine Imperative*, Emil Brunner suggested that unlike theologians of a generation or two before, many contemporary thinkers seem to have failed to recognize 'the subject of the individual and the community as a problem of adjustment.'[21] It has been the task of ethics to balance the mutual claims of the individual and the

---

[19]Ronald Preston, 'The Common Good,' *Ep Rev* 24 (January 1997), 17.
[20]Ibid.
[21]Emil Brunner, *The Divine Imperative*, trans. Olive Wyon, 2nd edn. (London: Lutterworth, 1937), 293.

community, while taking into account the rights of both, making the necessary adjustments in a just manner. Brunner describes the problem as it has been addressed in theology and philosophy throughout history

> The experience of humanity shows us how both these one-sided tendencies, a one-sided individualism and a one-sided collectivism, are perpetually involved in conflict with one another. Now it will be the tendency to break up the historically existing forms of community, to emancipate the individual, which will gain the upper hand, and then the pendulum will swing in the other direction, and the freedom of the individual will be suppressed by collectivism. This conflict already appears in Ancient Greece - for instance, between Socrates and the Athenian *Polis* - we see it again in the struggle for liberty at the close of the Middle Ages, in the Renaissance and the Reformation, and once more, in modern times, between the 'individualism of a Nietzsche, a Kierkegaard and an Ibsen,' one the one hand, and Socialism and Communism on the other.[22]

Brunner did not believe this to be a simplification of the problem, nor a misreading of history. He elaborated

> We do not perceive that this superficial classification violates historical reality, and 'lumps together' the most incompatible elements....On the other hand, however, if we go deeply enough, we see how closely Marxist Socialism and Communism is related to the individualism of the Enlightenment of the eighteenth century; what a great gulf lies between Luther's protest against the authority of the Catholic Church and the philosophy of Jean-Jacques Rousseau! The fact that an individual arises to protest against a collective force is an event which may mean all kinds of different things, just as a mass movement may mean many different things. Evidently, this problem demands some clear thinking, if this confusion is to be removed.[23]

Thus, it is fair to say that the confusion which still exists in ecumenical ethics today is, at least in part, a result of the failure of thinkers to think clearly on precisely this issue. In social ethics, more than any other theological field, the necessity to clarify and understand the intricacies of the relationship of the individual to the collective is apparent, yet seriously neglected. The pendulum-swing described by Brunner makes itself evident in a methodological analysis of Christian social ethics of the past century, such that we are able to witness the fact that the church has ended up in the state of confusion he indicated would arise when such aspects were not clarified. An examination of methodological elements with respect to individual and collective agency offers the potential of relativizing our present situation sufficiently to access some measure of objectivity by which our own theological presuppositions and philosophical tendencies might be evaluated.

---

[22]Ibid., 293-4.
[23]Ibid.

This task is all the more important because community, collectivity, common good, and individuality are far from static concepts, seeking to be defined once and for all. They constantly beg for re-examination and adjustment to the needs of an ever-changing society. While this will lead to some degree of ambiguity and partiality, we need not be defeated or discouraged. Rather, the partly transitory nature of such concepts may be understood as being 'very congenial to the dynamics of the Christian faith.'[24] When the resources of Christianity come to bear on these concepts and their concomitant issues, they may make the pathway far more clear, and not necessarily only for those within the Christian community.

Through this struggle to make sense of various approaches, I may not have succeeded in sorting out one clearly defined ethical method. However, I have become particularly aware of several things. First, that it is important and possible to come to recognise the advocates of various methods, and to understand the elements of the diverse plans they have set out for themselves and the church. This helps to identify better and worse ways of doing social ethics. Second, some methods relegated to the past have not been exhausted of their usefulness to the church, though their contemporary manifestations may end up looking quite different from their previous incarnations. Third, there is a socio-ethical mission for the church in a world that is often described as 'postmodern'. Indeed, such a mission is urgent. Recognising the diversity of the church need not nullify its potential to speak and act in ways that bear witness to its mission. Fourth, although social ethics are not entirely ambiguous, their complexity means that any suggestions such as those made here must be offered with humility and at least a degree of tentativeness. The things I have learned from conducting this study have strengthened my conviction that there must always be room for grace and mystery, as well as for confidence, in theology. Whether I have ended up as the Philosopher or the Fool is for the reader to decide.

---

[24]Preston, 'The Common Good,' 19.

CHAPTER 2

The Consciousness of God: Philosophical Impulses in Walter Rauschenbusch's Social Gospel Method

When I am in the consciousness of God,
My fellowmen are not far-off and forgotten,
But close and strangely dear.
Those whom I love
Have a mystic value.
They shine, as if a light were glowing within them.
Even those who frown on me
And love me not
Seem part of the great scheme of good.
(Or else they seem like stray bumble-bees
Buzzing at a window,
Headed the wrong way, yet seeking the light.)

Walter Rauschenbusch, The Little Gate to God

Introduction

In the introduction to a new edition of Walter Rauschenbusch's *A Theology for the Social Gospel,* Donald Shriver notes that Rauschenbusch shared the vision of many Protestants at the turn of the nineteenth century who believed 'that institutions and groups can repent. They can respond to the promise and presence of the Kingdom by advancing human relations to new planes of justice and love.'[1] The aspect of collective moral agency in Rauschenbusch's work is apparent and has been noted by most scholars who have sought to analyse any aspect of his thought. But scant attention has been paid to the method that led him to develop such a thoroughly social approach to Christian ethics. Of particular interest is how Rauschenbusch approached philosophy and theology, and how they, in turn, informed and directed his practical method. What sort of philosophy influenced Rauschenbusch's collective interpretation

---

[1]Donald Shriver, Introduction to *A Theology for the Social Gospel* by Walter Rauschenbusch, (1917; reprint, Library of Theological Ethics, Louisville, KY: Westminster/John Knox Press, 1997), xix.

of humanity and morality? Was it determined by his theology, or was his theology determined by it? Was his practical approach consistent with his theoretical method? In this chapter, I will seek to answer the first of these questions, considering how idealist philosophy shaped Rauschenbusch's understanding of moral agency in collective terms, how he developed the idea of collective consciousness, and how his approach to human solidarity may be distinguished from evolutionary ethics.

Philosophical Idealism and the Collective Idea

While many have noted the influence of various idealist philosophers on Rauschenbusch's method, few have elaborated on that influence, or explained how it contributed to Rauschenbusch's interpretation of social ethics. The particular concern here is to demonstrate how idealism, especially the approaches of Immanuel Kant and Josiah Royce, informed Rauschenbusch's collective understanding of personhood and ethics, and the nature of society. Moreover, it is essential to grasp how, through an idealist philosophy, Rauschenbusch's method balanced the role of the individual will with the moral agency of the community. An understanding of this philosophical basis will illustrate how Rauschenbusch's method allows for an essentially collective interpretation of moral agency, upon which his theology and practical programme are built.

In his thorough study of British idealism, Alan Sell has highlighted the varied expressions and interpretations into Christian thought-forms of this philosophical school.[2] When idealism was widely adopted and adapted by theologians and ethicists at the turn of the nineteenth century, such variety found increase at the hands of those representing diverse disciplines. As an historian, and not primarily a theologian or philosopher, Rauschenbusch elaborated an ethical method that combined numerous idealist influences as he sought to gather together several strands of thought across social-scientific and theological disciplines. The result was an eclectic mix of transcendent and immanent idealism, filtered often unsuccessfully through elements of Christian doctrine. A serious contradiction in his thought emerged from an attempt to borrow thought-forms and categories that did not easily reconcile with some statements he wanted to make about human nature from a Christian point of view. In spite of this contradiction, it is clear that idealism in a broad sense bequeathed to Rauschenbusch the tools he needed to construct a method based on a collective interpretation of humanity, where the role of the individual was present, but relegated to a subservient role *vis-à-vis* the community.

A discussion of idealism's influence on Rauschenbusch's development of the social idea begins with his response to the philosopher Immanuel Kant.

---

[2]Alan P. F. Sell, *Philosophical Idealism and Christian Belief* (Cardiff: University of Wales Press, 1995).

While Kant stressed the role of the individual moral agent in actions of the will, he also discussed the relationship between the individual and society as a whole. It was this aspect of his thought that captured Rauschenbusch's imagination. He borrowed from Kant the idea of an ethical commonwealth, to which and for which individuals were responsible. Such responsibility was not enforced by coercion, but represented a free association of individuals for the good of the community. Rauschenbusch affirmed Kant's interpretation

> The lofty mind of Immanuel Kant was inspired with a religious enthusiasm by contemplating the possibility of an ethical commonwealth, a kingdom of virtue, in which right action would not, as in the State, be due to coercion, but to the free devotion of all. He held that in the past the upward aspirations of the individual have been corrupted or checked by the influence of society, which was a social force dominated by evil; therefore a new organization of society is needed, consciously dedicated to righteousness, which will support and train the weak will of the individual. Such a Kingdom of God would be at once the highest good and the highest duty. Its realization is not like other duties from man to man, but is a duty that the race owes to the race, the duty of realizing its divine destiny. It is a duty so vast that it transcends the powers of man; God alone can bring it to reality. But because we feel the duty, we may conclude that the Ruler of the moral universe is behind it and is cooperating with us, and each of us must work for it as if all depended on himself.[3]

Perhaps no single statement more clearly portrays the philosophical foundation of Rauschenbusch's method than this description of Kant's approach.

Rauschenbusch immediately seized upon this interpretation of Kant as a philosophical expression of his own understanding of the kingdom of God, a community that would take the 'raw material' of human existence, and raise it to a higher level through conviction and co-operation. The mind of God, present in this new, dynamic community initiated by Jesus, would indwell the community and work out his will through a common bond of fraternal understanding, most often referred to as 'sympathy' or 'love'. Rauschenbusch saw how Kant's notion of the 'church' could assist his analysis and interpretation of the present social crisis and how the need for justice ought to be addressed, although, 'by "church" Kant meant primarily the complete organization of humanity under the moral law in a universal society,' rather than a formal institution. Kant 'contrasted the historical-ecclesiastical church with the pure religious faith of reason in a universal church and rejected most of the historic forms of the church, including the sectarian.'[4] Although critical

---

[3]Walter Rauschenbusch, *Christianizing the Social Order* (New York: Macmillan, 1912), 88-89. Cf. Immanuel Kant, *Religion within the Limits of Reason Alone*, trans. T. M. Greene and H. H. Hudson, (New York: Harper & Row, 1960), Section III.

[4]Donald Smucker, *The Origins of Walter Rauschenbusch's Social Ethics* (Montreal, PQ & Kingston, ON: McGill-Queen's University Press, 1994), 84.

of the church's socio-ethical expression throughout history, Rauschenbusch did not join Kant in his extreme renunciation of the institutional church, and remained an active member of ecclesiastical bodies throughout his lifetime. But Rauschenbusch embraced Kant's elaboration of the unity of the human race beyond ecclesiastical boundaries, constrained by will and reason to a universal duty to the good, preferring to speak of the fraternity of humanity rather than emphasise solely the formal and visible organisation of Christianity. In Kant's thought Rauschenbusch found the collective idea he was seeking - 'a familial organization of humanity in a voluntary, universal community of moral law, which is to say, the Kingdom of God.'[5]

Like most ethicists after Kant, whose work was done in his shadow and in reaction to his thought, Rauschenbusch could not embrace Kant's analysis *in toto*, and he joined with many who wanted to move idealism beyond the phenomenal-noumenal divide elaborated by Kant. This led him to make assertions about collective existence, which incorporated a degree of naturalism, especially in his more developed thought. For Rauschenbusch, the unity of the human race was not an abstract notion, but one that found real expression in familial relationships. In this respect, Rauschenbusch moved farther away from Kant as he wanted love to serve as the universal motif of basic human existence, finding expression in the natural realm and not only in relations of the will. For Rauschenbusch, perceiving love as a moral category and a natural instinct did not mean that moral action would be wholly determined, nor that the individual agent lacked moral freedom. As Harlan Beckley has explained, in Rauschenbusch's view, 'humans are agents capable of disposing of their interests. The task of moral agents, however, is not to free themselves from interests, but to order, balance, and integrate their natural interests into habits of character that serve the common good.'[6] According to Stephen Post, 'underlying this interpretation of love is a resistance to the Kantian conception of the moral agent as ahistorical, stripped of the special relations that develop over time between those in proximity, and as abstracted from the familial ties that in reality are such a large part of everyday moral experience for most of us.' Post concludes, 'Rauschenbusch was of course deeply informed by Kant in other respects. But judging from *Dare We Be Christians?* the author rejected the Kantian endeavour to transcend all empirical anthropology and human embeddedness in the phenomenal world of special relations.'[7]

Kant's notions of duty, freedom, and voluntary association in an ethical

---

[5]Ibid.

[6]Harlan Beckley, *Passion for Justice: Retrieving the Legacies of Walter Rauschenbusch, John A. Ryan, and Reinhold Niebuhr* (Louisville, KY: Westminster/John Knox Press, 1992), 73.

[7]Stephen Post, Foreword to *Dare We Be Christians* by Walter Rauschenbusch (1914; reprint ed., Cleveland OH: Pilgrim Press, 1993), viii.

commonwealth gave Rauschenbusch at least the rudimentary tools for building an ethical method that described the role of the individual moral agent as an aspect of collective agency. But Rauschenbusch wanted to go much further in developing a notion of the collective tendency as an expression of the immanent ideal, and turned to other thinkers to supply him with the raw materials for the naturalistic aspects of his thought, which incorporated notions of evolution and progress. Rauschenbusch was keen to interact with the thought of scholars from other disciplines, and he was challenged by them to take on board at least some elements of their evolutionary thought. It is interesting, for example, to note how closely his naturalistic views of the development of society resemble the progressive stages described by Wilhelm Wundt, who used evolutionary theory to undergird his argument that throughout human existence, even in primitive times, unity has been the naturally progressive impulse of human existence.[8]

It is important here to recognize that when Rauschenbusch's thought is being considered as a whole, some generalisations must be made in order to analyse his overall method, which has elements that are not always easily reconciled. A later discussion will demonstrate that Rauschenbusch's variance with Kant regarding naturalism was not always present in his work, and that when it did appear it represented a stark inconsistency in his thought. However, the overall tendency in Rauschenbusch's work was toward an increasing naturalism, which served to strengthen his desire to uphold society as the primary moral agent.

The aspects of idealist interpretation which assisted Rauschenbusch in hallowing the natural instincts of the human race may be found in the work of Josiah Royce, a contemporary of Rauschenbusch whose idealist thought found him wrestling with some of the issues raised for Christian ethics by modern science - issues which Kant may have anticipated but could not fully contemplate. Careful to emphasise the importance of collective existence without losing the individual in the ideal, Royce provided Rauschenbusch with the analysis he needed to balance his understanding of the individual and communal self.

Rauschenbusch described Royce as 'one of the ablest philosophical thinkers [the American] nation has ever produced,' paying tribute to him alongside Washington Gladden and Richard Ely, as men who 'had matured their thought when the rest of us were young men, and they had a spirit in them which kindled and compelled us.'[9] Though not uncritical of Royce's reflections on the

---

[8]See Wilhelm Wundt, *Ethics* [1886], vol. I, *The Facts of the Moral Life,* trans. Julia Gulliver and Edward Titchener (1886; reprint, London: Swan Sonneschein & Co., 1908), 227-293. Wundt provided an explanation of the evolutionary human impetus toward association through family, tribe, and organized society as evidence of the developing social instinct throughout human history.
[9]Rauschenbusch, *Christianizing the Social Order*, 9.

Christian religion, Rauschenbusch nevertheless was struck by his mentor's adaptation of Wundt's *Volkerpsychologie*, impressing Royce 'with the reality of super-personal forces in human life.'[10] Rauschenbusch quoted Royce at length on this idea

> There are in the world two profoundly different grades, or levels, of mental beings, namely, the beings that we usually call human individuals, and the beings that we call communities. Any highly organized community is as truly a human being as you and I are individually human. Only a community is not what we usually call an individual human being because it has no one separate and internally well-knit physical organism of its own; and because its mind, if you attribute to it any one mind, is therefore not manifested through the expressive movements of such a single separate human organism. Yet there are reasons for attributing to a community a mind of its own. The communities are vastly more complex, and, in many ways, are also immeasurably more potent and enduring than are the individuals. Their mental life possesses, as Wundt has pointed out, a psychology of its own, which can be systematically studied. Their mental existence in no mere creation of abstract thinking or of metaphor; and is no more a topic for mystical insight, or for phantastic speculation, than is the mental existence of an individual man.[11]

It was precisely with this notion of personhood and collective identity that Royce's version of idealism infiltrated Rauschenbusch's own method.

Rauschenbusch immediately took hold of this collective understanding of personhood and recognised it as a conception 'of great importance for the doctrine of sin.'[12] Linking it with his belief that the moral standard of groups has authority over the moral standard of individuals, whether positive or negative, he asserted that 'these super-personal forces count in the moral world not only through their authority over their members, but through their influence in the general social life.' Rauschenbusch highlighted the need for the church and its theology to embrace such a collective understanding of human moral agency: 'The social gospel realizes the importance and power of the super-personal forces in the community,' he argued

> It has succeeded in awakening the social conscience of the nation to the danger of allowing such forces to become parasitic and oppressive. A realization of the spiritual power and value of these composite personalities must get into theology, otherwise theology will not deal adequately with the problem of sin and

---

[10]Rauschenbusch, *A Theology for the Social Gospel*, 70.

[11]Josiah Royce, *The Problem of Christianity*, vol. I, *The Christian Doctrine of Life* (New York: Macmillan, 1914), 164-7. Cited by Rauschenbusch in *A Theology for the Social Gospel*, 70-1.

[12]Rauschenbusch, *A Theology for the Social Gospel*, 71.

redemption, and will be unrelated to some of the most important work of salvation which the coming generations will have to do.[13]

In this way, Rauschenbusch allowed the concept of corporate personality into his own theology in a defining role.

Never quite content to shed his pietistic heritage, Rauschenbusch did not trade completely an individualistic religion for a social one. Indeed, he felt that a 'perfect religious hope must include both: eternal life for the individual, the Kingdom of God for humanity.'[14] But as his thought developed, the role of the individual as a moral agent was increasingly submerged beneath that of the community. In this sense, moral freedom belonged more to the realm of the society than to the individual, since as members of society, individuals 'are free only within very contracted limits.'[15]

Responsible to and for the wellbeing of all members of society, the individual was truly free only when acting in the interests of the good of all. Conversely, the individual was subject to super-personal forces influencing the conditions of moral choice and behaviour, whether positive or negative. The mind of God, or the spirit of Christ, was seen to be at work in society countering the negative super-personal forces, and was assisted in the task of social reform as individuals assented to the social agenda in theory and practice. Following this line of thought, Rauschenbusch asserted boldly the necessary inter-dependence of God's self-revelation and social progress

> The social movement is one of the chief ways in which God is revealing that he lives and rules as a God that loves righteousness and hates iniquity. A theological God who has no interest in the conquest of justice and fraternity is not Christian. It is not enough for theology to eliminate this or that autocratic trait. Its God must join the social movement. The real God has been in it long ago. The development of a Christian social order would be the highest proof of God's saving power. The failure of the movement would impugn his existence.[16]

Moral freedom for the individual lay in the decision to participate in the social evolutionary process, which God was directing, or to refrain in egotistic selfishness. Loyalty to the ethical directive, which was essentially the spirit of community, ultimately defined Rauschenbusch's religion - a notion he borrowed undoubtedly from Royce's philosophy.

Conferring authority on the social consciousness was not representative of historical Christian doctrine, and Gerald Birney Smith observed correctly that Royce's 'substitution of the "spirit of the community" for the traditional conception of Christ as the unique founder of Christianity involves significant

---

[13]Ibid., 75-6.
[14]Rauschenbusch, *Christianity and the Social Crisis*, 107.
[15]Ibid., 360.
[16]Rauschenbusch, *A Theology for the Social Gospel,* 178.

consequences'-consequences which held true for Rauschenbusch's method. Smith elaborated the nature of these consequences, stating without disapproval

> Loyalty to the community implies an active participation in the *making* of the community, and thus lends to religion an active aspect in the place of the more passive dependence on the grace of God which characterizes the Christianity of the creeds. Thus…the actual content of the new religion of loyalty is such as to compel us to abandon the conception of Christianity as something specifically furnished to mankind by the unique advent of Christ. It is rather a social creation, and is therefore always subject to the vicissitudes of social evolution. Mankind, in loyalty to the great community ideal, must continually create the "spirit of the community," whose work is inspirational and co-operative rather than finally authoritative.[17]

Therefore authority, inasmuch as it exists at all, must be seen as intrinsic to the community.

Nothing in Rauschenbusch's method seems to conflict with the idea that moral authority rests within the community - rather, as illustrated above, his method confirms this popular contention of his contemporaries. The collective moral consciousness is seen to exist, by Rauschenbusch and others, as a powerful source of moral authority, against which no external appeal might prevail. The sentiment is summed up by another contemporary, Hastings Rashdall, in this way: 'If it were not merely our own individual judgement but that of our whole community, including its best and wisest, that were in collision with the judgement of the great teacher, then we could hardly contend that the *ipse dixit* of any authority, however justly venerated, ought to prevail against the voice of such a collective Conscience.'[18] At this point, the deification of the spirit of community moves dangerously close to taking form in Rauschenbusch's method, as he follows Royce's philosophical lead.[19]

Smith concluded his discussion of the consequences of Royce's argument thus: 'By assigning to this imminent spirit a superhuman reality, Professor Royce is enabled to identify it with the ultimate cosmic principle, and thus give to his religion of loyalty a cosmic-religious significance. But in the practical workings of religion, the content of worship and activity will be directed to the

---

[17]See Gerald Birney Smith's review of *The Problem of Christianity* by Josiah Royce in *AJT* 17 (October 1913): 638.

[18]Hastings Rashdall, *Conscience and Christ* (London: Duckworth, 1916), 30.

[19]Smith accused Rauschenbusch directly of the opposite methodological error. He believed Rauschenbusch to be making an appeal to the authority of an outdated and irretrievable source when he referred to the authority of Christ rather than the collective authority of the community. This criticism does not stand when it is recognized that for Rauschenbusch, Christ's authority was imminent in the community, and so in practical terms at least, moral authority did indeed rest with the collective consciousness. See G. B. Smith's review of *A Theology for the Social Gospel* in *AJT* 23 (October 1918): 583-588. Cf. Rauschenbusch's doctrine of God in Chapter 3.

social life that we as individuals share. Christianity has in this sense been humanized, even though the object of worship be defined in superhuman terms.' What becomes evident from this analysis is that Royce and Rauschenbusch, however unwittingly, took it upon themselves to redefine the nature of the Christian religion, and claim the authority to do so as members of the collective consciousness, which embodied the ideal. In this sense, Royce's modified idealism defines Rauschenbusch's method, although 'the term "absolute pragmatism," which Professor Royce himself uses, is not inappropriate.'[20]

Regardless of the label ascribed to Rauschenbusch, it is a variant of idealism that most significantly informed his thought. It led him to consider the significance of collective responsibility and personality as he interacted with the thought of many scholars, and gave him the philosophical tools to construct an ethical programme that interpreted humanity and prescribed its moral solutions in collective terms. Rauschenbusch's notion of collective consciousness developed further as he encountered another idealist philosopher, a nationalist who vigorously argued the crucial role of religion in building a collective consciousness capable of initiating and sustaining significant social change, as a step of evolutionary moral progress.

Developing the Idea of Collective Moral Consciousness

If Royce bequeathed to Rauschenbusch the philosophical idealism that allowed the Christian historian to conceive of moral existence in collective terms, then it was thinkers like the Italian nationalist Giuseppi Mazzini who encouraged Rauschenbusch to develop that notion into a more clearly defined philosophy of collective moral consciousness.[21] Scant attention has been paid to the influence of Mazzini, despite the fact that Rauschenbusch's personal assistant and early biographer made five references to Mazzini's effect on his work.[22] Donovan Smucker suggests 'it is difficult to determine which parts of Mazzini's vision influenced Rauschenbusch,' and places Mazzini among those of minor influence to Rauschenbusch's intellectual formation.[23] Despite this lowly estimation of his contribution, numerous references to Mazzini are to be found in Rauschenbusch's work, especially in early formative days, and Sharpe records Rauschenbusch's appreciation of Mazzini as a prophet 'to whom God has given an eye for the lessons of the past and an ear which he has laid on the beating heart of his own generation, and who, therefore, is able to tell what shall be.' Even a cursory reading of Mazzini's *Essays* leaves no doubt as to the

---

[20]G. B. Smith, review of Royce in *AJT*, 638.
[21]He was known in his English-language publications as Joseph Mazzini.
[22]See Dores Sharpe, *Walter Rauschenbusch* (New York: Macmillan, 1942). Cf. Smucker, *The Origins*, 115.
[23]Smucker, *The Origins*, 77.

reasons why Rauschenbusch regarded it as a religious book, 'a book of devotion.'[24] It is justifiable to argue that Mazzini influenced Rauschenbusch's philosophical development and provided a certain degree of practical inspiration, with the result that his presence would not be readily apparent in Rauschenbusch's work, especially when analysed from a largely theological or historical point of view. Although the influence of Mazzini on Rauschenbusch's complete body of work should not be overestimated, neither should it be overlooked. In particular, the argument being set forth here is that Mazzini contributed to, underscored, and solidified Rauschenbusch's philosophical conception of the solidarity of collective moral consciousness that existed within philosophical idealism, and demonstrated its religious and moral necessity, if not inevitability. In this sense, Mazzini stands as a representative of those thinkers who helped Rauschenbusch develop his philosophical method in its assumption of the collective moral unity of the human race. Mazzini's work exemplifies, therefore, the corporate thought patterns and assumptions that are keys to Rauschenbusch's method, and which have been neglected by much scholarship focused on the social gospel.[25] A brief survey of common themes in Mazzini and Rauschenbusch will demonstrate this point.

Mazzini perceived life as a mission, binding religion to duty for the betterment of humanity as a whole. The struggle for liberty achieved the freedom of the individual, which was a necessary precursor to the collective idea, but it focused too narrowly on human rights and neglected the realm of human duty, which was the natural evolution of the freedom attained. Mazzini turned to nature to define collective existence in relation to individual humanity. 'Now the law of the individual can only be deduced from the law of the species,' he asserted. 'The individual mission can only be ascertained and defined by placing ourselves upon an elevation, enabling us to grasp and

---

[24]Sharpe, *Walter Rauschenbusch*, 84.

[25]It may well be that the influence of Mazzini and other European reformers has been neglected as Rauschenbusch's 'Americanness' has been emphasized. Many scholars argue that the social gospel was a uniquely American movement, and attempt to define Rauschenbusch strictly within those parameters, perhaps overlooking the fact that he spent a good deal of time studying and traveling in Europe, and was only one generation removed from his continental European heritage. This brief overview of Mazzini's social thought demonstrates how Rauschenbusch borrowed significantly from European thinkers for some of his foundational ideas and was not simply a reflection of American liberal Protestantism. Cf. W. A. Visser't Hooft, *The Background of the Social Gospel in America* (1928; reprint, St. Louis, MS: The Bethany Press, n.d.); and Paul Phillips, *A Kingdom on Earth: Anglo-American Social Christianity, 1880-1940* (University Park, PA: The Pennsylvania State University Press, 1996). Visser't Hooft highlights the 'American-ness' of the movement, while Phillips explores the aspects of the movement held in common in North America and the United Kingdom, emphasizing the social gospel's trans-national nature, including its European influences.

comprehend the whole. We must reascend to the conception of *Humanity*, in order to ascertain the secret, rule, and law of life of the individual, of man. Hence the necessity of a general co-operation, of harmony of effort, - in a word, of *association*, - in order to fulfil the work of all.'[26] This notion of *association*, defined by many of Rauschenbusch's contemporaries as *fraternity*, was to serve as the new organising principle for ethics and all analyses of human behaviour. 'Now I believe that the time has arrived when the principle of association, solemnly and universally promulgated, should become the starting-point of all theoretical and practical studies,' Mazzini wrote, 'having for their aim the progressive organisation of human society, and be placed at the summit of our constitutions, our codes, and our formulae of faith. And I say, moreover, that the promulgation of a term directing our researches upon a path absolutely different from any yet tried, is sufficient to constitute, or at least to indicate, a new epoch.'[27]

True to the Kantian legacy, *duty* replaced an obsession with individual *right* as the watchword of this new epoch. Mazzini found *duty* to be most significant for collective progress, arguing that, 'Right is the faith of the individual. Duty is the common collective faith. Right can but organise resistance: it may destroy, it cannot found. Duty builds up, associates, and unites; it is derived from a general law, whereas Right is derived only from human will....'[28] When the concept of duty permeated society, Mazzini believed there would be no need for coercion to effect moral advancement: 'Societies based upon Duty would not be compelled to have recourse to force; duty, once admitted as the rule, excludes the possibility of struggle; and by rendering the individual subject to the general aim, it cuts at the very root of those evils which Right is unable to prevent, and only affects to cure.' Mazzini saw that duty, specifically the duty to sacrifice individualism for the amelioration of collective existence, required the ethical sanction and motivation provided by religion if it were to move beyond words to significant moral action.[29] Religion did not serve merely to hallow secular aims, but breathed a new collective consciousness into society. Mazzini writes almost prophetically

> The evil at the present day is, not that men assign too much value to life, but the reverse. Life has fallen in estimation, because, as at all periods of crisis and disorganisation, the chain is broken which in all forms of belief attaches it through humanity to heaven. It has fallen, because the consciousness of mutual human responsibility, which alone constitutes its dignity and strength, being lost together with all community of belief, its sphere of activity has become restricted, and it

[26]Mazzini, 'Faith and the Future,' *Essays: Selected From the Writings, Literary, Political, and Religious of Joseph Mazzini*, ed. and intro. by William Clarke (London: Walter Scott, 1892), 30.
[27]Mazzini, 'Faith and the Future,' 32n.
[28]Ibid., 38.
[29]Ibid., 140.

has been compelled to fall back upon material interests, minor passions, and petty aims. It has fallen, because it has been too much individualised; and the remedy lies in re-attaching life to heaven - in raising it again, in restoring to it the consciousness of its power and sanctity. The means consist in retempering the individual life through communion with the universal life; they consist in restoring to the individual that which I have from the outset called the feeling of *the collective*, in pointing out to him his place in the tradition of the species, in bringing him into communion by love and by works, with all his fellow-men. By isolating ourselves, we have begun to feel ourselves feeble and little; we have begun to despise our own efforts and those of our brethren towards the attainment of the ideal; and we have in despair set ourselves to repeat and comment upon the *"Carpe diem"* of the heathen poet; we must make ourselves great and strong again by association; we must not discredit life, but make it holy.[30]

Here, and elsewhere, Mazzini recognised the power of religion to unite and ignite the passions of people. 'The religious element is universal, immortal: it both universalises and unites,' he insisted. 'Every great revolution has borne its stamp, and revealed it in its origins or in its aims. Through it is association founded.'[31] For Mazzini, and later for the social gospel, religion would be equated with Christ, whose idealist interpretation meant humanity's progress was nearly assured from the foundation of the Gospel: 'We advance, encouraged by the sacred promise of Jesus; we seek the new gospel, of which, before dying, he gave us the immortal hope, and of which the Christian gospel is but the germ, even as man is the germ of Humanity.' Jesus was considered the great *Initiator* of a process that led forward in evolutionary progress. In contrast to many idealist thinkers, Mazzini did not perceive the future *telos* as inevitable, or progress as guaranteed apart from human effort; indeed, human effort was itself a part of the discovery of the Ideal. The attainment of progress depended on human effort as part of the natural and providential design. 'The Ideal is not within, but beyond us and supreme over us: it is not the *creation*, but the gradual *discovery* of the human intellect,' Mazzini writes

> The law which directs the discovery is named Progress: The method by which progress is achieved is Association - the association of all the human faculties and forces. The ultimate discovery of the aim of life is assured by Providential design, but time and space are given to us wherein to achieve it, and are therefore the field of liberty and responsibility for each and all of us. Our choice lies between evil, which is egotism, and good, which is love and sacrifice for the sake of fellow-men.[32]

The task for each individual, then, is to contribute to the development of an eschatological and religious fulfilment or synthesis for all of humanity and the

---

[30]Ibid., 146-7.
[31]Ibid., 44.
[32]Ibid., 331.

whole of life. Mazzini explains: 'Before us is the evolution of a future in which the two eternal elements of every organisation - the individual and humanity, liberty and association - will be harmonised; in which one whole synthesis, a veritable religious formula, will - without suppressing any in favour of the rest - embrace all the revelations of progress, all the holy ideas that have been successively transmitted to us by providential design.'[33]

The trend towards unity and association meant that efforts to promote political or economic reform were the very duty of each generation, in faithfulness to the past and the future. For Mazzini, this understanding of human existence could only begin with a collective interpretation of humanity, and end with a commitment to unified moral action. Individualism gave to humanity a sense of freedom and equality, but a rigorously individualistic interpretation of life leads humanity away from its designed fulfilment, and to the egoistic frustration of secular materialism

> But if we start from the point of view of the collective existence of Humanity, and regard social life as the continued development of an idea by the life of all its individuals, if we regard history as the record of this continuous development in time and space through the works of individuals; if we believe in the *copartnery* and mutual responsibility of generations, never losing sight of the fact that the life of the individual is *his* development in a medium fashioned by the labours of all the individuals who have preceded him, and that the powers of the individual are *his* powers grafted upon those of all foregoing humanity, - our conception will change...and we shall learn that it is not only our right but our duty to incarnate our thought in action.[34]

By now it is quite clear how the collective moral consciousness as a key idea might have developed in Rauschenbusch's mind as he encountered Mazzini and others who shared similar presuppositions and philosophies. Their ideas fed his ideas, even as he found in them the inspiration he needed for the task set before him as an individual. Rauschenbusch must have been stirred and strengthened by lines such as these

> Great ideas create great peoples. Let your life be the living summary of one sole organic idea. Enlarge the horizon of the peoples. Liberate their conscience from the materialism by which it is weighed down. Set a vast mission before them. Rebaptise them.... principles alone can generate revolutions. The question now agitating the world is a religious question Analysis, and anarchy of religious belief, have extinguished faith in the hearts of the peoples. Synthesis, and unity of religious belief, will rekindle it.[35]

The corporate idea did not only leave an imprint on Rauschenbusch's

---

[33]Ibid., 49.
[34]Ibid., 128-9.
[35]Ibid., 51-2.

thought, but it became the cornerstone of his method. Indeed, Rauschenbusch himself could have penned these words which summarise the approach of Mazzini and many others who influenced his thought: 'The cry of *"God wills it"* must be the eternal watchword of every undertaking like our own, having sacrifice for its basis, the people for its instrument, and Humanity for its aim.'[36] The notions of collective duty and self-sacrifice, the existence of a single moral consciousness in society, the need for a single organic theme on which to build one's thought and action, the power of religion to build a shared moral consciousness and provide moral sanction, the initiation by Jesus of a divine process, and the significant contribution of the present epoch in the unfolding of history are all ideas in Mazzini's work which found expression in Rauschenbusch's thought, and especially in his commitment to a collective understanding of human life.

Though present throughout Rauschenbusch's work, the influence of Mazzini and others who developed the concept of a collective moral consciousness is especially identifiable in an early, unpublished manuscript, in which Rauschenbusch considers the difference between individual and collective morality and decidedly emphasises the significance of the latter. In a paper entitled, 'Corporate Life of Humanity,' Rauschenbusch explains clearly his understanding of collective existence, and exhorts the students and staff of Rochester seminary to be committed to its aims and directions. He commends Tolstoi, Leibnitz, Hegel, Comte, Lessing, Dante, Bacon, and Mazzini for developing the corporate idea in philosophy and culture, and sets out the building blocks for this crucial aspect of his method in a revealing fashion.[37]

Rauschenbusch begins his argument by stating boldly: 'There are two moral beings both dear to the heart of God: man and humanity.'[38] He notes the significance of the individual, especially in Jesus' earthly ministry, and affirms the importance of spiritual renewal in individual souls. 'But behind the individual another ethical personality arises, shadowy and vast;' he writes. It is 'a macrocosmos, which also struggles and learns and sins and suffers and rises or falls, and in whose heart heaven and hell have fought for supremacy in a conflict that has lasted for ages and will last till the holy city of God is built on

---

[36]Ibid., 35.

[37]See Walter Rauschenbusch, 'The Corporate Life of Humanity,' unpublished lecture, 1896, Rauschenbusch Family Papers, Record Group 1003, Box 17, American Baptist Archives, Rochester, NY. In a hand-written note on the back of the paper, Seminary President Augustus H. Strong penned the following affirmation on October 19, 1896: 'The lecture of Rev. W. R. on the "Corporate Life of Humanity", delivered before our Seminary last Monday evening was so fresh and valuable a presentation of a great theme, that I wish to commend it to all theological sem's and to bespeak for it a hearing. We have rarely had a lecture which was more timely and inspiring. Both faculty and students united in praising it, both for its substance and for the manner of its delivery.'

[38]Rauschenbusch, 'The Corporate Life of Humanity,' 2.

earth. That is humanity.'[39]

Like Mazzini, Rauschenbusch first turns to an argument from nature to support his assertion. 'The human individual is not an isolated being. By his descent he is organically connected with the past of his race, bearing about in the impulses and forces that fashion his life the results of the developement [*sic.*] of past generations. By his power of originating new life he bears a similar organic relation to the future of the race, influencing by his deed to-day the life of coming generations to the end of time.'[40] Moreover, Rauschenbusch explains that, 'wherever a number of human beings live and work together, love and hate, and unite in the bonds of family and friendship, an organic, collective life is formed.' But this life is not perceived as some nebulous, non-personal entity - in fact, it possesses moral agency. In any such association, 'a sort of moral atmosphere is created. There are certain acknowledged ideas concerning right and wrong, a common norm which is applied to the actions of every member in the community and according to which praise or censure are distributed. The habits of thinking and working in common, the influences frequently passing from one to another, create a sort of corporate nervous system along which the common impulses can run and make united action possible.' By acknowledging the fact of corporate consciousness, Rauschenbusch recognises that it has positive and negative potential, as 'lofty corporate enthusiasm sometimes lifts mean men up beyond their own range of flight; corporate waves of anger, revenge or jealousy run through society and sweep the best and sanest from their feet.'[41]

As he traces the concept of collective morality through the Old and New Testaments, making observations regarding its present application, Rauschenbusch suggests that both the problem of human existence and its solution lie in the notion of corporate personality. 'In Christ and the Christian movement a tremendous impulse from God touched the people,' he writes. 'As a nation it rejected that power of salvation, thereby refined and increased the malignancy of the evil spirit, and fell a prey to the toxic forces secreted in its own life. Only by this view of the nation as a moral personality, which lives on and possesses moral continuity even though its citizens pass away, can the moral problems of history be solved. Though even then there is mystery enough to keep us humble,' he concedes wisely. Rauschenbusch's argument regarding the power of the collective moral consciousness gains strength for the contemporary reader when he points to the emergence and growth of nationalist movements, whose potentially horrific negative side he does not consider, though he correctly assesses nationalism's power to assert the collective will of the people. Nationalism is the 'tenacious' and 'collective struggle' of people 'which has re-made the map of Europe during this century and which is still

---

[39]Ibid., 3.
[40]Ibid. Cf. Walter Rauschenbusch, *Dare We Be Christians?*
[41]Rauschenbusch, 'The Corporate Life of Humanity', 4.

shaking Great Britain with the Irish question...and keeping up a perpetual ferment in the Balkan States,' he writes. Rauschenbusch's appreciation of nationalism as a force, which along with religion could build a powerful sense of moral consciousness in society as a whole, was undoubtedly related to his reading of Mazzini.

Like Mazzini, then, Rauschenbusch is committed to delineating the existence of a single moral consciousness in society, and he similarly believes in the power of religion to define and motivate it in particular directions. Rauschenbusch notes with enthusiasm Mazzini's observation that 'every great revolution demands a great idea to be its center of action; to furnish it with both a lever and a fulcrum for the work it has to do.'[42] For Rauschenbusch, as for Mazzini, the great idea or fulcrum for action in the revolution of the social gospel is the notion of association.

Rooted in the new epoch initiated by Jesus, religion provides the moral resources, the zeal, the impetus, and the motivation for the development of a common moral consciousness and subsequent basis for action. As Rauschenbusch's friend and colleague Leighton Williams expressed in 1907 on behalf of their fraternal organisation, The Brotherhood of the Kingdom

We believe that morals are the florescence of true religion and its true fruitage, but let us never confound the fruit with the roots...Morals apart from religion are cut flowers. They may retain their form and fragrance for a time after they are severed from the parent stem, but their life is gone and they must soon wither and decay.[43]

These words demonstrate the necessary connection that social gospel leaders at the turn of the century believed must exist between Christianity and social ethics. For Rauschenbusch, the necessary unity between religion and ethics is reinforced by his reading of Harnack, who argued that religion was 'the soul of morality, and morality the body of religion.'[44] 'It is enough,' he declared

If religion prepares men's minds for great economic changes and revolutions; if it foresees the new moral duties which these impose; if it knows how to adapt itself to them, and perceives the right moment at which to step in with its forces and do its work. A religion which aims at saving the soul and transforming the inner man, and which regards a change in outward circumstances as but a small matter in comparison with the power of evil, can only follow in the wake of earthly changes

---

[42]Rauschenbusch, *Christianizing the Social Order,* 41. Cf. Mazzini, *Essays,* 24.
[43]Leighton Williams, *The Reign of the New Humanity,* Amity Tract No.11 (August 8, 1907). Cited in *Foundations* I (January 1959): 26. The Brotherhood of the Kingdom was a group of men organized by Rauschenbusch to further the cause of the social gospel through propagation in church and academic circles.
[44]Adolf Harnack, *What is Christianity?* trans. T. B. Saunders (London: Williams and Norgate, 1901).

and exercise an after-influence; it is not qualified to lead the way in economic developments.[45]

With Harnack's analysis pointing towards the sense in which religion may serve as a source of moral authority for the social gospel, it becomes increasingly clear why Rauschenbusch believes religion is able to provide the moral resources required for significant social change.[46] Religion serves a rather utilitarian purpose as it is interpreted and employed for the achievement of a greater good amongst a greater number of people in society.[47]

At this point, Rauschenbusch echoes loudly the sentiments expressed by Mazzini, as he exhorts

> ...[a] great task demands a great faith. To live a great life a man needs a great cause to which he can surrender, something divinely large and engrossing for which he can live, and if need be, die. A great religious faith will lift him out of his narrow grooves and make him the inspired instrument of the universal will of God. It is the point at which the mind of man coincides with the mind of the Eternal. [48]

It is Rauschenbusch's primary concern that this faith be applied on a collective level in order to achieve the goals of the social revolution which he believes is initiated by Jesus and is reaching fruition in his generation. Again reflecting Mazzini's influence, Rauschenbusch emphasises that 'our moral efficiency depends on our religious faith. The force of will, of courage, of self-sacrifice liberated by a living religious faith is so incalculable, so invincible, that nothing is impossible when that power enters the field.'[49]

For Rauschenbusch, true religion is inseparable from ethics, and with Mazzini he regards the mind of Jesus as an example of the perfect union of religion and ethics, 'in which the consciousness of God and the consciousness of humanity blend completely.'[50] Taking up the challenge of Mazzini to find a

---

[45]Adolf Harnack, a paper read on May 17, 1894 at the Evangelical Social Congress held at Frankfurt-am-Main, in *Essays on the Social Gospel* by Adolf Harnack and Wilhelm Herrmann, trans. G. M. Craik, ed. Maurice A. Canney (London: Williams and Norgate, 1907), 18-19.

[46]See Christopher Lasch, 'Religious Contributions to Social Movements: Walter Rauschenbusch, the Social Gospel, and its Critics,' *JRE* 18:1 (Spring 1990): 7-26. Lasch contrasts Rauschenbusch's understanding of the authority of religion as providing moral resource with that of Niebuhr who saw the ethical import of religion as a critique of all human endeavour.

[47]Donovan Smucker believes this led Rauschenbusch into a Christ-of-culture concept, something Rauschenbusch has been accused of developing by some later critics. See for example H. Richard Niebuhr, *Christ and Culture* (New York: Harper and Bros., 1951).

[48]Rauschenbusch, *Christianizing the Social Order*, 40. Cf. Mazzini, *Essays*, 122.

[49]Rauschenbusch, *Christianizing the Social Order*, 41.

[50]Rauschenbusch, *A Theology for the Social Gospel*, 14.

single, organic idea on which to base thought and action, Rauschenbusch follows Mazzini's lead in regarding Jesus as the Initiator of a divine process in human society, and adopts the Kingdom of God as his organic, organising principle which embodies, expresses and empowers the collective consciousness of humanity.[51] Rauschenbusch also shares Mazzini's belief that an organic evolutionary tie bound the past, present, and future, and sees it as the responsibility of his generation to meet the social challenge as a legacy upon which future generations might build. In this way, the social impulse would continue to evolve throughout history.

The Source and Development of Collective Moral Consciousness

It is not entirely clear whether Rauschenbusch thought that the existence of a collective consciousness is of natural or supernatural origin, or both. It should be evident by now that Rauschenbusch stressed an evolutionary view of a developing solidaristic impulse, present in the natural order. But there are other points in his work where he argued that the natural state of human existence is individualistic, egotistical, and to be vigorously resisted. All elements of his thought considered, it becomes clear that Rauschenbusch wavered on the issue of whether humanity ought to battle against natural impulses, or build a society upon them. This aspect of his method must be described as a logical inconsistency rather than an intentional paradox. Despite such incongruity, it is clear that Rauschenbusch understood nature in moral terms.

Many inconsistencies in Rauschenbusch's view of human nature could be explained as reflecting development in his thought.[52] In most of his earlier expressions he argued generally that nature is something to be battled and defeated as the source of human egotism and collective strife. Some of his more mature thinking reveals a less thoroughgoing evolutionary ethic and one that is more solidly naturalistic. When tempered with idealism, his views of nature and history emphasise the elements of process and progress, and a potential teleology, such that he asserts: 'Human nature is the raw material for the Christian character. The spirit of Christ working in the human spirit is to elevate the aims, enoble the motives, and intensify the affections. This process is never complete. The Christian is always in the making. In the same way

---

[51]See Walter Rauschenbusch, 'The Kingdom of God,' an address given on January 2, 1913 in *The Social Gospel in America 1870-1920*, ed. Robert T. Handy (New York: Oxford University Press, 1966), 264-7.

[52]Rauschenbusch's belief in the negative force of natural impulses is affirmed as late as 1916 in *The Social Principles of Jesus*, and stands in stark contrast to the view affirmed elsewhere that suggests human nature need only be hallowed and extended. See, for example, the final chapter of *Christianity and the Social Crisis*, in which Rauschenbusch suggests human nature possesses immense latent perfectibility; and Walter Rauschenbusch, *The Social Principles of Jesus* (New York: Grosset & Dunlap, 1916).

human society is the raw material for Christian society. The spirit of Christ is to hallow all natural relations of men and give them a divine significance and value. This process too is never complete.'[53] Ethically speaking, the solidaristic impulses of humanity are seen to be present in nature but at least require identification and elevation if not recreation. Thus Rauschenbusch's ideal still depends on the participation of rational human beings to order those natural collective impulses into useful structures and practices.

It would be easy to identify and categorise Rauschenbusch's thought as simply affirming an idealistic interpretation and modification of evolutionary theories. But in his early more 'realist' days, and even in a devotional publication as late as 1916, Rauschenbusch describes natural impulses as persistent downward tendencies requiring confrontation in a constant battle to counter their negative and sinful effects. Rauschenbusch therefore expounds two very different and rather contradictory understandings of nature, evolution, and the development of the social principle.

The first approach - which could be seen to represent his earlier thought if not for the fact that he later employed it as a tool to encourage devotional enthusiasm - is thoroughly evolutionary, in the spirit of Herbert Spencer and T. H. Huxley. For Huxley, as for evolutionary ethics in general, history is understood as a cyclical process. The natural order is bound up in an endless cycle of life and death; the fight for survival ensues whilst the hostile environment is given to periods of blossoming and decay. In Huxley's view, social ethics are a matter of battling this natural tendency to decay - a matter of fighting against nature. Like a gardener who nurtures and tends a beautiful life-giving plot of land in a fight against the weeds and wilds, so humanity is able to prolong the development of life in a battle against the tendency to decay by nurturing and tending the ethics which preserve society in the midst of a hostile environment. He describes the process in this way

> I beg you to accompany me in an attempt to reach a world which, to many, is probably strange, by the help of a bean. It is, as you know, a simple, inert-looking thing. Yet, if planted under proper conditions, of which sufficient warmth is one of the most important, it manifests active powers of a very remarkable kind. A small green seedling emerges, rises to the surface of the soil, rapidly increases in size.... By insensible steps, the plant builds itself up into a large and various fabric of root, stem, leaves, flowers, and fruit, every one moulded within and without in accordance with an extremely complex, but, at the same time, minutely defined pattern. In each of these complicated structures, as in their smallest constituents, there is an immanent energy which, in harmony with that resident in

---

[53]Rauschenbusch, *Christianity and the Social Crisis,* 308-9.

all the others, incessantly works towards the maintenance of the whole and the
efficient performance of the part which it has to play in the economy of nature.[54]

According to Huxley's view, if left to its own devices, nature is unable to
sustain any particular manifestation of life. He observed that, 'no sooner has the
edifice, reared with such exact elaboration attained completeness, than it begins
to crumble.' In time, and 'By degrees, the plant withers and disappears from
view, leaving behind more or fewer apparently inert and simple bodies, just like
the bean from which it sprang; and, like it, endowed with the potentiality of
giving rise to a similar cycle of manifestations.' This explanation is, in fact,
'the Sisyphaean process, in the course of which, the living and growing plant
passes from the relative simplicity and latent potentiality of the seed to the full
epiphany of a highly differentiated type, thence to fall back to simplicity and
potentiality.'[55]

Such a cycle would seem to have no possibility of sustainability and little
ethical relevance. But Huxley allows that, if carefully worked by the gardener
and protected from the encroaching decay and wild influences of nature, the
blossoming plant could derive a sustained existence in an oasis in the midst of
nature's wilderness. He explains: 'If the fruits and tubers, the foliage and the
flowers thus obtained, reach, or sufficiently approach, that ideal, there is no
reason why the *status quo* attained should not be indefinitely prolonged.'[56] In
other words, an evolved humanity could carve out a society whose ethic was
sustainable, even as the processes of nature and history would seek to destroy
it.

At various points in his work, Rauschenbusch echoes this understanding of
nature as decay, and the importance of the battle against its destructive
influences, interpreting it in moral terms. At times he seems to adopt
completely Huxley's belief that 'the ethical progress of society depends, not on
imitating the cosmic process, still less in running away from it, but in
combating it.'[57] Against the moral optimism of many contemporaries,
Rauschenbusch describes early the evolution of humanity as a cycle, prone to
decline: 'It is not true that man tends by nature upward. It is the downward way
that is easy; the upward way is steep and toilsome.' Even in social expression,
Rauschenbusch observes a natural negative tendency, asking, 'What association
of men or what human institution does not sag downward?'[58] Sounding very

---

[54]T. H. Huxley, *Evolution and Ethics, and Other Essays*, Collected Essays vol. ix
(London: Macmillan & Co., 1894), 47.
[55]Ibid., 47-8.
[56]Ibid., 14.
[57]Ibid., 83.
[58]Walter Rauschenbusch, *The Righteousness of the Kingdom*, ed. and intro. by Max
Stackhouse (Nashville, TN: Abingdon Press, 1968), 281-2. This represents an early,
originally unpublished work of Rauschenbusch, discovered in the American Baptist
Archives.

much like one of his own later critics, he asserts: 'Let us have no illusions. The world will not evolve into a Kingdom of God by natural processes. It is uphill work. It is a battle. Every inch will have to be fought for.'[59]

These views cannot be easily dismissed as representing only Rauschenbusch's early and undeveloped thought. He later insists that, 'every step of approach toward the Kingdom of God must be won by conflicts.... Human nature needs a strong reenforcement to rouse it from its inherited lethargy and put it on the toilsome upward track.'[60] Rauschenbusch barely resembles the typical liberal Protestant when he declares that 'History laughs at the optimistic illusion that nothing can stand in the way of progress.' Reading Rauschenbusch in the light of Huxley's evolutionary ethic illuminates his sometimes confusing insistence that if the present social crisis should fail to bring about a lasting and just social order, then God would have to start the process all over again. In this regard, he suggests rather forcefully

> At the same time when Christianity has thus attained to its adolescence and moral maturity, there is a piercing call from the world about it, summoning all moral strength and religious heroism to save the Christian world from social strangulation and death.... It rests upon us to decide if a new era is to dawn in the transformation of the world into the kingdom of God, or if Western civilization is to descend to the graveyard of civilizations and God will have to try once more.[61]

Thus far, it would seem to be Rauschenbusch's view that progress towards social cohesion is not natural, assured, or determined. For him, the source of human progress lay outside of the natural order, and in accordance with his idealist philosophy, he locates it in the mind of God. He explains his developing views as follows

> And what, then, shall lift humanity up, if the force that raises it is not naturally inherent in it? .... One epoch of history cannot be greater and nobler than the one out of which it has grown unless an additional force has entered into its composition. Whence does that force come in human history?

> The same question has been raised concerning the asserted upward evolution of the organic world below man. If the higher forms of life have developed from the lowest, what has pushed them up? Those who believe in God have not hesitated to reply: God. He is immanent in the world, forever active and working. It is his

---

[59]Ibid., 283.
[60]Rauschenbusch, *The Social Principles of Jesus*, 158.
[61]Rauschenbusch, *Christianity and the Social Crisis,* 210.

force and his guidance which moulds his existing works into higher forms through his Kingdom. [62]

Not in human nature, but in the human spirit is teleological hope to be found: 'In them and in their work lies the hope of humanity's progress. The upward forces communicated through them have to overcome the downward inclination of flesh and blood, as life in the physical world overcomes the force of gravity.'[63] In *Christianizing the Social Order,* he further delineates the line between the natural order and the mind of God. 'We are apt to think that progress is the natural thing,' he writes, keen to point out the error of such thinking. 'Progress is more than natural,' he insists, 'It is divine.'[64] Are we to conclude then, that Rauschenbusch succumbs to some form of religious dualism?

It would perhaps be most fair to evaluate Rauschenbusch's evolutionary ethical views when balanced with comments which reveal a very different approach from that seen above, but which also grow out of his developing idealism. A demonstration of Rauschenbusch's contradictory dependence on naturalism for social ethics may be found in various works, but perhaps is explained most clearly in his exposition on love in the little volume *Dare We Be Christians?* For Rauschenbusch, in this work, love is the basic social category for all of the natural order. The natural predilection to love is observed amongst animals that live in community, and is experienced as a compulsion towards solidarity amongst humans. Rauschenbusch links closely the ideas of love and social progress using scientific evolution to prop up his argument. In this sense, love is as determined as it is free, and Rauschenbusch's law of love may be clearly distinguished from that of Kant.[65] Even in his earlier work, while reflecting Kant and Mazzini's influence by describing the obligation to love as *duty,* Rauschenbusch is clear that the sense of duty conforms to a natural and instinctual pattern: 'Love is the force that draws man and man together, the great social instinct of the race. It runs through all our relations and is the foundation of all our institutions.'[66] In many instances, Rauschenbusch clearly identifies love with the social instinct.

Interpreting science through idealism, Rauschenbusch offers his own understanding of evolution as 'survival of those who love the most.' He

[62]Rauschenbusch, *The Righteousness of the Kingdom,* 283-4. It is interesting to note that Rauschenbusch continues this thought through a quotation of Mazzini in his next paragraph.
[63]Ibid., 284.
[64]Rauschenbusch, *Christianizing the Social Order,* 30.
[65]Kant's ultimate category is law, accessed by reason, while Rauschenbusch's ultimate category is love, accessed by nature and reason. Cf. Kant, *Fundamental Principles of the Metaphysic of Ethics,* trans. Thomas Kingsmill Abbott (London: Longmans Green & Co., 1946); Smucker, 85.
[66]Rauschenbusch, *Christianizing the Social Order,* 262.

observes, 'Every step of social progress demands an increase in love, the history of evolution is a history of the appearance and the expansion of love. The first dawn of social cohesion appears in the love of parent animals for their young. The sympathetic type emerges as we ascend the scale of life. The offspring of love survive, propagate, and bequeath their capacity for love. Nature, by the power of life and death, weeds out the loveless and increases the totality of love in the universe.'[67] One cannot help but marvel at the survival and propagation of such anti-social creatures as the cuckoo and wonder what measure of love the enduring and prolific cockroach contributes to the totality of love in the natural world, when considering Rauschenbusch's conclusions. Yet, he uses this naturalistic view to further develop his understanding of human solidarity and community consciousness. Seeing only the positive aspects of social cohesion built on blood lines and nationalism, and following Mazzini's lead, Rauschenbusch sets forth these natural human bonds as evolutionary contributions to the development of the social consciousness

> In the history of man social organization began in groups that had common blood and the sense of kinship to bind them. Every enduring enlargement of political organization demands a basis of fellow-feeling, and love as well as common economic interests. Kings and statesmen have tried to patch nations and races together by treaties or coercion, but unless intermarriage has fused the blood, and religion and common suffering have welded the spirits of the people, empires have dropped apart again along the ancient lines of cleavage. The history of the Germans, the Italians and the Slavs in the nineteenth century and today consists largely of the effort to undo the artificial cobbling and stitching of kingcraft and to allow the nations to coalesce in commonwealths along the lines marked out by national love and race coherence.[68]

Though we might wince at these comments from the perspective of twenty-first-century democratic pluralism, their power is felt when the history of intervening years is considered. While Rauschenbusch may seriously underestimate the negative potential of such 'natural' social bonds, he correctly identifies them as being amongst the most enduring of social cohesions. It is, however, a methodological error in his philosophy that causes him to embrace all social impulses as expressions of 'love' and thus fail to consider that not all natural social 'feelings' promote good will or justice, especially when evoked by nationalism or religion.

At this juncture, Rauschenbusch seems to agree with the Kantian conception that moral progress is the very goal of nature, as he softens his stance against natural progress by marrying a view of evolutionary science with the doctrine

---

[67]Rauschenbusch, *Dare We Be Christians?* 26.
[68]Ibid., 26-7.

of God's immanence.[69] He suggests

> The spread of evolutionary ideas is another mark of modern religious thought. It has opened a vast historical outlook, backward and forward, and trained us in bold conceptions of the upward climb of the race. There is no denying that this has unsettled the ecclesiastical system of thought, much as the growth of tree roots will burst solid masonry. But it has prepared us for understanding the idea of a Reign of God toward which all creation is moving. Translate the evolutionary theories into religious faith, and you have the doctrine of the Kingdom of God. This combination with scientific evolutionary thought has freed the Kingdom ideal of its catastrophic setting and its background of demonism, and so adapted it to the climate of the modern world.[70]

Rauschenbusch should perhaps be permitted some latitude when considering this stark inconsistency in his work, as he undoubtedly wrestles with the development of his own thoughts on evolution and the social impulse, and the potential impact evolutionary theories might have on more conservative elements of his constituency. In his last work, he concludes a discussion of sin with this qualifying admission: 'Of course evolutionary thought has radically changed the conceptions about the origin of the race for those whose thinking is done under the influence of evolutionary science.'[71] He does not finally confess where his own sympathies lie, though he indicates that theology should never contradict what is scientifically held to be true. It is, however, at those points where the idealist influence is most obvious that he turns to nature for support for an ethical system that has the social impulse as its centre. Though it is now apparent that Rauschenbusch contradicts himself over whether the natural impulse should be hallowed and empowered by Christianity or overcome by it, it is also clear that he understands nature in moral terms.[72]

Rauschenbusch's tendency to interpret nature in moral terms, both positively and negatively, is connected to his struggle to understand evolutionary processes both as natural and supernatural. His confusion of these determinants seems to arise from his convoluted idealism, which here elevates transcendent mind over immoral matter, and there immerses mind in natural immanence, which directs the development of the human race through social bonds of love and solidarity. In certain instances, Rauschenbusch does not seem to take

---

[69]Cf. Roger Sullivan, *Immanuel Kant's Moral Theory* (Cambridge: Cambridge University Press, 1989), 236.

[70]Rauschenbusch, *Christianizing the Social Order*, 90.

[71]Rauschenbusch, *Theology for the Social Gospel*, 43-4.

[72]Though related in some ways to the concept of naturalistic fallacy, this aspect of Rauschenbusch's thought is best illuminated by his understanding of evolution, rather than a debate regarding the naturalistic fallacy. For a discussion of the naturalistic fallacy and evolution see A. G. N. Flew, *Evolutionary Ethics* (London: Macmillan, 1967), 37-8.

positive moral cues from nature. Following Huxley's lead, he joins the battle against nature but does not finally reject nature's moral order; he simply replaces a positive interpretation with a negative one. Flew rightly accuses Huxley of 'going too far' in 'replacing a positive connection by a negative rather than by no connection at all,' and Rauschenbusch may be similarly accused, especially considering his belief in an omnipotent Creator.[73] These expressed views stand in obvious contrast to those where he observes positive morality present in nature, particularly in social expressions of humans and animals.

In other cases, where Rauschenbusch seems to affirm certain natural impulses, it is his idealism that rescues him from a strictly evolutionary ethic, though his use of terms draws him dangerously close to adopting evolutionary moral categories. With idealism conditioning his thought, it is not easy for Rauschenbusch to maintain a dualist position. Rauschenbusch's idealism leads him to highlight God's immanence, and Royce helps him to understand evolution as a mere present expression of an eternally past and future ideal.[74] Royce's model allows for a history of observable evolution with or without obvious progress, as a mere temporal expression of the eternal mind of God. But Royce also makes room for the possibility of moral progress in a biological evolution that could not make moral demands of its own accord.[75] In this instance, Royce and Rauschenbusch stand on consistent philosophical ground. 'For if you are, however mistakenly, committed to the belief that the whole universe is an expression of the intentions of an omnipotent and righteous author, then this belief provides you with a positive reason both for accounting nature good and for speaking of intentions in this connection,' Flew allows.

---

[73]Ibid., 50.

[74]See Josiah Royce, *The Spirit of Modern Philosophy* (Boston and New York: Houghton Mifflin Co., 1892), 326-336. For Royce, the universe stretches infinitely into the past and future. Nature may be perceived as 'winding down' or 'evolving' merely as a present temporal reality within infinity. He believed these issues were what made philosophy necessary - to offer explanations beyond what biology was able to understand or explain.

[75]See Royce, *The Spirit of Modern Philosophy*, 337-8. Royce argues: 'What if the foregoing paradoxes of the world of the "running down" energy, and of the endlessly consolidating matter, were due to the fact that we have been trying to give an hypothetical account of an absolute world-process in terms of human forms of conception and of experience? What if the truly complete world-process does not occur in time at all, but can only be conceived "under the form of eternity," as Spinoza would have said? .... What if both the permanent laws and energy of nature on the one hand, and what we know as the process of evolution on the other, were but the temporal sign of something whose significance is to be otherwise conceived?' In contrast to Kant, Royce looks to philosophy to provide at least speculative propositions that point beyond what is merely observable, and ultimately finds the key in the concept of 'consciousness'.

Under such circumstances, the theologian will at least have a reason for pursuing an evolutionary method where the secularist does not.[76]

Although Rauschenbusch does not finally embrace evolutionary ethics, his method must be described nevertheless as evolutionary, and progressive. Considering the way idealism informs his view of nature and evolution, helping Rauschenbusch to interpret nature and love in terms of solidarity and collectivity, the accusation that he has a utopian expectation of a 'fulfilment of history in history' cannot stand.[77] It is clearly a fulfilment not an historical *finis* that Rauschenbusch anticipates, since he 'cannot conceive of finite existence or of human happiness except in terms of growth.'[78] It is fair to say, then, that 'Rauschenbusch was an optimist about progress, though not progress unto perfection.'[79]

It is important to recognise that history, not nature, was the fundamental category of Rauschenbusch's thought.[80] This means that 'history rather than nature offered proof that evolution was progressive and teleological.'[81] He may thus be grouped with those evolutionary theologians who 'shifted the evidence of nature to the arena of history and looked for evidence of human progress in the increasing prosperity and morality they believed signified an almost Christian nation.' As Janet Fishburn writes, social gospel advocates represented part of a methodological shift 'to the "new" evolutionary interpretation of history as their defense against [reaction to] Darwin.'[82] Darwinism really had no arguable goal, no teleology and no ethical meaning. As with Huxley's bean analogy, nature was part of an endless cycle of life and death. It became clear to

---

[76]Flew, *Evolutionary Ethics,* 50.

[77]Reinhard Hutter, 'The Church: Midwife of History or Witness of the Eschaton?' *JRE* 18:1 (Spring 1990): 38. Cf. Richard Dickinson, 'The Church's Responsibility for Society: I. Rauschenbusch and Niebuhr: Brothers Under the Skin?' *RL* XXVII:2 (Spring 1958).

[78]Rauschenbusch, *A Theology for the Social Gospel,* 233.

[79]Harlan Beckley, *Passion for Justice,* 48. Harry Emerson Fosdick suggests that Rauschenbusch had one of the more realistic and balanced views of progress amongst his contemporaries. See Fosdick's 'Interpretation of the Life and Work of Walter Rauschenbusch, in *A Rauschenbusch Reader: The Kingdom of God and the Social Gospel* (Benson Landis, New York: Harper and Brothers, 1957).

[80]Stackhouse makes this suggestion in his introduction to *The Righteousness of the Kingdom.* Cf. David Alan McClintock, 'Walter Rauschenbusch: The Kingdom of God and the American Experience' (Ph.D. diss., Case Western Reserve University, 1975). McClintock examines Rauschenbusch's theory of history, which he sees as central to his social gospel thought.

[81]Darlene Pietz, *Solidarity as Hermeneutic: A Revisionist Reading of the Theology of Walter Rauschenbusch,* American University Studies Series VII vol. 122 (New York: Peter Lang, 1992), 128.

[82]Janet Forsyth Fishburn, *The Fatherhood of God and the Victorian Family: The Social Gospel in America* (Philadelphia, PA: Fortress Press, 1981), 49.

some that evolutionary science needed a more purposeful direction and moral interpretation 'before its integration into American social and Christian thinking would be possible.' For 'without a teleology, the evolutionary process seemed amoral, and devoid of priorities which could define the process as progress.'[83]

Rauschenbusch's teleology then, ultimately marries the eschatology of the Kingdom of God with the concept of evolution in modern science, and he does not recognise any difficulty with their relationship. 'Any doctrine about the future of the race which is to guide our thought and action, must view it from distinctly Christian, ethical points of view, and must not contradict what is historically and scientifically certain,' he writes.[84] Idealism gives Rauschenbusch the raw materials for interpreting nature *qua* nature, and interpreting the natural order as an expression of the mind of God. Understood in historical rather than scientific terms, social evolution reveals a progressive process, which is increasing the social consciousness of humanity, and nurturing the bonds of love and unity. This aspect of his method contributes significantly to his belief that the structures of society can and will be reformed to the benefit of humanity as a whole. But his collective application of idealism leads Rauschenbusch into methodological difficulties as he attempts to reconcile scientific and social theory with Christian doctrine, as this early analysis reveals, and as the following study will confirm.

---

[83]Ibid.
[84]Rauschenbusch, *A Theology for the Social Gospel*, 208-9.

CHAPTER 3

The Fatherland of the Soul: Theological Impulses in Walter Rauschenbusch's Social Gospel Method

So it is when my soul steps through the postern gate
Into the presence of God.
Big things become small and small things become great.
The near becomes far and the future is near.
The lowly and despised is shot through with glory,
And most of human power and greatness
Seems full of infernal iniquities
As a carcass is full of maggots.
God is the substance of all revolutions;
When I am in him, I am in the Kingdom of God
And in the fatherland of my Soul.

Walter Rauschenbusch, The Little Gate to God

Introduction

Considering the title of Rauschenbusch's best-known work, it may not be difficult to confirm the suspicion arising from the study of Rauschenbusch's philosophical method - namely, that his theology was constructed to conform to his philosophy and reflected clearly a reinterpretation of 'traditional' theological concepts into collective categories. Rauschenbusch admitted this was his task in *A Theology for the Social Gospel*: '...to show that a readjustment and expansion of theology, so that it will furnish an adequate intellectual basis for the social gospel, is necessary, feasible, desirable, and legitimate,' and to offer 'concrete suggestions how some of the most important sections of doctrinal theology may be expanded and readjusted to make room for the religious convictions summed up in "the social gospel".'[1] He justified this approach through an appeal to the authority of the collective consciousness, arguing, 'All those social groups which distinctly face toward the future, clearly show their need and craving for a social interpretation and application of

---

[1]Walter Rauschenbusch, *A Theology for the Social Gospel*, 1.

Christianity'.[2] Rauschenbusch revealed his philosophical bias even more clearly when he suggested that, 'The argument of this book is built on the conviction that the social gospel is a permanent addition to our spiritual outlook and that its arrival constitutes a stage in the development of the Christian religion.'[3] Moreover, he argued, 'The individualistic gospel has taught us to see the sinfulness of every human heart and has inspired us with faith in the willingness and power of God to save every soul that comes to him. But it has not given us an adequate understanding of the sinfulness of the social order and its share in the sins of all individuals within it.'[4] A collective interpretation of theology is what Rauschenbusch proposed to offer in response to this perceived neglect.

Having established the centrality of the philosophical concept of 'solidarity of consciousness' in Rauschenbusch's thought, it becomes evident through an examination of his theology that this theme not only remained present in his elaboration of major theological categories, but it largely shaped his doctrinal reinterpretations which themselves reinforced his philosophical ideas. This position will be argued through an examination of three aspects of Rauschenbusch's theology, as his elaboration of the doctrines of humanity, Jesus Christ, and the church are considered.

When Rauschenbusch's rejection of metaphysics in favour of ethics is considered in relation to his theology, the pragmatic leanings of his variant idealism are emphasized. This means Rauschenbusch developed a theological method that began with the human situation and moved from there to consider the role of God in relation to the human problem. The doctrines of sin and salvation were primary, and their interpretation largely influenced Rauschenbusch's conception of God and correlative doctrines. This is not an accidental method, but one that Rauschenbusch developed with clear intent: 'Now, the doctrines of sin and salvation are the starting-point and goal of Christian theology. Every essential change or enlargement in them is bound to affect related doctrines also.'[5] Following Rauschenbusch's method, this meant that the doctrines of sin and salvation were reinterpreted according to a collective understanding of humanity, and their social interpretation influenced the doctrinal development of the concept of God. The culmination was the kingdom of God idea, which Rauschenbusch believed was able to knit the various elements of social doctrine together into a coherent method of interpretation, and which effectively replaced a traditional understanding of the church.

---

[2] Ibid., 3.
[3] Ibid., 2.
[4] Ibid., 5.
[5] Ibid., 167.

Christian Anthropology

Rauschenbusch's doctrine of humanity is expressed through his exposition of the solidarity that binds humanity together in sin and salvation. Rauschenbusch believes that nowhere is the need so great for socialising theological concepts than in the Christian doctrine of sin, defined over and against the kingdom of God as the 'kingdom of Evil.' He bemoans his perception that theology 'has not given adequate attention to the social idealizations of evil, which falsify the ethical standards for the individual by the authority of his group or community, deaden the voice of the Holy Spirit to the conscience of individuals and communities, and perpetuate antiquated wrongs in society. These social idealizations are the real heretical doctrines from the point of view of the Kingdom of God.'[6] The matter of how Rauschenbusch has attained this privileged viewpoint aside, it becomes increasingly clear that he intends to use a doctrine of original sin, redefined as the kingdom of evil, to further build his argument for the existence of a collective consciousness. For help on this matter, he turns to the theologian Friedrich Schleiermacher, whom he describes as 'one of the really creative minds of Protestant theology.'[7]

Collective Sin

In his discussion of human sin, it is clear from the very outset that Rauschenbusch agrees with Schleiermacher that 'the sin of the individual has its source in something beyond and prior to his own existence.'[8] And yet, original sin 'is at the same time so really the personal guilt of every individual who shares in it that it is best represented as the corporate act and the corporate guilt of the human race.' The subsequent recognition of the corporate nature of sin 'is likewise recognition of the universal need of redemption.'[9] Rauschenbusch appeals to Schleiermacher's interpretation of sin as possessing an intrinsic and extrinsic collective nature, and offers the following translation of several paragraphs of Schleiermacher's *Der Christliche Glaube*

> If now, this sinfulness which precedes all acts of sin, is produced in every individual through the sinful acts and condition of others, and if on the other hand every man by his own free actions propagates and strengthens it in others; then it is something wholly common to us. Whether we view this sinfulness as guilt and as conscious action, or as a principle and condition of life, in either aspect it is something wholly common, not pertaining to every individual separately or

---

[6]Ibid., 78.

[7]Ibid., 92.

[8]Friedrich Schleiermacher, *The Christian Faith*, English translation of the second German Edition, ed. H. R. Mackintosh and J. S. Stewart (Edinburgh: T&T Clark, 1928), 279. For a collection of Schleiermacher's ethical writings, see Friedrich Schleiermacher, *Introduction to Christian Ethics*, trans. John C. Shelley, (Nashville: Abingdon, 1989).

[9]Schleiermacher, *The Christian Faith,* 285.

referring to him alone, but *in each the work of all, and in all the work of each.* In fact we can understand it justly and completely only in this solidarity. For that reason the doctrines dealing with it are never to be taken as expressions of individual self-consciousness, but they are expressions of the common consciousness.[10]

Rauschenbusch borrows this definition of sin as a collective reality, though he filters it through his reading of Albrecht Ritschl, who modified Schleiermacher's view, while holding fast to an understanding of sin's corporate nature.

Ritschl exerts the single most significant influence over Rauschenbusch's theology, and Rauschenbusch describes him as, 'another incisive and original thinker.' Rauschenbusch appeals to Ritschl to bolster his definition of sin as a collective reality. Ritschl, says Rauschenbusch, 'adopted this solidaristic conception of sin, and its correlated ideas in the doctrine of salvation, as the basis of his theological system.' Rauschenbusch concurs that 'this, and not the theory of subjective religion which is commonly quoted in connection with his name, is Schleiermacher's epoch-making contribution to theology,' and agrees with Ritschl that this collective understanding 'is one of the fundamental conditions of religion, without which it can neither be rightly understood or rightly lived.'[11] Ritschl's own description of Christianity as the ethical religion *par excellence* testifies to the moral core of his theology, though he disagrees with Schleiermacher regarding the definition of the collective dimension of sin

---

[10]Rauschenbusch, *A Theology for the Social Gospel*, 92-3. Cf. Schleiermacher, 288. Rauschenbusch's translation is very close to that of later English translations. His ready access to German works (owing to his bilingualism) and the extent to which he often borrowed from them reveal a far less uniquely American view than some scholars attribute to Rauschenbusch. Cf. Willem Visser't Hooft, *The Background of the Social Gospel in America*. Visser't Hooft's stated goal was to discover the influences that led to a distinctly American Christian movement, and to establish it as a theological development apart from European influence. He wrote, 'We shall find that a number of influences at work in America originated in the country itself and that of the influences from abroad many were so thoroughly nationalized that their foreign aspect was forgotten and their nature changed.' Visser't Hooft's early analysis has long stood as the predominant view regarding the unique and independent nature of the social gospel. Paul Phillips has recently examined some of the connections between the social gospel in America and Britain. See *A Kingdom on Earth: Anglo-American Social Christianity 1880-1940*. But European influences have been largely ignored by most interpretations of the social gospel. Considering Rauschenbusch's extensive contacts with Europe and the fact that most of his reading and intellectual mentors were European, the unique 'American-ness' of Rauschenbusch's theology has perhaps been overestimated and overstated.
[11]Rauschenbusch, *Theology for the Social Gospel*, 93-4.

as *original*.[12]

For Schleiermacher, the universal self-consciousness that inhibits the emergence of humanity's God-consciousness is defined generally as original sin. Rather than an inherited alteration of human character, such sinfulness is described more as a condition in which all of humanity participates through a common bond.[13] While Ritschl affirms Schleiermacher's collective interpretation of sin, he prefers to describe the corporate elements as belonging to *the kingdom of sin*, a concept intended to replace that of original sin. Asserting his notion of the kingdom of sin, Ritschl vigorously argues that humans 'can only regard ourselves as sharing its guilt when we not only attribute to ourselves our own sinful actions as such, but at the same time calculate how they produce sin in others also, although we may possess no complete or distinct idea of the extent of these effects.'[14] At the same time, Ritschl suggests, the effects are manifested 'in the blunting of our moral vigilance and our moral judgement,' as a form of sinful federation with others which affects everyone.[15]

Ritschl describes it as 'a merit in Schleiermacher to have formed the above conception of common sin, in which are to be included all particular actions. Only he did wrong in inserting it under the traditional heading of original sin, to which it bears very little resemblance.'[16] Ritschl prefers to abandon the concept of original sin, as it is bound to interpret sin in metaphysical terms as an inherited corruption, after the traditions of Augustine and Luther. His intention is to define sin as grounded in 'the self-determination of the individual will' and to describe its elements of self-striving as wilful defiance against God rather than as any sort of original law.[17] Sin in its individual and collective forms, along with its individual and collective results, is to be described anew as the kingdom of evil. Ritschl's denial of original sin in its traditional definition emphasises the principle of moral freedom, and reveals the influence of Kant on his system. The resulting discrepancy between Schleiermacher and Ritschl may be of some help in explaining Rauschenbusch's contradictory understanding of human nature as exhibiting both the selfish tendencies of original sin and latent perfectibility, discussed in the previous chapter.

Rauschenbusch borrows several of these theological elements from Ritschl

---

[12]Albrecht Ritschl, *The Christian Doctrine of Justification and Reconciliation*, ed. English translation., H. R. Mackintosh and A. B. Macaulay (Edinburgh: T & T Clark, 1902), 526. For relevant studies of Ritschl see: A. E. Garvie, *The Ritschlian Theology* (Edinburgh: T&T Clark, 1899); James Orr, *Theology and the Evangelical Faith* (London: Hodder & Stoughton, 1898); James Richmond, *Ritschl: A Reappraisal. A Study in Systematic Theology* (London: Collins, 1978).
[13]Schleiermacher, *The Christian Faith*, 291ff.
[14]Ritschl, *Justification and Reconciliation*, 338.
[15]Ibid.
[16]Ibid., 339.
[17]Ibid., 349.

and Schleiermacher, and builds them into a collectively defined understanding of sin, which considers the solidarity of humanity across boundaries of society and generation. With Ritschl, he rejects the traditional interpretation of the fall and original sin as an 'unvarying racial endowment', active in every individual, and 'which can be overcome only by the Grace offered in the Gospel and ministered by the Church. It would strengthen the appeal of the social gospel,' he argues, 'if evil could be regarded instead as a variable factor in the life of humanity, which it is our duty to diminish for every young life and every new generation.'[18] Rauschenbusch does not deny that there is a significant relationship between sin and the individual, allowing that sin's 'quality, degree, and culpability vary according to the individual, according to his social freedom, and his power over others.'[19] But even in this connection, he is keen to emphasise the social aspect of individual action and attitude. Once again, contrary to other elements of his argument, he describes sin as part of human nature, though humans are guilty of sin only inasmuch as individual will and reason participate in it. Defining sin as a sliding scale of self-interest, expressed as sensuousness, selfishness, and godlessness, Rauschenbusch regards the worse forms of sin as those that offend the good of humanity, and the universal good. 'The definition of sin as selfishness furnishes an excellent theological basis for a social conception of sin and salvation,' he writes.[20] Moreover, the social gospel is able to make a significant contribution towards socialising and vitalising these doctrines.

According to Rauschenbusch's social interpretation, sin is never 'a private transaction between the sinner and God. Humanity always crowds the audience-room when God holds court.' Sin is enacted not against God only, but against God-in-humanity. Rauschenbusch believes that democratising the theological conception of God yields an understanding of sin as transgression against humanity where God is present within human society. He sees it as an ethical imperative that God and humanity be bound together in any doctrine of sin, which logically abandons sin to the realm of individual action against the collective social interest.

Rauschenbusch does not follow this line of argument logically, however. He believes not only that sin has collective consequences, but that it has social origins as well. The transmission of sin is clearly a social phenomenon in Rauschenbusch's method, as he attributes more moral authority to society as a whole than to its individual members. In his view, individuals will succumb to sin largely to the degree in which specific sins are advocated or condemned by the wider society. 'A group may be better or worse than a given member in it,' he writes. The group 'may require more neatness, fortitude, efficiency, and hard work than he is accustomed to... On the other hand, if a group practices evil, it

---

[18]Rauschenbusch, *Theology for the Social Gospel*, 43.
[19]Ibid., 45.
[20]Ibid., 47.

will excuse or idealise it, and resent any private judgement which condemns it.' In such cases, evil 'becomes part of the standards of morality sanctioned by the authority of society. This confuses the moral judgement of the individual.' The moral authority of society is an important key to understanding Rauschenbusch's method, as he believes strongly that 'religious faith in the individual would be weak and intermittent unless it could lean on permanent social authorities.' Similarly, in the individual, sin is 'shame-faced and cowardly except where society backs and protects it.' [21]

Sin as a collective reality for Rauschenbusch is also expressed in his description of super-personal forces. He recognises early the existence of evil forces that fall outside of individual responsibility, describing their public manifestations as 'the devil's spider webs,' before which evangelical Christians 'sometimes reverently bow,' praising them as 'mighty works of God.'[22] Ideas developed by later critics are actually found here in Rauschenbusch's thought as he describes evil forces as social institutions which have idealised themselves at the expense of those who do not benefit from their existence. In particular, he cites the example of capitalism as a system held in reverent regard by its beneficiaries, but which carries grave moral consequences for those who do not possess a vested interest in an expanding profit margin.[23] Such evil collective forces are equated generally with institutions that have 'fallen from a better estate,' and as their goals become idealised, they exert whatever pressure is necessary in order to succeed. Similarly, the greater potential for good which an organisation possesses, the greater evil it is capable of when it succumbs to selfish, sinful tendencies.[24] Rauschenbusch does not separate finally the sinful condition from the sinful act, as humanity is ultimately responsible for changing these super-personal forces, which are described as corporate personalities capable of moral action, including repentance.

Rauschenbusch reflects Ritschl's idea of humanity's *justitia originalis* when he suggests the possibility of collective repentance.[25] However, he recognises that repentance is a moral act made possible by Jesus Christ, who represented

---

[21]Ibid., 62.

[22]Rauschenbusch, *Christianity and the Social Crisis*, 349.

[23]Ibid., 350-1.

[24]Rauschenbusch, *Theology for the Social Gospel*, 72-3. Cf. Jan Milic Lochman, *The Faith We Confess: An Ecumenical Dogmatics*, trans. David Lewis (Edinburgh: T & T Clark, 1984), 225-6. Lochman describes sin as both condition and act, stressing the non-personal nature of the sinful forces that exist in the economic and social order. Wolfhart Pannenberg acknowledges the communal and individual aspects of sin elaborated by Kant, Schleiermacher and Ritschl, but suggests that any theological understanding of 'sins' should not be divorced from the biblical notion of the human condition of 'sin'. See Wolfhart Pannenberg, *Anthropology in Theological Perspective*, trans. Matthew J. O'Connell (Edinburgh: T & T Clark, 1985).

[25]Cf. Ritschl's doctrine of sin in *Justification and Reconciliation*, 327-384.

the ultimate expression of humanity's God-consciousness, and who founded a new and dynamic kingdom of God to replace the kingdom of evil. Subsequently, humanity's God-consciousness is expressed as a universal brotherhood, whose practice of Christian ethics was made possible through a racial salvation. Though he never denies a place for preaching the individual salvation of souls, Rauschenbusch believes finally that a corporate problem demands a corporate solution.[26]

Christological Considerations

The social gospel conception of God was examined in the previous chapter in connection with Rauschenbusch's idealism, and most contemporary theological social thought was generally in keeping with that school of philosophy. W. A. Visser't Hooft attributed the resultant theology to a blend of Puritan revivalism and Enlightenment liberalism, and he hinted at, but neglected, a study of the social gospel's idealist philosophy.[27] However, regardless of whether social gospel theology is traced through philosophy or history, the subsequent doctrine of God is the same: 'God is to be identified with the norms which we find as it were inscribed into the universe. Thus He is the indwelling law of all things, in nature as natural law, in man as the rational and ethical law of human life, as reason and conscience.'[28] God's 'function is therefore to strengthen these forces that are already given in human life rather than to reveal His Will continuously to man. Revelation is universal.... Transcendence does not mean an absolute difference from, but rather an addition to humanity. Similarly divine and human reality stand in a continuous relationship with each other.'[29]

The moralised conception of God that emerges from this theology suppresses 'the notion of God's Sovereignty in the interests of his love and benevolence for humanity.'[30] The notion of God's Fatherhood becomes the primary focus of doctrine, in an expressed hope that it will bring humanity back to a proper perception of the life and religion of Jesus, and subsequently, the spirit of Jesus will be expressed in communal life. This doctrine lay at the heart of what social theologians preferred to call 'democratised' or 'democratic' ethics as opposed to those more traditional 'authoritarian' ethics - 'that God is

---

[26]Further discussion of the relationship between the individual and the collective consciousness in Rauschenbusch's theology may be found below in an examination of his conception of the kingdom of God.

[27]Even Donovan Smucker, who provides a study of the origins of Rauschenbusch's social ethics, offers only passing references to his developing philosophical idealism.

[28]Visser't Hooft, 170.

[29]Visser't Hooft suggests that the lack of awareness of the inability of social gospel thinkers to reconcile this philosophy with their conception of a personal God led many to an antithetical position towards the doctrine of God. They did not realize they could not have it both ways. See Visser't Hooft, 170-171.

[30]Ibid., 174.

the immanent co-worker, toiling with his children, and that salvation is a process of co-operation with God.'[31] It becomes immediately apparent that even the social gospel doctrine of God is really an extension of the theology of humanity, which is itself derived from principles of idealist philosophy. G. B. Smith stated approvingly of Rauschenbusch, 'It is only in so far as God is concerned with human welfare that this social theology has any place for him.'[32]

Considering Rauschenbusch's philosophy, and his anthropology, the primary questions become: *What sort of Christ was required for the solution of humanity's most basic problem Was Jesus to be regarded more as God's revelation or humanity's achievement?* It is largely true that 'in his Christology Rauschenbusch shows the strong influence of the Ritschlian point of view. Jesus appears as a unique individual who taught a perfect theology so far as the social gospel is concerned.'[33] But it will be further demonstrated that in social gospel thought, as expressed in Rauschenbusch's work, the life of Jesus represented both a revelation of God and an achievement of humanity that confirmed the solidarity of the human race and initiated a corporate solution to the problem of corporate sin. Essentially, 'as initiator of the kingdom, the important thing about Jesus is his moral will and his social sympathy. It is his "unity with the will of God," rather than a divine essence which describes his significance. Schleiermacher's definition of Jesus in terms of a perfect God-consciousness is reproduced with the social rather than the individual-mystical emphasis.'[34] In this way, Rauschenbusch is able to maintain the primary significance of collective moral life.

Jesus the Social Reformer

Methodologically, Rauschenbusch acknowledges that the kind of Christ he portrays depends largely on the perceived problem of humanity. He is firm in his contention that this is the only way of doing Christology, suggesting that 'Theologians have always tried to make their christology match with their conception of salvation.'[35] Moreover, he believes that such conceptions are only partial estimations of the whole doctrinal picture, as he argues that in the past, 'each conception of salvation made a pragmatic selection and construction of the facts. Each was fragmentary, but without necessarily excluding other series of ideas.' Following this pattern, 'the social gospel, without excluding other

---

[31]Eugene Lyman, 'Social Idealism and the Changing Theology,' *AJT* 17 (October 1913): 643.

[32]Gerald Birney Smith's review of 'A Theology for the Social Gospel,' *AJT* 22 (October 1918): 584.

[33]Ibid., 585-6.

[34]Ibid., 586. Cf. Rauschenbusch, *Theology for the Social Gospel*, 154.

[35]Rauschenbusch, *Theology for the Social Gospel*, 147.

theological convictions, demands to understand that Christ who set in motion the historical forces of redemption which are to overthrow the Kingdom of Evil.' Despite an attempt not to dismiss previous doctrinal conceptions of Christ, Rauschenbusch nevertheless asserts, with a degree of historical arrogance, that the quest of the social gospel to uncover a more comprehensive and collective interpretation of Christ 'is surely not an illegitimate interest. It is a return to the earliest messianic theology; whereas some of the other christological interests and ideas are alien importations....'

Seeking further justification of his method, Rauschenbusch suggests that previous to his own theological attempt, 'The speculative problem of christological dogma was how the divine and human natures united in the one person of Christ,' but now 'the problem of the social gospel is how the divine life of Christ can get control of human society. The social gospel is concerned about a progressive social incarnation of God.'[36] Rauschenbusch is seemingly unaware that there are other possible approaches to a moral Christology, quite distinct from the social gospel, and yet similarly unconcerned with metaphysical speculations.[37] He is content to posit the social gospel approach ultimately as the correct one.

This is not to say that Rauschenbusch claimed Jesus as the champion of any particular manifestation of the social movement. He wanted to guard against any attempt to marginalise Jesus as the exclusive representative of any specific party involved in social reform. Rauschenbusch sought to free Jesus from socio-political labelling and affirmed his universal relevance as he argued that

> Jesus was not a social reformer of the modern type. Sociology and political economy were just as far outside of his range of thought as organic chemistry or the geography of America. He saw the evil in the life of men and their sufferings, but he approached these facts purely from the moral, and not from the economic or historical point of view. He wanted men to live a right life in common, and only in so far as the social questions are moral questions did he deal with them as they confronted him.[38]

Evident here is Rauschenbusch's desire for a moral and thoroughly collective interpretation of Christ's life and teaching. Jesus was more than a social hero - he was the initiator of the modern social process. Jesus stood in the tradition of the prophets, and was counted among them, but his life and achievement were seen as a realisation of their hope and faith.

As more than a mere teacher of morality, 'Jesus had learned the greatest and

---

[36]Ibid., 147-8.
[37]See for example the work of Peter Taylor Forsyth, who was a contemporary of Rauschenbusch, but who understood the significance of the Cross of Christ in a very different way in the midst of a changing social climate.
[38]Rauschenbusch, *Christianity and the Social Crisis,* 47.

deepest and rarest secret of all - how to live a religious life.'[39] Jesus' life was an accomplishment of complete unity in consciousness between God and humanity, in Rauschenbusch's view

> Jesus had realized the life of God in the soul of man and the life of man in the love of God. That was the real secret of his life, the well-spring of his purity, his compassion, his unwearied courage, his unquenchable idealism: he knew the Father. But if he had that greatest of all possessions, the real key to the secret of life, it was his highest social duty to share it and help others to gain what he had. He had to teach men to live as children in the presence of their Father, and no longer as slaves cringing before a despot. He had to show them that the ordinary life of selfishness and hate and anxiety and chafing ambition and covetousness is no life at all, and that they must enter into a new world of love and solidarity and inward contentment. There was no service that he could render to men which would equal that.[40]

Considering this very clear statement about Jesus' life and purpose, it becomes evident that the Jesus of the social gospel was considered at least as equally important for what he demonstrated, as what he achieved. His life of illustration and example was a primary part of the solution to humanity's problem of selfishness. Jesus' acquisition of the consciousness of God, and embodying that consciousness in everyday activity was the path to be followed by everyone who would walk in the footsteps of the Elder Brother.[41] Even in this respect, Rauschenbusch's social gospel Christology consistently displayed a solidaristic interpretation and application.

Atonement for Social Sin

Rauschenbusch carried forward his collective understanding of Christ in a discussion of the atonement, where he continued to borrow heavily from Ritschl. He dismissed traditional interpretations of the atonement, describing theories of ransom, satisfaction, and substitution as 'post-biblical ideas...alien from the spirit of the gospel.'[42] They proved inadequate as their social origins and applications were originally absent or later stripped away. And so he claimed the methodological right to develop a new Christology based on the needs and desires of the contemporary social context. To this end, he justified his method, arguing that

---

[39]Ibid.

[40]Ibid., 48.

[41]This idea characterized the general ethos of the period, and is expressed clearly in the hymnody that emerged at the same time as the social gospel. See for example, Washington Gladden's *O Master, Let Me Walk with Thee,* and William Merrill's *Rise Up, O Men of God.*

[42]Rauschenbusch, *Theology for the Social Gospel,* 243.

our dominant ideas are personality and social solidarity. The problems which burden us are the social problems. Has the death of Christ any relation to these? Have we not just as much right to connect this supreme religious event with our problems as Paul and Anselm and Calvin, and to use the terminology and methods of our day? In so far as the historical and social sciences have taught our generation to comprehend solidaristic facts, we are in a better situation to understand the atonement than any previous generation.[43]

For Rauschenbusch, the ultimate significance of the cross was Jesus' action of opposition to the collective sin that sought to destroy him, and finally crucified him. Jesus bore the sins of humanity in so far as he withstood to the point of suffering the social forces that led finally to his death. Accordingly, Rauschenbusch developed a thoroughly contextualised Christology, offering new interpretations of old doctrines based on the impetus and sentiments of the contemporary social movement.

Protestant liberals welcomed Rauschenbusch's theological and Christological contributions, as they expressed theologically what essentially was social practice in and outside of the churches. One leading social thinker, G. B. Smith commented approvingly on Rauschenbusch's adaptation of the atonement, 'It is not a forensic or vicarious penalty which Jesus bears. It is the actual consequence of actual sins of which we are guilty. The redemptive power of his death is found in its capacity to evoke repentance from us, in its revelation of divine, self-sacrificing love, and in its enforcement of prophetic religion.' He noted further that, 'In this exposition comes a curiously anthropomorphic representation of the effect of the death of Jesus on God,' citing Rauschenbusch's suggestion that, 'The death of Jesus must have been a great experience for God.... If the principle of forgiving love had not been in the heart of God before, this experience would fix it there. If he had ever thought and felt like the Jewish Jehovah, he would henceforth think and feel as the Father of Jesus Christ.'[44] Smith compared this with another of Rauschenbusch's statements: 'He [Jesus] not only saved humanity; he saved God. He gave God his first chance of being loved and of escaping from the worst misunderstandings conceivable.'[45] Considering these rather odd theological assertions, Smith quite correctly wondered 'if such statements would have been made if the author had not been labouring under the apologetic necessity of giving some kind of content to the traditional conception of the atonement as removing an obstacle to God's ability to forgive.' [46]

Rauschenbusch encountered such methodological trouble when he attempted

---

[43]Ibid., 244.

[44]Cf. Rauschenbusch, *Theology for the Social Gospel,* 264.

[45]Cf. Ibid., 175. One might be forgiven for detecting a ring of Marcionism in such statements.

[46]G. B. Smith, review of 'A Theology for the Social Gospel,' 587.

to make the social gospel 'fit' into traditional theological categories. As these statements suggest, he succeeded neither in clarifying his own solidaristic views of Christology, nor in transforming old categories into new ones. In this sense, Rauschenbusch might have better served his task of developing a theology for the social gospel by refraining from forcing social gospel concepts into traditional categories, and allowing himself to describe social gospel theology in more positive terms. On this point, Smith's critique of Rauschenbusch's method is more sweeping, accusing Rauschenbusch of failing to follow consistently a collective approach. 'In the final analysis,' Smith writes, Rauschenbusch 'appeals to a single authority in history, and denies a truly social method.' He argues, 'the result is inconsistent.... The social conception, which is so admirably evident in the content of the message, has not been carried over into the realm of method. The author gives us a social gospel, but not a social way of theologizing....This is the language of a theology which justifies its doctrines by appeal to a superhuman authority rather than by consulting the exigencies of social life.'[47]

Despite the confidence with which Smith offers his critique of Rauschenbusch's failure to provide a thoroughly socialised Christology, it cannot withstand evidence to the contrary. Rauschenbusch's inconsistent use of language often leads to confusion, and as Visser't Hooft points out, the lack of depth in theological reflection frequently fails to weed out these inconsistencies. If forced to clarify this issue, the weight of evidence would place Rauschenbusch's theological method squarely where Smith said it ought to be, in the realm of social life, with the experience of collective humanity as its authority. This conclusion may be clearly drawn from his doctrines of humanity and salvation, as they emerge from his philosophical presuppositions. Despite occasional language that might indicate the contrary, Rauschenbusch's methodological practice shows generally that his very understanding of the person and work of Christ is thoroughly dependent on the present needs of society as a whole. His idealism confirms that the authority of society, the social gospel, and Jesus are one and the same. Smith is perhaps too ready to take Rauschenbusch's words and categories in *A Theology for the Social Gospel* at face value, and thus fails to examine his methodological practice, which is very much a 'social [and contextual] way of theologizing.'

Nevertheless, it may be suggested that Rauschenbusch describes a Jesus who is less than a Christ, who demonstrated more than he achieved.[48] If

---

[47]Ibid., 588.

[48]Theological conservatives were not so welcoming of social gospel theology as their liberal counterparts. Social gospel chronicler Charles Hopkins has noted several voices of opposition, including the editor of the *Biblical Repertory and Princeton Review* who, as early as 1868, scathingly dismissed the growing social impulse, suggesting that 'The advocates of spiritualism, of woman's rights, of social changes of nearly every kind, have nearly all of them been touched with a liberalism amounting to deism, and are

Rauschenbusch's Jesus is simply the exemplar Christ, the great teacher and elder brother of the human race, the social gospel may be accused of denying the uniqueness of the person and work of Christ, or at least of dismissing the importance of the interpretation of Jesus' atonement through the ages of Christian history. Rauschenbusch's belief is that every understanding of the cross of Christ is contextual, and so his theological assertions are to be considered at least as valid, if not more valid, than those that preceded the social gospel. Historical hubris notwithstanding, Rauschenbusch's view follows consistently his belief in the progressive nature of the realisation of the mind of God in humanity. For the social gospel, the revision of theology to speak from and to the new collective reality represents a stage of growth in humanity, brought about by an increasing presence of God-consciousness in humanity as a whole, and made possible by Jesus' original achievement. Jesus represented continuity of revelation as he stood in the tradition of the Old Testament prophets, and his aim, like John the Baptist, 'was the realization of the theocracy.'[49] Unlike the prophets who went before, Jesus did not merely preach about the kingdom, but he represented its fulfilment.

Rauschenbusch refers to Jesus as 'infinitely above' the prophets, suggesting a difference of degree rather than quality, deferring to Wellhausen's description of Jesus' 'superiority'.[50] Rauschenbusch is keen to highlight Jesus' firm position amongst the prophets in order to bolster his contention regarding the inseparable connection between prophetic religion and the social life of the nation. But he finally admits that Jesus 'was not merely an initiator, but a consummator. Like all great minds that do not merely imagine Utopias, but actually advance humanity to a new epoch, he took the situation and material furnished to him by the past and moulded that into a fuller approximation to the divine conception within him.'[51] Thus Rauschenbusch contends that the difference between Jesus and the former prophets is, in fact, qualitative - 'Jesus incarnated a new type of human life and he was conscious of that.'[52] In this aspect of Christology, Rauschenbusch demonstrates that the mind of God is

---

inclined to reject as authoritative the Old and New Testament writers. *Biblical Repertory and Princeton Review*, 40, 1868, 126-7, cited in Charles H. Hopkins, *The Rise of the Social Gospel in American Protestantism 1868-1915*, (1940; reprint, New Haven, CT: Yale University Press, 1967), 16. Rauschenbusch encountered some of his greatest opposition from millenarians, and spent a good deal of time countering their views in the early days of his fraternal organization, 'The Brotherhood of the Kingdom.' See, for example, 'Our Attitude Toward Millenarianism,' *The Examiner* (24 Sept. and 1 Oct. 1896), reprinted in Winthrop Hudson ed., *Walter Rauschenbusch: Selected Writings* (New York: Paulist Press, 1984), 79-94.

[49]Rauschenbusch, *Christianity and the Social Crisis,* 53.

[50]Ibid. Rauschenbusch refers the reader to Wellhausen's *Isrealitische und Judische Geschichte*, Chapter 24.

[51]Ibid., 54.

[52]Ibid., 60.

ultimately concerned with the social life of humanity, as revealed in the personality and teaching of Jesus who, though unique, stood in the prophetic tradition with primary concern for the life of the human community rather than the human individual.

Rauschenbusch is not so single-minded in his efforts as to deny the significance of individual encounters with the historical Jesus, or the Christ of faith. In his life and preaching, he clings tenaciously to an evangelical view of the importance of individual appropriation of faith, but vehemently argues that the salvation of the individual was not Jesus' primary motive. He admits, 'Jesus worked on individuals and through individuals, but his real end was not individualistic, but social, and in his method he employed strong social forces...his end was not the new soul, but the new society; not man, but Man.'[53] Motivated and empowered by a unique level of God-consciousness which enabled him to appreciate the collective nature of moral life, Jesus was uniquely qualified to initiate and fulfil what was foreseen by the prophets. He fulfilled his mission successfully through initiating the kingdom of God. The kingdom of God as a dynamically progressive concept provides Rauschenbusch with the key doctrine of his theological method, satisfying the requirements of his philosophical basis and lending a structural framework to his method of ethical practice.

The Kingdom of God, the Church, and Society

In the previous chapter, I pointed to some of the ways in which philosophical idealism made Rauschenbusch's adoption of the kingdom of God as a unifying concept possible. Here, in a brief analysis of his theology, several elements have been identified that make its adoption as a unifying concept necessary. Humanity is portrayed as being bound up in a social moral existence, with a common spiritual problem. Jesus Christ, through his unique achievement of human God-consciousness, taught and demonstrated a social salvation for the problem of social sin. Appropriation of the Christian faith may well begin with each individual, but Rauschenbusch needs a bigger vision that will tie his collective vision together, giving it power and direction for the practical task of

---

[53]Ibid., 60-1. Dietrich Bonhoeffer makes a similar statement in his writings, regarding the two-fold relationship Christ has with individuals and the community. Cf. Dietrich Bonhoeffer, *The Cost of Discipleship* (London: SCM Press, 1959). Significant similarities between Rauschenbusch's thought, and that which would emerge later from Germany, including that of Bonhoeffer and Jürgen Moltmann's theology of hope, reinforces the argument that European influences were more significant for Rauschenbusch than often assumed. Cf. Jürgen Moltmann, *Jesus Christ for Today's World*, trans. Margaret Kohl (Minneapolis, MN: Fortress Press, 1994). Beginning on p. 24, Moltmann provides a practical method of social ethics to be pursued in the interests of the kingdom of God, which is strangely akin to Rauschenbusch's programme for Christianizing the social order.

social reform. He believes the church has failed in its mission to carry out this task, and so rejects traditional interpretations that equate the kingdom of God with the church. With evangelical intensity and fervour, he adopts the kingdom of God as the organising principle, empowering dynamic, and evolutionary goal of his ethical theory and practice. His use of the kingdom motif satisfies the demands of his philosophy for an imminent, evolutionary, progressive ideal accessible by the common consciousness, and the demands of his theology for a universal and inclusive body to battle against and ideally replace the sinful structures of society that corrupted the moral integrity of individuals and communities. Rauschenbusch's assumptions of philosophy and theology are united in the ideal of the kingdom, initiated by Jesus in a unique but natural fashion.

Reflecting on the early struggles of his faith, Rauschenbusch described the agony of wrestling with the failure of the church to communicate any notion of social salvation, and the criticism he felt he had received as a result of his views on the social problems of the day. He explained how he began to identify the need for a greater concept to bring his strands of social and theological thought together

> Now for a time, as these things got into my mind, the necessity came to me of combining this with the religious life that was so strong in me. I had personal religion. I now had that large social outlook, and how was I to combine the two things? I needed a unity of life - faith. A real religion always wanted unity. It wants to bring the whole world into one great conception that can inspire and fill the soul. It sees one God, it wants one world, and it wants one redemption. That is faith.... And that was the real difficulty in my thought all the time - how to find a place, under the old religious conceptions, for this great task of changing the world and making it righteous; making it habitable; making it merciful; making it brotherly.... But where could I get it with my old Christianity - with my old religion?[54]

The idea of the kingdom of God 'offered itself as the real solution' for Rauschenbusch's problems. As a key concept and organising principle, it met his personal need of faith, and his intellectual need for a theological idea that satisfied the demands of his idealist philosophy. With the kingdom of God he discovered

> Here was a religious concept that embraced it all. Here was something so big that absolutely nothing that interested me was excluded from it. Was it a matter of personal religion? Why, the kingdom of God begins with that! The powers of the kingdom of God well up in the individual soul; that is where they are born, and that is where the starting point necessarily must be. Was it a matter of world-wide

[54]Walter Rauschenbusch, 'the Kingdom of God,' a speech given January 2, 1913 at the Central YMCA, Cleveland, reprinted in Robert T. Handy ed., *The Social Gospel in America, 1870-1920* (New York: Oxford University Press, 1966), 266-7.

missions? Why, that is the kingdom of God, isn't it - carrying it out to the boundaries of the earth. Was it a matter of getting justice for the workingman? Is not justice part of the kingdom of God? Does not the kingdom of God consist simply in this - that God's will shall be done on earth, even as it now is in heaven? And so, wherever I touched, there was the kingdom of God. That was the brilliancy, the splendour of that conception - it touches everything with religion. It carries God into everything that you do, and there is nothing else that does it in the same way.[55]

It was Albrecht Ritschl who was largely responsible for reintroducing the idea of the kingdom to Protestant theology, and it is not surprising that Rauschenbusch seized upon the notion during one of his visits to Germany.[56] Most scholars agree that Ritschl bequeathed to Rauschenbusch the kingdom motif with its collective emphasis and social nature, but Harlan Beckley is keen to highlight the differences between their views, especially considering Rauschenbusch's reliance upon sociological thought as an advantage not available to Ritschl.[57] Beckley suggests that 'Rauschenbusch's sociological understanding of the kingdom separated him from the idealism of many liberals.'[58] However, it is clear that in using the term 'idealism,' Beckley must be referring to an eschatological utopianism and not the philosophical idealism characteristic of Rauschenbusch's method. In fact, Rauschenbusch' view of the kingdom affirms his philosophical idealism, and gives it a specific form of theological expression.

From a brief examination of Ritschl's view of the kingdom, it becomes quite apparent that Rauschenbusch borrows much of it for his own elaboration. Many of Rauschenbusch's theological and philosophical assumptions are illuminated by even a cursory overview of his mentor's theology of the kingdom. Ritschl suggests that humans exist in nature as individuals in multiplicity. As such, humans rely on the idea of God for their moral development but in turn, God's moral goals for humanity 'cannot be attained save through the means furnished by our natural endowment.'[59] The outworking of these relationships reveals a complete unity of purpose. Thus

---

[55]Ibid., 267.

[56]Rauschenbusch wrote, 'In 1891 I spent a year of study in Germany, partly on the teachings of Jesus, and partly on sociology. That is a good combination and likely to produce results.... So Christ's conception of the Kingdom of God came to me as a new revelation. Here was the idea and purpose that had dominated the mind of the Master himself.' See Rauschenbusch, *Christianizing the Social Order,* 93.

[57]Donovan Smucker attributes Rauschenbusch's theological perspective of the kingdom largely to Ritschlianism, filtered through Anabaptist sectariansim. See *The Origins of Walter Rauschenbusch's Social Ethics*, 42; Cf. Harlan Beckley, *A Passion for Justice*, 37. Rauschenbusch made this distinction himself in *A Theology for the Social Gospel*, 139.

[58]Beckley, 37.

[59]Ritschl, *Justification and Reconciliation*, 280.

...if we must conceive God as necessary to guarantee our personal morality and our moral fellowship, we must recognise that the entire universe is designed to serve this Divine end; for otherwise we could not view even our moral life as an object of Divine care. The whole universe, therefore, considered thus as the precondition of the moral kingdom of created spirits, is throughout God's creation for this end.[60]

In order for humanity to be perceived as akin in nature to the Divine Will, 'it would be necessary to conceive the human race as a unity in spite of its natural multiplicity, a unity which is other than its natural genetic unity.' The conception for which Ritschl searched is found 'in the idea of the Christian community, which makes the Kingdom of God its task.' [61]

Long before Rauschenbusch seized upon the kingdom as a unifying concept for his own method, Ritschl was illustrating how the kingdom is able to transform the conflicting moral will of many individuals into a single, moral consciousness which possessed both will and agency. He explains

This idea of the moral unification of the human race, through action prompted by universal love to our neighbour represents a unity of many which belongs to the realm of the thoroughly defined, in other words, the good will. The multitude of spirits who, for all their natural and generic affinity, may yet, in the practical expression they give to their will, be utterly at variance, attain a supernatural unity through mutual and social action prompted by love....It is an essential characteristic of the Kingdom of God that, as the final end which is being realised in the world and as the supreme good of created spirits, it transcends the world, just as God Himself is supramundane. The idea of the Kingdom of God, therefore, gives a supramundane character to humanity as bound to Him, *i.e.* it both transcends and completes all the natural and particular motives which unite men together.[62]

Ritschl is quick to point out that the origin of the community that 'is called on to form itself by union into the Kingdom of God' depends on Christ alone as its founder, and as its Lord to whom it must render obedience. Ritschl's view provides a glimpse into the way Rauschenbusch would develop not only the idea of collective consciousness, but the notion that individuals, groups, institutions and societies could exercise moral agency through solidarity in sin and repentance, as the kingdom of God grows in their midst.

Collectivity of consciousness is not to be equated with the church, visible or invisible. It becomes important for Ritschl to contrast the broadly unifying concept of the kingdom from the institution of the church. 'In order to preserve the true articulation of the Christian view of the world,' he writes, 'it is necessary clearly to distinguish between viewing the followers of Christ, first,

---

[60]Ibid.
[61]Ibid., 280.
[62]Ibid., 280-1.

under the conception of the Kingdom of God, and secondly, under the conception of the *worshipping community*, or the Church.'[63] Ritschl is keen to make a distinction between actions of spiritual devotion and those of moral significance. Believers in Christ constitute a church as they explicitly express their faith to God in prayer, but constitute the kingdom of God 'in so far as, forgetting distinctions of sex, rank, or nationality, they act reciprocally from love, and thus call into existence that fellowship of moral disposition and moral blessings which extends, through all possible gradations, to the limits of the human race.'[64] The clear distinction between church and kingdom is a necessary one for Ritschl, affirming the universality of his theological programme. But such an all-encompassing theory raises the difficult question of moral intent, and whether or not action may precede, or provisionally establish, belief.[65]

Again, Rauschenbusch borrows extensively from Ritschl in the formation and exposition of his thought, as even a brief examination of his view of the Kingdom reveals. For Rauschenbusch, the kingdom is an evolutionary and progressive ideal, conceived as a Messianic theocracy with a real and present hope for the establishment of a 'perfected' social order.[66] He elaborates early

---

[63]Ibid., 284.

[64]Ibid., 285. Ritschl here refers to Schleiermacher's distinction between action that is symbolic (representative) and action that is organising (disseminative).

[65]These questions of Ritschl, and subsequently of Rauschenbusch, anticipate similar questions that will be raised later against process, liberationist and other idealist theologians who advocate the doctrine of 'crypto-Christians', suggesting that people may be unknowingly justified by political action. Rauschenbusch clearly had no difficulty ascribing Christianity to anyone involved in social work, regardless of professed belief. At this point his idealism and immanentism become most concrete. Moreover, the connection sometimes suggested between the social gospel and liberation theology is highlighted as Rauschenbusch asserted that social workers not only do redemptive Christian work, but participate in the cross of Christ and 'the thin red line' of Christian history as they suffer for the sake of others. Nevertheless, the religious person engaged in social work is considered superior: 'Other things being equal, a man of religious faith and temper is always the wiser and stronger. The religious souls are the master souls.' See Walter Rauschenbusch, *Unto Me* (Boston, New York, and Chicago: The Pilgrim Press, 1912).

[66]Rauschenbusch's perception of the Kingdom as a messianic theocracy is highlighted in his posthumously published book *The Righteousness of the Kingdom*, 79ff. The political notion of a messianic theocracy reveals his reliance upon Mazzini, again in an earlier, formative period of Rauschenbusch's thought. The perfection of the social order in history was to be considered more as a progressive, anticipated hope than an actual, eschatological realization. Mark Chapman agrees that 'the charge that he succumbed to the cult of inevitable progress cannot be substantiated.' See Mark Chapman, 'Walter Rauschenbusch and the Coming of God's Kingdom,' *The Kingdom of God and Human Society: Essays by members of the Scripture, Theology and Society Group*, ed. Robin Barbour (Edinburgh: T & T Clark, 1993, 175).

and in great detail his understanding of the Kingdom and its significance for Christian thought and practice, writing extensively on behalf of the Brotherhood of the Kingdom, an organised group of churchmen interested in the new social Christianity, of which he was co-founder. In these writings and elsewhere he outlines his understanding of the meaning and significance of the concept of the kingdom of God.

In an article written in 1892 for *The Examiner*, Rauschenbusch details his understanding of the kingdom as 'A Conquering Idea.'[67] In his opening sentence he pays tribute to Ritschl as 'the great theologian, who has himself done more, perhaps, than any other man to rehabilitate that idea in the theological thought of Germany.' He bemoans the near loss of the term 'kingdom of God' from the Christian vocabulary, with the result that the remaining conception of the kingdom 'has been so pruned and so tangled up with other conceptions that its original force has been largely lost.' The problem, as he sees it, is threefold: the Christian hope of perfection was transferred from the kingdom on earth to life after death and millenarian expectations; the kingdom as a collective ideal was replaced by the idea of individual salvation; and the idea of the kingdom became mistakenly swallowed up in the idea of the church. Rauschenbusch is willing to see the truth in these aspects of the kingdom, but argues they are aspects only; 'When taken as parts of that larger idea, and recognized in their relation to it, they are good and indispensable. When taken as a substitute for it, they work mischief.'[68] Such mischief had been worked, from his perspective, to the point that Christianity risked losing its dynamism as a movement, if it had not already done so.[69]

Rauschenbusch elaborates the most significant results of the three-fold problem, which he identifies as robbing the kingdom concept of its moral force

> The substitution of heaven for the kingdom of God on earth has pushed Christianity from an offensive to a defensive attitude, has substituted asceticism for a revolutionary movement. The domination of individualism has fostered religious selfishness and crippled the missionary impulse. The substitution of the church for the kingdom has made Christianity one-sided, has made philanthropy a side-show, and has left the bulk of human life unsanctified even in theory.[70]

---

[67]Walter Rauschenbusch, 'A Conquering Idea,' *The Examiner* (31 July 1892), in *Selected Writings*, 71-74.

[68]Ibid., 72-3.

[69]H. Richard Niebuhr seems to offer corroboration of Rauschenbusch's view when he suggests in that dynamic faith is to be distinguished from institutional religion. Here he affirms but seeks to move beyond the sociological analysis provided by Henri Bergson. H. Richard Niebuhr, *The Kingdom of God in America* (New York: Harper and Bros., 1937), 11ff.

[70]Walter Rauschenbusch, 'A Conquering Idea,' *Selected Writings*, 73.

Even at this early stage, the influence of Ritschl is clear. The immanent and universal nature of the kingdom, its collective significance over individual relevance, and the distinction between church and kingdom may find specific application in Rauschenbusch's sociological analysis, but are very much a part of the inheritance he receives from his theological mentor.

In his discussion of the kingdom, the primacy of the collective over the individual is emphasised, and Rauschenbusch rails against millenarians who look for an otherworldly salvation rather than partake in the salvific activity of the social gospel. Their views are individualistic and apocalyptic, trading moral action for asceticism, optimistic pragmatism for pessimistic resignation. Rauschenbusch believes such views are harmful to the social gospel in particular, and to Christianity in general, perceptively suggesting that 'eschatology is usually loved in inverse proportion to the square of the mental diameter of those who do the loving.'[71] Nevertheless, his criticisms are usually polite, issuing from serious and thoughtful concern, and he ends one article directed toward millenarianism with the challenging question, 'which will do more to make our lives spiritual and release us from the tyranny of the world, the thought that we may at any moment enter into the presence of the Lord, or the thought that every moment we are in the presence of the Lord?'[72]

Rauschenbusch is not oblivious to the eschatological assertions made by his contemporaries from the opposite direction, but he is summarily dismissive of their proposals, directing his attention to what he perceives as the more dangerous perspective.[73] Rauschenbusch argues that the significance of the kingdom for Jesus was its present dynamic power, not its final consummation, whether anticipated by Jesus himself, or his followers. Rauschenbusch clarifies his thinking on this issue thus

> Like the old prophets, Jesus believed that God was the real creator of the kingdom; it was not to be set up by manmade evolution. It is one of the axioms of religious faith to believe that. He certainly believed in a divine consummation at the close. But the more he believed in the supreme value of its spiritual and moral blessings, and in the power of spiritual forces to mould human life, the more would the final act of consummation recede in importance and the present facts and processes grow more concrete and important to his mind.'[74]

Despite the fact that the kingdom was understood to be initiated and consummated by God, and not by mere human effort, 'it still remained a social

---

[71]Rauschenbusch, *Theology for the Social Gospel*, 209.
[72]Rauschenbusch, 'The Brotherhood of the Kingdom,' *Selected Writings*, 94.
[73]See Rauschenbusch's chapter on eschatology in *Theology for the Social Gospel*, 208-39, and especially 218-20 for his direct response to this issue. In contrast, Schweitzer's 'consistent' eschatology allowed only for an 'interim' kingdom ethic. Cf. Albert Schweitzer, *The Quest of the Historical Jesus* (1906; London: SCM, 2000).
[74]Rauschenbusch, *Christianity and the Social Crisis*, 63.

hope. The kingdom of God is still a collective conception, involving the whole social life of man. It is not a matter of saving human atoms, but of saving the social organism. It is not a matter of getting individuals into heaven, but of transforming life on earth into the harmony of heaven.'[75] The kingdom of God, as founded by Jesus and as a present and continuing reality was to be seen as essentially social in its growth and aim, and that view took precedence over any eschatological concerns, apocalyptic or otherwise.

As demonstrated previously, Rauschenbusch believes in a collective consciousness of humanity, and sees the conditioning of that consciousness as the key to social moral reform. The kingdom of God serves as the means of achieving unity of moral consciousness, as the immanence of God permeates humanity, and individuals surrender their individual rights, accepting the responsibility for the moral wellbeing of the society as a whole. In this sense, God needs individuals and individuals need God, but the goal is always the social salvation of the human race. For Rauschenbusch, the collective consciousness does not possess a well-defined personality, but is clearly attributed with moral will and agency. Individuals are not 'swallowed up' in the collective consciousness, but are seen as responsible for individual actions as well as the actions of the society of which they are part. As the kingdom grows, and society is transformed, entire social organisms will come to 'repent' and be sanctified, and in turn join the fight for social justice against collective forces of evil in what may be described essentially as a class struggle. The struggle will be a fight and will not always come easily. The affinity of the social gospel to liberation theology and dependency theory is once again highlighted as Rauschenbusch suggests the relationship between individual and collective forces

> Any social work that deals with the causes of misery involves fighting, for the causes of misery are never only in the people who are miserable. They are chiefly in those who profit by their misery. The lower tenth of society is submerged because the upper tenth is riding on the other nine tenths and putting the heads of some under water. The word redemption means literally emancipation and liberation from slavery. It involves making the exploiters quit exploiting. But if any one tries to make them stop they will strike back and hurt him. No one will move very far on the way of social relief without colliding with strong and active forces, perhaps with the controlling forces of society, and being punished for his interference with their income.[76]

The difficulty Rauschenbusch has in sorting out the exact relationship of the individual to the collective moral agent is highlighted in passages such as these. With the absence of more disciplined reflection, he fails to define the collective personality more clearly than simply to suggest its existence in relation to the

---

[75]Ibid., 65.
[76]Rauschenbusch, *Unto Me*, 26-7.

individual. But at least the kingdom of God motif provides him with a collective force with which to counter the kingdom of evil, and he is convinced theologically that the conversion of the individual is inexorably bound to the conversion of the social order. 'If any new principle is to gain power in human history, it must take shape and life in individuals who have faith in it,' Rauschenbusch argues. Those of faith 'are the living spirits, the channels by which new truth and power from God enter humanity.' Exercising faith leads to self-sacrifice for the common good: 'To repent of our collective social sins, to have faith in the possibility and reality of a divine life in humanity, to submit the will to the purposes of the kingdom of God, to permit the divine inspiration to emancipate and clarify the moral insight - this is the most intimate duty' of religious souls 'who would help to build the coming Messianic era' of humanity.[77]

Since the kingdom is to be perceived as a messianic theocracy, with relevance for all of creation and not only the self-designated believers in Christ, it is not to be equated with the church but to encompass all of society. Wherever the fight for social reform is being carried out, within or without the church, Rauschenbusch believes there is the kingdom. Those who engage in the social struggle, he writes, 'are in the direct line of apostolic succession. Like the Son of Man they seek and save the lost. Their work is redemptive work....they are treading step by step in the footprints of Jesus of Nazareth.' Specifically, 'they are doing Christian work when they do social work, even if they themselves disclaim religious motives or even repudiate religious faith.'[78] In this sense, the kingdom is a universal concept that promotes unity and the spirit of association, and transforms everything it touches with the dynamic power to change.[79]

The church, on the other hand, is seen by Rauschenbusch as old and stale, 'a perpetuation of the past', whereas the Kingdom represents the 'power of the coming age.'[80] Only as the church is vitalised by the life of the Kingdom is it considered as a living and vibrant force, fulfilling its role as 'the social force in salvation.'[81] Rauschenbusch believes the church is too prone to idealising itself

---

[77]Rauschenbusch, *Christianity and the Social Crisis*, 352.

[78]Ibid., 12-14.

[79]Social gospel advocates were responsible for fostering unity and association in a number of areas. They were particularly active in the formation of the Federal Council of the Churches of Christ in America, which was among the first national ecumenical bodies formed in the United States, and which served as a forerunner to American participation in the Life and Work and Faith and Order movements that preceded the formation of the World Council of Churches. See Charles MacFarland, 'The Progress of Federation Among the Churches,' *AJT* 21 (July 1917): 392-410; and Peter G. Mode, 'Aims and Methods of Contemporary Church-Union Movements in America,' *AJT* 24 (April 1920): 224-51.

[80]Rauschenbusch, *Theology for the Social Gospel*, 129-30.

[81]Ibid., 119.

in the life of the people, and he regards with scepticism Royce's high view of the church as *the* central idea in Christianity, suggesting; 'This slighting of Jesus is one of the most unsatisfactory elements in Royce's thought.'[82]

Rauschenbusch never forgave the church for holding him back from his desire to meet the social needs he encountered as a young man, with the result that his attitude to the church is reflected most often in negative, rather than positive terms. Though he remained a churchman all of his life, his historical appreciation of the individualistic and materialistic failures of the church consistently coloured his vision. After Royce, he agreed that the church fosters loyalty, and is able to temper individualistic faith with a reminder that salvation for the individual is by membership into a community that had salvation. At its best, the church is seen as a community of devoted religious minds, which is able to direct the spiritual resources of faith toward the social aims of the Kingdom, and invest it with enthusiasm and commitment. The spirit of Jesus is the mark of its authority, demonstrated by its effect on the lives of its members, and those surrounding it. Practical, ethical import is Rauschenbusch's chief concern for the church. Jesus' 'conditional form of predicating the saving power and spiritual authority of the church' is, for Rauschenbusch, 'only one more way of asserting that in anything which claims to be Christian, religion must have an immediate ethical nexus and effect.'[83]

Believing strongly in the separation of church and state, Rauschenbusch holds that the church might be a significant force for social change, when it allows the spirit of Christ to permeate its life. 'If the Church tries to confine itself to theology and to the Bible, and refuses its larger mission to humanity, its theology will gradually become mythology and its Bible a closed book,' he warns.[84] But he also contends that the evolution of the Christian spirit had led the church to a 'stage in its development where it is fit and free for its largest social mission.'[85] The church could ignore the world in ascetic departure, tolerate the world and conform to it, or condemn the world and seek to change it. The growth of the kingdom offers opportunity for the church to lead the way in social reform if it becomes an instrument of God in the intended task. 'The Church, too, has its own power and future at stake in the issues of social development,' Rauschenbusch suggests. 'Thus the will of God revealed in Christ and in the highest manifestations of the religious spirit, the call of human duty, and the motives of self-protection, alike summon Christian[s]...singly and collectively to put their hands to the plough and not to look back till public

---

[82]Ibid., 127.

[83]Ibid., 129. Rauschenbusch's rather low view of the Church may be attributed to the Anabaptist influence of his father, and his own continued interest in Anabaptist history. See for example, Smucker, 30-73; Paul Minus, *Walter Rauschenbusch: American Reformer*, 82.

[84]Rauschenbusch, *Christianity and the Social Crisis*, 339.

[85]Ibid., 343.

morality shall be at least as much Christianized as private morality now is.'[86]

The church, then, is to serve as an instrument of the kingdom in Christianizing the whole of society, bringing the consciousness of God to full fruition in the community of humanity, in the present life. The steps to be taken in Christianizing society are specific and concrete in Rauschenbusch's programme, involving most radical change for the economic sector, as the area of social life not yet permeated by Christian ethics. In his practical method, Rauschenbusch's idealist philosophy and kingdom theology are united in a programme of reform that envisages the complete permeation of human life by Christian principles of love and justice. The way this was to work out in ecumenical method on the international scene will be considered after an examination of another, very different approach to social ethics, which moves to the fore when the optimism of the social gospel is no longer the order of the day.

---

[86]Ibid.

CHAPTER 4

How Weak We Are: Philosophical Impulses in Reinhold Niebuhr's Realist Method

O Lord, you have made us very great. Help us to remember how weak we are, so that we may not deny our kinship with the creatures of the field and our common dependence with them upon summer and winter, day and night. O Lord, you have made us very small, and we bring our years to an end like a tale that is told; help us to remember that beyond our brief day is the eternity of your love.

Reinhold Niebuhr

Introduction

For all of the comparisons made between Rauschenbusch and the man who succeeded him as the most influential mind in American ecumenical Christian social ethics, it is clear that Reinhold Niebuhr stands apart in at least one significant respect - his method of social ethics has been dissected from almost every perspective, leading advocates from various camps to claim him as their own, and others to reject his method outright.[1] Moreover, various philosophical impulses in his method have been criticized and analysed from these many points of view, leaving a deeply rutted path to tread for those who would seek to follow his footprints through the social ethics playing field.

---

[1]Ronald Stone has suggested that Niebuhr's tendency to be always controversial accounts in part for the broad attention his work has received. See Ronald H. Stone, *Professor Reinhold Niebuhr: A Mentor to the Twentieth Century*, (Louisville, KY: Westminster/John Knox Press, 1992), xi. From feminist to fundamentalist, scholars have found it impossible to ignore Niebuhr, and have interpreted him in various ways. Hans Hofmann describes Niebuhr as 'resolved to be more orthodox than the orthodox fundamentalist,' (*The Theology of Reinhold Niebuhr* trans. Louise Pettibone Smith [New York, NY: Charles Scribner's Sons, 1956], 114), while Gordon Lewis has described him as a 'total relativist.' (Gordon Lewis and Bruce Demarest, eds., *Challenges to Inerrancy* [Chicago, IL: Moody Press, 1984], 173.) Catholic and conservative economist Michael Novak is a self-described Niebuhrian, as are several liberation theologians. (Michael Novak, *The Spirit of Democratic Capitalism* [New York, NY: Simon and Schuster, 1982].) Niebuhr has been acclaimed and criticized from both ends of the theological spectrum, and every point in between.

In a relatively recent work, Robin Lovin advances significantly the contemporary relevance of Niebuhr's work, providing clarity for the present task, which seeks to understand how Niebuhr's realism led him to a social ethic that advocated a thoroughly ecumenical collective moral agency, without allowing for the exercise of that agency in acts of repentance. Lovin writes with the goal of finding a basis for moral agreement in society rooted in Niebuhrian realism, and offers an excellent study of the philosophy, theology, and practice of realism.[2] However, while clearly presenting the way in which Niebuhr's realism is able to inform the contemporary situation, Lovin pays only scant attention to some aspects of Niebuhr's philosophical heritage. In particular, while offering adequate treatment of Niebuhr's pragmatism, he neglects completely the legacy of existentialism bequeathed by Soren Kierkegaard. Pragmatism and existentialism are of key importance for the present task because they influence significantly Niebuhr's conception of the self, which is a crucial aspect of his ethical programme. Niebuhr's understanding of the self led him to recognize individual and collective elements of sin, but to advocate repentance on behalf of individuals only. His embrace of this paradox as an intentional dialectic, and not as an inconsistency in his method, distinguishes him most clearly from Rauschenbusch, with whom he shared many other aspects of moral thought.

What was presented as a contradiction in Rauschenbusch's method - namely, the conflict between human nature and freedom - was refined by Niebuhr to form an intentional dialectical tension, revealing a more systematic, and reasoned approach than the earlier idealist programme of Rauschenbusch. For Niebuhr, human freedom meant there were theoretically no limits to the possibilities of human brotherhood, while human nature meant collective existence would never ascend to its potential heights in reality.[3] Rauschenbusch's imminent idealism suggested few real ethical limits for a collective humanity indwelled by God, while Niebuhr's sober realism affirmed there were infinite possibilities but limited realities.

Yet, it is not readily apparent how Niebuhr could advocate moral agency for groups in acts of commission, but not in acts of repentant transformation. The change wrought in society by or on behalf of any particular group, or society as a whole, would only ever be partial, qualified, and in some way, self-serving. This rather pessimistic stance sets him even further apart from Rauschenbusch, as does his refusal to allow for the possibility of repentance on behalf of groups who possess generally negative moral agency. How is it that he could agree with Rauschenbusch regarding the social nature of humanity, describe in detail the moral agency of communities, and yet deny in practice the positive aspects

---

[2]See Robin Lovin, *Reinhold Niebuhr and Christian Realism* (Cambridge: Cambridge University Press, 1995).
[3]Reinhold Niebuhr, *The Nature and Destiny of Man*, vol II, *Human Destiny* (New York, NY: Charles Scribner's Sons, 1943), 85.

of that same moral agency? How does his assessment affect the Christian perceptions of responsibility for sin, and knowledge of revelation? These questions will be addressed in the course of the following two chapters, as Niebuhr's ethical methodology is examined, with particular reference to his understanding of the difference between individuals and groups as ethical agents.

It has been noted that Niebuhr's approach to social ethics has been studied, analysed, critiqued and adopted by representatives across the theological spectrum. The goal of this section, then, is not to wander over ground that is already marked with many well-trodden paths, but to present Niebuhr's method as a philosophical contrast to that of Rauschenbusch, despite many common elements and influences.[4] Specifically, it will be demonstrated how Niebuhr's method allowed for the existence of moral agency on behalf of individuals and groups, but asserted the individual would always occupy a different moral space from groups. Although Niebuhr upheld the moral ideal of love, full realisation of the transcendent nature of that ideal would always be beyond the grasp of humanity's common ethical life. Repentance would be possible on behalf of individuals, but the best society could hope for as a whole, was a proximate form of justice, enabled by common grace. Niebuhr's method reveals a continuous striving for a closer approximation of love in society, with the acknowledgement that the ideal is unattainable in history. The Bible is used as symbol and myth in their fullest sense, pointing to realities which may be partially accessed by human reason, but which also confirm human limitations. The result is a democratic, consultative process, geared toward an ideal ethic, whose immediate goal is the greatest possible justice for the greatest number of people, but whose ultimate goal is always beyond reach. Methodologically speaking, groups and individuals participate in a continuous devising and revising of policies and approaches, balancing the power and interests of all parties, while neither attaining a fulfilment of justice, nor surrendering the struggle in despair.

What aspects of Niebuhr's philosophy and theology allowed him to pursue this method of social ethics? In what way did his approach differ from the idealism of Rauschenbusch, and what distinguished his thought in his own lifetime? To what degree did his philosophy inform his theology and ethical *praxis*? Niebuhr's consistent affirmation of the negative moral agency of groups, and his denial of some positive aspects found in Rauschenbusch's idealism, reflect clearly his own philosophical and theological presuppositions, and subsequently inform his ethical method. To demonstrate this, a brief statement of Niebuhr's 'realist' method will lead into a discussion of the philosophical impulses that informed his approach, and a discussion of the necessary theological implications will follow in the proceeding chapter.

---

[4]Cf. Richard Dickinson, 'Rauschenbusch and Niebuhr: Brothers under the skin?' *RL* 27 (Spring 1958): 163-171.

Christian Realism

Niebuhr's Personal and Theological Context

Like Rauschenbusch, Reinhold Niebuhr was raised in a German-American family of the manse, though a generation further removed from his immigrant roots. He shared with Rauschenbusch the discipline and piety of his religious background, though educated in the Lutheran and Reformed theology of his German Evangelical Synod rather than the Baptist tradition which had formed Rauschenbusch's faith heritage - a difference which remains apparent throughout any comparison of their thought. Introduced by his father to theology and biblical study from a young age, and after completing studies at Yale, Niebuhr went on to spend thirteen years working out their practical significance in pastoral ministry in Detroit. Here, in industrial America, Niebuhr gained the experiences and insights that would challenge him and feed his work in ethics in the years to come as preacher, writer, lecturer, and teacher of ethics at Union Theological Seminary in New York City. As he faced the injustices experienced by his parishioners in a rapidly industrializing urban centre, Niebuhr early realized that, 'I was up against an industrial city, and I saw that human nature was quite different than I had learned at Yale Divinity School.'[5] Meeting social gospel advocates like the Episcopal Bishop Charles Williams, whom he later described as his 'mentor and guide,' led him to the conviction that charity should not be a substitute for justice, and to his subsequent commitment to socialist and pacifist movements.[6] Through his experiences, 'The social conscience Niebuhr had acquired from his pietist heritage became transformed to include not only charitable endeavours but promotion of legislation protecting industrial workers and their families.'[7] As the Ford motor company expanded its control over a large labour force, Niebuhr reacted strongly against such unmitigated power, writing in true social gospel style in his journal in 1927: 'What a civilisation this is! Naïve gentlemen with a genius for mechanics suddenly become the arbiters over the lives and fortunes of hundreds and thousands. Their moral pretensions are credulously accepted at full value. No one bothers to ask whether an industry which can maintain a cash reserve of a quarter of a billion ought not make some provision for its unemployed.'[8]

---

[5]Robert McAfee Brown, *The Essential Reinhold Niebuhr: Selected Essays and Addresses* (New Haven, CT: Yale University Press, 1986), 20.
[6]Reinhold Niebuhr, *Man's Nature and his Communities* (New York: Charles Scribner's Sons, 1965), 11.
[7]Charles C. Brown, *Niebuhr and His Age: Reinhold Niebuhr's Prophetic Role in the Twentieth Century* (Philadelphia, PA: Trinity Press International, 1992), 24.
[8]Reinhold Niebuhr, *Leaves from the Notebook of a Tamed Cynic* (New York: DeCapo, 1976), 154-5.

Initially, Niebuhr found the social gospel of Rauschenbusch and others to be an attractive model of social ethics, based on the liberal theology in which he was saturated at Yale and elsewhere. While critical of many liberal proposals, Niebuhr's first book was essentially a restatement of the social gospel, 'grounded in the still dominant Ritschlian theology of the American Protestant milieu in the 1920's... it called for a fusion of religious goodwill and reason to solve urgent problems of modern civilisation - a strategy Niebuhr five years later criticized as inadequate....'[9] Despite the fact that the social gospel's optimistic liberal assumptions about people and society originally appealed to him, they led eventually to unresolved tensions in his mind as his early idealism collided with his pastoral experience. When this happened, he was forced to confess, 'humans are never as good as their ideals.'[10] In trying to meet the needs of his congregation, Niebuhr later admitted that his time in the pastorate was a period of formation and growth. He wrote; 'Even while imagining myself to preach the Gospel, I had really experimented with many modern alternatives to Christian faith until one by one they proved unavailing.'[11] Eventually, Niebuhr decisively rejected prevailing imminent, idealist socio-political interpretations of the gospel because their persistent utopianism refused to take the reality of human sin seriously. This insight came to him as he developed 'a deeper sense of sin as a social and personal reality.'[12]

As Niebuhr faced pastoral challenges, and as the international situation deteriorated, he increasingly questioned the ability of classical liberalism to provide adequate answers to the current crisis. He made note of Augustine's comment that 'the truest interpretations of the Christian faith may come in such crises when a proud culture is humbled,' and observed that 'all forms of modern secularism...whether bourgeois or humanist or Marxist or Nazi, contained an implicit or explicit self-glorification.'[13] This discovery allowed him to make 'a decisive break with the social gospel synthesis, opening a way for the soul to save itself beyond the necessities of society and politics.'[14] Donald Meyer has described Niebuhr's eventual break with old dominant theological trends in this way: 'Social gospel pastors tried to give positive and economic content to religious ideas. Niebuhr's thought, on the other hand, was a gradual theological elaboration of what was at first merely socio-ethical criticism. He was unable to ground his "timely" analysis of the crisis in the

---

[9]Brown, *Niebuhr and His Age*, 22.

[10]Niebuhr cited in Ibid., 33.

[11]Niebuhr cited in June Bingham, *Courage to Change: An Introduction to the Life and Thought of Reinhold Niebuhr* (New York: Charles Scribner's Sons, 1972), 19.

[12]Brown, *Niebuhr and His Age*, 35.

[13]Cited in Ibid., 62-3.

[14]Donald B. Meyer, *The Protestant Search for Political Realism, 1919-1941* (Westport, CT: Greenwood Press Publishers, 1960), 240.

West except in "timeless" theological categories.'[15] For Niebuhr, the role of theology was to lead social ethics, not *vice-versa*.

Niebuhr was soon hailed as leader of the movement of American theologians away from the fold of the old liberalism, whose 'persistent attacks upon liberal doctrines of divine immanence, human efficacy, and cultural accommodation were certainly predicated upon the incipient doctrines of divine transcendence, human sinfulness, and cultural resistance.'[16] Although 'American neoorthodoxy began as a theological corrective...its critique of liberalism eventually developed into a constructive and self-sustaining theological program,' which set the theological agenda for two decades.[17] As the movement's acclaimed spokesman, Niebuhr's lasting mark was made chiefly through his application of these theological and philosophical developments to the realm of social ethics.

While Niebuhr's reputation grew in America, so did the neoorthodox theology of Karl Barth and Emil Brunner on the Continent. Like Rauschenbusch, Niebuhr's bilingualism allowed him access to Continental thought before English translations were available, and he interacted with both Barth and Brunner, though he preferred the theology of the latter. In 1928, Niebuhr met Brunner, who later recalled the significance of the meeting: 'What I said in my lecture about sin led to an animated and passionate discussion. The concept of sin in those days had almost disappeared from the vocabulary of enlightened theologians. But I sensed how this basic term seemed to stimulate Niebuhr, and set fire to his imagination.'[18]

Despite many similar elements, Barth never stimulated Niebuhr's thought to the same degree as Brunner.[19] Niebuhr accused Barth of ignoring the social and ethical dimensions of faith, yet in many ways, the two theologians had much in common. Joseph Bettis writes, 'Both recognised that social ethics was decisive for theological reflection during their generation. And both recognised that in order to deal with social ethics adequately they would have to develop a way of thinking about theological problems very different from the tradition of

---

[15]Ibid., 238.

[16]Dennis Voskuil, 'Neoorthodoxy,' *Reformed Theology in America*, ed. David Wells (Grand Rapids, MI: Eerdmans, 1985), 253.

[17]Ibid., 255.

[18]Emil Brunner, 'Some Remarks on Reinhold Niebuhr's Work as a Christian Thinker,' *Reinhold Niebuhr: His Religious, Social, and Political Thought*, ed. Charles Kegley (New York: Pilgrim Press, 1984), 82.

[19]Brunner wrote, 'Theologically he has no doubt learned most from the dialectical theology, which for him was more understandable, more accessible, and more easily digestible in my version than in Karl Barth's.' Ibid., 83. Nevertheless, Brunner would accuse Niebuhr of failing to give credit to the sources of his ideas, particularly European thinkers such as himself. Ibid., 86-7.

nineteenth-century Protestant liberalism they inherited.'[20] Though they held in common an existential emphasis on faith inherited from extensive reading of Soren Kierkegaard, Niebuhr never shared the depth of Barth's pessimism about human nature and social organisation. In 1960, Niebuhr wrote, 'Barth has long since ceased to have any effect on my thought, indeed he has become irrelevant to all Christians in the Western world who believe in accepting common and collective responsibilities without illusion and without despair.'[21] Niebuhr could not readily embrace Barth's version of neoorthodoxy, rejecting the serious disjunction that Barth drew between time and eternity. Niebuhr found many areas of contact between God and the human person, as later examination will reveal. As a result, Niebuhr sought a balance between God's immanence and transcendence, whereas Barth was not willing to concede any ground to immanence theology. This discrepancy between two great thinkers would find its greatest manifestation in the ethical realm, as Niebuhr wrote bluntly: 'Karl Barth's belief that the moral life of man would possess no valid principles of guidance, if the Ten Commandments had not introduced such principles by revelation, is as absurd as it is unscriptural.'[22]

In spite of his disagreement with Barth, it is accurate to describe Niebuhr as the father of American neoorthodoxy.[23] A theological ethos with a renewed emphasis on the ethical transcendence of God and the reality of human sin, led him to pioneer the movement in a dynamic way. While intent to smash the same liberal icons, Niebuhr undertook the task through a slightly different method from his colleagues on the European continent. The approach he would prefer would interpret theology intentionally from the perspective of humanity, would embrace elements of pragmatism and existentialism, find expression in society and politics, and be drawn under the banner of 'Christian realism.'

Niebuhr's Developing Moral Realism

In general terms, Niebuhr's realism emerged out of a school of philosophical, theological, and political thought led by Americans such as D. C. Macintosh, John Bennett, and Niebuhr himself.[24] As a self-confessed pragmatist, Niebuhr

---

[20]Joseph Bettis, 'Theology and Politics: Karl Barth and Reinhold Niebuhr on Social Ethics After Liberalism,' *RL* 48 (Spring 1979): 53.

[21]Niebuhr cited in ibid., 55.

[22]Niebuhr, *Human Destiny*, 254.

[23]Brunner criticized the unfortunate use of this label, since 'in all the world there is nothing more unorthodox than the spiritual volcano Reinhold Niebuhr. For most people "orthodoxy" means something like spiritual conformism, while Niebuhr is a true son of independent non-conformism. The term 'radical-Protestant' would suit him very much better.' Brunner in Kegley, ed., *Reinhold Niebuhr*, 82-3.

[24]Cf. Douglas Clyde Macintosh, ed., *Religious Realism* (New York: Macmillan, 1931). Macintosh was one of Niebuhr's teachers, whose ideas would have influenced his intellectual development.

was less interested in developing well-constructed theological doctrines, and more concerned to offer a practical application of absolute principles to a world inhabited by sinful humanity. Niebuhr's realism, then, rejected idealist and utopian philosophies, preferring a more balanced, less ruggedly contextual approach to human behaviour. It assumed the existence of moral truths that apply universally, beyond individual relativities and circumstantial particularities, since 'the moral realist holds that the truth of moral claims depends on a state of affairs that exist independently of our moral beliefs.'[25] As Robin Lovin points out

> in the parlance of contemporary philosophy, this is to say that Christian Realism is a version of moral realism. Moral ideas can be true or false. Moral statements are not only expressions of emotion or reports of the speaker's attitudes and preferences, as non-cognitivist theories would have it. Moral statements make claims about what is the case and of the evidence we marshal to support those ideas.[26]

Thus, while Rauschenbusch appealed to the emerging unified moral consciousness of the community to validate his moral claims, Niebuhr believed that certain moral claims were valid in and of themselves, as derived principles.

Moral principles, derived from the ideal of love revealed on the cross of Christ, could only be partial reflections of the ideal, which itself symbolizes judgement of human efforts to attain the ideal. Accordingly, the objective of social ethics is always incomplete, since 'social achievements provide no final goal.' Potential of the human person, both negative and positive, becomes the key to understanding our capability of building a better social order. 'The dynamics of history are driven by the human capacity always to imagine life beyond existing limitations. Biblical faith gives vision and direction to that capacity for self-transcendence, but we are best able to challenge and channel our powers when we also understand what is really going on,' writes Robin Lovin.[27] What was really going on, Niebuhr believed, was a power struggle rooted within the self's perceptions of its own finiteness, a condition dramatically magnified on a collective level. Thus, Niebuhr upheld the fact of a real moral ideal, but believed equally in the real limitations of human achievement.

Niebuhr's realism set him apart from Rauschenbusch's social gospel, and distanced him from his own flirtation with Marxist idealism. Lovin attributes Niebuhr's shift to his desire for justice to bear real, observable fruit

> The devotion of revolutionaries to their cause is real enough, but it is unrealistic because the goals they espouse will not finally end social conflict and usher in the

---

[25]Lovin, *Reinhold Niebuhr and Christian Realism*, 13.
[26]Ibid., 12.
[27]Ibid., 1.

age of peace they promise. Moral ideas may be fervently held and actively practised, and to that end they will have real effects. To be realistic in Niebuhr's sense, however, they must also be true.[28]

The identification and application of a 'realistic' ethic could be no easy task. Yet, 'no one is more conscious than [Niebuhr] of the problems and difficulties involved in relating an absolute, transcendent norm to the contingencies of particular situations.'[29] A commitment to the task of Christian realism led Niebuhr to the theoretical and practical use of a dialectical method, reflected in his theology and practical ethics. The dialectical approach was necessary, from Niebuhr's point of view, as it provided the only means of taking all factors of the human moral situation into consideration. In his own words

> The ethical fruitfulness of various types of religion is determined by the quality of their tension between the historical and the transcendent. This quality is measured by two considerations. The degree to which the transcendent truly transcends every value and achievement of history, so that no relative value of historical achievement may become the basis of moral complacency, and the degree to which the transcendent remains in organic contact with the historical, so that no degree of tension may rob the historical of its significance.[30]

This dialectical tension characterized Niebuhr's realism constantly and consistently, as it served as his framework for understanding humanity, society, theology, and ethics, and gave his method the coherence he believed was necessary for its philosophical validity.[31]

It is partly Niebuhr's Christian realism that has made him difficult to label, allowing him to be claimed as mentor by conservatives and liberals alike.[32]

---

[28]Ibid., 11-12.

[29]Gordon Harland, *The Thought of Reinhold Niebuhr* (New York: Oxford University Press, 1960), 193.

[30]Reinhold Niebuhr, *An Interpretation of Christian Ethics* (New York: Meridian Books, 1956), 18.

[31]Cf. Reinhold Niebuhr, 'Coherence, Incoherence, and Christian Faith,' *USQR*, VII (January 1952): 11-24.

[32]Robert Ayers attributes misappropriation of Niebuhr's thought to a failure to grasp his epistemology and ontology. 'It may be that Niebuhr was at fault for not dealing with the issues of methodology, epistemology, and ontology in a direct, simple, and systematic way in separate essays so that his positions in these areas would be immediately obvious. Had he done so perhaps some of the confusion concerning his theological positions could have been avoided.' Robert Ayers, 'Methodological, Epistemological, and Ontological Motifs in the Thought of Reinhold Niebuhr,' *MT* 7 (January 1991): 169. Cf. Kenneth Durkin *Reinhold Niebuhr* (London: Geoffrey Chapman, 1989), 177-180. Durkin points to the discussion between Niebuhr and his friend Paul Tillich as a clarification of some of these issues. See Paul Tillich, 'Reinhold Niebuhr's Doctrine of Knowledge,' in Kegley, ed., *Reinhold Niebuhr*, 89-98.

Niebuhr's realism 'was not a formal doctrine or even a set of positions on issues. It was a dynamic orientation towards the world, a cultivation of tension in one's apprehension of it.... The living of Christian realism promoted changes of opinion as the Christian constantly renegotiated the balance between taking the world as it was and demanding that it embody higher standards of justice.'[33] According to Richard Fox, there is no peace for a Christian realist like Niebuhr, 'only an occasional deep breath before the next in a never-ending series of re-examinations.'[34] This statement, perhaps more than any other, captures the spirit of Niebuhr's ethical method, which managed to hold in creative dialectical tension the transcendent ideal and human limitations, the potential of humanity, and the judgement of God. Fox suggests that the genius of Niebuhr's realism 'was its capacity to generate an active commitment to social and political action while holding that action under the sanction of divine judgement.' He further identifies this as the reason why Niebuhr's realism appealed to different schools of ethical thought

> At its best Christian realism was a distinctively modern yet identifiably traditional faith. It grasped the fundamental relativity of modern existence, the need to remain open to new experience, and the stultifying smugness of religion or piety that failed to appreciate the brokenness of human life. But it also grasped the enduring promise of historic orthodoxy, which viewed human nature as 'determined' yet still 'free' to devote itself to good or to evil in this earthly vale of tears.[35]

This method of Christian realism, with its elements of naturalism and pragmatism, was applied to nearly every area of human social life - economics, ethics, and politics. As Niebuhr became a celebrated figure on the national political scene, and in international ecumenical circles, a realist method characteristic of his thought came to dominate the field of social ethics in an intense period of post-war crises. Throughout this time, Niebuhr remained committed to the ideal of love and its realistic application in a striving for proximate justice. In his view, the varied results achieved through the consultative process of balancing power never negated the attempt.

Niebuhr's stated objective was to place theology before philosophy and ethical method, and an examination of his approach will later reveal a degree of success in this respect.[36] Yet, the presuppositions of his realism so defined his

---

[33]Richard Fox, 'Reinhold Niebuhr - The Living of Christian Realism,' *Reinhold Niebuhr and the Issues of Our Time*, ed. Richard Harries (London & Oxford: Mowbray, 1986), 10.

[34]Ibid., 22.

[35]Ibid., 22-23.

[36]N. H. G. Robinson confirms that, as Niebuhr's thought developed, 'his theology ...acquired a clearer position of precedence over his political philosophy than was the case at an earlier stage.' *Christ and Conscience* (London: James Nisbet, 1956), 110.

thought that they became, in some senses, prescriptive to his theology, through which he filtered and sometimes corrected his realism until the various elements of his method formed a coherent, dialectical whole. Coherence was, in fact, one element of Niebuhr's philosophy that will be explored in a brief discussion, along with the influence of pragmatism and existentialism on his social thought. Together, these elements of philosophy helped Niebuhr to construct an ethical method that was committed to a theological view of the limitations and possibilities of collective human life and activity.

Rejection of Idealism

In his *magnum opus*, Niebuhr approached the philosophical task directly, tackling each major philosophy of human nature, and refuting it with a statement of its inadequacy to explain some key element of human existence. As Niebuhr saw it, the basic task in understanding human nature was to determine to what degree humans were intimately bound by or connected to their natural environment and its necessities, and to what degree they were free to transcend the natural world. One scholar describes Niebuhr's dilemma in this way: 'If the self is identical with the natural world, then it is no more than one of the animals. If the self completely transcends the natural world, it is absorbed into a timeless eternity'.[37] In order to explore this dynamic of human existence more fully, Niebuhr compared various views of humanity, rejecting them in favour of a Christian perspective that did not resolve the dilemma, but held both aspects in creative dialectical tension. None of the classical or liberal views of humanity could explain the existential situation in a way that satisfied Niebuhr's observations. In his own words

> The obvious fact is that man is a child of nature, subject to its vicissitudes, compelled by its necessities, driven by its impulses, and confined within the brevity of the years which nature permits its varied organic form, allowing them some, but not too much, latitude. The other less obvious fact is that man is a spirit who stands outside of nature, life, himself, his reason and his world.... How difficult it is to do justice to both the uniqueness of man and his affinities with the world of philosophies, which describe and emphasize the rational faculties of man or his capacity for self-transcendence to forget his relation to nature and to

---

Niebuhr's friend John Bennett was eager to confirm that, although Niebuhr's theology developed through interaction with his ethical thought and activities, in the final analysis, 'Niebuhr's social ethics are immediately controlled by his theology.' John C. Bennett, 'Reinhold Niebuhr's Social Ethics,' Kegley, ed., *Reinhold Niebuhr*, 102.

[37]Bob E. Patterson, *Reinhold Niebuhr* (Peabody, MA: Hendrickson, 1977), 64.

identify him, prematurely and unqualifiedly with the divine and the eternal; and of naturalistic philosophies to obscure the uniqueness of man.[38]

Niebuhr found it necessary to spend the first several sections of the volume refuting the claims of those philosophies that identified humans too closely with nature, or offered too much credibility to their rational faculties. He concluded that modern understandings of humanity had a single and common source of error: 'Man is not measured in a dimension sufficiently high or deep to do full justice to either his stature or his capacity for both good and evil or to understand the total environment in which such a stature can understand, express and find itself.'[39]

In an effort to provide some balance to this dilemma, Niebuhr embarked on an exploration of the main strands of philosophical thought influencing dominant perceptions of the human situation. In the first volume of *The Nature and Destiny of Man* he explored the contributions and pitfalls of materialism, rationalism, idealism, and existentialism, offering his conclusions in a fairly methodical manner. The end result of his philosophical foray was a skilful exposition of deficiencies in several approaches, where he succeeded in a demonstration that 'truth is always seen in sharper contours when contrasted distinctively against error.'[40] This would leave the way clear for an assertion of his realist position, and his definition of the superiority of the Christian view. Perhaps what is most revealing about Niebuhr's critique of several philosophical schools is the way it defines most explicitly the influences against which he reacted, and what methodological weaknesses he hoped to avoid.

Niebuhr launched his attack against pure rationalism and idealism in various classical and modern expressions, centred on the problems of vitality and form, individuality, and conscience. His arguments flowed from a conviction that 'it is infinitely easier to admit the fact of the double milieu than it is to explain the relation between the two sides without corrupting one or the other....'[41] He defined *vitality* as human impulses and drives; *form* as the unities, cohesions, and differentiations of life. Both vitality and form are present in human nature and spirit, where human freedom provides the potential for good or evil actions, though natural vitalities provide greater attraction to sinful behaviour than those that exist in the spirit, as a result of its capability for self-transcendence.

Accusing Platonic thought of negating the value of the body and emphasizing the essential value of *nous*, Niebuhr saved his harshest critique for modern idealists, arguing that 'Kantian idealism throws the impulses of nature

---

[38]Niebuhr, *The Nature and Destiny of Man*, vol. I, Human *Nature* (New York: Charles Scribner's Sons, 1941), 3-4.

[39]Ibid., 124.

[40]Edward John Carnell, *The Theology of Reinhold Niebuhr* (Grand Rapids, MI: Eerdmans, 1951), 46.

[41]Ibid.

more completely into an outer darkness than any form of Greek classicism.'[42] Hegelianism received the same negative brushstroke, as he accused that approach of being a 'rationalized version and corruption of the Christian view of the unity of human life and the dynamic quality of historical existence.'[43] Such philosophies fall into a dualistic error that 'has the consequence for the doctrine of man of identifying the body with evil and of assuming the essential goodness of mind or spirit.'[44] Being true to the whole of human experience means acknowledging that humans consist of more than simply rational mind. Thus, 'Niebuhr contends that the idealistic premise follows only when one is not true to the full content of his experience. An existentially sensitive mind is no less conscious of the reality of physical impulses as being part of his real self than he is that the potentialities of ratiocination are properly his.'[45]

If thoroughgoing rationalist philosophies led to an overemphasis of mind, other idealisms identified humanity too closely with history and nature. After engaging the thought of Karl Marx and Friedrich Engels, Niebuhr explained how their methods submerged freedom and reason beneath nature and matter. This form of idealism compromised human individuality, making 'finite reason so continuous with divine or cosmic reason that essential individuality is finally lost.'[46] Although 'idealistic philosophy always has the advantage over naturalism in that it appreciates [the] depth of human spirit...it usually sacrifices this advantage by identifying the universal perspective of the self-transcendent ego with universal spirit. Its true self therefore ceases to be a self in a true sense and become merely an aspect of universal mind.'[47] Once again, idealism was seen as failing to maintain a proper balance of vitality and form, and neglected the seriousness of the time-eternity dialectic for human history. The consequences of such errors are of crucial ethical significance, as delineated by one Niebuhr scholar: 'If the individual is nothing, justice for the individual is nothing. And if time is nothing, justice for the individual in time is nothing. Whenever either individuality or time is corrupted, a respect for degrees of justice within history, which alone prevents social betterment from merging with social indifference, is destroyed.'[48] The 'common failure' of various idealistic or Romantic methods 'to achieve their avowed aim of establishing human individuality on a sure foundation suggests that the Christian concept is more in tune with reality' than other approaches.[49] Niebuhr

---

[42]Niebuhr, *Human Nature,* 32.

[43]Ibid., 32-33.

[44]Ibid., 7.

[45]Carnell, *The Theology of Reinhold Niebuhr*, 47.

[46]Ibid. Carnell points out that Niebuhr is well aware of other forms of idealism which do not necessarily eliminate the possibility of individualism.

[47]Niebuhr, *Human Nature,* 75.

[48]Carnell, *The Theology of Reinhold Niebuhr*, 49.

[49]William John Wolf, 'Reinhold Niebuhr's Doctrine of Man,' in Kegley, ed., *Reinhold Niebuhr*, 311.

concluded that idealism in its purely rationalistic forms, and naturalism in its materialistic manifestations are to be rejected on such grounds.

By this stage, it should be clear that Niebuhr approached the ethical problems of society from a very different position from Rauschenbusch. While he was willing to acknowledge a degree of collective moral existence, he made it clear that he viewed society as derived from the human individual, and not *vice-versa*. He was keen to guard against the liberal tendency toward construction of an immanent God and a perfectible humanity, having learned at least some of the lessons of nationalistic assertions that lead to war. But how did Niebuhr construct this belief? Why did he assert the inferiority of the collective consciousness to that of the individual, and what implications does it have for his ethical method? For answers to these questions, we must turn to some of the constructive elements of Niebuhr's thought, which were developed in various ways from scholars as diverse as Soren Kierkegaard and William James.

Existential Impulses

Perceiving the self as 'primarily an active rather than contemplative organic unity,' the human is far more than an organic unity in Niebuhr's view. 'It has the spiritual capacity of transcending both the natural process in which it is immersed and its own consciousness. As consciousness is the principle of transcendence over process, so self-consciousness is the principle of transcending consciousness.' Niebuhr employed this understanding in his attack upon the idealism of liberal Protestantism, though he remained appreciative of its advantages over materialism. He turned to Kierkegaard to help explain how the self is lost in idealism to become merely an aspect of universal mind, compromising individuality.[50] Kierkegaard supplied him with the 'paradox of faith' that 'the individual is higher than the universal, that the individual determines his relation to the universal by his relation to the absolute, not his relation to the absolute by his relation to the universal.'[51] According to Niebuhr, failure to recognize the fact that 'every self is a unity of thought and life in which thought remains in organic unity with all the organic processes of finite existence,' falsifies the problem of sin, as absolute and critical idealism have done, to varying degrees.[52] How this understanding works out in Niebuhr's thought in contrast to that of Rauschenbusch is made clearer in his critique of Royce, whose ideas were heartily endorsed by the social gospel advocate.

Niebuhr offered Royce's thought as an example of the inability of absolute idealism to come to terms with what he describes as 'the Christian idea' of

---

[50]Carnell suggests that Kierkegaard 'bequeathed to Barth, Brunner, and Niebuhr their dialectical framework.' Carnell, *Theology*, 33.

[51]Niebuhr, *Human Nature*, 75.

[52]Ibid., 78.

selfhood. He affirmed Royce's desire to preserve an adequate concept of individuality, acknowledging that Royce's Absolute 'is a mosaic which requires the variety of individuality for its richness.' But Royce's definition of individuality was insufficient for Niebuhr: 'by individuality Royce means particularity and not the distinctive depth of spirit which distinguishes human individuality from the particularity of nature...'. He furnished the following quotation from Royce to illustrate his point: 'Any finite idea is so far a self, and I can, if you please, contrast my present self with my past or my future self, with yesterday's hopes or tomorrow's deeds, quite as genuinely as with your inner life or with the whole society of which I am a member, or with the whole life of which our experience of nature is a hint, or, finally with the life of God in its entirety.' For Niebuhr's understanding of Royce, this meant that 'Finite selfhood is thus in the same category as any finite reality while ultimate selfhood is nothing short of the Absolute. For the Absolute is defined by Royce as "our very selfhood in fulfilment".' Royce suggested further that, 'from the point of view of the Absolute the finite beings never fall away. They are where they are, namely in and of the Absolute Unity.' This understanding clearly runs counter to Niebuhr's desire to explain evil as being rooted in self-consciousness, as a later examination of his theology will demonstrate. 'Put in terms of Christian doctrine,' Niebuhr wrote, 'Royce's view is that each man is Christ from the perspective of God while he is both creature and sinner only from his own perspective. Or it might be fairer to say that in his view man's finiteness is sinful only as its exclusiveness and discreteness have not yet been transcended in a rational perspective which logically culminates in God's perspective.' Niebuhr attributed Royce's misunderstanding to an error in equating the biblical and Platonic views of humanity, suggesting that such a view leads to the conclusion that 'universal mind is the "Christ" of redemption.'[53]

In contrast to Royce, Niebuhr described Kierkegaard as interpreting 'the true meaning of human selfhood more accurately than any modern, and possibly any previous, Christian theologian.' Kierkegaard's existential elaboration of selfhood captured Niebuhr's attention, and he quoted him in explanation of some of his own thoughts on the subject

> The self is the conscious synthesis of the limited and the unlimited which is related to itself and the task of which is to become a self, a task which can be realized only in relation to God. To become a self means to become concrete. But to become concrete means to be neither limited nor unlimited, for that which must become concrete is a synthesis. Therefore development consists in this: that in the eternalization of the self one escapes the self endlessly and in temporalization of the self one endlessly returns to the self.[54]

---

[53]Ibid., 78-9.
[54]Ibid., 171.

Appropriating Kierkegaard's analysis of the self gave Niebuhr a framework for developing an understanding of humanity that replaced the old emphasis on the collective consciousness with a renewed appreciation of the individual moral person.

Moreover, Niebuhr viewed groups as human creations with a different existential constitution from the individual self. As extensions of the individual, societies and social structures have equal potential for positive achievement and tyrannical destruction. The expression of pride on a group level becomes particularly destructive when it is used to extend the will-to-power over other groups and institutions, in a false assertion of human immortality. Groups may come to exhibit characteristics of personality but lack the conditions of self-hood which enables self-reflection, self-transcendence, and even repentance. In other words, in direct contrast to Rauschenbusch's approach, Niebuhr's method does not support the concept of society possessing a moral consciousness *per se*, and so moderation and limitation of its power may only come in relative terms, through interaction with other societies and groups that judge and balance its pretensions. The result will be expressed in a form of justice, which may be described as divisible.

Niebuhr remained consistently clear in his acknowledgement of the significant difference between individual and collective consciousness. In *An Interpretation of Christian Ethics* he wrote

> It is possible for individuals to be saved from this sinful pretension, not by achieving an absolute perspective upon life, but by their recognition of their inability to do so. Individuals may be saved by repentance, which is the gateway to grace. The recognition of creatureliness and finiteness, in other words, may become the basis of man's reconciliation to God through his resignation to his finite condition. But the collective life of mankind promises no such hope of salvation, for the very reason that it offers men the very symbols of pseudo-universality which tempt them to glorify and worship themselves as God.[55]

Niebuhr had much to say throughout his work about the collective existence of humanity, but always upheld a clear distinction between social and individual morality. The distinction lay in the selfhood of the individual, which allowed the positive aspects of the freedom of the soul to experience victory over the impulses of self-interest. In contrast to the Christian promise of new life for individuals who 'die to self,' grace must be relevant to social existence in a different way, since 'collective forms of life do not have the exact integrity of the individual soul; nor do they have as direct an access to divine judgement and grace...'.[56] The theological implications of this statement will be drawn out further in the following chapter, but suffice it to say at this stage that Niebuhr

---

[55]Niebuhr, *Ethics,* 85.
[56]Niebuhr, *Christian Realism and Political Problems* (New York: Charles Scribner's Sons, 1953), 111.

conceived of an existential, and moral, difference between humans in their individual and collective forms, rooted in his understanding of Kierkegaard's anthropological interpretation.[57]

True to his dialectical method, Niebuhr eventually offered a specific and brief survey of philosophical theories of community existence, through a critique of idealist and realist approaches in a later work entitled, *Man's Nature and His Communities.* In this historical survey representing his most mature thought, he dismissed the idealism of the Greek philosophers as placing too much 'confidence in the virtue and power of reason as the source of the social and moral order.'[58] Although Aristotle embraced more 'realist' interpretations than Plato, they both placed too much confidence in the ability of reason to modify and correct social behaviour, and so ignored the actual power structures, which they took for granted. The actual historical situation demonstrated that 'reason never operates in a vacuum, and that the presuppositions with which it begins - individual or social - make it the servant, rather than the master, of the vital impulses of human life.'[59] Niebuhr believed this 'ideological taint' in the operation of the rational faculty, which placed undue confidence in the development of reason remained unanalysed until the nineteenth century when Marx and Freud described theories of rationalization and ideology, which married idealism and realism, and failed to consistently describe either theory. For example, Niebuhr described Marxism as little more than 'an old form of religious self-righteousness,' which is realistic about the bourgeoisie 'sinners' but idealistic about the 'Messianic class.'[60] The intervening history was similarly characterized by a 'bewildering confusion of realism and idealism,' expressed in more and less helpful combinations, from Paul, Augustine, and Luther, to Aquinas, Hobbes, and Locke.

According to Niebuhr, what most theories failed to take into considerable account were the forces of self-interest and power that corrupt every attempt at social or political organization. Power is not to be understood as a substitution for the ideal of love in social relationship, applied either intentionally or

---

[57]In Kierkegaard's explanation of faith, we find clues as to the source of Niebuhr's understanding of belief, which precludes collective commitment, as it is based on an existential predicament of the individual self. Kierkegaard asserted, 'Faith is precisely the contradiction between the infinite passion of the individual's waywardness and the objective uncertainty. If I am capable of grasping God objectively, I do not believe, but precisely because I cannot do this I must believe.' Soren Kierkegaard, *Concluding Unscientific Postscript*, trans. David Swenson (Princeton, NJ: Princeton University Press, 1944), 182. See further John Heywood Thomas, *Subjectivity and Paradox* (Oxford: Blackwell, 1957), ch. 3 and 151-8.

[58]Niebuhr, *Man's Nature and His Communities* (New York: Charles Scribner's Sons, 1965), 25-26.

[59]Ibid., 26.

[60]Ibid., 27.

unwittingly, but power is viewed as a corruption of love itself.[61] The distinction, though subtle, is an important one for Niebuhr, as it guards against an unwarranted pessimism about the human social situation, and defends his position against accusations of dualism.[62] If the distinction is valid, he offered, 'it would point to the residual force but not the effacement, of the higher, or wider, or nobler loyalty, however much corrupted by the lower one.'[63] Though this meant nations would have the potential to act in favour of a broader interest, it was not considered to be a likely outcome, and certainly not possible apart from considered self-interest. According to Niebuhr's realism then, hope for better forms of justice lay not in the possibility of humans laying aside national self-interest in favour of a larger common human interest, but in demonstrating how a larger common interest could benefit the national self-interest.[64]

Despite a seemingly pessimistic tone, Niebuhr believed the realism of this interpretation provided for better forms of justice to improve the life of society and the lives of its members, as moral perfection stands as a revealed symbol of judgement and not an achievable utopia. This view intensifies, rather than nullifies, the necessity for increased efforts toward the alleviation of evil and suffering in society. While human reason and virtue are limited, Niebuhr insisted as a moral cognitivist, 'that the degree of imagination and insight with which disciplined minds are able to enter into the problems of their fellow men and to enlarge the field of interests in which human actions take place, may materially improve human happiness and social harmony.' Moreover, 'a religious ethic which holds such achievements in contempt discredits itself, particularly in a generation in which the problems of man's aggregate existence have become so great that their slightest alleviation must be regarded as a boon to mankind.'[65]

Experience and history were thus important philosophical categories for Niebuhr, as he embraced a modified pragmatism to assist in the building of an ethical apologetic. While Niebuhr believed 'ultimately the acceptance of the truth of the Gospel is a gift of grace which stands beyond worldly wisdom' and is unable to 'compel conviction on purely rational grounds, there is nevertheless a positive apologetic task.'[66] This task 'consists in correlating the

---

[61]See ibid., 53-7.

[62]See Kenenth Hamilton, 'Created Soul - Eternal Spirit: A Continuing Theological Thorn,' *SJT* 19 (March 1966): 29-30. Hamilton accuses Niebuhr of an ostensible biblical corruption in failing to maintain body-spirit unity. This is a misunderstanding of Niebuhr's position, possibly attributable to a misreading of Niebuhr's sometimes awkward dialectical approach.

[63]Niebuhr, *Man's Nature and His Communities*, 57.

[64]At least some international political systems theorists, such as Hans Morgenthau, would apply Niebuhr's analysis of human nature to international political behaviour.

[65]Niebuhr, *Ethics,* 88.

[66]Reinhold Niebuhr, *Faith and History* (London: Nisbet, 1949), 187.

truth, apprehended by faith and repentance, to truths about life and history, gained generally in experience. Such a correlation validates the truth of faith in so far as it proves it to be a source and centre of an interpretation of life, more adequate than alternative interpretations, because it comprehends all of life's antinomies and contradictions into a system of meaning and is conducive to a renewal of life.'[67]

Pragmatist Impulses

Implicit in Niebuhr's definition of apologetics is a rejection of any type of philosophy that might seek metaphysical knowledge of God through sheer ratiocination. Niebuhr borrowed from William James a pragmatic approach that rejected the high limits of metaphysics proposed by the idealists.[68] James bid farewell to dogmatic theology with the assertion that 'ratiocination is a relatively superficial and unreal path to the deity.'[69] But James, and Niebuhr after him, still recognized the rational quality of humanity, and suggested that philosophy offered helpful tools to sift out 'unworthy formulations,' test hypotheses, assess verifiability, refine definitions, distinguish between 'innocent over-belief and symbolism,' and as a result, 'offer mediation between different believers and help to bring about consensus of opinion.'[70] Philosophy would not work in a conceptual vacuum, nor operate in isolation from concrete life experience. Rather, experience would provide the questions, verify the answers, and prompt reconstructions of belief and practice. It is this pragmatic method that led Niebuhr to claim to stand firmly in the tradition of William James.[71] Niebuhr's pragmatism, then, does not depend on the employment of reason alone to attain truth, but relies on the unfolding of history to reveal and test truth, apprehended in a limited way by humans through experience.[72]

Human experience, however, could not be self-interpreting, and depended ultimately on faith to provide historical meaning. Robert Ayers describes the influence of James' empirical-pragmatic epistemology on Niebuhr, making

---

[67]Ibid.

[68]In a sentence dismissing the possibility of metaphysics, James wrote, 'So much for the metaphysics of God! From the point of view of practical religion, the metaphysical monster which they offer to our worship is an absolutely worthless invention of the scholarly mind.' Though Niebuhr would perhaps not go quite this far, the influence on his thinking of this philosophical challenge is apparent. William James, *Varieties of Religious Experience* (1902; reprint, New York: New American Library of World Literature, 1958), 340.

[69]Ibid., 341.

[70]Ibid., 346-7.

[71]Niebuhr wrote to a friend, 'I stand in the William James tradition. He was both an empiricist and a religious man, and his faith was both the consequence and the presupposition of his pragmatism.' Cited in Bingham, *Courage*, 224.

[72]Cf. Lovin, *Reinhold Niebuhr and Christian Realism*, 40.

reference to his acknowledgement of science as a means of gaining knowledge of the natural world, and his understanding that the experiences of daily life form a basis for theories about the meaning of life 'beyond the narrow scope of scientific thinking.'[73] As Niebuhr built on James' 'radical empiricism,' he argued that facts and experiences have no meaning apart from a principle of interpretation. For Niebuhr, that principle was faith, whose 'criterion of meaning comes by means of a special revelation which provides clues to the meaning of life and history without abolishing all mystery.'[74] With faith as his ultimate category, Niebuhr's pragmatism 'cannot demonstrate that ideological systems, social theories, or religions are true, but it can show that one or another of them provides a better way of anticipating future events and making choices in light of the likely outcomes.'[75] Though pluralism is defended in a pragmatic method, relativism is confronted since people 'can hardly be indifferent to an argument that Christianity provides such an account [of human life] more adequately than other systems, even if that pragmatic demonstration fails to "prove" that all human claims and interests are limited in the way that the Christian idea of God implies.'[76] Thus, the Christian approach is seen by Niebuhr and the realists as relevant to all of human life, regardless of whether everyone in broader society shares Christian faith and presuppositions.

For Niebuhr, what history and experience have demonstrated, and faith in God's revelation proved coherently, is that love is the foundational moral law, and that humans are generally rational and social beings, but far from perfectly so. The law of love is relevant, therefore, insofar as it serves as a transcendent ideal, attainable only in proximate measures of justice, derived rationally through a pragmatic process. The transcendent ideal subsequently judges human efforts to establish justice, encouraging ever greater approximations, while establishing the impossibility of achieving moral perfection. A method of coherence tells us best what means are necessary to produce desired outcomes and thus achieve better forms of what will ever only be a proximate form of moral justice. Coherence also not only encourages revision, but its pragmatic elements demand it. Developing a method of coherence, Niebuhr demonstrated how ethical principles could be successfully applied through pragmatic means.[77]

In an article written in 1951, Niebuhr explicated his understanding of coherence in a very clear and helpful way. He began with this statement

---

[73]See Robert Ayers, 'Methodological, Epistemological, and Ontological Motifs in the Thought of Reinhold Niebuhr,' 162.

[74]Ibid., 163.

[75]Lovin, *Reinhold Niebuhr and Christian Realism*, 49.

[76]Ibid., 40.

[77]Cf. John C. Bennett, 'Theologians of our Time: Reinhold Niebuhr', *ExpTim* (May 1964): 237-40.

The whole of reality is characterized by a basic coherence. Things and events are in a vast web of relationships and are known through their relations. Perceptual knowledge is possible only within a framework of conceptual images, which in some sense conform to the structures in which reality is organized. The world is organized or it could not exist; if it is to be known, it must be known through its sequences, coherences, causalities, and essences.[78]

Despite this strong statement at the outset of his discussion, Niebuhr was not unaware of the criticisms and philosophical pitfalls of such an approach.[79] In fact, he described four 'primary perils to truth in making coherence the basic test of truth,' and accordingly modifies his method of coherence to conform to certain theological premises.[80] In particular, he criticised attempts to derive moral principles from natural law, and from the subjective self as postulated by Kierkegaard.[81] While both natural law and existentialism influenced Niebuhr's own system, he was nevertheless aware of their weaknesses, and in the realm of moral discourse, preferred to balance such philosophical influences with theological and dogmatic aspects of Christian belief. In this way, he held consistently a dialectical tension between practical ethics and ideals, reason and faith, natural law and revelation, indicating that

faith in the sovereignty of a divine creator, judge, and redeemer is not subject to rational proof, because it stands beyond and above the rational coherences of the world and can therefore not be proved by an analysis of these coherences. But a scientific and philosophical analysis of these coherences is not incapable of revealing where they point beyond themselves to a freedom which is not in them, to contradictions between each other which suggest a profounder mystery and meaning beyond them.[82]

An apologetically defensible theology and ethic which reached such a balance could sufficiently take its rightful place in wider academic and public discussion, if it managed to hold fast 'to the mystery and meaning beyond coherences' while maintaining 'a decent respect for the order and meaning of

---

[78]Niebuhr, 'Coherence, Incoherence, and Christian Faith,' 155. Stanley Grenz's recent post-foundationalist proposal positing a theological method of coherence based on a 'mosaic' of belief, and drawing from Pannenberg's theology, sounds hardly new or novel in light of Niebuhr's thought. See Stanley Grenz, 'Beyond Foundationalism: Is a Nonfoundationalist Evangelical Theology Possible?' *JCTR* 1998: [http://apu.edu/~CTRF/papers/ctrfpapers.html].
[79]Cf. Caroline Simon, 'Christianity and Moral Knowledge,' *Christian Theism and Moral Philosophy* eds. Michael Beaty, Carlton Fisher, and Mark Nelson (Macon, GA: Mercer University Press, 1998), 107-144.
[80]Niebuhr, 'Coherence, Incoherence, and Christian Faith,' 155.
[81]Cf. C. Stephen Evans, 'A Kierkegaardian View of the Foundations of Morality,' in Beaty et. al. eds., 63-76.
[82]Niebuhr, 'Coherence, Incoherence, and Christian Faith,' 167-8.

the natural world.'[83]

Although Niebuhr's coherence did not surrender to ethical relativism, it upheld the value of an open and pluralistic society. With the law of love serving as an ethical standard at least as a symbol of judgement, an authoritative moral standard existed, though in practice it was considered unattainable, since all actions are historically contingent. This would mean no particular group in society, nor any society as a whole could make absolute moral claims about itself in relation to others, and all would benefit from the interaction and interplay with other perspectives. Such social interaction is the very thing that saves individuals from their own self-interest, and as such is regarded by Niebuhr as a form of grace

> If these analyses are at all correct, they point to the fact that the law of love is indeed the basis of all moral life, that it can not be obeyed by a simple act of the will because the power of self-concern is too great, and that the forces which draw the self from its undue self-concern are usually forces of 'common grace' in the sense that they represent all forms of social security or responsibility or pressure which prompt the self to bethink itself of its social essence and to realise itself by not trying too desperately for self-realisation.[84]

Groups experience the same 'common grace' as they modify one another, and are caused to behave in ways that are not too deterministic for self-realization on a collective level, and consequently strive toward a broader form of justice.

Consequently, we see groups functioning as personalities, but without the same moral capacity of the individual to repent and sacrifice its own self-interest in complete surrender to a more broadly encompassing good. In fact, Niebuhr could not describe group behaviour in strictly ethical terms at all. So strong did he consider collective egoist impulses to be, that he contended group behaviour should be discussed in political, rather than ethical parlance. Christianity, then, participates as one group among many in the public realm, corrected by its encounters with other groups, even as it seeks to bring its own particular views of justice to the fore. 'The adherent of religion must come to terms with the historic facts,' wrote Niebuhr, 'that in all collective behaviour religious piety is likely to sanctify historical and contingent viewpoints.' Furthermore, he believed, such tendencies are magnified in religious collective behaviour: 'Historically speaking, religious piety is more apt to be found claiming the divine for an ally of its own partial viewpoints - "It has seemed good to the Holy Spirit and to us" - rather than showing a humble awareness of the relative aspects of all historical loyalties or as bringing forth the fruits of repentance for shortcomings as judged by the transcendent God.'[85] In other words, although Christianity may point to the truth, it does not necessarily

---

[83]Ibid., 168.
[84]Niebuhr, *Man's Nature and His Communities*, 95-6.
[85]Ibid., 85.

embody it, and grace demands its participation in an open society to modify its own prideful claims and self-serving assertions. Christianity was required additionally to participate in the open society to provide a similar modifying influence for other groups, and to contribute positively to the formation of justice. Accordingly, Niebuhr could conceive of no distinct line dividing Christian social ethics from social ethics in general. In this regard, his understanding of the relationship between Christianity and society moved more closely to Augustinian and Reformed conceptions than Lutheran.[86]

Natural Law

Despite protestations and statements otherwise, there has been much debate amongst scholars over the degree to which Niebuhr subscribed to an ethical theory of natural law, and whether it affected his method negatively or positively.[87] The transcendent nature of the law of love is constantly maintained by Niebuhr, but the appropriation of love in forms of justice is made possible by a degree of moral reason, which allows moral agents to consent to the establishment of a universal moral community. Although reason may be flawed, and the moral community corrupt, there is within the human creature the capacity to think and act in ways that suggest Niebuhr was not keen to abandon natural law thinking altogether, despite his frequent critiques of natural law 'excesses.'[88]

Emil Brunner believed it was Niebuhr's inability to properly balance his understanding of natural law with his conception of the social norm of justice that led him to yield few concrete solutions to ecumenical ethical problems. Brunner wrote

---

[86]While Gabriel Fackre notes that Niebuhr has rarely been considered in the context of Reformed theology, he suggests there is reason to see him as standing in the Reformed tradition. See Gabriel Fackre, 'Reinhold Niebuhr,' in David Wells, ed., *Reformed Theology in America*. G. Brillenburg Wurth disagrees that Niebuhr ought to be considered as standing in the tradition of the Reformers. See Wurth, *Niebuhr* trans. David H. Freeman, International Library of Philosophy and Theology Modern Thinkers Series, ed. David H. Freeman (USA: Presbyterian and Reformed Publishing Co., 1975), 36 & 41. Despite Wurth's protests, a strong argument for placing Niebuhr in a Reformed theological context may be easily made, and he was, in any case, ecclesiastically Reformed.

[87]See Niebuhr, *The Children of Light and the Children of Darkness* (New York: Charles Scribner's Sons, 1944), 188ff. Cf. Paul Ramsay, 'Love and Law,' in Kegley, ed., *Reinhold Niebuhr*, 143-188; Robert Fitch, 'Reinhold Niebuhr's Philosophy of History,' in Kegley, ed., *Reinhold Niebuhr*, 367-386.

[88]John C. Bennett, 'Theologians of Our Time: Reinhold Niebuhr,' *ExpTim* (May, 1964): 239-40.

Niebuhr has taken occasion publicly to dissociate himself from the traditional 'natural law' doctrine, because for him this is inseparably bound up with the Aristotelian-Thomistic system, and anyone who is somewhat familiar with the history of the 'natural law' philosophy will understand this reservation on the part of a New Testament-oriented thinker. All the more urgent, however, becomes the question what 'justice' could mean to a Christian who wants to distinguish it from the supreme ethical norm of love....Niebuhr himself is very clear on the fact that justice is not the same thing as love, but that justice is the proper norm for the social order. All the more necessary might it be to make clear what justice is as distinguished from love and in what relation justice stands to love, the sovereign norm for Christian ethics.[89]

Brunner believed that this deficiency in Niebuhr's method explained a particular criticism 'that has often been levelled against Niebuhr's social ethics' regarding the difficulty of applying justice in concrete situations.[90] The solution to this problem would not necessarily mean resorting to a method based on natural law, 'made up of timelessly valid ethical demands,' which Niebuhr rightly warred against. But Niebuhr 'must be able to make clear the relationship' of the moral obligations 'posed by justice to the supreme ethical principle of love.'[91] In Brunner's view, Niebuhr failed to account for the relationship between love and justice adequately.

Part of the confusion may have resulted from a 'perpetual battle' waged by Niebuhr on two fronts - 'on the one side against Catholic stereotypes of natural law, and on the other side against the moral relativists, especially when they are protestant theologians.'[92] His dialectical method also contributed to the problem of identifying the degree to which Niebuhr would embrace natural law principles, as he viewed moral obligations as related, but not identical to, the law of love. Paul Ramsey concluded that in Niebuhr's view there is, in effect, 'only one natural and essential law; the rest is application.'[93] Nevertheless, 'certain "principles" of justice, as distinguished from formulas or prescriptions, were indeed operative, such as liberty, equality, and loyalty to covenants; but these principles will be recognized as no more than the law of love in its various facets.'[94] The spirit of justice may be described as identical as the spirit of love, except in love's highest level where it is described as 'purely sacrificial and engages in no calculation of what the due of each man may be.'[95] The law of love, as the norm for individuals is transmuted into the law of justice for

---

[89]Brunner, in Kegley, ed., *Reinhold Niebuhr*, 84.
[90]Ibid., 84-5. This issue is discussed further in chapter five of the present study.
[91]Ibid., 85.
[92]John Bennett, 'Reinhold Niebuhr,' 239.
[93]Paul Ramsey, 'Love and Law,' in Kegley, ed., *Reinhold Niebuhr*, 167. Cf. Niebuhr, *Faith and History*, 198-203.
[94]Niebuhr, *Christian Realism and Political Problems*, 135.
[95]Ibid.

social ethics, and its principles reflect and participate in this revealed law. But the development of particular moral applications from this law belongs to the realms of reason and history, and therefore becomes at times, less distinguishable from natural law.

This discussion is an important one because it is central to any attempt to understand the benefits and pitfalls of a 'realist' approach to the development and application of moral principles in society. If Niebuhr's view of human freedom and reason do not differ significantly from a natural law approach, then in what sense is his method to be distinguished from Rauschenbusch's idealist method, which depended heavily on natural law? Niebuhr believed his view was distinct from Rauschenbusch's in several crucial ways, most of which are best described from the perspective of his Christian anthropology. Although the present discussion has demonstrated that the division of Niebuhr's philosophy from his theology is both undesirable and impossible, it is to a primarily theological discussion that we must now turn in order to fill in some of the blanks left so far in this portrayal of Niebuhr's ethical method. Questions of the role of authority, human freedom and sin, atonement, and society, find the greatest potential for satisfaction in Niebuhr's constructive theology.

A topic so great as the philosophical impulses of Niebuhr's ethical method can hardly be touched upon in a chapter of this length. Nevertheless, the ground has been laid to understand the realist approach Niebuhr took to issues of love and justice, and their application to the life of society. Though individuals are the primary moral agents for Niebuhr, based on his existential pragmatism, and rejection of most forms of idealism, he nevertheless saw community as the place where the individual life of faith was to be applied. Niebuhr's realism and pragmatism meant that his appreciation for methodological coherence would extend to his practice of ethics on an ecumenical level, where individual and collective agency were balanced in a process of study and dialogue. Such study and dialogue would rest upon a certain degree of ethical ambiguity, but the process ought always to strive towards an application of justice that moved society beyond present attainments. However, Niebuhr's development of this approach depended as much, if not more, on theological impulses than philosophical ones. His deep appreciation of the nature of sin, of the transcendent judgement of the Cross, and the significance of God's grace to the ethical task move to the fore in an examination of his theology, which he considered as prior to philosophy, and to which we now turn.

CHAPTER 5

What We Know As Truth: Theological Impulses in Reinhold Niebuhr's Realist Method

What we know as truth is determined by peculiar and individual perspectives. Pressures of environment, influences of heredity, and excellencies and deficiencies of teachers help to determine our life philosophies. We ought therefore to hold them with decent humility and a measure of scepticism. But if we permit ourselves to be tempted into a complete subjectivism and scepticism by these facts, we put an end to all philosophy and ultimately to civilization itself. For civilization depends upon the vigorous pursuit of the highest values by people who are intelligent enough to know that their values are qualified by their interests and corrupted by their prejudices.

Reinhold Niebuhr

Introduction

Although Niebuhr was conversant with philosophy and ethics, his method rested firmly upon strong theological convictions. To his mind, the Christian account of life offered a far more complete, and real description of what lay behind human motivations, and the impulses of history, than any other philosophy or ideology. For Niebuhr, the strength of the Christian view of humanity is found in its nature as a revealed religion which emphasizes equally the transcendence and immanence of God, and balances the image of God and creaturely necessities in humanity. As Niebuhr proposed, there are theological corruptions of ethical understanding within Christianity as well as philosophical corruptions without. He believed mysticism, for example, overemphasizes the immanence of God, equating the depths of the human soul with eternity. Other errors stress transcendence, such that any possibility of God acting in history is logically precluded. The relevance of achieving a proper view of transcendence and immanence, without becoming embedded in ontological and metaphysical categories, was central to Niebuhr's anthropological assertions, and subsequently, his ethics: 'The most important characteristic of a religion of revelation is this twofold emphasis upon the transcendence of God and upon

His intimate relation to the world. In this divine transcendence the spirit of man finds a home in which it can understand its stature of freedom. But there it also finds the limits of freedom, the judgement which is spoken against it, and, ultimately, the mercy which makes such a judgement sufferable.'[1] The insights of Christian revelation provided Niebuhr with the theological elements of his method, whereby humans are perceived as spiritually self-transcendent as bearers of the image of God; weak, dependent, and finite creatures in relation to the natural world; inevitably but not necessarily involved in denial of their dependence and finitude which leads to evil and sin, as humans seek to escape the anxiety produced by such denial. Grace accessed through Jesus Christ offers a direct link to forgiveness and repentance for the individual, but politics must be substituted for ethics on a collective level.

Myth and Symbol

Niebuhr sought the objectivity provided by authoritative revelation for a realist approach that took all aspects of human nature and freedom seriously, but he did not want to be bound to the literal authority of any singular interpretation of the text. The struggle to find ethical, religious, scientific epistemological balance in his method, led him to embrace a mythical understanding of Scripture and revelation, which would serve as the ethical foundation for his methodology. Since he believed that Christian doctrine must maintain a tension between the actual and the ideal in order to bear ethical fruit, he assumed that 'this tension must first illumine the ethical problems of history without sanctifying any actual condition in history, and second, be credible in light of modern science and experience. For Niebuhr, the concept of myth functioned to resolve both these problems.'[2]

To abandon traditional doctrines that were no longer intellectually acceptable to the modern world was to baptize modern science and philosophy as the ideal - a position that Niebuhr rejected. At the same time, while orthodoxy was preferable to liberalism, Niebuhr believed its religious truths are 'still embedded in outmoded science' and 'its morality is expressed in dogmatic and authoritarian moral codes' which have 'lost both religious and moral meaning.'[3] This dilemma was solved for Niebuhr by employing the concepts of myth and symbol in the interpretation of Christian revelation. He preferred to think of Christian truths as embodied in myths, rather than literal language since 'what is true in the Christian religion can be expressed only in symbols which contain a certain degree of provisional and superficial deception.'[4]

---

[1] Reinhold Niebuhr, *Human Nature*, 126.
[2] Beckley, *Passion for Justice*, 257.
[3] Niebuhr, *An Interpretation of Christian Ethics*, 14.
[4] Reinhold Niebuhr, *Beyond Tragedy* (New York, NY: Charles Scribner's Sons, 1937), 3.

Comparing the temporal process to an artist's canvass, Niebuhr described it as a single dimension upon which two dimensions must be recorded. 'This can be done only by symbols which deceive for the sake of truth,' leaving the human grasp of truth always in a provisional state.[5] Because biblical accounts of creation, fall, atonement, and judgement cannot be fully rationalized, they have 'been an offence' to philosophers and scientists alike. Deep religious truths can only be expressed in such myths, however, in terms that outrage reason, because they describe concepts that are beyond rationalization. Describing Christian truths as embodied in mythical form did not negate the value of the truth they possessed, and through his approach, Niebuhr hoped to preserve his ability to interact with biblical revelation seriously, without alienating the modern mindset. This understanding of revelation as myth is to be distinguished from Rudolf Bultmann's programme of demythologization, which sought to interpret biblical myth consistently, but was dismissive of much of the historical element that Niebuhr wanted to preserve.[6]

Niebuhr saw myth as a particular strength of the Christian religion over and against other philosophies of human life. As opposed to rational or non-mythical religions which 'tend to define the ideal in terms of passionless form and the world of actuality as unqualifiedly evil, it is the virtue of mythical religions that they discover symbols of the transcendent in the actual without either separating the one or identifying it with the other.[7] He explained

> This is perhaps the most essential genius of myth, that it points to the timeless in time, to the ideal in the actual, but does not lift the temporal to the category of the eternal (as pantheism does), nor deny the significant glimpses of the eternal and the ideal in the temporal (as dualism does). When the mythical method is applied to the description of human character, its paradoxes disclose precisely the same relationships in human personality which myth reveals and more consistent philosophers obscure, in the nature of the universe.[8]

Harlan Beckley suggests that myth was really 'the key to Niebuhr's retrieval of Christian doctrines because it expresses truth paradoxically. It uses symbols from the temporal world that point to a transcendent dimension of reality.' Though the ideal is never attainable within temporal existence, myth nevertheless contains 'the ultimate truth about how humans ought to live

---

[5]Ibid., 6.
[6]Cf. Rudolf Bultmann, *Jesus Christ and Mythology* (London: 1960). Niebuhr later regretted his own use of the term 'myth', saying, 'I am sorry I ever used it, particularly since the project for 'demythologising' the Bible has been undertaken and bids fair to reduce the Biblical revelation to eternally valid truths without any existential encounters between God and man.' 'Reply' in Kegley ed., *Reinhold Niebuhr*, 439.
[7]Niebuhr, *Ethics*, 79-80.
[8]Ibid., 80.

together within history.'[9] Interpretations of 'myth' and 'symbol' suited Niebuhr's dialectical method, and satisfied the theological needs of his primary ethical concerns.

Niebuhr's approach to Scripture was not always widely received, and he was criticized from both conservative and liberal directions. Conservatives criticized Niebuhr vigorously on his view of the Bible, especially in his outright rejection of orthodox approaches.[10] In his examination of Niebuhr's position, E. J. Carnell notes that Niebuhr attempted to take the middle road of the realist, capitulating to the demands of science while rejecting the orthodox view of the Bible as God's objective revelation, true in whole and part: 'Niebuhr, thus, is fully congenial to destructive higher criticism,' he writes. 'While refusing to go as far as the liberal who supposes that the Bible is just man's search for God in written form, Niebuhr halts far short of historical Protestantism. The Bible contains truth only at those points where it supports both the dialectical interpretation of history and the existential assurances within the race and the individual.'[11] Carnell asserts that Niebuhr has failed to break with liberalism with respect to epistemology, arguing that 'he has simply enlarged the "kernel" of Biblical truth to include *Heilsgeschichte*. But both the kernel-husk theory of the Bible and the tendency to divorce theology from history remain.'[12]

For certain fundamentalists who preferred to cling to the verbal plenary inspiration of Scripture, Niebuhr's mythical approach was completely unacceptable, leading them to close themselves to his theological and ethical insights.[13] Yet, perhaps it was easier for Niebuhr to dismiss criticism from conservatives with whom he had little contact than to bear the accusations from

---

[9]Beckley, *Passion for Justice*, 260. Beckley notes that Niebuhr later exchanged use of the word 'myth' for 'symbol' as a result of the sceptical connotation of 'myth', though for Niebuhr their function was the same.

[10]Cf. Reinhold Niebuhr, *Reflections of the End of an Era* (New York, NY: Charles Scribner's Sons, 1934), 122. Niebuhr wrote: 'In one sense all Orthodox Christian theology has been guilty of the sin of profanity. It has insisted on the literal and historic truths of its myths, forgetting that it is the function and character of religious myth to speak of the eternal in relation to time, and that it cannot therefore be a statement of temporal sequence.'

[11]E. J. Carnell, *The Theology of Reinhold Niebuhr*, 119-20.

[12]Ibid., 119n.

[13]See Gordon Lewis and Bruce Demarest, eds., *Challenges to Inerrancy: A Theological Response,* Chicago, IL: Moody Press, 1984. In Lewis' article entitled, 'The Niebuhrs' Relativism, Relationalism, Contextualization, and Revelation,' he argues that Scripture must be understood as being human and divine 'just as' Jesus Christ was human and divine, and therefore rejects Niebuhr's work outright. Cf. E. J. Carnell, 'Conservatives and Liberals Do Not Need Each Other,' *CT* (May 1965): 39. It seems extreme to accuse Niebuhr of acquiescing to Harnack's hermeneutic, especially considering the equally strong attacks that were launched at his method from the opposite direction. Cf. Adolf Harnack, *What is Christianity?* 1901.

his liberal colleagues who branded him a 'biblicist' for attempting to take Scriptural revelation seriously at all.[14] Despite the arguments that followed Niebuhr's approach to Scripture and revelation, in true pragmatist fashion, many scholars now suggest that history has proved the place of Niebuhr's method within the broad Reformed tradition.

Theology from Below

Niebuhr's theological understanding actually begins with his doctrine of humanity, which rests on a primarily ethical basis. If it is true, as James Gustafson argues, that Niebuhr develops his theology from ethical considerations, then his decision to begin a more systematic theological elaboration with the condition of humanity is not surprising.[15] Gustafson argues convincingly that all theologians and ethicists fall somewhere between these two positions: the theism of Barth or the ethicism of Kant, with most weight of preference being placed in one or the other direction. 'This weight, if it does not determine of form and content totally, makes a difference at critical points in the development of a position,' says Gustafson, denying the validity of the dialectical approach as a means of escaping the reality of his statement.[16] Niebuhr's ethical concerns led him to ethical consideration of the human situation with its emphasis on freedom and sin, as opposed to Barth's approach, which began with God and developed an ethic based on grace. Indeed, Niebuhr's entire theological system appears to be rooted in ethical concerns, existentially discerned, and approached through reason as a 'theology from below.' In his own understanding, 'every philosophy of life is touched with anthropocentric tendencies. Even theocentric religions believe that the Creator of the world is interested in saving man from his unique predicament.'[17] Considering his philosophical understanding of the self, and the divine-human encounter in revelation, it follows that Niebuhr cannot conceive of any other

---

[14]Paul Tillich defended his friend from such 'outside' attacks, stating, 'They do not see how far away from any mechanical supernaturalism and from any authoritarian Biblicism Niebuhr's thought actually is.' Paul Tillich, ' Reinhold Niebuhr's Doctrine of Knowledge,' in Kegley, ed., *Reinhold Niebuhr*, 96. Niebuhr in turn makes it clear that what he wants to do is find a balanced view. 'Any liberalism which transmutes the experience (of divine forgiveness) into a philosophical proposition which can be intellectually accepted, and any Biblicism which changes belief from repentance and commitment to the mere acceptance of historical propositions, equally rob the experience of its resource of 'wisdom and power'. Niebuhr, 'Response,' in Kegley, ed., *Reinhold Niebuhr*, 519.

[15]See James Gustafson, 'Theology in the Service of Ethics: An Interpretation of Reinhold Niebuhr's Theological Ethics,' in Richard Harries, ed., *Reinhold Niebuhr and the Issues of Our Time* (London & Oxford: Mobray, 1986), 24-45.

[16]Ibid., 25.

[17]Niebuhr, *Human Nature,* 3.

theological starting point apart from a doctrine of humanity.

Niebuhr's intense concern for apologetics contributed to the centrality of anthropology in his method. He understood objective revelations of God concerning personhood and historical action to be 'absurd from a strictly ontological standpoint,' leading him to dismiss metaphysical discussions in his theology.[18] His good friend Paul Tillich often criticized him for his reluctance to consider ontology as a valid theological exercise, and especially for failing to recognize the ontological presuppositions that supported his own ethical method. Tillich argued specifically that Niebuhr's discussion of sin can not be addressed apart from ontological categories, suggesting quite correctly that when Niebuhr rejected sin as comprising part of humanity's essential nature, he stepped clearly into ontological territory.[19] Moreover, Niebuhr's refusal to place primary theological focus on ontology does not mean that his method was void of ontology, or that he was unaware of the ontological dimensions of his system.[20] In fact, Ronald Stone points out that Tillich simply could not acknowledge Niebuhr's epistemology because of its 'strangeness' to his thought: 'Niebuhr stood in the empirical tradition of William James, which was anathema to German idealism.'[21] It was a clear attempt to avoid unhelpful ontology that led Niebuhr to embrace the reading of Christian revelation as myth, since it allowed him to 'advocate an apologetic that would make clear the ontologically ambiguous status of the concept of personality and history. In the midst of such ambiguities,' he felt room must be left 'for the nonrational, so that the message of God's relationship to creation as evidenced in the symbols of the Bible can be spoken.'[22] So while ontological considerations are an inevitable part of any theological system based on revelation and expected to have ethical import, Niebuhr was consistently and fairly clear that his purpose was apologetic, his basis and outcome was ethical, and his focus was the predicament of humanity in history.[23]

---

[18]Reinhold Niebuhr, 'Intellectual Autobiography,' in Kegley, ed., *Reinhold Niebuhr*, 19.

[19]See Paul Tillich, 'Sin and Grace' in H. R. Landon, ed., *Reinhold Niebuhr: A Prophetic Voice in Our Time* (Greenwich, CT: Seabury, 1962), 27-41.

[20]Cf. Robert Ayers, 'Methodological, Epistemological, and Ontological Motifs in the Thought of Reinhold Niebuhr,' *MT* 7 (January 1991), 159.

[21]Ronald Stone, *Reinhold Niebuhr: Prophet to Politicians* (Nashville, TN: Abingdon, 1972), 148.

[22]Stanley Grenz and Roger Olson, *Twentieth-Century Theology* (Downers Grove, IL: InterVarsity Press, 1992), 101-2.

[23]As Alan Sell has noted, ethical and ontological concerns can hardly be separated in theology, since 'logically Christology takes precedence over soteriology: Christ can only do what he does because he is who he is.' Nevertheless, 'in history and in the believer's experience we come to an understanding of who Christ is via what he has done.' See Alan P. F. Sell, *Philosophical Idealism and Christian Belief* (Cardiff: University of Wales Press, 1995), 194-195.

Anthropological Considerations

For Niebuhr, Christian myth adequately described the existential predicament of humanity, by expressing the truth of humanity's dual nature as created beings, who bear God's image in possessing freedom over nature.[24] Arguing that all logical concepts of derivation begin and end with the doctrine of God's creation *ex nihilo*, which affirms the potential height of the human spirit, Niebuhr is careful to emphasize the positive nature of the freedom of self-transcendence that represents the *imago dei*. For his purposes, the doctrine of 'creation *ex nihilo* keeps the relations between time and eternity fluid enough to allow for historical progress, and yet rigid enough to keep history tensionally responsive to absolute norms of obligation.'[25] The paradox that results within humanity, of being at once free and dependent, leads Niebuhr to make some specific conclusions regarding the limits and possibilities of humans as image-bearers.[26]

Niebuhr refused to equate the image of God with reason, suggesting the *imago dei* entails more than the mind of humanity either as individuals or collectively. He was willing to admit reason as a part of the image, but freedom, or self-transcendence is the key element, which is present in the human spirit. Niebuhr's affection for Augustinian theology becomes apparent here, as 'the most profound theologians, beginning with Augustine, have associated the image of God with a human capacity to transcend reason, world, and the self.'[27] Unlike Luther, who argued that the image of God is all but obliterated in humanity as a result of the fall, Niebuhr believed that positive human potential remained intact, though tainted. This is a helpful distinction, since the reception of revelation and human responsibility for sin would be precluded if humans no longer bore the capacity for existential encounter with the Divine.[28] Niebuhr affirmed the capacity humanity possesses for ethical good, in accordance with God's declaration at creation, and embodied in the

---

[24]This is not to be seen as a strict dualism, but a coherent tension, expressed similarly in Luther's *simul justus et peccator*. Gustaf Aulen highlights this paradox as an important Reformation doctrine. See Gustaf Aulen, 'Criticism, Claim, and Confidence: The Realism of the Christian Conception of Man,' *Int,* 3 (April 1949): 131- 41.

[25]Carnell, *Theology of Reinhold Niebuhr*, 55.

[26]The image of God in humanity is best considered in concert with Niebuhr's appraisal of original justice. Though intimately connected, the concepts of image and original justice are not identical. The image relates the historical to the eternal in God, while original justice relates the historical to the eternal in humanity. For Niebuhr, 'the concept of the image of God was secondary to that of original justice.' Cf. a discussion of the image of God in Wolfhart Pannenberg, *Anthropology in Theological Perspective*, trans. Matthew J. O'Connell (Philadelphia, PA: Westminster, 1985), 55ff.

[27]Beckley, *Passion for Justice*, 265.

[28]See Gabriel Fackre, *The Promise of Reinhold Niebuhr*, 37. Fackre narrows down Niebuhr's description of the image of God to describe it simply as, 'The structure through which God makes his presence felt in the conscience of man...'

freedom of self-transcendence. Herein lies human potential, creativity, and capacity for love and justice. As humans enjoy the capacity to transcend all the necessities of nature and exercise freedom of spirit, they are to find ultimate fulfilment of their freedom by subjecting themselves to God. Niebuhr concluded: 'Under the influence of Augustinian ideas, Christian theology consistently interprets the image of God in terms of the rational faculties of the soul, but includes among these the capacity of rising to the knowledge of God and (when unspoiled by sin) of achieving blessedness and virtue by reason of subjecting its life to the Creator.'[29]

The Nature of Sin

From Niebuhr's perspective, the very ability to transcend nature allows humanity to recognize its ultimate connectedness to it, and therefore to finitude and dependence.[30] Anxiety emerging from such recognition leads not necessarily, but inevitably, to sin - a doctrine Niebuhr found 'most lacking in the modern mindset.'[31] The very capacity for self-transcendence, which the image of God yields in humanity, is misused as humans refuse to acknowledge their creatureliness.

As Daphne Hampson notes in her feminist critique of Niebuhr's concept of sin, he is thoroughly dependent on Kierkegaard for his categories of analysis.[32] She writes: 'Kierkegaard, in *The Concept of Dread* and elsewhere, says that man is a double, both tied-to-nature and spirit, having both necessity and possibility. It is this duality, this *Zweispaltung*, which gives rise to anxiety, to *Angst*. Niebuhr, taking this as given, says that in this situation of anxiety man tries to discard his contingent nature and soar to pretensions of absoluteness.'[33] Borrowing here from the Christian tradition from Augustine to Luther, Niebuhr views sin as 'that self-centredness whereby the creature in his *hubris* pretends to be adequate of himself, and so sets himself up in the place of God, refusing

---

[29]Niebuhr, *Human Nature,* 158. The Creator-creature distinction is consistently maintained by Niebuhr. Individual or collective existence are never submerged or dissolved in the divine personality, though they find their fulfilment in acknowledgement of a dependent relationship.

[30]Niebuhr admits his own dependence on Schleiermacher for at least part of this analysis, but insists that the human experience of God entails more than an experience of 'unqualified dependence.' *Human Nature,* 128.

[31]Grenz and Olson, *Twentieth Century*, 103.

[32]Daphne Hampson, 'Reinhold Niebuhr on Sin: A Critique,' in Harries, ed., *Reinhold Niebuhr and the Issues of our Time*, 46-60. Hampson provides a concise and perceptive description of Niebuhr's concept of sin, and Carnell likewise argued that it was questionable 'whether one can appreciate Niebuhr fully until he understands his historical lineage in Kierkegaard.' Carnell, *Theology*, 71. Niebuhr himself professed Kierkegaard to be 'the greatest of Christian psychologists.' *Human Nature,* 44.

[33]Hampson, 'Reinhold Niebuhr on Sin,' 46.

to be dependent.'[34] Anxiety is not sinful in and of itself, rather, it is the very presence of that anxiety that makes sin inevitable. Anxiety over the recognition of humanity's finitude leads the ego to make itself the centre of existence, and through its pride and will-to-power, it attempts to subordinate other life to its will, or becomes submerged in its vitalities. 'Anxiety, as a permanent concomitant of freedom, is thus both the source of creativity and a temptation to sin...when anxiety is conceived it brings forth both pride and sensuality.'[35] Hampson is correct in her observation that Niebuhr depends on Kierkegaard's analysis of anxiety to derive his understanding of sin. This in itself, however, does not render his observations incorrect. In fact, there is a strong biblical basis for recognizing the nature of sin as pride, as Niebuhr acknowledges.[36] Niebuhr's conclusions here are easily acceptable within the framework of scriptural revelation, but it is important to recognize that the source of his thought is rooted in existentialism rather than revealed truth.

Throughout Niebuhr's analysis, the dialectical tension between the image of God and human sinfulness is consistently maintained. He writes

> The fact is that man is never unconscious of his weakness, of the limited and dependent character of his existence and knowledge. The occasion for his temptation lies in the two facts, his greatness and his weakness, his unlimited and his limited knowledge, taken together. Man is both strong and weak, both free and bound, both blind and far-seeing. He stands at the juncture of nature and spirit; and is involved in both freedom and necessity. His sin is never the mere ignorance of his ignorance. It is always partly an effort to obscure his blindness by overestimating the degree of his sight and to obscure his insecurity by stretching his power beyond its limits.[37]

Ronald Stone attributes Niebuhr's understanding of anxiety and sin to his reading of Heidegger's *Sein und Zeit*. Drawing on Heidegger's analysis in order to explain 'how anxiety is simultaneously the cause of man's achievements and the precondition of his sin, Niebuhr concludes that 'man knows his life is limited, but he does not know where the limits are. No achievement represents perfection, and there is no place for man to rest in his struggle to escape his finitude.' Given human nature, anxiety is inevitable and necessary, but only when the situation is misinterpreted does it produce a rebellion by man against the law of love.[38] In the anxious search to escape human finitude, humanity must either acknowledge its finitude and subject itself to God, or assert itself in sin, rebelling against God. Where trust in God, or faith is not present, sin inevitably results, on both individual and collective levels.

---

[34]Ibid.
[35]Niebuhr, *Human Nature,* 185-186.
[36]Ibid., 180.
[37]Ibid., 181.
[38]Stone, *Prophet to Politicians*, 97.

SIN AS PRIDE

Niebuhr describes sin specifically as pride or self-love, which is expressed through human will-to-power, and sensuality.[39] He deals most extensively with the sin of pride, which is expressed in different forms. Pride of power, intellectual or moral pride, spiritual pride, and collective pride all find their roots in anxiety's soil, while 'lack of trust in God leads to egotistic self-assertiveness in individual and collective life.'[40] In all of its forms, pride is an expression of the individual's desire to assert a will-to-power, which overestimates its ability to overcome the limits of nature and finitude. 'Man falls into pride, when he seeks to raise his contingent existence to unconditioned existence.'[41] In the assertion of their will-to-power, humans seek to make people and nature subservient to their egos in a search for secure existence. This also may be expressed on intellectual, moral, and spiritual levels, as individuals are convinced that they possess final truth. The resulting injustice for those subject to this assertion of power is obvious.

Furthermore, particular programmes and agendas may be asserted at the expense of others, with no recognition that all corporate systems manifest the consequences and extensions of human pride and remain under the judgement of eternal principles.[42] This is an extremely helpful observation that serves as a reminder that no human system of ethical action or thought is capable of embodying truth in its entirety. It also explains a major flaw of the kinds of ethics and theology that fall prey to this very temptation. Potential for growth comes when this will-to-power is weakened, and humans come to 'recognize that for each of us the school of thought where we feel most at home is not the only theology which is enlightening.'[43] Niebuhr's elaboration of sin as pride and

---

[39]Niebuhr's conception of the will-to-power seeks to be biblical and stands in contrast to Friedrich Nietzsche's use of the term. Niebuhr wrote that in Nietzsche's view, '...the creation of too broad and too narrow forms for the expression of the will-to-live or the will-to-power, proves the impossibility of penetrating to the paradox of human spirituality from the perspective of romanticism.' Moreover, Niebuhr critiqued that, 'romanticism, at least in its fully developed Nietzschian form, substitutes brutality for hypocrisy and asserts the particular and unique, whether individual or collective, in nihilistic disregard of any general system of value.' *Human Nature,* 39, 91.

[40]Bob Patterson, *Reinhold Niebuhr,* 88.

[41]Niebuhr, *Human Nature,* 186.

[42]Carnell points out a significant aspect of Niebuhr's thought that required clarification. If no claims to final truth are valid, then Niebuhr's own claim that the *agape* of Jesus Christ is the norm for humanity must be called into question. Carnell states, 'It would seem, therefore, that the sin is not so much that a claim to finality *per se* has been made, but rather that the wrong type of a claim has been advanced. *If this is not valid, then Niebuhr has no more right than his opponent to make a claim to finality; for a principle which undermines everything undermines itself also.*' See Carnell, *Theology,* 79.

[43]This comment was made with respect to the theological ferment of the sixties, but carries a continually valuable caveat that characterises Niebuhr's approach. See Albert

will-to-power provides useful building blocks for developing an understanding human nature that explains why humans behave ethically as they do. It provides an apologetic tool as it draws observations from common human experience, and suggests a way forward for further reflection.

SIN AS SENSUALITY

Unlike the sin of pride, sensuality seeks not so much to assert selfhood as to confirm self-love, as it indulges the individual in the drives and desires of nature. If pride is sin rooted in spirit, sensuality is sin rooted in nature. Finding the anxiety of finitude unbearable, sensuality either seeks to enhance the ego, or to escape it completely. Yet, as sensuality is indulged, the anxiety only grows in increasing torment. Patterson summarized Niebuhr's description of the cycle in this way: 'Sensuality begins with self-love or self-gratification. Futility soon ensues, and sensuality becomes self-escape in forms of indulgence that soon reach a point where they defeat their own ends. When a sensuous process is deified it proves disillusioning, and a plunge into unconsciousness is made.'[44] The allusion to a Pauline description of the struggle between spirit and flesh makes adequate reference to the human refusal to acknowledge the very existence of such tension, in the midst of an indulgent sensuality.

It is unfortunate that Niebuhr did not elaborate the concept of sensuality to the same extent as the sin of pride. His inclusion of materialism, drunkenness, and sexual indulgence or perversions as sins of sensuality leaves many open avenues for understanding his social ethics, especially in the contemporary age where individuals often are more interested in accumulating goods and experiences, turning inward on themselves, to the neglect of society as a whole. Harlan Beckley has noted that this aspect of Niebuhr's analysis stands in relative isolation to the rest of his thought, since he never worked out its implications for justice as he did with the sin of pride. Niebuhr's neglect carries significant implications: 'Had he integrated sin as an escape from freedom into his theory and conception of justice, Niebuhr might have had more to say about the dangers of passivity in the face of injustice.' Beckley's observations carry particular relevance to the present study, as passivity may be perceived as a collective weakness of the western church. It is regrettable that Niebuhr never developed the implications of his thought in this regard. 'Although he criticized Protestant orthodoxy and neo-orthodoxy for "defeatism" in the early thirties and again in the second volume of *The Nature and Destiny of Man*, Niebuhr was far more concerned about injustice resulting from inordinate assertions of power than about injustice as a consequence of refusing to exercise our

---

H. van den Heuvel, 'The Honest to God Debate in Ecumenical Perspective,' *ER* 16 (3, April 1964): 289. E. J. Carnell also warned early that 'Conservatives must be careful not to define saving faith too narrowly.' E. J. Carnell, *The Case for Biblical Christianity*, ed. Ronald H. Nash (Grand Rapids, MI: Eerdmans, 1969), 123.
[44]Patterson, *Reinhold Niebuhr*, 93.

freedom to achieve relative justice.'[45]

COLLECTIVE EGOISM

Although the will-to-power may be modified on an individual basis through faith, justice, and love, the problem is compounded on a collective level. On a collective level, sin is not conditioned by conscience, as individuals submit to an ethic, or rather politic, of a lower common denominator. The insecurity, egotism, and greed, which drive individual sin is significantly compounded on a group level. As groups make 'unconditional claims for their conditioned values,' they mistake their natural particularities such as race or nationhood for values of universal significance.[46] Pride causes them to ignore the injustice that may grow out of their assertions of power, and overlook the sinfulness inherent in their own systems. Niebuhr writes: 'Whenever the group develops organs of will, as in the apparatus of the state, it seems to the individual to have become an independent centre of moral life. He will be inclined to bow to its pretensions and to acquiesce in its claims of authority, even when these do not coincide with his moral scruples or inclinations.'[47]

Paradox once again moves to centre stage in Niebuhr's method. The very fact that individuals need to relate to the community for their own self-identity is corrupted as they seek to extend their own sin through collective structures. As 'individual decisions and achievements grow into, as well as out of, the community and find their final meaning in the community,' so do individual pretensions seek fulfilment in and through the community.[48] But unlike Locke, who believed that the democratic social contract gave rational agency to the majority, Niebuhr could not find much room for optimism when he considered how competing elements of society used power to extend particularistic self-interests.[49]

In Niebuhr's view, groups lack the freedom for self-evaluation that emerges on an individual level through self-transcendence. Being unable to distinguish between healthy self-criticism and self-destructive inner conflict, moral rebels and criminals are treated together as enemies of the group system. For Niebuhr, collective egoism represents the very essence of sin

> Collective pride is thus man's last, and in some respects most pathetic, effort to deny the determinate and contingent character of his existence. The very essence of human sin is in it. It can hardly be surprising that this form of human sin is also most fruitful of human guilt, that is of objective social and historical evil. In its

---

[45]Beckley, *Passion for Justice*, 272-3.
[46]Niebuhr, *Human Nature*, 213.
[47]Ibid., 208.
[48]Niebuhr, *The Children of Light and the Children of Darkness,* 50.
[49]Reinhold Niebuhr, *Man's Nature and His Communities,* (New York: Charles Scribner's Sons, 1965), 44. Cf. John Locke, *Two Treatises of Government,* chap 8, par. 96.

whole range from pride of family to pride of nation, collective egoism and group pride are a more pregnant source of injustice and conflict than purely individual pride.[50]

The problem appears insurmountable, but it is not hopeless. 'Niebuhr contends that neither the individual nor the state can understand its true limitations until it sees itself from beyond itself, *i.e.*, until the voice of God is heard speaking to and against the ego.' The implied Christian perspective, which balances the time-eternity dialectic, is 'gained only within Biblical presuppositions.'[51] Even though love and justice cannot come to bear on a group in the same way they do in the lives of individuals, grace allows a measure of love and justice to be worked out in society, for the ethical betterment of the collective and its individual agents.[52] Niebuhr confessed that he sometimes gave a more pessimistic interpretation of society than he intended, and clarified the role of common grace at work in the social life of humanity.[53]

Despite Niebuhr's clarification regarding the role of common grace at work in society and its organizations, it should be abundantly clear that his understanding of collective humanity differed significantly from that of Rauschenbusch. Where Rauschenbusch highlighted the positive potential of collective allegiances, including nationalism, Niebuhr largely sought to identify the negative tendencies of such common consciousness to exacerbate and multiply humanity's sinful pretensions. Thus, while 'secular and religious idealists hoped to change the social situation by beguiling the egoism of individuals, either by adequate education or by pious benevolence,' Niebuhr insisted that 'collective self-regard of class, race and nation is more stubborn and persistent than the egoism of individuals.'[54] In other words, while Rauschenbusch thought Christian love could relate directly to society, magnified in a collective consciousness that shared particular values, Niebuhr thought that the collective consciousness manifested in group behaviour

---

[50]Niebuhr, *Man's Nature and His Communities*, 213.

[51]Carnell, *Theology*, 85.

[52]See Niebuhr, *Man's Nature and His Communities*, 57ff. Here, Niebuhr explores the political possibilities of creative freedom. 'The importance of establishing this residual creative freedom in collective man lies not in the possibility of subordinating the lower to the higher or wider interest - but in the possibility that even a residual loyalty to values, transcending national existence, may change radically the nation's conception of the breadth and quality of its 'national interest.' This approach has the purpose of balancing Aristotelian naturalism, Lutheran scepticism, Hobbesian cynicism, and Lockean rationalism, and Marxist optimism. In this volume, Niebuhr is keen to ensure that only a faint line be drawn between saving grace (which bears on the lives of individuals) and common grace (which is worked out in collective existence).

[53]Ibid., 95-6.

[54]Ibid., 14-15.

demanded a mediation of Christian love, which balanced all interests in a practical form of justice. Justice was necessary as a practical application of Christian love, because despite their most noble intentions, humans were bound inevitably to sin. It remains to be seen from Niebuhr's method, however, how humans could be responsible for sin, which was described as 'inevitable.'

INEVITABILITY AND RESPONSIBILITY

Following the definition of Kierkegaard that 'anxiety is the dizziness of freedom,' Niebuhr wanted to assert the significance of the observation that 'the same freedom which tempts to anxiety also contains the ideal possibility of knowing God.'[55] He believed that 'if man knew, loved and obeyed God as the author and end of his existence, a proper limit would be set for his desires including the natural impulse of survival.'[56] In reality, however, people do not acknowledge their creaturely dependence. As they assert their pride and desire for power, they confirm the pre-existent condition of original sin.

Though he later regretted his use of the term, Niebuhr's understanding of original sin contributes to the formation of his contention of responsibility despite inevitability.[57] In Niebuhr's thought, the inevitability of sin is due not simply to the strength of temptation, but to a presupposed human condition. This precondition is present in the creation myth, because creation implies the dialectic of freedom and dependency, with its resultant anxiety, which presents the temptation for sin. Without the temptation, sin would not exist, and without prior sin, temptation would not exist. Niebuhr points to the myth of the fall of the devil to argue for the precondition of sin as any assertion of self that grows out of freedom and finitude. Herein lies the paradox that renders sin inevitable, but not necessary. The freedom which lies in the self-transcending image of God leaves humanity with a choice, whereby humans are aware of their participation in sin, and thus do not escape accountability.

Hans Hofmann notes that 'Niebuhr will never deny either the burden of sin or the freedom of man which is the first condition of responsibility.'[58] If humanity could rationalise or educate its way out of sin, the inevitability of

---

[55]Niebuhr cites Kierkegaard's *Begriff der Angst*, upon which he is thoroughly dependent for this analysis. He elaborates: 'The anxiety of freedom leads to sin only if the prior sin of unbelief is assumed. This is the meaning of Kierkegaard's assertion that sin posits itself.' Niebuhr is not content to adopt a purely existential understanding of sin as anxiety, as he includes the most important element of sin as rebellion against the loving will of God. See *Human Nature*, 252-254.

[56]Niebuhr, *Human Nature*, 253.

[57]See the preface of the later edition of *Human Nature*. Niebuhr does not regret the content of his description of original sin, rather the use of the term, which had little relevance for the modern mind. Thus, his intention does not represent a change in position so much as a desire to clarify the apologetic task in which he was engaged.

[58]Hans Hofmann, *The Theology of Reinhold Niebuhr*, trans. Louise Pettibone Smith (New York: Charles Scribner's Sons, 1956), 197.

original sin would be denied, and if humanity was so utterly submerged beneath the marks of sin so as to obliterate the image of God, they could not be considered accountable for sin. According to Niebuhr, accountability for sin is confirmed by the conscience: 'The fact of responsibility is attested by the feeling of remorse or repentance which follows the sinful action.' It is important to notice that conscience does not establish guilt, but rather confirms it. As the self contemplates the sinful act, 'it discovers that some degree of conscious dishonesty accompanied the act, which means that the self was not deterministically and blindly involved in it.' The result of such contemplation will lead to remorse and repentance, which 'are similar in their acknowledgement of freedom and responsibility and their implied assertion of it. They differ in the fact that repentance is the expression of freedom and faith while remorse is the expression of freedom without faith.'[59] Though Niebuhr acknowledges the possible complacency that may emerge in the conscience through deception and habitual patterns of action, he maintains individual accountability for sin, arguing 'that habitual sin can never destroy the uneasy conscience so completely as to remove the individual from the realm of moral responsibility to the realm of unmoral nature.'[60] Again, Hofmann offers a helpful summary of Niebuhr's thought

> Sin belongs to the unfathomable mystery of God, who never lets sinful man fall out of His hand nor from the domain of His seeking love. Else the God who is Almighty would not be also absolute love and would not be the only true and just judge. Man's conscience, which so long as it speaks at all testifies that man in his original state decreed by God is truly a person, and accuses him of perversion, is based upon this understanding of sin and proves its correctness. It is man, loved by God, loved in freedom and endowed with will, man at the meeting place of finiteness and freedom, of nature and spirit - it is only this man who can really sin. Sin is the final, almost unbelievable, denial by man of the basis of his own existence.[61]

Niebuhr's observations are helpful and insightful as they identify sin as rooted in the will of humanity, something which liberalism had gone to great lengths

---

[59]Niebuhr, *Human Nature*, 255. Niebuhr writes further regarding the difference between remorse and repentance: 'The one is the 'Godly sorrow' of which St. Paul speaks, and the other is 'the sorrow of this world which worketh death.' It is, in other words, the despair into which sin transmutes the anxiety which precedes sin.'
[60]Ibid., 256.
[61]Hofmann, *Theology*, 197-198. Recognising Niebuhr's thought as not completely original, Hofmann reads 'between the lines here the experience of a vital and honest man, an experience such as we find in Augustine's *Confessions*. The thinking parallels Luther's statement that by our power much is accomplished, surprisingly much, but not the whole. Just when we desire to do the whole, to complete our great and foolish rejection of our own potentiality as given and ordained by God, we fall helpless and hopeless, in our fall pulling down everything around us.'

to deny. Indeed, his conclusions represented a great step forward for theological anthropology.[62]

ORIGINAL JUSTICE

According to his understanding of the creation myth, Niebuhr does not hold to a temporal state of perfection prior to the fall.[63] He assigns such belief to a literal and false reading of the biblical account. Perfect essence is regarded as the true nature of humanity as God intended at creation, known only through the revelation of Jesus Christ, who displayed the true essence of human nature. For both natural and spiritual elements of human nature, there is a corresponding intended perfection. While natural law corresponds to the natural essence of humanity in its perfected state, love is the corresponding principle of perfection to the spirit. The corresponding elements of perfection are not only desirable for humanity, but they serve as its requirements, and are possible because humanity's essential nature, though corrupted, is not destroyed by sin. Niebuhr is aware of the possibility that such concessions to human self-esteem may contribute to the sin of pride, yet he is anxious to correct the 'errors' of the Protestant doctrine of total depravity, and the Catholic understanding of the *donum supernaturale*. The perfection of humanity's essential nature serves as law to individuals through self-transcendent memory of essence corrupted but not destroyed, a law not completely external to individuals, but 'written on their hearts.' Niebuhr recognizes that these laws are not simple possibilities for humanity, but rather they are to be understood as ultimate possibilities.

Love becomes the most significant moral requirement, because unlike any law or system of justice, it binds human spirit to human spirit, in a way that

---

[62]Carnell's analysis is particularly interesting. He writes: 'One of the most glaring lacunae in Niebuhr's system protrudes here. Niebuhr tells us very clearly why *sinning* (on his definition of sin) is inevitable - it is because men persistently refuse to remain within their appointed limits. But what Niebuhr does not oblige to explain with persuasion is why this *refusing* is inevitable. He rejects the notion that there is a sinfulness in the race that has come down through Adam through natural heredity – 'an Augustinian corruption,' in his words. But may it not actually be that man is far more constitutionally sinful than existentialism is willing to concede? How else can we explain the refusal of man to remain within his limits? When an automobile continually breaks down, one soon suspects that there is a constitutional deficiency in the machine. What, likewise, of man?' Carnell, *Theology*, 92. Carnell is correct in his criticism regarding the desirability of recognising sin as a constitutional deficiency. However, even though Niebuhr does not explicitly describe original sin as an inherent constitutional corruption, the notion is not completely foreign to his thought. Sin may not be seen as total destruction of essential nature, but it is certainly regarded as a corruption. See *Human Nature*, 269, 275-276. In any case, Niebuhr stands apart from his liberal colleagues who argue the virtues and potentialities of humanity, while he consistently reiterates the inevitable sinfulness of humanity.
[63]Cf. Pannenberg, *Anthropology*, 56, n.

transcends natural particularities. 'The law of love is thus a requirement of human freedom; and the freedom of the self and of the other both require it.'[64] Love as the *justitia originalis* of human nature carries particularly demanding moral requirements, and represents the fulcrum of all of Niebuhr's theological and political writing

> In its freedom it constantly rises above...laws and rules and realizes that they are determined by contingent factors and that they fall short of the ultimate possibility of loving the neighbour 'as thyself'. A sense of justice may prompt men to organize legal systems...through which a general sense of obligation toward the needy neighbour is expressed. But no such system can leave the self satisfied when it faces particular needs among those who are the beneficiaries of such minimal schemes of justice. The freedom and uniqueness of the other also raise moral requirements above any scheme of justice.... Love is thus the end term of any system of morals. It is the moral requirement in which all schemes of justice are fulfilled and negated.... It does not carefully arbitrate between the needs of the self and of the other, since it meets the needs of the other without concern for the self.[65]

To what degree the original righteousness of love may be realized in the history of sinful humanity becomes Niebuhr's obvious concern, to which he directs his attention in *Human Destiny*, volume II of *The Nature and Destiny of Man*. This will be addressed below from the perspective of Niebuhr's Christology, as his view of the solution to the basic problem of human existence further enlightens an evaluation of his ethical method.

Thus, Niebuhr described in balance the existential problem of humanity as being rooted in the dialectical tension between humans as bearers of freedom in God's image, and humans as dependent and finite creatures. But Niebuhr's greatest theological strength is his recognition of the human condition of sin, which holds certain anthropocentric tendencies in check. Sin as pride, will-to-power, and sensuality applies itself well to a social ethic that sees misappropriation and use of power as a significant human problem, and the indulgence of self-love as a significant factor in the neglect of social ethics on behalf of certain groups and individuals. Likewise, the notion that groups are deceived by sin to imagine their particularities to be universally valid and true, leads to a call for confession and repentance. Niebuhr's establishment of responsibility for sin despite inevitability offers an important anthropological re-evaluation of relativistic tendencies in ethics, and suggests the notion of spiritual judgement or accountability, related to original justice in humans. Love as the expression of original justice offers a way forward for balancing individual and collective anthropology in social ethics. The full meaning of love in the *agape* of Christ's will is revealed in Niebuhr's Christological

---

[64]Niebuhr, *Human Nature*, 295.
[65]Ibid.

solution to the existential problem of sin.

Christological Impulses

Niebuhr's Christological presentation was not particularly systematic, but it informed important aspects of his method nonetheless. By his own admission, Christology eventually became central to his thought and crucial to his anthropology, though he never elaborated it dogmatically.[66] Interpreting the revelation of Christ in history in relation to his time-eternity dialectic, and from the existential perspective of its meaning for humanity, Niebuhr found in Christology a norm for ethical motivation and moral authority. In the tradition of the Reformation, Niebuhr 'moved from the benefits of Christ to his promises, from what Christ does to us to what he is for us.'[67] Hans Hofmann noted that Niebuhr's Christology was intended to be nothing more than an analysis of the truth about *Christus pro nobis* and *Christus in nobis*, and yet Paul Lehmann has shown how a re-reading of Niebuhr's theology from the perspective of his Christology reveals 'a fresh and rewarding discovery of an intrinsic unity.'[68] As Lehmann has made clear, one would not expect an extended treatment of Christology in a treatise on human nature and human destiny, referring to Niebuhr's *magnum opus* and most systematic elaboration of his theology. Nevertheless, in Niebuhr's examination of what Christ has done in and for humanity, as the second Adam and as the Son of God, the anthropological significance becomes clear. 'Plainly, if unobtrusively, Niebuhr's account of Jesus Christ is the presupposition of his anthropology.'[69]

As for his theology in general, Niebuhr's Christology grew out of a rejection of liberal Protestant formulations of optimism and triumphalism, which left the problem of evil either defeated or unresolved. It was his concern to challenge such simplified notions of history, which do justice neither to the power of love nor the seriousness of sin. Niebuhr wrote

---

[66]Niebuhr writes: 'The situation is that I have come gradually to realise that it is possible to look at the human situation without illusion and without despair only from the standpoint of the Christ-revelation. It has come to be more and more the ultimate truth.... I have come to know with Pascal that only in 'simplicity of the Gospel' is it possible to measure the full 'dignity' and 'misery' of man. Thus the Christological center of my thought has become more explicit and more important. But...I have never pretended to be a theologian, and so I have elaborated the Christological theme only in the context of inquiries about human nature and human history. See Niebuhr, 'Response,' in Kegley, ed., *Reinhold Niebuhr*, 439

[67]Patterson, *Reinhold Niebuhr*, 105.

[68]See Hofmann, 204f.; Paul Lehmann, 'The Christology of Reinhold Niebuhr,' in Kegley ed., *Reinhold Niebuhr*, 253.

[69]Lehmann, 'Christology,' 254.

If the revelation of history's meaning is given through vicarious suffering of a guiltless individual or nation this means one of two things. It may mean that vicarious love is a force in history which gradually gains the triumph over evil and therefore ceases to be tragic. This is the optimistic interpretation which liberal Christianity has given the Cross of Christ. According to this interpretation the power of love in history, as symbolized by the Cross, begins tragically but ends triumphantly. It overcomes evil. But the idea of the suffering servant in history may also mean that vicarious love remains defeated and tragic in history; but has its triumph in the knowledge that it is ultimately right and true. Such a tragic conception still leaves the problem of the evil in history unresolved.[70]

For Niebuhr, the concepts of revelation and history are inseparable. History gives humanity its freedom and its accompanying sinful assertions of self-interest, and at the same time bears the redeeming activity of God. Hans Hofmann observes; 'Because history is the bearer of God's redeeming activity moving towards its goal, and also at the same time the bearer of man's self-will and rebellion, intolerable tension exists between the redemptive will of God and the sinful will of man, between grace and sin.'[71] Dialectical tension must remain the motif for interpreting the action of Jesus Christ in history, which implicitly rejects liberal representations of the human situation. Any interpretation that does not take freedom, sin, or history seriously 'must be judged inadequate and false not only on the grounds of biblical Christology but above all from the viewpoint of realistic anthropology and ethics.' If Christ is nothing more than the 'ideal man' whose perfect example may be emulated, then 'in the background there lies an idealistic and optimistic conception of man, who is in the last resort self-sufficient and who is capable (in the essence of his humanity reached in Christ) of being himself the ultimate ideal and norm.'[72]

Jesus Christ reveals to humanity the law of love, which transcends history, even as it enters history. It is a super-historical norm in the sense that it reveals the infinite possibilities of human life, which yet remain unattainable by humanity in history as it consistently falls short of the revealed ideal. In this Christological explanation, Niebuhr shows that 'there is in the human situation both more and less than was imagined by the all too simple anthropology which is at the background of liberal Christology.... By its lineality the humanizing conception of Jesus disturbs this dialectic of human existence.'[73] Niebuhr's dialectical method is maintained in his ethical interpretation of the Cross of Christ. Here, the connection between revelation and history is plainly illustrated, while the human dialectic is held in proper perspective.

---

[70]Niebuhr, *Human Destiny,* 45.
[71]Hofmann, *Theology,* 204.
[72]J. M. Lochman, 'Realism in Niebuhr's Christology,' *The Scottish Journal of Theology* 11 (1958): 256.
[73]Ibid.

But what of the significance of the Cross of Christ? Did Niebuhr place any value for human life on the atonement, or was it considered irrelevant for ethics? The meaning of the Cross could only really be understood in the context of God's relationship to humanity. In this sense, an ethical interpretation is maintained, even for soteriology. Hans Hofmann summarizes Niebuhr's thought on this point: 'Only to man in true relatedness to Himself does God in Christ reveal Himself as He is, as the God who in His redeeming love claims man for Himself in order that man may carry that love with its restoring power into society and so be directed toward the goal at the end of the days....Only in that relatedness can man comprehend the true meaning of his own existence and all of history.'[74]

Even as Niebuhr sought to rebut the claims of liberal Christology, he was equally intent to correct the 'mistakes' of the orthodox understanding of Jesus Christ. Although he moved in an increasingly orthodox direction throughout the development of his Christology, Niebuhr refuted orthodoxy's expression of Christology in metaphysical categories. 'According to Niebuhr, the orthodox dogma holds in contrast to the Liberal conception a basic truth when it asserts that Jesus Christ is the fullness but also the transcendent norm of humanity,' wrote J. M. Lochman in the *Scottish Journal of Theology*. 'But even this dogma misrepresents the final truth when it tries to express the symbolic and dialectical truth about the revelation of God in the terms of Greek metaphysics.'[75] For Niebuhr's existential thinking, such a theological model reduced faith and overemphasized human capacity to know the unknowable. Niebuhr believed that whenever attempts are made to express Christological truth in metaphysical terms, 'this means, in effect, that an ultimate truth, transcending all human wisdom and apprehended by faith, is transmuted into a truth of human wisdom and incorporated into a metaphysical system.'[76] Niebuhr's goal became the successful interpretation of the 'metaphysical dogma' about the two natures of Christ in 'more personal ethical concepts.' It was, for example, important for Niebuhr that Jesus was sinless, especially as he who was more than human revealed the 'impossible possibility,' thus depicting the 'basic dialectic character of our situation. It is anthropologically relevant and for that reason more comprehensible to the modern man than metaphysical concepts'- a statement which points again to Niebuhr's apologetic and ethical concerns over his desire to offer dogmatic constructions.[77]

As a presupposition of his anthropology, Niebuhr's Christology is built upon the same existential methodology. His rejection of metaphysics in favour of ethics is apparent throughout his Christological elaboration, and he specifically states his preference in this respect

---

[74]Hofmann, *Theology*, 205.
[75]Lochman, 'Realism,' 258-259.
[76]Niebuhr, *Human Destiny*, 62.
[77]See Lochman, 'Realism,' 261.

Theologies continue to elaborate systems which either claim the authority of the Cross for the relative norms of history or which raise the perfection of the Cross and the sinlessness of Christ to a position of irrelevance. But meanwhile Christian faith has always understood, beyond all canons of common sense and all metaphysical speculations, that the perfection of the Cross represents the fulfilment- and the end -of historic ethics.[78]

This abandonment of metaphysics in favour of ethics represents both a strength and a weakness in Niebuhr's thought. In one sense, it avoids unhelpful arguments about Christ's nature and sharpens his focus in the ethical direction he intends. But it also overlooks the inherent connection between metaphysics and ethics in Christology and carries the potential to undermine traditional Protestant views of the incarnation and atonement - doctrines that have significant ethical import. Moreover, it neglects important aspects of pneumatology and ecclesiology, both of which are crucial to Christian ethics.

Despite Niebuhr's reaction to orthodox Christology, Paul Lehmann argues plausibly that Niebuhr gradually moved from 'a less and less implicitly to a more and more explicitly evangelical Christology.'[79] From the very earliest writings, Lehmann suggests, Niebuhr 'concentrated upon the gulf between Christianity and contemporary culture and upon the anthropological consequences of that gulf.' For Niebuhr, 'neither orthodox nor liberal interpretations of the Christian faith have given relevant expression to the insights of Christian faith, so that its truth and power have been obscured.'[80] In his twentieth-century version of 'the benefits of Christ,' Niebuhr relied on a Liberal Protestant framework to underscore the contemporary relevance of Christianity in general and Christology in particular. But true to his Reformed heritage, he eventually shifted from a concern for the relevance of Christ to an interest in the truth of Christ, 'and in so doing made contemporary sense of the Christological insights of orthodoxy.' Although Niebuhr started with 'the benefits of Christ,' this beginning gave 'contemporary meaning and effectiveness to the *Christus in nobis*.'[81] Niebuhr's Reformed roots played a role in keeping him theologically grounded

> Unlike the Christology of medieval and Protestant scholasticism, the Reformers broke fresh ground for understanding and interpreting the person and work of Jesus Christ by stressing the link between Christology and anthropology. Niebuhr's Christology stands in this tradition and shares its movement from the

---

[78]Niebuhr, *Human Destiny*, 75.
[79]See Lehmann, 'Christology,' 263. 'Evangelical' in this sense refers to the universal nature and relevance of the Christ event.
[80]Ibid., 263-4.
[81]Ibid., 264.

benefits to the promise, from the *Christus in nobis* to the *Christus pro nobis*, from what Christ is and does in and to us to what He does and is for us.[82]

The connection between anthropology and Christology is maintained through Niebuhr's conceptual shift, though its point of reference has changed. As Lehmann sums up, 'The turning point in the theology of Reinhold Niebuhr is the point at which the concern for the relevance of Christianity is stated less and less with reference to the human situation to which the Christian faith is relevant and more and more with reference to the truth of the Christian faith by which the human situation is illumined and resolved.'[83] Niebuhr's shift leads him to attempt to interpret humanity in light of Christology, and once *Christus in nobis* is rediscovered, he is able to move once more to the relevance of *Christus pro nobis*.

Niebuhr's discussion of *Christus pro nobis* centres on the revelation of new creation. Jesus Christ as the second Adam presupposes a first Adam. What is to be known about the perfection of humanity in a first Adam can be known only as Christ has revealed it, since perfection of humanity is never realised in history. Niebuhr re-interprets the orthodox understanding of Christ as human and divine in terms of the 'paradoxical relation of a divine *agape*, which stoops to conquer, and the human *agape*, which rises above history in a sacrificial act.'[84] This explanation of the doctrine preserves the dialectic of the possibilities and limitations of history. As the possibilities and limitations of history are revealed and affirmed in their significance for humanity, themes of grace and atonement become particularly relevant to Niebuhr's method.

Niebuhr understood grace as having a two-fold nature. It is both truth and power - truth as it confronts humanity with the 'impossible' ideal in Christ; power as that which makes the truth 'possible' in history. Christ as the second Adam revealed the perfection of human nature that is part of human essence, but perfection is impossible to achieve or demonstrate within history, which involves freedom and finitude. Christ as the Son of God revealed the divine love of God whose grace offers forgiveness for sin and empowerment to strive for proximate justice even in the midst of sinful conditions, out of gratitude for God's great love. Spiritual regeneration is the resulting process from acknowledgment of Christ as second Adam and Son of God. Niebuhr centred on three aspects of Galatians 2:20: 'I am crucified with Christ: nevertheless I live; yet not I, but Christ liveth in me....'. In this verse he saw an explanation of the process of regeneration, wherein the converted self confesses new life as the result of divinely infused power. 'Niebuhr maintained that the new life, a product of the grace of God, is a reality; but the new life is never a fully accomplished reality. It is fully accomplished in intention rather than

---

[82]Ibid., 265.
[83]Ibid.
[84]Niebuhr, *Human Destiny*, 71.

achievement. Grace does not completely remove the contradiction between God and man.'[85]

Wanting both to support and deny aspects of the sovereignty of divine grace, Niebuhr preserved human responsibility by 'interpreting God's electing grace and man's free will as an existential relation. He said that the relation cannot be subjected to a precise logical analysis. Free will as a force working independently of grace is true on one level of experience (the sinful self), while God's grace as the exclusive source of human redemption is true on another level (faith).'[86] In this way, existential conversion 'is theoretically as repetitious in the individual as the experience of the 'fall' itself...the dialectic is broken if the conversion experience is not kept as much a marching of truth within history as the experience of falling.'[87] As Niebuhr wrote, 'The shattering of the self is a perennial process and occurs in every spiritual experience in which the self is confronted with the claims of God, and becomes conscious of its sinful, self-centred state.'[88] Here, Niebuhr departed from orthodox understandings of conversion, which 'the classic Reformers taught with singleness of mind...was a unique experience in man and was not repeated.'[89] Although such a view carries immense ethical significance, and may be helpful to a constructive understanding of moral development, it appears to rest on a rather limited view of the atonement.

Yet, Niebuhr is quick to dismiss liberal understandings of the atonement, which misinterpret the meaning of the incarnation, and the need of humanity.[90] In Niebuhr's thinking, 'there can be no simple abrogation of the wrath of God by the mercy of God.' The atonement is a complex notion whereby 'the wrath of God is the world in its essential structure reacting against the sinful corruptions of that structure; it is the law of life as love, which the egotism of man defies, a defiance which leads to the destruction of life. The mercy of God represents the ultimate freedom of God above his own law; but not the freedom to abrogate the law.' This mystery is grasped only as God's justice and forgiveness are recognized together as one. Knowledge of the divine mercy through God's justice and forgiveness brings humanity to despair, without which 'there is no possibility of the contrition which appropriates the divine forgiveness.' Moreover

---

[85]Patterson, *Reinhold Niebuhr*, 114.

[86]Ibid., 115.

[87]Carnell, *Theology*, 189.

[88]Niebuhr, *Human Destiny,* n.5, 109.

[89]Carnell, *Theology*, 190.

[90]Niebuhr accuses Hastings Rashdall of being 'a typical Anglican rationalist,' by undermining the importance and the significance of the atonement. *Human Destiny,* 59. Cf. Hastings Rashdall, *The Idea of Atonement in Christian Theology* (London: 1919). This volume upholds an 'exemplar' theory of atonement, rejecting substitutionary theories as incompatible with modern conceptions of justice.

it is in this contrition and in this appropriation of divine mercy and forgiveness that the human situation is fully understood and overcome. In this experience man understands himself in his finiteness, realizes the guilt of his efforts to escape his insufficiency and dependence and lays hold upon a power beyond himself which both completes his incompleteness and purges him of his false and vain efforts at self-completion.[91]

For Niebuhr, this appropriation of righteousness, through human realization of guilt and reception of forgiveness through grace, represents the significance of the atonement. This conception stands in critical contrast to other explanations.

Niebuhr especially criticizes historical orthodox positions, which he accuses of falling prey to Greek metaphysics, to the peril of faith and existential understanding. It is Niebuhr's misunderstanding of the nature of sin that leads to this somewhat truncated version of the atonement. If sin is not something that humans do *against* God, then there is no need of a Christ who reconciles them metaphysically *and* existentially *to* God. In Carnell's view, Niebuhr's Christology reveals that he does not really take sin seriously at all, since God's judgment is represented only in the tensions of human existence

Man is only in an existential predicament. He does not stand under the wrath of a severe God into whose hands it is a fearful thing to fall. The transition from sinfulness to eternal salvation is rather painless. Sin will easily be forgiven, for God will take all of our sins into and upon Himself. Niebuhr speaks very often of judgement, but his descriptions are always informed with a half-hearted liberalism. God is pictured in a way man *hopes* that He is, and not according to the way Jesus Christ warned in advance that He actually *is*.[92]

While the truth probably lay somewhere between Niebuhr's view and that of his conservative critic, the result is that Niebuhr does not faithfully balance the dialectic of God's justice and mercy. For in the end, God's justice is swallowed up in his mercy, and the need of humanity for a radical, metaphysical solution to sin is watered down to a simple recognition of human finitude. At this point, Lochman correctly insists that we encounter Niebuhr 'at the frontier of religious idealism dressed up as "realism" and in the Christological sphere we are near a certain form of docetism.'[93]

To be fair, it needs to be pointed out that Niebuhr's Christology matured with the rest of his thought, and the progression of time saw a moderation of his idealist tendencies. Niebuhr himself wrote in 1939 that his early Christological thought contained all of the 'theological windmills' against which he was then

---

[91]Niebuhr, *Human Destiny,* 56-57.
[92]Carnell, *Theology*, 201.
[93]Lochman, 'Realism,' 258.

fighting so vigorously.[94] At the same time, it must be argued that he never fully recovered from those early liberal influences on his thinking, as Lochman has demonstrated convincingly. Lochman points out significant weaknesses of Niebuhr's Christology, which remain central to his analysis throughout its development. While Niebuhr's dialectic 'has some justice done to it by traditional Christology,' there are 'traces of a methodological approach which make it questionable from a theological point of view.' The major weakness of Niebuhr's methodology is that its symbolism leads to a Christological formulation where 'we find in Jesus Christ an illustration, a reflection of the general problems of anthropology and ethics rather than a unique and concrete event in which the real God in the real man intervenes in our history' - another result of a complete neglect of metaphysics.[95]

Niebuhr's view contrasts sharply with those of some neo-orthodox contemporaries. He rejected outright Barth's denial of the *Anknupfungspunkt*, which Niebuhr believed 'exists in man by virtue of the residual element of *justitia originalis* in his being.'[96] Moreover he wrote: 'The relation between the truth, apprehended in God's self-disclosure, and the truth about life which men deduce through a rational organization of their experience, might best be clarified through the analogy of our knowledge of other persons.' Niebuhr's affection for analogous reasoning became very apparent in his Christology. Yet, even so, Niebuhr maintained that the other self cannot be understood in the depths of personality unless he speaks. 'Only the "word" of the other self, coming out of the depth or height of his self-transcendence can finally disclose the other "I" as subject and not merely object of our knowledge. Only this communication can give the final clue to the peculiar behaviour of the other.'[97] The revelation in Christ is acknowledged, but its relevance reduced to what it reveals of humanity, rather than what it reveals of God. 'For Niebuhr

---

[94]See Reinhold Niebuhr, 'Ten Years That Shook My World,' *CC* 56 (April 26, 1939): 542.

[95]Lochman, 'Realism,' 256-257. While Patterson argues, 'Niebuhr eventually came to the place in his Christology where he emphasized equally well the truth of the Christian faith and the relevance of this truth to the human situation,' (Patterson, *Reinhold Niebuhr*, 105), it seems questionable whether such a dialectical balance was ever explicitly reached. This is at least partly due to Niebuhr's failure to elaborate his doctrinal understanding in a more systematic fashion. To be fair, his intention was always to provide a foundation and motivation for human behaviour rather than offer elaborate doctrinal explanations. But Niebuhr's symbolic interpretation of the Cross-Resurrection event does little justice to his understanding of history and its significance as a solution for the human situation.

[96]Niebuhr regarded Brunner as being closer to the truth on this issue, as he engaged in vigorous debate with Barth. Niebuhr conceded that Barth was successful in pointing out inconsistencies in Brunner's work, but argued that alone did not prove him wrong. See *Human Destiny*, 64.

[97]Niebuhr, *Human Destiny*, 65.

Christology is relevant so far as it explains this [dialectical] view of world and of man. In so far as it contradicts this it is rejected.'[98] Thus, Niebuhr consistently based his Christological analysis on existential observation, adjusting the orthodox understanding as deemed necessary, rather than allowing the historical witness to serve as a potential corrective to his own theology. In this sense, though his theology logically preceded his philosophy, ethics played the primary and determining role in his method. As for many Christologies of Niebuhr's time, it may be said that 'the price paid for a more plastic and to the modern man more comprehensible formulation of the fundamental meaning of history is too high.'[99] Especially significant for ethics is Niebuhr's binitarian approach to theology, which neglects the ongoing role of the Holy Spirit in the world, particularly in relation to efforts of justice. This concern, among others, will be addressed more fully in relation to Niebuhr's understanding of the kingdom of God.

Kingdom of God

Before a practical application of Niebuhr's theology can be understood, his view of the kingdom of God requires brief clarification and reflection. This aspect of his thought is not abundantly clear, as he offers no distinct definition of what constitutes the kingdom. It may be derived from his discussion of the kingdom and justice that he embraces an Augustinian understanding of the eschatological kingdom, toward which all of humanity moves, under the grace of God. Niebuhr is not so naïve as to think that the kingdom is ever achieved by a sinful humanity, but he sees the employment of law and politics as tools that move humanity toward the kingdom in increments of history.[100] It is difficult at this juncture to balance Niebuhr's usual scepticism with such apparent optimism. He is eager to point out, however, that it is not a view of human progress towards some utopian future that he has in mind. Rather, his doctrines of the image of God, original justice, and the grace of God in Christ allow the possibility of improvement and progress, for temporal human existence. In this underdeveloped aspect of his thought, the lines between individual and collective agencies, and particular and general communities become blurred. Although Niebuhr does not equate the kingdom with the world, neither does he clearly distinguish it from the world.

Part of Niebuhr's failure to clarify the distinction between the kingdom and the world may be rooted in his neglect of pneumatology and ecclesiology, and how they bear on the human situation as he describes it. He mentions his belief that it is the Holy Spirit who brings about repentance and faith, but he does not elaborate the role of the Spirit working through the kingdom to bring about

---

[98]Lochman, 'Realism,' 262.
[99]Ibid., 263.
[100]Niebuhr, *Human Destiny*, 244-286.

transformations of humanity, or human society.[101] Nor does he specify how the Holy Spirit works through the church to confront the world with the realities of the kingdom of God. Contrary to Niebuhr's belief, it is not in an unregenerate humanity but in the church where God meets the world in Christ, through the power of his Holy Spirit.

These weaknesses bear particular relevance when Niebuhr's application is taken into consideration. He would be the first to acknowledge that his concepts of balance-of-power and democratic capitalism have been accorded too much credence, given the realities of human nature. Even as he stood on the edge of a 'potential international community,' he suggested that it would

> be constructed neither by the pessimists, who believe it impossible to go beyond the balance of power principle in the relation of nation to each other; nor by the cynics, who would organize the world by the imposition of imperial authority without regard to the injustices which flow inevitably from arbitrary and irresponsible power; nor yet by the idealists, who are under the old illusion that a new level of historic development will emancipate history of these vexing problems.[102]

Rather, he argued that the new world must be built by those who are resolute, who 'when hope is dead will hope by faith; who will neither seek premature escape from the guilt of history, nor yet call the evil, which taints all their achievements, good. There is no escape from the paradoxical relation of history to the Kingdom of God.'[103] Many of those who have applied Niebuhr's ideas doggedly and unswervingly to theology, politics, ethics, and history, have failed to follow his own caveat. Niebuhr's warning, and his challenge, reminds those who seek to apply his anthropology to social ethics to examine their own systems and applications, constantly and consistently. This is particularly relevant, as some Christian social ethicists have come to understand that

> our social systems are not eternal or absolute but reflect the ambiguous nature of humankind and the angelic guardians of culture. Our institutions are not just a constraint on sin...they themselves are full of sin. The structures of social life contain both good and bad. Because of the hold of self-interest we will tend to see only the good in those social forms which favor our interests unless we have a

---

[101]Cf. ibid., 112. Niebuhr's doctrinal weakness with respect to pneumatology is particularly glaring here, as he attempts to explain the role of the Holy Spirit in human transformation. Later, in his discussion of the kingdom, pneumatology is either completely absent, or confused with his doctrine of grace.

[102]Ibid., 285.

[103]Ibid., 285-6.

strong theology of sin. Our social life is fallen with us, and no social system is beyond the need of reform or perhaps even of reconstitution.[104]

Freedom to re-evaluate and reconstitute social systems is possible when humanity sees its social organizations in light of the kingdom of God. The kingdom which is an eternal reality directed by the Spirit of God allows humanity to see its own structures as finite, meaning reform and renewal are possible. Such a view of the kingdom of God strengthens Niebuhr's argument that human endeavours are always tainted by sin, and humanity must be careful to recognize the tentative nature of all its efforts.

Niebuhr's understanding of the eschatological sanction for ethics, as service in the kingdom of God, is best summed up in the following statement by Carnell: 'What man does in history makes a difference in eternity.'[105] This is the single most important conclusion of Niebuhr's thought which must be appropriated into any theoretical-ethical construction. Christ stands as the revelation of eternity to a humanity in turmoil of sin because of its refusal to accept its finite nature. The revelation of the essential ethical nature of humanity makes striving for the ethical ideal possible, even as judgement stands over human existence and at the end of history. There is a need for humanity to be convinced of its finiteness, that it might accept this revelation, and understand the necessity of ethical social action in history. For those Christians who have accepted the revelation and judgement of Christ, there is a need to demonstrate continually the ethical sanction embodied in that revelation, and the responsibility for justice embodied in judgement. Niebuhr's 'mythical' interpretation of eschatological symbols notwithstanding, the very meaning of history in the interim between *telos* and *finis* as found in the notion of service and self-sacrifice for the kingdom of God validates his eschatological ethical sanction.

Thus, Niebuhr had aspects in common with Rauschenbusch, but significant areas of difference. One finds it difficult not to think that had Rauschenbusch been alive to encounter Niebuhr's ideas after the war, he would have been more friend than foe to the latter ethicist. What Niebuhr managed to achieve to a far greater degree than the idealists, and even than many realists, was a balanced view of individual and collective moral agency, with the freedom of ethical transcendence belonging primarily to the individual. He achieved this balance in the midst of a generally consistent philosophy and challenging theology, though sometimes giving methodological pride of place to ethical, rather than theological concepts, interpreting the latter in light of his experience of the former. Because of the consistency and general integrity of his thought, his influence in political and social ethics would stretch around the world, leaving

---

[104]Stephen Charles Mott, *Biblical Ethics and Social Change* (New York and Oxford: Oxford University Press, 1982), 14.

[105]Carnell, *Theology*, 181.

an enduring if compromised legacy in the ecumenical bodies where his approach and similar methods were discussed, practiced, refined, and redefined.

CHAPTER 6

Something in Common? Applying Moral Idealism and Realism in an Ecumenical Setting

Is it strange that I love God?
And when I come back through the gate,
Do you wonder that I carry memories with me?
And my eyes are hot with unshed tears for what I see.
And I feel like a stranger and a homeless man
Where the poor are wasted for gain,
Where rivers run red,
And where God's sunlight is darkened by lies?

Walter Rauschenbusch,
The Little Gate to God

God, give us grace to accept with serenity the things that cannot be changed, courage to change the things that should be changed, and the wisdom to distinguish the one from the other.

Reinhold Niebuhr

Introduction

Thus far we have explored how two individual thinkers, though representative of broader schools of thought, pieced together their theological and philosophical approaches to social ethics in clearly divergent forms. What remains to be discovered in this chapter is how these elements expressed themselves in terms of practical ethical methods, both of which had wide appeal amongst Christians from across the ecumenical spectrum, and in broader society. In turn, they represent the two most significant approaches to social ethics in ecumenical circles in the pre- and post- war periods of the twentieth century. The social gospel dominated the ecumenical social agenda in many western circles until well after the time of the First World War. Its optimism, however, met with increasing opposition, and the theological divide was highlighted as ecumenical co-operation developed globally. The formation of the World Council of Churches after the Second World War saw Niebuhrian-style realism dominate the social ethics agenda, making its most significant contribution in the form of the 'Responsible Society' principle, which emphasized the obligation of humans to one another to promote justice, pursue peace, and recognize that every structure is imperfect and subject to the judgement of prophetic voice. A realist approach to social ethics remained prevalent in the WCC from its inception until the mid sixties. By this time, the Cold War was an abiding reality, and the voices of Christians from various sectors in the third world were being raised and heard. These voices often found cohesion in ideology, and became loud proponents of Marxist revolution and socialist liberation, forcing realist methods to be overlooked in favour of more dramatic - if finally less effective - approaches to social change.

Rauschenbush's Social Ethics

The influence of Rauschenbusch's ideas on the development of a major approach to social ethics in national and international ecumenical circles should not be underestimated. He was consulted by individual leaders of politics and commerce, and was sought after as a contributing member to numerous organizations and institutions.[1] Despite the eventual demise of his own Brotherhood of the Kingdom, its interests were picked up and carried on in various bodies that sought to apply the social concerns of Christianity to society at large.[2] The presence of a biographical file on Rauschenbusch at the World Council of Churches library, though brief, testifies to his enduring legacy to the thought and practice of ecumenical social ethics on an international scale.[3]

One of his greatest legacies became embodied in the social creed of the Federal Council of Churches in America, a document adopted as the centrepiece of social concern amongst the Protestant churches, and about which churches found wide agreement. Selecting his causes carefully, and refraining from active participation in meetings as a result of his deafness, Rauschenbusch nevertheless agreed to correspond with other social pioneers from the Council, who developed the document, 'The Social Creed of the Churches.'[4] Though most scholars agree that his contribution to the formation of the Council was significant, Rauschenbusch's personal secretary went so far as to assert that, 'In the light of the actual happenings perhaps it would be just to say that the Federal Council of Churches of Christ in America *is* the lengthened shadow of

---

[1] Dores Sharpe, *Walter Rauschenbusch* (New York, Macmillan, 1942), 403-419.
[2] Paul Minus, *Walter Rauschenbusch: American Reformer* (New York: Macmillan, 1988), 173-176.
[3] WCC Biofile 280.99.99.OPQR.
[4] Minus, *Walter Rauschenbusch*, 173. Minus agrees with Sharpe regarding the long shadow of Rauschenbusch in ecumenical social ethics, indicating that 'In subsequent years, Rauschenbusch continued to give his counsel generously to this ecumenical body built upon theological and social convictions close to his heart.'

Walter Rauschenbusch.'[5] If such a statement is true at all, it must bear particular relevance to the role that Rauschenbusch played in the development of the social creed, which endured for years as the heart of Christian social thinking in North America, and whose legacy is felt to this day.

The creed stated clearly the stand that churches ought to take on issues of freedom, poverty, and justice. It suggested the adoption of ethical principles, drawn from the current understanding of love's direct relevance to contemporary social problems. It stated, 'We deem it the duty of all Christian people to concern themselves directly with certain practical industrial problems.' To this end, the churches 'must stand' for particular rights and laws for the betterment of all in society. The statement ends with a word to those whose needs they sought to address: 'To the toilers of America and to those who by organized effort are seeking to lift the crushing burdens of the poor, and to reduce the hardships and uphold the dignity of labor, this Council sends the greetings of human brotherhood and the pledge of sympathy and of help in a cause which belongs to all who follow Christ.'[6]

The stamp of Rauschenbusch - especially of his theological and philosophical thought - is apparent. Yet, a fair criticism may be directed toward this creed, and some of its underlying assumptions. It assumes, as Rauschenbusch's approach has revealed, a singular collective moral will, or at least the possibility of the establishment of such a moral will, based on the gradual, evolutionary determinism of the kingdom of God. That Rauschenbusch believed all Christians could and would reach similar conclusions regarding the practical application of broader social principles was evident. He acknowledged early in his career, however, that a concrete approach should be spelled out for those to whom the solutions did not seem so readily apparent. Thus through propagation and education, the ideals of the kingdom would be realized in all of society. Referring to a paper that he had delivered at an earlier date, he told one audience that in the previous discussion

> several of you criticized the lack of a programme, the absence of suggestions how our social conditions could be made better. It was not within the scope of that paper to develop a plan of action, and yet the complaint was just. Discussions of social questions usually drag us out of the City of the Present with its crooked but definite streets and alleys, and leave us facing the fields of the Future, where only a net-work of calf-paths invites our hesitating feet. It is so much easier to criticize the present than to construct the future. The one requires merely an open ear and

---

[5] Sharpe, *Walter Rauschenbusch*, 406.
[6] Ibid., 405.

eye for the evils thick about us, and sympathy enough to hate wrong. The other
requires that very rare faculty, a constructive imagination.[7]

Rauschenbusch was, therefore, not as naïve as some may accuse him
regarding the difficult necessity of building an inclusive and constructive
method that would lend practical effect to the high ideals of broad Christian
principles. 'If some one, like myself, is young and good-natured enough to
respond to the demand and attempts to construct a positive programme,'
Rauschenbusch wrote, 'he sails between Scylla and Charybdis. If he goes into
tangible details that appeal to the imagination, his critics bid him go back to his
home in Utopia. If he confines himself to large guiding principles, they want to
know if we are to risk the future of our civilization on such glittering
generalities. So the most experienced social thinkers are slow to take their seat
on the Delphic tripod.'[8] It was therefore with utmost humility and caution that
he presented his practical method, but he grew in confidence as his ideas and
the social gospel gained momentum and popularity. His desire for a single land
tax after the manner detailed by Henry George; for industrial and labour
reform; and for a socialist economy to replace the present capitalist system
while preserving individual freedoms and property rights were outlined clearly
and rather boldly in his later work, *Christianizing the Social Order.*

In this, his last book, Rauschenbusch demonstrated how he thought love
could be translated and applied directly to the problems of society. That
brotherhood would triumph over individualism and fraternity over selfishness
he had no doubt, as social salvation stood central to the gradual transformation
of secular society into the kingdom of God. Conviction and commitment on
behalf of Christians would yield unity of interpretation and purpose for the
redemption of collective institutions and structures, while resisting the
revolutionary impulse of non-Christian transformation. He was aware that not
all Christians agreed with his approach, especially millenarians, and he
reserved special criticism for their avoidance of the social question.
Rauschenbusch believed that if they would only surrender their doctrine of
unbelief, despair, and 'pious pessimism', they would recognize their error and
be convinced of his social solutions. As it was, he found them strangely akin to
the revolutionary socialists, 'who discourage gradual improvement and stake
their hopes on a sudden overturning which shall change the "system" and make
all things new.' Rather than cutting 'the nerve of present efforts,' by holding
fast to a mistaken eschatology, doctrinal clarity would lead them to stand
instead with his method.[9] Methods which advocated rapid change by revolution

---

[7]Walter Rauschenbusch, 'How can the Aims of the Social Movement be Realized?'
unpublished paper, American Baptist Historical Archives, Rauschenbusch Family
Papers, Record Group 1003, Box 19, 2.
[8]Ibid.
[9]Ibid., 7.

or *parousia* were to be rejected on similar grounds, as they in turn rejected Rauschenbusch's outline of a gradual, evolutionary social transformation.

It becomes readily apparent that Rauschenbusch had neither the intention, nor the philosophical and theological means to rigorously address, assimilate, or otherwise draw into his method those Christians who chose to distance themselves from his approach to social transformation. Though concerned for the negative effect dissenters could have on the overall progress of change, his strategy for their involvement was to persuade them to abandon falsely-held beliefs and doctrines, and join the social gospel movement. The way for unity to manifest itself in this movement was for all Christians to join in 'what God was doing in the world' through church groups and secular organizations, and whose purpose and direction should be evident to all thinking, caring people. With a theology based on premises of idealist philosophy, Rauschenbusch's method had no means of mediating positions or disputes apart from issuing an invitation to become part of God's purposes in creation through the social realisation of his kingdom. This represents a particular problem inherent in the ethical methodology of idealist philosophy or theology - those who differ are not readily integrated into a system or approach. Similarly, it points to particular methodological challenges to be addressed by those theologies which make exclusive moral claims about how theological truth is to be applied in the practical realm.

By his own admission, Rauschenbusch's ethical wisdom and accompanying method were defined by specific parameters including: the teachings of Jesus Christ accessed through Scripture; the general convictions of the Christian conscience; the common consent of the best social groups of the past; and the bent of the most prophetic movements of the present.[10] In his day, as in many days before and since, there existed 'more honest will to "do something" than clear understanding of what is to be done.'[11] Rauschenbusch drew from his specified resources the wisdom that he felt addressed the present problems most effectively, reinforcing at every turn those observations made previously about his philosophical and theological impulses.

When Rauschenbusch turned his attention toward delineating a programme of social ethics, he managed to balance his parameters with less consistency than he intended. Even by his own admission, his methodological discussion focused more on economic theory than a discussion of Scriptural teachings, giving the impression that his 'high religious ground' had 'sagged down to the level of mere economic discussion.'[12] He insisted this is a false impression, however, since his 'sole concern is for the Kingdom of God and the salvation of men,' where 'a full salvation also includes the economic life.'[13]

---

[10]Rauschenbusch, *Christianizing the Social Order*, 406.
[11]Ibid.
[12]Ibid., 458.
[13]Ibid.

Apart from his own insistence to the contrary, however, it is difficult to see how Rauschenbusch developed his economic theory from the parameter he defined as the teachings of Jesus. At this stage of his argument, he used ethical principles rather than the words of Jesus to establish his programme, perhaps acknowledging by omission the extreme difficulty inherent in deriving specific economic theory from the gospels. It might be fair to say that Rauschenbusch's identification of this parameter was his way of indicating the foundational nature of his ethical task, or at least acknowledging the existence of ethical norms. Making such a deontological assumption is, however, a far methodological distance from deriving specific applications of love to society, with direct reference to Christ's teachings. It would seem that Rauschenbusch avoided addressing this difficulty and instead depended rather heavily on the other parameters of common Christian consciousness, and past and present social theory, leading to a decidedly teleological approach to ethics.

His appeal to the common consciousness is evidenced in his assumption of the universal interpretation of certain social expressions in history, and his reliance upon sermonic persuasion to convince his audience. What he fails to come to terms with is the fact that his interpretation of the collective conscience relies heavily on the subjective nature of his own moral consciousness, which travels the methodological road from the particular to the universal. Thus, his method of persuasion is contextual and anecdotal, relying heavily on case studies, personal examples, and story-telling, which illustrate the points he attempts to make, while trying to substantiate such cases by introducing broader sociological theory.

Rauschenbusch drew heavily from sociologists and economists in developing his programme, acknowledging the broad significance of the growing social impulse being generated within society. He was especially fond of Richard Ely, and in this respect the parameters of past and present social theory were often narrowed to the contemporary context. Nevertheless, there can be no doubt that his system was strengthened by his interaction with theorists and thinkers from outside the theological realm. Such contacts encouraged him to consider at least, the broader implications of his own ideas, and the need for effective ethical method to involve not only theologians, but also experts from a variety of fields of study. His work was regularly strengthened by collaboration with colleagues across denominational lines, and through studies produced by church and secular bodies.

Another particular difficulty that emerges from his discussion is the matter of Rauschenbusch's target for reform. It is clear that Rauschenbusch longed for the transformation of society and believed in the social salvation of the human race. Yet individuals, especially wealthy and powerful ones, were recognized as having particular responsibility and thus possessed a moral agency quite distinct from the agency possessed by a society as a whole. While Rauschenbusch hinted at the relationship between groups and individuals, the outworking of his method did not always make clear exactly to whom his comments were addressed, and how the different aspects of agency were to be held in creative tension. It would seem, therefore, that a social ethic which addresses these differences, and specifies linguistically and practically the role of one regarding the other is preferable to one which assumes the existence of dual agency without defining its inherent tensions and independent vagaries.

A question remains, however, regarding the identity of Rauschenbusch's target audience. Did he write and speak primarily *to* the church or *for* the church? Certainly, in a practical sense, he sought to engage both tasks, and he did not force a sharp distinction between his comments aimed externally at politicians, leaders and society at large, and those aimed internally at church leaders and members. In this sense, his theological and philosophical belief in the universality of God's kingdom led him to stress continuity between the church and the world, and lent credibility to the church as a significant moral voice in larger society. The church had not only the freedom and the right to speak to society, but the duty to address society's ills and identify areas and means for improvement. As a social gospel leader, he saw himself as merely giving voice to that social process which God had initiated and was causing to evolve in the world, with or without the church.[14]

His firm belief in God's activity in the world was what led him, on occasion, to specifically address the church itself. In this regard, his comments usually centred on the admonition to the churches to join the social gospel movement, and not neglect their unique role and duty to form the moral core of society. This conforms to his desire for renewal inside and outside of the church, as he wrote: 'We must change our economic system in order to preserve our conscience and our religious faith; we must renew and strengthen our religion in order to be able to change our economic system. This is a two-handed job; a one-handed man will bungle it.'[15] Discriminatory remarks aside, it is clear that Rauschenbusch saw the particular need from time to time to address the church specifically, as he singled it out for active participation in social reform. But even when Rauschenbusch addressed the church directly, it was never with the intention of isolating the moral life of the church from that of the rest of society. Rather, the entire point of church renewal was the outward influence it exacted through the moral life of those who were members not only of churches, but of political and social communities as well.

Here, the role of the individual conscience vis-à-vis the collective conscience is manifested in Rauschenbusch's method. The religious conversion of individuals became a cornerstone of his approach, as he argued

---

[14]Though the church was seen to have a special role to play in the social movement, Rauschenbusch believed that God's activity would carry on through the social movement, even if the church had to be bypassed. *Christianizing the Social Order*, 458. Similar sentiments are expressed throughout Rauschenbusch's *Christianity and the Social Crisis.*

[15]Rauschenbusch, *Christianizing the Social Order*, 459-60.

God wants to turn humanity right side up, but he needs a fulcrum. Every saved soul is a fixed point on which God can rest his lever. A divine world is ever pressing into this imperfect and sinful world, demanding admission and realization for its higher principles, and every inspired man is a channel through which the spirit of God can enter humanity. Every higher era must be built on a higher moral law and a purer experience of religion. Therefore the most immediate and constant need in christianizing the social order is for more religious individuals.'[16]

Lest doubts begin to rise over Rauschenbusch's commitment to the concept of the collective consciousness, it must be stressed that even this 'fulcrum' power of the individual is derivative of and dependent on the social aspects of human existence. 'This power of the individual rests on the social cohesion of mankind,' he writes. 'Because we are bound together in unity of life, the good or the evil in one man's soul affects the rest.'[17] The salvation of individuals was necessary precisely because of their inexorable connection with the rest of humanity.[18]

Apart from his call to the churches for the religious renewal of individuals, he also called on them to take their rightful place in leading the social movement that was of God's origin. This would happen by laying aside old doctrinal disputes, and finding unity across denominations in the social task of the present

> To become fully Christian the churches must turn their back on dead issues and face their present tasks. There is probably not a single denomination which is not thrusting on its people questions for which no man would care and of which only antiquarians would know if the churches did not keep these questions alive. Our children sometimes pull the clothes of their grandparents out of old chests in the attic and masquerade in long-tailed coats and crinolines. We religious folks who air the issues of the sixteenth century go through the same mummery in solemn earnest, while the enemy is at the gate.[19]

By contrast, the unity of churches would prove a powerful social force, if together they could find ways of laying aside doctrinal differences. 'To become fully Christian and to do their duty by society the churches must get together. The disunion of the Church wastes the funds entrusted to it, wastes the abilities of its servants, and wastes the power of religious enthusiasm or turns it into antisocial directions.'[20] By 'perpetuating trivial discussions in which scarcely any present-day religious values are at stake,' he felt the churches were denying

---

[16]Ibid., 460.

[17]Ibid., 461.

[18]Rauschenbusch affirmed that, 'Our religious individuality must get its interpretation from the supreme fact of social solidarity.' Ibid., 465.

[19]Ibid., 463.

[20]Ibid.

the power of God, and neglecting their duty to society. As a united force, the church subsequently would 'get salvation by finding the purpose of its existence outside of itself, in the Kingdom of God, the perfect life of the race.'[21]

Much of this may remind us of the slogan of the earliest international ecumenical conferences: 'Doctrine divides, service unites.' The philosophical and theological considerations of the social gospel dominated the ecumenical agenda in those early years, and the methods identified in Rauschenbusch's social ethics manifested themselves in ecumenical circles until well after the time of the First World War. Despite the 'blip' on the unity sonograph during the period 1914-1918, those concerned with Christian social ethics nevertheless maintained a positive, idealist, social gospel approach, which prevailed at the first international, ecumenical conference on Life and Work held in Stockholm in 1925. There, the social gospel method took on a global ecumenical significance, whose impulses and resonance are still to be felt in ecumenical circles to the present day.

The Social Gospel at Stockholm

At Stockholm, social gospel leaders from North America and Western Europe sought to avoid divisive doctrinal arguments and focus strictly on the social issues facing the churches. They felt that progress could be made by concentrating on the practical issues, and leaving debates over theology to another body. Therefore, 'Stockholm was dominated by what turned out to be a simplistic idea: Doctrine divides but social cooperation unites. It concentrated on the social responsibility of the churches, assuming that doctrinal discussions could be left to the Faith and Order movement....'.[22] In Stockholm, advocates of the social gospel found allies from various churches and countries. Thus, the programme to which Rauschenbusch had committed his life, found expression in these early ecumenical meetings.

John Bennett has noted the continuity of the movement through the difficult war years, with the result that, 'The social gospel [still] had considerable momentum in the United States and it had great influence in Stockholm. In spite of the tragedy of the First World War and profound moral frustration because of its results, adherents of the social gospel were still very optimistic about realizing aspects of the kingdom of God in history, as a result of human progress.'[23] The Federal Council of Churches of Christ in America was a major sponsor of the Stockholm conference, whose ethos was present in the Letter of Invitation 'declaring that "the world's greatest need is the Christian way of life not merely in personal and social behaviour but in public opinion and its

---

[21]Ibid., 464.
[22]John C. Bennett, 'Breakthrough in Ecumenical Social Ethics,' *ER* 40 (April 1988): 134.
[23]Ibid.

outcome in public action,'' a goal involving the responsibility of "putting our hearts and our hands into a united effort that God's will may be done on earth as it is in heaven".' In true social gospel style, 'it was an ample undertaking expressed in confident language.'[24] Despite the significant American influence, it became evident at Stockholm that 'the Social Gospel Movement was not merely an American phenomenon. The aspirations it expressed were a major preoccupation of Protestant thought throughout the world.'[25]

Thus, 'Stockholm began with the assumption that social concern united while doctrine divides,' but 'at its first session it was confronted by a profound theological difference which made agreement on social responsibility impossible.' Bennett notes that the Stockholm meeting records the comments of an Anglican bishop from England, who 'expressed the hope that the kingdom of God could in large measure be realized in this world.' Subsequently, 'a speaker from Germany stated the conviction that there was no relation between the kingdom of God and human efforts to achieve justice and peace in this world.' Although the German delegate 'represented a small minority at Stockholm…his view was widely held at that time in the Protestant churches and it was the sort of theological difference with which the Faith and Order movement had not been dealing.' This debate over the possibility and degree of human participation in the building of God's kingdom 'was an extreme case of theological differences which were important' for future social debates.[26] It also highlighted a theological-ethical divide between a pietistic Lutheranism, an Episcopal state-Anglicanism, and a more activist Reformed view.[27]

Therefore, limiting the scope of the conference to united practical action and leaving theological differences to the Faith and Order movement appears to have proved inadequate. Too many questions of theology and methodology arose which required debate before decisions on social action could be taken. Edward Duff summarizes the issue by asking questions that remained unsolved at Stockholm

> But on what levels of action should Christian forces function? By providing a
> Christian programme to match the socialist programme, as one delegate

---

[24]See Edward Duff, *The Social Thought of the World Council of Churches* (London, New York, & Toronto: Longmans, Green, & Co., 1956), 28.

[25]Ibid., 25. Duff cites examples from Western Christendom - Germany, France, Switzerland, Sweden, Britain, etc. Even British participants, though believed to be more prophetic leaders with a 'theologically more sophisticated understanding of the church in relation to society…were more optimistic about possible Christian achievements in history than was the trend' in later conferences. Bennett, 134. Bennett is referring in particular to the leadership of William Temple.

[26]Bennett, 135.

[27]The Lutheran tendency towards a 'two realm' ethic lay particularly behind the German opposition to the social gospel. Though it found a limited voice at Stockholm, it represented a significant theological difference to the activism of the social gospel.

suggested? Or by serving as the "soul" for the new instruments of international political and social collaboration, as another delegate urged? A sometime Professor of Ethics called attention to the difficulties of applying Christian principles to concrete problems, given the complicated structures of modern social living and the consequent danger either of meaningless generalizations or of unauthoritative private opinions. Was united practical action possible without unity of faith? The current slogan announcing that "doctrine divides but action unites", was soon seen as no adequate answer to the irrepressible question of the significance, indeed of the need, of theology. The American delegate who remarked: "All you do in theology is useless for our practical task", revealed the widespread, probably dominant, instrumental conception of Christianity as providing inspiration for human betterment.[28]

The issues requiring attention made their appearance at the beginning of the conference, and remained at its close. The Rt. Rev. Theodore Woods, Bishop of Winchester and preacher of the opening service declared: 'We believe in the Kingdom of Heaven. We are conspirators for its establishment. That is why we are here. That is the meaning of this Conference.'[29] He was later rebuffed by a Lutheran Bishop: 'Nothing could be more mistaken or more disastrous than to suppose that we mortal men have to build up God's Kingdom in the world.'[30]

While 'the division of opinion concerned the reason for calling the Conference - to determine the role of religion in social life; it raised the question as to whether there could be a specifically Christian judgement on social problems.' In more than one opinion since, 'the problem was of more than academic interest: "When pressed to their source the differing attitudes towards Christian duty were seen to be rooted in theological differences," the Chairman of the Life and Work Executive Committee was later to note.'[31] Duff points out that

> the Chairman, Archbishop Nathan Söderblom of Stockholm, in a letter summarizing his impressions two months after the Conference, put his finger on the touchstone of divisions: 'Is the Kingdom of God a force immanent in humanity, a programme to be advanced by energetic and enthusiastic human activity? Or is it a judgment and a salvation wrought by God, working in an inscrutable fashion, through the ages to the fulfillment of history, a specifically divine activity before which we must bow in adoration even though it escapes poor human comprehension?'[32]

---

[28]Duff, *Social Thought*, 29-30.

[29]Ibid., 30.

[30]Ibid., 30-31. The speaker is identified as the Rt. Rev. Ludwig Ihmels, Bishop of Saxony.

[31]Ibid., 31.

[32]From *'La Conference Universelle du Christianisme Practique,'* 2, cited in Duff, *Social Thought,* 31, n.2.

Various theological differences and philosophical approaches to social ethics revealed that the task of finding a unified method of tackling difficult social questions would not be easy. W. A. Visser't Hooft reports in his biography, that during and after Stockholm, 'German theologians attacked American *Aktivismus* and American churchmen criticized the otherworldly quietism of the continental theologians'. In the USA it was a current joke that the Germans had adapted the hymn, *Rise up, O men of God* in this way

> Sit down, O men of God
> His Kingdom he will bring
> Whenever it may please His will
> You cannot do a thing.[33]

With such a divergence of opinion, it is not surprising that no concrete decisions were taken at Stockholm.

Despite this divide in perception of how to approach social issues, there was, in those early days at least, a sense amongst the majority that the social gospel had finally awoken the churches to the reality of social problems and needs. There was a strong sense that the individualism that had marked the life of the churches would need to yield to a new social understanding that would turn the attention of the churches outward to political and social life within countries and on a global scale. While 'the conference showed that the Churches had to do much more serious thinking about both the nature of the problems and the Christian approach to them,' it nevertheless solidified for the first time, the ecumenical commitment to address social ethics on an international level.[34]

Paul Abrecht has summarized the basic presuppositions which characterized the social thought of the conference, among which may be recognized a concise expression of the social gospel approach

> The rejection of the prevailing static conception of human nature and society, and the refusal to interpret the Christian doctrine of sin and the fall of man as an argument against working for social betterment.
>
> The insistence that God is at work in the protest movement within society, and that man must co-operate with him in realizing his will to establish his Kingdom.
>
> The rejection of all atomistic and mechanistic conceptions of society such as were dominant in the hey-day of *laissez-faire* capitalism.
>
> The insistence that men are largely shaped by their social environment, and the conviction that social structures can be altered in order to promote better conditions of human life.

---

[33]W. A. Visser't Hooft, *Memoirs* (Geneva: WCC, 1987), 26.
[34]Paul Abrecht, 'The Development of Ecumenical Social Thought and Action,' *The Ecumenical Advance: A History of the Ecumenical Movement,* vol. II, 1948-1968, 3rd ed., ed. Harold E. Fey (Geneva: WCC, 1993), 236.

The emphasis on the role of the State and the community in regulating various aspects of social life and in developing new and more just patterns of society.

The concern for the solidarity of men and for equality of opportunity as a vital element in the Christian understanding of social reform and social change.[35]

Abrecht further notes that

It has been said that the Stockholm Conference of 1925, by endorsing these ideas, gave an ecumenical blessing to the social gospel movements which has already gained momentum in the United States, Great Britain, and many countries of Europe. It would perhaps be more true to say that the Churches incorporated certain insights of these movements into their thinking, while remaining critical of some of the conclusions which the movements themselves drew from these insights.[36]

Despite the wide sympathy and agreement regarding social gospel analysis, Abrecht points to the more cautious notes which were being sounded behind the scenes at Stockholm, and whose resonance was to be felt even more strongly with the advent of the Second World War.

Methodologically speaking, therefore, the conference did not strive, nor was it able, to provide a specific, authoritative, comprehensive, and uniting approach to the social issues of the day. Ans van der Bent noted that the only official utterance of the conference was its official printed message

It contained expressions of penitence for the churches' failure to do their duty and affirmed their obligation to apply the gospel 'in all realms of human life - industrial, social, political and international'. But it described the primary mission of the church as 'to state principles and assert the ideal, while leaving to individual consciences and to communities the duty of applying them with charity, wisdom and courage'; and it looked beyond the churches for 'allies in this holy cause' - youth, those seeking after truth by whatever way and the workers of the world, many of whom 'are acting in accordance with these principles.' Thus Stockholm did not offer 'precise solutions' or put the results of its 'friendly discussions' to a vote.[37]

Leaving ethical application of the ideal to individuals and communities may be a valid approach, but in this case at least, it was more an expression of an inability to move discussion to any meaningful stage rather than an intentional

---

[35]Ibid., 237.

[36]Ibid.

[37]Ans J. van der Bent, *Commitment to God's World* (Geneva: WCC, 1995), 12. Cf. The Message of the Stockholm Conference, *The Stockholm Conference 1925: Official Report*, ed. G. K. A. Bell (London: OUP, 1926), 710-16, cited in *The Ecumenical Movement: An Anthology of Key Texts and Voices*, ed. Michael Kinnamon and Brian E. Cope (Geneva: WCC and Grand Rapids, MI: Eerdmans, 1997), 265-7.

commitment to the individual moral agent.

N. Söderblom's closing sermon at the conference confirmed the view that the assembly was to serve the purpose of inspiring the churches to action. The value of praxis over doctrine was thus emphasized, even at these early ecumenical meetings. Declaring that the churches had to learn to listen and act, rather than just speak to issues, Söderblom exhorted, 'words are not enough. Words are cheap. We must give ourselves.'[38] 'Divisions and silence' have impeded the Saviour's work, while unity and action will rally people and countries 'to a confidence in the inner light and its attending moral courage....'[39] Despite the rallying cry of the conference, it became clear to many that the divisions were not simple ones, to be dealt with by laying them aside, or pretending they did not exist. To the contrary, if any concrete, united moral action were to be taken at all, not only was a deeper theological basis needed, but it would have to include a mechanism for dealing with divergent approaches and opinions.[40]

Niebuhr's Social Ethics

As dissatisfaction with social gospel idealism became more widespread, it found particular resonance with the young pastor and theologian in America who articulated an increasingly popular position within theological and ecumenical circles. Reinhold Niebuhr's Christian realism offered an alternative method for addressing social and political issues, which dealt more practically with the complexities of applying Christian principles to social ethics. His ideas resonated widely, so that by the Oxford conference in 1937, his Christian realism was the dominant position amongst delegates, and by 1948 in Amsterdam, it ruled the social ethics agenda. Social gospel idealism did not completely disappear in this period, but its advocates were forced into a decidedly marginalized position within the field of ecumenical ethics.

Even in his earlier years, Niebuhr was actively advocating a social ethic that took into consideration the very different moral nature of individuals and groups. He wished to emphasize especially the impossibility of making direct applications of love to politics or society. In contrast to Rauschenbusch, who believed that love was not only the ultimate moral category but that it was immediately applicable to all areas of human life, Niebuhr refused to accept the direct appropriation of love in social ethics. He noted that from the time of Rauschenbusch, 'it has been rather generally assumed that it is possible to abstract an adequate social ethic for the reconstruction of society from the social teachings of Jesus...that guidance for the adjustment of every political

---

[38]N. Söderblom, Sermon of the Closing Service, in *The Stockholm Conference 1925: Official Report*, 741-45.

[39]Ibid., cited in Kinnamon and Cope, eds., *Ecumenical Movement*, 17.

[40]Abrecht, 'The Development of Ecumenical Social Thought and Action,' 238.

and economic problem could be found in his words, and that nothing but a little logic would serve to draw out the "social implications" of his teachings.[41] Niebuhr suggested that energy spent explicating such positions was 'vainly spent and has served to create as much confusion as light.' His objections were clear and succinct

> There is indeed a very rigorous ethical ideal in the gospel of Jesus, but there is no social ethic in the ordinary sense of the word in it, precisely because the ethical ideal is too rigorous and perfect to lend itself to application in the economic and political problems of our day. This does not mean that the ethic of Jesus has no light to give to a modern Christian who faces the perplexing economic and political issues of a technological civilization. It means only that confusion will be avoided if a rigorous distinction is made between a perfectionist and absolute ethic and the necessities of a social situation.[42]

Niebuhr clarified his view by explaining how Jesus' ethic was a personal ethic, though not strictly an individualist one. 'His ethic was an ethic of love,' after all, 'and it therefore implied social relationships. But it was an individual ethic in the sense that his chief interest was in the quality of life of an individual.'[43] Though apparently disinterested in social and political issues, Jesus further advocated and demonstrated an ethical ideal of 'complete disinterestedness' or total selflessness. The kind of impartiality demanded by the ethic of Jesus can be neither disavowed nor achieved

> We cannot disavow it because it is a fact that the prudential motive destroys the purity of every ethical action. We have the right to view the social and personal consequences of an action in retrospect, but if we view it in prospect we have something less than the best. So powerful is the drive of self-interest in life, however, that this ideal is as difficult to achieve as it is to disavow. It remains, therefore, as an ideal which convicts every moral achievement of imperfection, but it is always a little beyond the realm of actual human history.[44]

Niebuhr firmly believed that 'No Christian, even the most perfect, is able "always" to consider the common interest before his own,' and such an individual is certainly 'not able to do it without looking at the common interest with eyes colored by his own ambitions.'[45] If such complete selflessness were an historical possibility, then political justice would become an exercise in

---

[41]Reinhold Niebuhr, 'The Ethic of Jesus and the Social Problem,' *RL,* (Spring 1932), in *Love and Justice: Selections from the Shorter Writings of Reinhold Niebuhr*, ed. D. B. Robertson, Louisville, KY: Westminster/John Knox Press, 1957, 30.
[42]Ibid.
[43]Ibid.
[44]Ibid., 32.
[45]Reinhold Niebuhr, 'Justice and Love,' *Christianity and Society* (Fall 1950), in D. B. Robertson ed., 27.

perfect love, and 'many irrelevant sermons and church resolutions would become relevant. Unfortunately there is no such possibility for [individuals]; and perfect disinterestedness for groups and nations is even more impossible.'[46] This thought of Niebuhr's seems to imply an ideal so transcendent as to be barely relevant to human activity in the real world, and a practical ethic that is only relatively applied.[47]

Although perfect love, which the ideal *agape* demonstrated and demands, is impossible to achieve, Niebuhr believed it may be approximated in personal relationships through actions of mutual love. In personal relationships, an individual is able to consider the needs of others in relation to the self, and lay aside selfish interests, at least to the degree in which faith and grace are present. The fact that one's own interests are considered at all makes the moral action less than the perfect selflessness demanded by *agape*, but love is still applied to a helpful, if less than ideal degree.

As demonstrated in the previous chapter, Niebuhr contended that in collective relationships, the interest of the self is not only asserted but also magnified. The ability to achieve Christ-like disinterestedness is even further removed from the realm of possibility. Though the ideal of Jesus may be used as 'a vantage point from which to condemn the present social order...we are in error when we try to draw from the teachings of Jesus any warrant for the social policies which we find necessary to attain to any modicum of justice.'[48] In contrast to the social gospel approach, 'we may be right in believing that we are striving for a justice which approximates the Christian ideal more closely than the present social order, but we are wrong when we talk about achieving a "Christian social order".'[49]

While Rauschenbusch advocated the possibility and potential of collective conversion, leading to social justice and peace, Niebuhr made a crucial observation and subsequent clarification of human group behaviour. He pointed out that not only are human agents less able to dismiss self-interest in a group which inevitably magnifies and extends their egoism, but they are at once members of various groups which may have competing interests. The possibility of a single collective consciousness, exercising a single moral will in a singularly self-sacrificing manner simply does not exist.

Nevertheless, the cross of Christ stands as the norm and law of moral life; it is an impossible possibility that empowers and judges human striving. A

---

[46]Ibid.

[47]Harlan Beckley insists that Niebuhr's early writing reveals an idealism that never tempted Rauschenbusch. Niebuhr conceded that some of his early work was flawed for this reason. See Beckley, *Passion for Justice*, 37 & 199.

[48]Cf. P. T. Forsyth's advocacy of ethical principles over precepts. See Anna Robbins 'Forsyth on Gospel and Society: A Matter of Principle,' *P. T. Forsyth: Theologian for a New Millennium* (London: URC, 2000), 210.

[49]Niebuhr, 'The Ethic of Jesus and the Social Problem,' in D. B. Robertson, ed., 33.

delicate balancing of philosophy, doctrine, and reason is required to avoid falling into the abyss of moral despair, though the practitioner of social ethics would find it necessary to 'skirt the edge of cynicism' in order to maintain a proper perspective in the pursuit of justice. In Niebuhr's method, justice was the manifestation of *agape* in social life, just as mutual love was the manifestation of *agape* in individual ethics.[50]

While guarding against prideful and self-righteous approaches, and despite his protestations to the contrary, some believed Niebuhr's method left little room for creativity in the actual development and application of justice in society. His seemingly negative view meant that in practice, assertions of power could be balanced only by counter assertions of power. There was never a sense of having reached a solution to any given problem, rather there seemed simply to be an ongoing discussion of issues in an attempt to better understand, and sometimes respond to ethical problems. The acceptance of human limitations, and resultant ethical ambiguity left some frustrated with the approach.[51]

Emil Brunner suggested it was precisely for this reason that ecumenical ethics did not make more progress in the period dominated by Niebuhr's realism. Niebuhr's deficiency in explaining what justice actually *is* in real terms supported the criticism levelled against his ethics that they failed to bridge the gap between moral criticism and ethical application. Brunner explained that the failure to more explicitly describe the nature and content of justice was the source of a significant criticism of Niebuhr's method

> Brilliant as Reinhold Niebuhr is in his analysis of existing social conditions or of historical movements and cultural trends, this critical analysis seldom gives rise to definite, concrete ethical postulates for social action. We who, in various ecumenical study groups, often marveled at the brilliance of his analysis, nevertheless noted time and again this deficiency between criticism and construction. And the reason for this is evident: the lack of an adequate concept of justice.[52]

Brunner may have been expressing frustrations that emerged from struggling with a method which offered no easy answers to ethical problems, and whose advocates often had to be satisfied with lesser approximations of justice than some would like. With the benefit of hindsight, however, we might marvel at the degree of unanimity achieved, and the amount of ethical work that was accomplished in this period of ecumenical history.

Whether Niebuhr had an inadequate concept of justice or too adequate a

---

[50]Niebuhr, 'Justice and Love,' in D. B. Robertson, ed., 28.

[51]This was the outcome of Emil Brunner's concern referred to previously, regarding Niebuhr's understanding of natural law. He felt that Niebuhr's method was unable to provide any concrete solutions because of the ambiguous relationship of love to justice.

[52]Emil Brunner in Kegley, ed., *Reinhold Niebuhr*, 84-5.

concept of human nature to be led to the self-confidence of ethical solutions may be debated. Nevertheless, John Bennett has been eager to point out that 'one of the great misinterpretations of Niebuhr is the idea that he is the great pessimist of modern theology.'[53] He points to Niebuhr's openness to the 'creative possibilities of justice' and emphasizes the roles of theology, faith, and hope in Niebuhr's programme.[54] Though Bennett sees great areas of commonality between Niebuhr and Brunner, he believes that 'Niebuhr is never as satisfied as Brunner seems to be that a particular policy at a particular time is the will of God. Nor does the receiving of the justifying grace of God enable Niebuhr to move ahead with as untroubled a conscience.'[55]

Though Bennett rightly balances Brunner's critical assessment with Niebuhr's own claims of hope and justice, his analysis does beg the question of how any progressive applications of justice are to be made with such lack of confidence and trepidation of action. It may be true that every human action is marred by sin and self-interest, but confidence in God and his indwelling Holy Spirit are where Christians find a source of sanctifying grace beyond themselves to rise above prideful inclinations and seek higher forms of justice. At this point, even his friend Bennett is forced to admit that 'in Niebuhr's formal analysis of love there is a missing link as we seek to relate love to social ethics.'[56] Though this 'missing link' may be presupposed in Niebuhr's thought as a whole, Bennett does not 'find it clearly described or clearly related to the types of love which he describes.'[57]

The irreparable disjunction that Niebuhr describes between the moral ideal of love revealed on the cross of Christ, and human life, calls into question the relevancy of the ideal, and thus the moral accountability of those agents who are the objects of grace.[58] Though Niebuhr often would protest otherwise, his method sometimes leaves gaps that are difficult to bridge. For example, Brunner rightly wonders precisely what it is that Niebuhr hopes for in Christ, and to what extent there stands a reality behind his eschatological symbols. Niebuhr may well have believed in doctrines of justification and grace, but it is very difficult in practice to skirt the rather slippery edge of cynicism without falling into its grasp.[59] In Niebuhr's theory, love may challenge justice to embody ever-higher forms, but as for most methods, it is difficult to achieve this outcome in practice.

While Niebuhr corrected the errors of idealism by countering its naïve

---

[53]John Bennett, 'Reinhold Niebuhr's Social Ethics,' in Kegley, ed., 103.
[54]Ibid., 105. Cf. Niebuhr, *Human Destiny,* 72.
[55]Ibid.
[56]Ibid., 111.
[57]Ibid.
[58]Cf. G. H. C. MacGregor, *The Relevance of the Impossible: A Reply to Reinhold Niebuhr* (London: Fellowship of Reconciliation, 1941).
[59]Cf. Niebuhr, *Human Destiny*, 72f.

optimism with the realism of a doctrine of transcendence, he was left with his own difficulties in describing the content of an ethic that was both relevant and relative. There can be no question that Niebuhr attempted to tread necessarily between two very dangerous precipices, something that all social philosophers must do, as Rauschenbusch noted. Yet, it is possible that such a method is preferable to many alternatives. According to Wurth, Niebuhr's approach safeguarded him 'from falling into an unmotivated, superficial optimism, and at the same time, kept him from a Lutheran quietism which lacks the courage to relate the gospel of Christ to the questions of the concrete world of today.'[60] A discussion between Barth and Niebuhr, following from the World Council of Churches in Amsterdam in 1948, illustrated the delicate balance that Niebuhr tried to strike between the unfounded optimism of the pre-war period, and the morally paralysing approach of German neo-orthodoxy.[61]

Niebuhr agreed with Barth that no programme of social ethics could be described as distinctively 'Christian,' nor that human effort was able to bring the kingdom to fruition in society. Even early on, Niebuhr suggested; 'the Barthians are quite right…in protesting against the easy identification of the Kingdom of God with every movement of social reform and social radicalism that has prevailed in American Christianity in particular and in liberal Protestantism in general.' He affirmed that 'those of us who dissociate ourselves from the easy optimism of modern liberalism and who believe that a just society is not going to be built by a little more education and a few more sermons on love have particular reason to reorient our thinking on this matter so that we will not come forward with a social ethic involving the use of force and coercion and political pressure of every kind and claim the authority of Jesus for it.'[62] Niebuhr saw no room for either optimism or defeatism, and argued accordingly for the development of principles of justice, which would operate within boundaries that balanced coercion and freedom.

Justice became the practical application of love in society, but was also related directly to moral law. The problem of love and law is usually defined by Niebuhr as the problem of the relation of duty to grace. Together, they represent the dialectical tension within humans, as they are at once subject to and transcendent over nature. The 'essential nature' of humans yields certain moral necessities, but it is differentiated from a deterministic natural law because grace allows the transcendent self to approximate love in higher forms of self-sacrifice. 'Love is a curious compound of willing through the strength of the sense of obligation and of willing not by the strength of our will but by the strength which enters the will through grace.'[63] Subsequently

---

[60]G. Brillenberg Wurth, *Reinhold Niebuhr*, 39.

[61]Ibid., 39f.

[62]Niebuhr, 'The Ethics of Jesus and the Social Problem,' *Love and Justice*, 33.

[63]Reinhold Niebuhr, *The Essential Reinhold Niebuhr: Selected Essays and Addresses*, ed. Robert McAfee Brown (New Haven, CT: Yale University Press, 1986), 146.

Grace, whether 'common' or 'saving,' has meaning only when life is measured at the limits of human possibilities, and when it is recognized that there are things we ought to do which we cannot do merely by the strength of our willing, but which may become possible because we are assisted by the help which others give us by their love, by the strength which accrues to our will in moments of crisis, and by the saving grace of the Spirit of God indwelling our spirit.[64]

The manifestations of love, which follow from law, are described as justice, based as they are on coercion rather than freedom. Justice, therefore, is related to both law and love. It is the end result of the law on one hand, and the instrument of love on the other.

In Niebuhr's view, there is finally less dialectical tension between law and love than is assumed most often in Catholic and Reformation ethics. One relies on a Stoic-Aristotelian rationalism and the other on a rigid understanding of scriptural authority, but the result is the same - they are 'too certain about the fixities of the norms of law.'[65] Niebuhr makes his view clear: 'All law, whether historical, positive, scriptural, or rational, is more tentative and less independent in its authority than orthodox Christianity, whether Catholic or Protestant, supposes, even as it is more necessary than liberal Protestantism assumes.' Here lies the heart of his practical approach to ethics, and he anticipates the charge of relativism, which would come from several quarters. He attempts to counter the charge by explaining that, 'The final dike against relativism is to be found not in these alleged fixities, but in the law of love itself. This is the only final law, and every other law is an expression of the law of love in minimal or in proximate terms or in terms appropriate to given historical occasions.'[66]

Nevertheless, Wurth called Niebuhr's realist approach a 'theology of accommodation,' which is ecumenical in its composition, but synthetic and compromising in its development. 'The new theology is more adapted to the needs of twentieth century man,' he concedes. To its credit, 'it contains dialectical tension, is less strange to reality, and has a better understanding of the tragic depths of human life' than its forebears. But in its application, Wurth argues that Niebuhr's thought has too much in common with nineteenth-century theology, as 'it accommodates the gospel in its deepest kernel to the dominant spirit of the time, and has received its stamp from the dominating philosophy of the day.'[67] Wurth is specific regarding the deepest flaw in Niebuhr's method. 'It lacks a clear cut biblical starting point,' he argues. 'In

---

[64]Ibid., 146. Niebuhr's description of love is differentiated from the social gospel conception of love, which regards short-term self-negation as a means to long-term self-fulfilment. It therefore falls far short of Niebuhr's notion of love as completely selfless sacrifice, which tempers grace with 'bourgeois prudence.' Cf. Ibid.,152.
[65]Ibid., 159.
[66]Ibid.
[67]Wurth, *Niebuhr*, 40.

every respect there appears a misunderstanding of the biblical relationship between the Creator and the creation. In its place is substituted the Kierkegaardian dialectical opposition between time and eternity.'[68] In practical terms, Niebuhr is said to suffer from a 'lack of insight into the meaning of the law of God as a norm for our human life, for creation in its entirety.' By contrast, 'if, in the spirit of biblical revelation, Niebuhr had understood the meaning of the law of God as the vital law not only for the individual but also for society, he would then not have been forced to compromise his realistic position in this unacceptable manner.'[69]

Wurth, Carnell, and others like them, find common ground in criticizing Niebuhr's method for being too compromising, accommodating or synthesizing. They have argued that Niebuhr's method leaves him with an ethic that is, at best, subjective and relative. Yet even Niebuhr's own admission regarding the relativity of the ethical task does not reflect its relation to the rest of his system, and he believed accusations of subjectivity to be unfounded. 'Professor Carnell is concerned to know upon what basis one can maintain the absoluteness of the Christian faith while recognizing the relativity of any formulation of the meaning of the faith and the corruption of the experience to which it is subject,' Niebuhr explains. 'My answer is that the faith proves its absoluteness precisely where its insights make it possible to detect the relativity of the interpretations and to question the validity of any claim, including our own, that we have been redeemed. At those points it is proved that faith has discerned and is in contact with the "true" God and not with some idol of our imagination.'[70] Despite his enthusiasm in addressing these concerns, Niebuhr did not regard such criticisms of his approach as 'substantive', thereby revealing the particularly broad ecumenical potential of his method.

While many scholars have made feasible criticisms of Niebuhr's method, the majority of critics have failed to communicate an alternative, which both rectifies the perceived errors of his realism, and offers a workable solution to the problem of relating biblical truth to the real moral world. It is easy to say that the absolute law of God is relevant to all of society, as it is to individuals. It is much more difficult to show how it is so, and how it translates into ethical practise, in ecumenical circles and in wider society. It is a great credit to Niebuhr's method that he recognised the important difference between individual and social ethics, and the interplay between them. That he was successful in achieving a large measure of unity and relevancy, if not always concrete solutions, was confirmed by his prominent role in ecumenical discussions, and in public life in general. Niebuhr and his colleagues were able to provide the ecumenical movement with a 'deeper theological basis,' required

---

[68]Ibid., 40-1.
[69]Ibid.
[70]Niebuhr, 'Response,' in Kegley, ed., 519.

to move social ethics forward from Stockholm.[71]

Niebuhr's hesitancy to offer concrete solutions to every ethical issue pioneered and drove a method of ecumenical social ethics which focused on study and dialogue, in an attempt to wrestle with the ambiguities and paradoxes which characterized human existence. Since social ethics was, at best, a precarious enterprise, a willingness to work from principles rather than precepts, and to highlight possibilities rather than policies was necessary if ecumenical efforts were to have any degree of effectiveness. Despite the critics of this method, it would come to dominate the ecumenical ethical agenda for nearly two decades, and generally characterize the greatest degree of unity ever achieved in ecumenical ethics on an international level.

Niebuhr's Realism Applied in the WCC

Not surprisingly, considering his widespread reputation, Niebuhr played a key role in the early ecumenical conferences, which focused on issues of church and society, as precursors to the formation of the WCC. At Oxford in 1937, and Amsterdam in 1948, he was a central figure involved in elucidating relevant theological and methodological concerns for ecumenical social ethics. Representing the significant theological shift from the dominant position at Stockholm, Niebuhr 'made one of the most influential addresses at Oxford interpreting the relation of Christian faith to secular political events.' Along with a paper by Brunner which was circulated widely, it 'did a good deal to mediate to the conference theological insights which mark the difference between Oxford and Stockholm. They, together with the world events on everyone's mind, created a greater realism in interpreting choices and confronting Christians in the world than had been characteristic of the kind of liberal Protestant theology that guided social concern and strategy in the churches.'[72] In place of 'doctrine divides, service unites,' the spirit of Oxford emphasized the sentiment, 'Let the church be the church.' The message of the conference put it this way: 'The first duty of the church, and its greatest service to the world, is that it be in very deed the church - confessing the true faith, committed to the will of Christ, its only Lord, and united in him in a fellowship of love and service.'[73]

One thing the reports of the Oxford conference accomplished was a clarification of the distinction between important concepts such as community, association, and state. It celebrated the gift of social life, while acknowledging the sinful ambiguity of human existence.[74] Issues of race and nationalism were

---

[71]Abrecht, 'The Development of Ecumenical Social Thought and Action,' 238.
[72]Bennett, 'Breakthrough in Ecumenical Social Ethics,' 135.
[73]Ibid., 137.
[74]Bennett attributes the frequent use of the word 'ambiguity' in these documents to Niebuhr's influence.

also discussed, and the notions of Christian citizenship, loyalty, freedom, and responsibility were moved to the fore in the reports from various sections. The influence of realism is apparent throughout the conference reports, and the mark of Niebuhr's ethical method is particularly clear in the report on the Church and the economic order.[75] Bennett explains

> The report is based on two theological ideas. One is that the kingdom of God is the source of both hope and judgment. It is wrong to say that it has no relation to the goals of justice for which we are striving and it is wrong to identify it with some particular social system. Reinhold Niebuhr's influence is clear in the formulation of this position. The second idea is that justice rather than love is the standard by which the economic order should be judged and yet these are not to be separated because love should will justice. Justice is defined as 'the ideal of a harmonious relation of life to life'. It presupposes 'the sinful tendency of one life to take advantage of another' and it seeks to check this tendency 'by defining the rightful place and privilege which each life must have in the harmony of the whole and by assigning the duty of each to each'. The process of achieving justice involves coercion in restraining the evil-doer. The realism that characterized Oxford in general is expressed in the statement that 'it cannot be assumed that the practice of Christian love will ever obviate the necessity for coercive political and economic arrangements'.[76]

Moreover, realism dictated that Christianity could not be identified solely with any particular economic system, while utopianism, materialism, and disregard for the dignity of the individual, were identified as particularly worthy of rejection by Christians.

But while theology and terminology were clarified within an ecumenical context, and the understanding of social life advanced, was anything concrete achieved? Did the shift in philosophy from Stockholm to Oxford and Amsterdam and subsequent conferences in the 1950s yield any more practical result in the development of an ecumenical ethic? While 'ambiguity' was the hallmark of the Oxford meeting, did it really 'find a way to resolve the important theological-ethical disagreements and disputes which blocked progress at and after Stockholm'?[77] Paul Abrecht believes it did. In direct opposition to Wurth's accusations, Abrecht argues

> By emphasizing the provisional character of all Christian efforts at social and economic policy-making, the Oxford conference helped avoid the danger of churches making ecclesiastical/theological commitments to contemporary social-ideological fashions. By its emphasis on cooperation with the social sciences and on the contribution of the Christian laity, it helped to prepare the way for a new

---

[75]Bennett confirms this in 'Breakthrough.'

[76]Bennett, 'Breakthrough,'137.

[77]Paul Abrecht, 'From Oxford to Vancouver: Lesson from Fifty Years of Ecumenical Work for Economic and Social Justice,' *ER* 40 (April 1988): 149-50.

type of Christian social thinking, avoiding the kind of ecclesiastical pontification and moralizing on social and economic issues which had so often in the past characterized the churches' thought and action.[78]

Within the study of ecumenical ethics, many scholars and participants believe this realist method to be a touchstone for Christian ethics, suggesting that social ethics become most confused when Churches move away from the foundation laid at Oxford. The value of the method lies more in its processes than its product. The roles of study and dialogue are primary, while specific solutions are regarded with some suspicion. The debate of ideas yields better forms of justice, as the pretensions of one group are balanced by the interests of another. Where positions seem irreconcilable, conversation continues as an expression of a commitment to social justice.

Perhaps one of the clearest manifestations of the realist approach was embodied in the principle of 'The Responsible Society', which found documentary expression at Amsterdam, and later at Evanston in 1954. As the ethos of the WCC moved from 'staying together' to 'growing together', the emphasis on ethics, and its relevance to the whole of society, increased. While the conferences yielded multifaceted statements and discussions on issues of moral significance, the sum of their thought is best expressed and understood in this concept which came to dominate ecumenical ethical understanding. The Responsible Society as a socio-ethical concept embodied Niebuhr's dialectical relationship between time and eternity, transcendence and immanence, human freedom and human nature, love and justice. It highlighted the moral life of Christians as individuals, who were yet part of a wider society encompassing church, nation, and state, and exempted Christianity from identification with any particular political or economic system. The Responsible Society concept was thus described

Man is created and called to be a free being, responsible to God and his neighbour. Any tendencies in State and society depriving man of the possibility of acting responsibly are a denial of God's intention for man and His work of salvation. A responsible society is one where freedom is the freedom of men who acknowledge responsibility to justice and public order, and where those who hold political authority or economic power are responsible for its exercise to God and the people whose welfare is affected by it.

Man must never be made a mere means for political or economic ends. Man is not made for the State, but the State for man. Man is not made for production, but production for man. For a society to be responsible under modern conditions it is required that the people have freedom to control, to criticise and to change their governments, that power be made responsible by law and tradition, and be

---

[78]Ibid., 150.

distributed as widely as possible through the whole community. It is required that economic justice and provision of equality of opportunity be established for all the members of society.[79]

This principle found wide, if not universal agreement, and was used as a guide for ecumenical ethics for several years. Amongst scholars and ecumenical participants alike, it is almost universally agreed that the realist approach, most visibly manifested in the principle of the Responsible Society, was to remain the distinctive feature of ecumenical ethics well into the 1950s.[80]

However, it would be inaccurate to present Niebuhr's method as the only one present at the Oxford conference and in the period following. Just as there were several positions in evidence at Stockholm, so there were at Oxford, and Amsterdam. Though the realist approach of Niebuhr and his colleagues dominated, it took its place amongst others that jostled for position on the social ethics agenda. In his official report on Oxford, J. H. Oldham summarized the three most important theological perspectives presented to the conference

A Christian ethics based on principles derived from New Testament teaching especially the Sermon on the Mount, representing the position of Stockholm.

A personal ethics of salvation - suspicious of 'Christian social programmes' - was held by several continental theologians who maintained that the Christian ethic could not be identified with that of the Sermon on the Mount. Thus Professor Emil Brunner of Zurich argued that 'The Christian Church has no right to lay down a social programme, because it is not its business to establish any kind of system. It is doubtful whether we ought to speak of a Christian ethic at all, since an ethic means something which has an independent existence and which once for all lays down rules for the various relations of life.'

A Christian ethics of justice derived from the love commandment. This view emphasized the prophetic mission of the Church in relation to the family, the nation, the state, economics and culture. In contrast to the first position, it stressed the reality of evil and the difficulty of direct applications of the love commandment.[81]

---

[79]The World Council of Churches, 'Report of Section III: The Church and the Disorder of Society,' *The Church and the Disorder of Society*, Man's Disorder and God's Design, vol. 3 (London: SCM Press, 1948), 200-201.

[80]Richard Dickinson describes the Responsible Society as an ecumenical 'doctrine which was to influence ecumenical social ethics for 15 years.' 'Changing Ecumenical Perspectives on Economic Development: A contribution to an on-going discussion,' *Development Assessed: Ecumenical Reflections and Actions on Development* (WCC Unit III Justice, Peace and Creation, Geneva, 9-12 January 1995): 27.

[81]The Oxford Conference (1937), official report, 27-32. Cited in Paul Abrecht, 'The Development of Ecumenical Social Thought and Action,' 239.

The first view outlined by Oldham is the one that was predominant in the heyday of the social gospel and at Stockholm, where moral agency was attributed to the individual, whose conscience was derivative of a universal consciousness that reflected the immanence of God. The second view was championed by theologians such as Emil Brunner, and some of its impulses may be detected in the midst of more recent approaches to Christian ethics, though they rest on very different philosophical grounds.[82] The third approach was that which dominated at Oxford and Amsterdam, particularly expressed in the notion of the Responsible Society and similar documents. At subsequent ecumenical conferences, largely in response to totalitarian social and political movements, the notion of group agency was expressed at the level of society, whose moral agency was derivative of the individual, and made possible by intentional and free consent. The notion of community was preferred to association, as it indicated a whole people with varied concerns, as opposed to a group organized around a single interest.[83] John Bennett has explained how the ecumenical conference participants managed to develop and maintain in this idea, a balanced view of the nature of humanity in social expression

> This community of neighbours who are in so many ways interdependent Oxford called a 'gift of God' and within it are our primary loyalties and responsibilities: from our experience in community we become social beings. But immediately the conference gave the other side of the picture. All forms of community from family to nation, while gifts of God, 'partake of both good and evil; they are of God and also of human sin.' 'Man's pride, greed, fear, idolatry infect them all.' Throughout the Oxford reports we find strong expressions of a very realistic view of humanity which is the product of everyday experience and of large events illumined by theology. It is not dogmatic pessimism or cynicism, far from both, but sees humanity as characterized throughout by ambiguity, one of Reinhold Niebuhr's favourite words.[84]

For realists of the period, the term 'ambiguity' embraced the theological concept of sin, understood in a collective sense, which protected the realist or neo-orthodox approach from the rather arrogant triumphalism of the social gospel, and the smug isolationism of extreme conservatism. In the face of the totalitarian challenge, it did not surrender to quietism, but left room for

---

[82]If social gospel idealism lives on in the liberation cause, and post-war idealism carries on in various guises, it may be possible that the position of Brunner finds modified post-modern expression in the radical orthodoxy of scholars such as John Milbank and Stanley Hauerwas. Certainly the suggestion that the church does not 'have an ethic' as such, is a theme they share.

[83]John C. Bennett, 'Breakthrough in Ecumenical Social Ethics: The Legacy of the Oxford Conference on Church, Community, and State (1937),' *ER* 40 (April 1988), 137. See J. H. Oldham and W. A. Visser't Hooft, *The Church and its Function in Society*, Church, Community, and State, vol. 1 (London: George Allen & Unwin, 1937).

[84]Ibid.

mystery, recognizing the tentative nature of ethical conclusions reached by individuals and groups, and encouraged an ongoing programme of study, dialogue, and revision. At the same time, it did not ignore the possibilities of justice, achievable under grace, pursued in an attitude of cultural and historical humility, and faith. As demonstrated previously, Niebuhr and others with him perceived the necessity of embracing ambiguity, and they sought to build upon their understanding of group behaviour and consciousness in the ecumenical task, while never undermining the importance of individual moral agency.

For the realists, ambiguity in ethics resulted necessarily from the recognition of the limits of human striving, and the proneness of groups to prideful self-assertion of global proportions. In the midst of this post-war understanding, the church was not seen as immune from this tendency to assert itself in expressions of power, and was responsible for its own errors of commission and neglect as a human collective. But as the church, this group was called to practice and demonstrate repentance, in social life generally, in personal relationships, and in the lives of individuals. Again, moral responsibility was upheld, as individuals were called upon to repent as members of the larger group. Collective consciousness was largely seen still as derivative of the individual moral agent, and responsibility was not divorced from human action. The Amsterdam report addressed the condition of collective sin, and the conflicts that may arise between various collective interests as a result, but whether regarded as condition or act, it was seen clearly as a human responsibility. As the report 'deals with the difficulty of deciding when the primary loyalty to family, to neighbours nearest to us and to nation conflicts with loyalty to God,' it upholds the individual as the one who must decide between competing loyalties. Moreover, it expressed the belief that although 'The abuses of loyalty to community are universal in our secularized society which generally lives at least on the edge of idolatry', nevertheless, 'All Christians are called to repentance as they see themselves in the light of the claim upon them of God as revealed in Christ.'[85] The universal nature of sin never negated the responsibility of Christians to repent of their part in its collective manifestations.

During these post-war years, and leading into the 1960s, 'The method of work ...was non-institutionalized and decentralized, depending much on local initiative. The purpose was to draw in laymen and theologians interested in applying ecumenical criteria to the problems of society in particular areas. In this way the staff gained experience and tested the capacity of the ecumenical movement to encourage the new and creative thinking asked for by the First Assembly.'[86] And yet, for increasing numbers of ecumenical participants, the

---

[85]Ibid. Bennett notes that the report managed to emphasize the evils of nationalism and racism without mentioning Germany by name, thus seeking to maintain unity in a complex environment.

[86]Abrecht, 'The Development of Ecumenical Social Thought and Action,' 244.

notion of the Responsible Society would eventually yield as much frustration as confidence. For, as Brunner made clear, although it enjoyed general consensus as a *principle,* it didn't say much about *policy,* and offered little specific guidance for direct ethical action. There was also a sense amongst some that the reason for broad agreement regarding the Responsible Society was due to a neglect or even intentional oversight of serious doctrinal differences, masking the fact that many participating groups and individuals were yet poles apart in method and understanding. The result, such critics say, was that the notion of the Responsible Society could not last even as a guiding principle, since it was dated in time and embraced more division than was immediately apparent.

More than wrestling with *principles*, and their application through a study-dialogue process, it was increasingly felt by some that *action* was required. Some in the WCC felt that the movement should seek increasingly to speak for the churches as well as to the churches. The form that action should take became the next focus of debate in ecumenical ethics, a debate that has endured to the present day. Would the realist method give theoreticians and practitioners what they needed to bridge the gap between *doxa* and *praxis*, or was a return to idealism preferable? Or would a new method offer more promise for progress?

CHAPTER 7

Beyond Ambiguity: Methodological Diversity and a Plea for Integrity

When you spell things out you're accused of politics. If you don't spell them out, you're accused of being an interesting social philosopher.

Derek Warlock

A good deal of confusion could be avoided, if we refrained from setting before the group, what can be the aim only of the individual; and before society as a whole, what can be the aim only of a group.

T. S. Eliot

Without a common and focal Gospel we fall easy victims to limitation of a more serious kind - to the idiosyncrasies of an individual, the fashion of an age, or the egoism of Humanity.

P. T. Forsyth

Introduction

The founding of the WCC, and its development, offered opportunities for the expression of various ethical methods in documentary form, through reports, studies, and official utterances. While some elements of Rauschenbusch's social gospel method are evident in early ecumenical documentation, Niebuhr's realist method is apparent in many documentary forms, especially in the first decade following the inception of the WCC. Available evidence reinforces the notion that philosophical trends eventually do find their way into Christian ethical speech and practice. Through this chapter, I intend to demonstrate how the social gospel and realist methods outlined previously - and others - have been reflected in WCC reports and statements. Particularly, I shall examine the kinds of discourse produced in such reports and statements, and consider to what degree they reflect various philosophical and theological assumptions, especially regarding collective and individual moral agency. Though the purpose here is to demonstrate the fact that ethical discourse represents various theological and philosophical presuppositions, I will also make suggestions about the type of discourse which might be most helpful, along with some preferred methodological aspects. These will be reshaped into an approach of integrity, by which other ethical methods may be evaluated.

Types of Ecumenical Moral Discourse

To this point, we have seen how different methods of social ethics resulted from divergent philosophical and theological presuppositions, highlighted in the relationship of the individual to the collective moral agent.[1] These presuppositions largely governed the ways in which ethical issues were approached, and the kinds of ethical statements that were issued. If, as these studies of Rauschenbusch and Niebuhr have indicated, the way in which the moral agent is perceived largely determines the procedure and final results of ethical deliberation, is this confirmed in the types of statements and reports issued by the World Council of Churches? Do such statements confirm the strategic role of philosophy and theology in practical method?

In a paper presented to the Church and Society Working Committee in 1987, James Gustafson identified four types of discourse identified from WCC publications and documents.[2] In his research, he observed 'that what is called social ethics in the WCC literature covers a lot of bases, addresses a lot of issues, is relevant to very different audiences, and is written in many different ways...'. Nevertheless, he was able to designate four general types of statements, which he describes as 'prophetic, narrative, ethical and policy discourse.'[3]

Prophetic moral discourse is described by Gustafson as 'taking two distinguishable forms: that of indictment and a more utopian form.' Indictment attempts to illustrate the dramatic fall of human society, and points 'to the *roots* of moral and social waywardness,' rather than specific policies. It acknowledges that 'fundamental values or orientations of social life are the source of the fault,' and its language is motivating, evoking a sense of urgency or crisis. The utopian form 'proclaims an ideal state of future of affairs,' providing incentive and motivation. Its language is vivid, alluring, and 'appeals to human idealism.'[4]

Narrative moral discourse contends that narratives 'function to sustain common memory in a community; narratives shape the moral ethos of a community and provide its moral identity.' Individual moral identities and

---

[1]This concept will be considered further with respect to collective responsibility later in this chapter, and throughout the present study.

[2]James M. Gustafson, 'An Analysis of Church and Society Social Ethical Writings,' *ER* 40 (April 1988): 267-278.

[3]Ibid., 268. Gustafson elsewhere employs the use of 'base points' and sources for Christian ethical writings, which he does not elaborate here. His desire to identify the basis for and coherency of ethical statements is set aside here in order that he might simply describe the type of statements he encountered in ecumenical ethics, and discover if there is any sense of unity between them. Cf. James Gustafson, *Ethics from a Theological Perspective,* vol. 2, *Ethics and Theology* (Chicago: University of Chicago Press, 1984).

[4]Ibid., 269.

consciences are formed by the stories of the collective, whose stories and parables are used at the point of moral decision.[5]

Ethical moral discourse describes 'more philosophically self-conscious and rigorous modes of moral argumentation,' which are 'concerned to find the rational grounds of autonomous ethics which might be backed by Christian convictions but which can be shared with non-believers.' Discussion often revolves around types of ethics identified by moral philosophy, and is intent to clarify use of concepts, definitions, and logical argument. It may often involve a casuistic-style practice to recommend particular forms of action.[6]

Policy moral discourse is described as having many features, but is distinguishable from ethical discourse by its starting-point: 'Whereas ethical discourse asks as the first question, "What ought we to do", in policy discourse the first question is likely to be, "What is going on?".'[7] It seeks to balance desirable results with possibilities, assumes the position of responsible moral agency, draws from a wide field of expertise, assesses power dynamics, focuses on technicalities, and perceives a short time frame for affecting change.

Gustafson observed that all of these types of moral discourse were present in WCC literature, and it may further be noted that the various streams often run concurrently, with one type sometimes dominating for a period of time. This would concur with Oldham's account of the presence of at least three approaches to social ethics at Amsterdam.[8]

It is widely agreed that several strands of various methods have been present at any given time within the larger programme of the WCC. Further, the present study has shown that ethical methods are not to be taken at face value, but are understood to represent complex webs of theological and philosophical influences. Gustafson suggests that all forms of discourse are required for a well-rounded ethical programme, so long as their respective functions and audiences are defined and understood.[9] But are the results of divergent methods to be so easily reconciled? Are any particular associations to be made between Gustafson's typology and the methods of social ethics that dominated the WCC during various periods of history in the twentieth century? If so, might these forms of discourse themselves represent the kind of differences in perception between the moral individual and collective, such as we have seen already in the thought of Rauschenbusch and Niebuhr? Do they make assumptions about

---

[5]Ibid.

[6]Ibid.

[7]Ibid., 270.

[8]Oldham's account is cited in the previous chapter.

[9]The task of providing clarity in social ethical issues appears not only to have been neglected by the WCC, but virtually ignored, hence the resulting state of 'confusion.' Ronald Preston believes this state has resulted from a loss of quality of dialogue, analysis, and study in social ethics in the WCC. Ronald Preston, *Confusions in Christian Social Ethics* (London: SCM Press, 1994).

the nature of individual and collective moral agency based on theologies and philosophies that are incompatible, or is there a method, expressed in a type of discourse, which embraces them all, or one that is preferable?

Paul Abrecht, who has written extensively as a participant and observer of ecumenical social ethics within the WCC, offers a particularly helpful historical perspective. The dictum that those who forget history are bound to repeat it may be aptly applied to the pursuit of ecumenical social ethics during the twentieth century. In Abrecht's wise words, 'The repetition of past errors is not confined to financiers and stockbrokers. The ecumenical movement and the churches also have trouble coming to terms with their history.'[10] The churches may recognize the crisis of the moment, but have met frustration in efforts to move the agenda forward in any unified, productive sense. An ignorance of history has led many ecumenical ethicists to propose strategies that actually repeat the mistakes of the past, and others to reject ecumenical co-operation at all because it is seen as compromising Christian doctrine in its pursuit of ideology.[11] Still others find themselves unable to think of a distinctly 'Christian' ethic, arguing that Christian formation cannot conceive of any other kind.[12] The resulting polarization sells short the rich legacy of commitment to positive theology and ethical method that characterized the ecumenical movement from the beginning. Through learned method and shared experience, early ecumenical participants forged a dialectical style which sustained dialogue and supported action, through interaction of theologians and lay expertise, even when agreement was far from universal. Sadly, conflict and confusion are inevitable when we know neither where we are headed, nor from whence we have come.[13]

---

[10]Paul Abrecht, 'From Oxford to Vancouver: Lessons from Fifty Years of Ecumenical Work for Economic and Social Justice,' *ER* 40 (April 1988): 147.

[11]For an account of the shifting relationship between evangelicals and ecumenism, see David J. Bosch, "Ecumenicals" and "Evangelicals": a Growing Relationship?' *ER* 40 (July-October 1988), 458-472; Bryant L. Myers, 'A Funny Thing Happened on the Way To Evangelical-Ecumenical Cooperation,' *IRM* 81 (July 1992): 397-407; C. Rene Padilla, 'Wholistic Mission: Evangelical and Ecumenical,' *IRM* 81 (July 1992): 381-2; Cecil M. Robeck, 'A Pentecostal Looks at the World Council of Churches,' *ER* 47 (January 1995), 60-69. During the sixth WCC Assembly at Vancouver in 1983, several evangelicals wrote a letter critiquing the 'fuzzy' use of language and theology, to the detriment of both, and the undermining of the individual moral agent. See *MS* 23 (1984): 130.

[12]See for example Stanley Hauerwas, *After Christendom?* (Nashville, TN: Abingdon Press, 1991).

[13]Paul Abrecht points to two books in particular, both published in 1987 - Ulrich Duchrow, *Global Economy: a Confessional Issue for the Churches?* Geneva: WCC; and Charles Elliott, *Comfortable Compassion? Poverty, Power and the Church,* London: Hodder & Stoughton. Regarding the two books, Abrecht says, 'Both claim to build on ecumenical experience. Yet both omit much of the ecumenical record on economic

What is perhaps most surprising is that the method developed at Oxford and Amsterdam under the influence of Niebuhr and like-minded cohorts has faded so quickly into history, when its integrative and coherent approach to study, analysis and dialogue produced a general consensus which endured for more than a decade, and which largely 'still applies.' Abrecht notes that, 'no other ethical approach or methodology has been articulated which has commanded a similar measure of ecumenical agreement or support. It remains still today an influential option in ecumenical social thought despite subsequent challenges from other theological-ethical views.'[14]

It is from this perspective that we approach another article written by Abrecht, reacting to the typology put forward by Gustafson.[15] At the outset, Abrecht acknowledges that ecumenical social thought and action are 'in the view of a number of observers, in some "disarray and confusion". There is a great diversity of theological-ethical perspectives underlying the different programmes, involving contrasting views of human nature and of the possibility of realizing freedom, social order, peace and justice in history.'[16] Attempts to ignore these differences by a refusal to examine theological and ethical variety 'has inevitably contributed to further disorder and disagreement in defining the theological-ethical basis of ecumenical social thought.'[17] Abrecht asserts that an acknowledgement of the existence of fundamental theological-ethical differences is helpful, if not essential, along with an admission that these divergent methods have their very 'origins in the history of ecumenical work on social questions.'[18]

Abrecht adopts Gustafson's typology and applies it to the dominant method of each significant historical period in ecumenical ethics in the twentieth century. He is not uncritical in this adoption, but he believes Gustafson's typology to be 'helpful in examining the various (and often conflicting) views on social ethics in the ecumenical movement today; it also suggests possibilities

---

justice. Both base their proposals for change in ideas, especially with respect to economic ethics, which the ecumenical movement has examined and rejected in the past.' 'Oxford to Vancouver,' 148. Ronald Preston similarly laments the loss of ecumenical memory. Cf. Ronald Preston, *Confusions in Christian Social Ethics*, London: SCM Press, 1994), 173. Concern for accountability and ecumenical memory was more recently stated in *The Report of the Unit I Committee to the Central Committee* of the WCC, meeting 11-19 September 1997 in Geneva. Document No. 1.3, WCC archives box 37.97.01, 4f.

[14]'Oxford to Vancouver,' 150.

[15]Paul Abrecht, 'Competing forms of Discourse in Ecumenical Social Thought or Ecumenical Experience with different Forms of Ethical Discourse,' *Towards a New Humanity: Essays in Honour of Dr. Paulos Mar Gregorios,* ed. K.M. George and K. J. Gabriel (Delhi: SPCK, 1992), 30-45.

[16]Ibid., 30.

[17]Ibid., 31.

[18]Ibid., 32.

of dialogue between these diverse approaches.'[19] Unsurprisingly, Abrecht identifies the early movement for Christian Life and Work (1919 to 1930) with *prophetic* discourse; the period 1930-1947 with *ethical* discourse; the inception of the WCC and the notion of the Responsible Society (1948-1966) with the development of *policy* discourse; and the period of liberation theology (1969-1991) with *narrative* and *prophetic* discourse. In addition to this breakdown, I would identify the most recent interval of history more particularly with *narrative* discourse.

Connections Between Discourse and Method

Based on Abrecht's association of Gustafson's moral discourse typology with ecumenical history, I intend to examine a statement or section of report from each historical period which represents the type of moral discourse described, and discover what theological and philosophical assumptions about individual and collective moral agency might support or be derived from such a statement. Whether the statement arises from or points toward individual, group, or universal action will be considered, and the resulting implications for how moral truth and responsibility are perceived will be described. The potential of such a statement to reflect unity and yield results will be similarly assessed.

Prophetic Discourse and the Social Gospel

The only official utterance to emerge from the meeting at Stockholm in 1925 was the message from the *Universal Christian Conference on Life and Work.*[20] Described as 'carefully prepared and modestly phrased,' the document made passing reference to the war and its consequences, but 'is much less dated than might have been expected, and in its enunciation of central ecumenical themes is a worthy prelude to the many similar ecumenical documents which have followed it.'[21] It contains elements of confession and repentance, affirms the responsibility of the church in the public realm, but leaves specific application to individuals and groups. At the same time it acknowledges a certain universality to human existence, and asserts that it is the duty of the church to state ideals, and encourage education toward social consciousness while

---

[19]Ibid., 34.

[20]*The Stockholm Conference 1925: Official Report*, ed. G. K. A. Bell (London: Oxford University Press, 1926), 710-716.

[21]Nils Ehrenström, 'Movements for International Friendship and Life and Work 1925-1948, *A History of the Ecumenical Movement 1517-1948*, eds. Ruth Rouse and Stephen C. Neill, 4th edn, Geneva: WCC, 1993, 547. Ehrenström further notes the extreme responses to the conference: 'Acclaimed by some as the most important ecclesiastical happening of the century, inaugurating a new epoch in Christian history, the Conference was condemned by other contemporaries as a dismal failure or, even worse, as a device of the devil.' 550.

working for the kingdom of God. It recognizes that 'the world is too strong for a divided Church,' and thus sets aside 'for the time our differences in Faith and Order,' so that 'united practical action in Christian Life and Work' might be undertaken.[22]

It becomes evident from even a cursory reading that this statement clearly reflects the prophetic typology described by Gustafson, and assigned to this historical period by Abrecht. In essence, it reflects the social gospel mood, which found philosophical and theological expression in the thought of leaders like Rauschenbusch and many others. The elements of indictment are present since it confesses, 'before God and the world the sins and failures of which the Churches have been guilty, through lack of love and sympathetic understanding.' Such indictment is not without optimism: 'The call of the present hour to the Church should be repentance, and with repentance a new courage springing from the inexhaustible resources which are in Christ....'.[23] However, the statement does not address specific situations but reflects more broadly on the present state of affairs in the economic, social and international political realm, conceding: 'We have not attempted to offer precise solutions, nor have we confirmed by a vote the results of our friendly discussions. This was due not only to our respect for the convictions of individuals or groups, but still more to the feeling that the mission of the Church is above all to state principles, and to assert the ideal, while leaving to individual consciences and to communities the duty of applying them with charity, wisdom and courage.'[24] This fits well the utopian aspect of prophetic typology, confirmed by its closing statements affirming young people, workers of the world, and truth-seekers by whatever means, and confirming a shared aspiration for a 'just and fraternal social order...according to God's design.'[25]

Gustafson has noted some of the pitfalls of prophetic discourse, suggesting that

> it is legitimate and important, but not sufficient. It dramatizes; it undercuts meagre preoccupations about means to short-range ends; it stirs human moral sentiments. Rigorous ethical writings and policy statements cannot do that. But by being in focus on the root of the evil it cannot inform incremental choices made by persons and institutions where good and bad are commingled, and where 'trade-offs' have to be defended. By being in focus on an ideal future, it often has little to say about means to shorter range ends in view.[26]

It may be encouraging to note that 'speaker after speaker' at the conference reverted 'to the Cross of Christ as the centre of unity in which the Churches

---

[22]Stockholm Report, section I, para 2 & 3.

[23]Ibid., section I, para 3.

[24]Ibid., section I, para 9.

[25]Ibid., section III, para 12.

[26]Gustafson, 'An Analysis,' 269.

experience already the fact and the promise of Christian unity,' for it reveals a sense of a source of unity pointing beyond the gathered community at Stockholm.[27] But if Christ's social immanence was the primary understanding of his meaning for the church, it is not surprising that 'the conference deliberately eschewed formal theological-ethical argument. The work for social justice, peace and world order was assumed as a priority which needed no new theological-ethical validation...[it] seemed to suggest that such discourse would only hamper or delay the realization of the prophetic vision.'[28]

Building on Gustafson's observations of the potential weaknesses of prophetic discourse, and in light of our previous examination of Rauschenbusch's idealism, we can understand quite readily some of the motivation and means of the Stockholm statement, along with its scope and intent. Its main category of thought was the kingdom of God, an inclusive, global community, with alliances outside of the church that affirm its universality.[29] While it affirmed Church loyalties, the statement supported a broader view of the Kingdom, admitting, 'we cannot confine this appeal to the Churches, for we gratefully recognize that we now have many allies in this holy cause.'[30] Though it left action to individuals and communities, it was a desire to avoid division and preserve unity that led to a dismissal of specific content. If the individual were derivative of the community, as for the social gospel, united action would result on a local level since it would become clear though propagation and education what the mind of God desired for social and political existence. This would be confirmed through social, political, and economic movements of all kinds, not just those within the churches. Thus the lines between individual, church, and world became blurred.

Believing that God indwelled the world with a single purpose for humanity would lead those at Stockholm to defer disagreements in hope that they would disappear at the level of local action. Publishing statements such as this one, in a prophetic style of discourse, glossed over differences and superficially presented the church as embodying a united front, for the purpose of social reform. As with Rauschenbusch's method, and for the same reasons, it neglected any means of mediating dissenting opinion. Despite the setback to the social gospel programme presented by the Great War, necessitating an admission of human guilt, the approach remained optimistic, hopeful, and teleological, since God's truth was being revealed in various forms through social movements around the world. So, while both individuals and communities are often acknowledged as moral participants, the primary stress was still on the universal bond of a humanity united by the cross of Christ. Individual and community differences were not taken into account in the

---

[27]Ehrenström, 'Movements,' 548.
[28]Abrecht, 'Competing Forms of Discourse,' 35.
[29]Stockholm Report, section III, para 11 & 12.
[30]Ibid., section III, para 12.

development of the statement, nor were individuals and communities left with any resources for living out the spirit of the statement made at Stockholm.

Disillusionment with the optimism of the social gospel would lead many theologians to question the methods of this first ecumenical gathering. The inability of broad affirmations to make any ethical difference and the dismissal of significant differences between Christians challenged some to seek a different approach to practising ethics together as churches. Realism and neo-orthodoxy were replacing idealism as the dominant philosophies of the day, and the shift in general mood would be felt and manifested at ecumenical gatherings leading up to and following the Second World War, including the preparatory studies for the inception of the World Council of Churches in 1948.

Ethical Discourse and Moral Realism

When attempting to identify a document for analysis from the period associated with the *ethical* type of discourse, the task becomes slightly more complicated than for the first, since the theologians of the day were busy producing myriad study volumes of theological-ethical reflection on the eve of a new war, and analysing the division and collapse of optimistic forms of thought.[31] To find expression of Niebuhr's ideas is no difficult task, as his imprint is everywhere to be found, from the Oxford meeting in 1937 to the formation of the WCC at Amsterdam in 1948 and beyond. However, in order to limit this study to a single statement representative of the dominant approach of the period concerned, the *Report of the Oxford Conference on Church, Community and State* must be consulted. This document not only represents a move away from the idealism that characterized the Stockholm gathering, but in the opinion of some, 'it remains to this day the most comprehensive statement on problems of church and society and Christian responsibility.'[32] Perhaps it is true that 'most church historians would agree that "no ecumenically organized reflection on theology and social ethics since Oxford has matched it in quality and thoroughness".'[33] For this reason, if no other, 'Scholars today would do well to re-visit the papers, discussions and official reports of the Oxford Life and Work

---

[31]In preparation for the first WCC Assembly alone, four major volumes were prepared which dealt with the question, 'What has the Church to contribute to society in its present extremity?' With such heavy-weight theologians as Niebuhr, Brunner, Ellul, Oldham, Tillich, Bennett and others contributing, the material may be biased toward a western perspective, but the value of the studies cannot be denied, nor have their appreciation of the complexities of Christian social ethics been surpassed. See the series *Man's Disorder and God's Design*, including *The Universal Church in God's Design, The Church's Witness to God's Design, The Church and the Disorder of Society, The Church and the International Disorder* (London: SCM Press, 1948).

[32]Ans van der Bent, *Commitment to God's World*, 17.

[33]Ans van der Bent, cited in Michael Kinnamon and Brian Cope eds., *The Ecumenical Movement: An Anthology of Key Texts and Voices* (Geneva: WCC, 1997).

Conference. What had begun at Stockholm became a deeper, more theological, more systematic and structural analysis of the economic and political orders.'[34] According to Ans van der Bent

> with 300 delegates, named by more than 120 churches in 45 countries, Oxford was more a working conference than Stockholm. The impressive preparations presented an adequate consensus of opinion of the different ecclesiastical traditions. The attendance of distinguished scholars and persons experienced in political affairs guaranteed a note of actuality and proportion in the conference's pronouncements. The study volumes, especially in the Oxford theme, served to stimulate thinking in theological faculties, in forums and among lay groups. While the direct comment on the reports solicited from the churches was 'disappointingly meagre', according to Visser't Hooft, he attributed this to the fact that 'most churches had as yet no corporate and relevant teaching on the problems of society and felt, therefore, unable to express and official opinion on the findings of Oxford.'[35]

Despite its largely 'western' perspective, the great theological ability of the participants and resulting study materials yielded a document of great scope and relevance, whose import would last well into the post-war period.

Rather than issuing broad confessions or platitudinous affirmations, the Oxford report began with a sense of tension between the gospel and the world, observing, 'In the midst of such a world, torn and disrupted and feverishly seeking a way out of its troubles, the church of Jesus Christ has to preach its message and fulfil its task.' It then asks, 'What is it to say? How is it to act? What are individual Christians to believe and do?'[36] True to the description of Gustafson, that the approach is analytical, and of Abrecht, that its starting-point is theology, the report seeks to draw implications from Christian resources to bear on the reality of the world situation. From the outset there is a clear acknowledgement of the church's collective responsibility and the individual Christian's responsibility to respond to issues of universal significance.

The theological basis of what follows is plainly laid out: the call to penitence and faith is described, and ethical direction sought from God in his self-revelation given supremely in Jesus Christ. Further, it is stated in contrast to the social primacy at Stockholm, that 'the first task of the church, now as always, is to make known the gospel, and to assert the claim of Jesus Christ as the incarnate Word of God to the lordship of all human life.'[37] Here we see ethical

---

[34]Richard D. N. Dickinson, 'Changing Ecumenical Perspectives on Economic Development: A contribution to an on-going discussion,' *Development Assessed: Ecumenical Reflections and Actions on Development* (WCC Unit III Justice, Peace and Creation, Geneva, 9-12 January 1995), 24.

[35]Van der Bent, *Commitment to God's World,* 16-17. Cf. W. A. Visser't Hooft, *The Ten Formative Years 1938-1948* (Geneva: WCC, 1948), 28.

[36]Section I; 1. The World Today.

[37]Section I; 2. The Call to the Church.

reflection being firmly rooted in Christian categories, which affirm the universality of human existence, and the need for particular response to the preaching of the gospel. The report proceeds to describe the permeation of human life by sin - including the life of the church - and the resulting tension for individual Christians who seek to make difficult ethical choices in a world characterized by ambiguity

> The difficulties arise in the main because the Christian finds himself called upon at every point to act in relation to systems or frameworks of life which partake of both good and evil; they are of God and yet also of human sin. The orders of family, community, people, nation, are part of the God-given basis and structure of human life without which the individual would have no existence at all; yet man's sin - his pride, greed, fear, idolatry - has infected them all. Hence the Christian who has seen the perfect will of God in Christ and would serve that will in the midst of his fellow men finds himself in perpetual tension and conflict. He accepts thankfully his community in order to live and to work in it and for it; yet if he would work in it and for it for Christ he must be in continuous protest against it.[38]

The tension facing each individual, and the ambiguity resulting from how to live out Christian truth in a complex world is not only spoken of in the report, but is also reflected in the amount of discussion and preparatory work which characterized and preceded the conference. In other words, it was contained not only in what the conference participants said, but how they approached the ecumenical ethics task from the outset.

The need for diligent, constant, and consistent study and dialogue was highlighted by the method advocated by the report, which was to be humble, reflective, and open to revision. The report stated, 'The difficulty of deciding how far in particular instances Christians should go in cooperation with ways of life which are in greater or less degree contrary to God's will is often great, and the danger of self-deception is always present. No general principle of guidance can be laid down.' Rather, the 'tragic and continuous tension...between the pure ideals of the kingdom and the unredeemed community of men in which it has to live and bear its witness' must be embraced and endured. Surrendering the difficulty of tension is traitorous to Christ. There can be no easy way to do Christian social ethics, and they will always be characterized by a provisional nature. The hand of Niebuhr is particularly evident here, as the report indicates, 'Where [the church] must join in what it feels to be a partial approach to the perfect will of Christ, it must keep its spirit sensitive and humble by continual acknowledgement before God of the sin of mankind which is wresting the gifts of God to evil ends, and in which it is itself implicated.'[39]

J. H. Oldham's description of 'middle axioms' does not feature in this part

---

[38]Ibid.
[39]Ibid.

of the report, but is presupposed by it. This is confirmed in an outline of the approach in the volume *The Church and Its Function in Society,* produced as part of the Oxford process.[40] The idea was that no universally-valid principles could be laid down for all time, nor could individual Christians be excused from moral responsibility, much less abdicate such responsibility by being directed to action by church hierarchies. Thus there was a need for provisional definitions of ethical behaviour, in between the demands of the gospel and the particularities of a specific situation. This idea is reflected in the report, which seeks to describe generally what the Christian attitude should be in various contexts. It manages, therefore, to preserve the responsibility of the individual agent while acknowledging the complexities and perplexities of collective life.

The report further recognizes the multiplicity of collectives that participate in the wider sphere of human existence. It affirms nationhood and race as gifts of God, whilst warning these may too easily provide vehicles for the extension of sinful egoism.[41] Based on this theological premise, an early and prophetic recognition of the potential for human sin to be expressed in movements of equality and liberation is found in the report. It states, 'Many voices in all nations are lifted in these days in favor of a more just international order and the removal of inequalities of opportunity. The achievement of the practical results can only be retarded if through the overeagerness of some the impression is created that equality of opportunity is sought not as an end in itself but as a means of reversing in their favor inequalities such as now exist.'[42] The realist rejection of idealist premises is evident, and complete.

The report does not leave churches, individuals, and groups in a state of morally paralysed cynicism, however. The theological underpinnings of the method make it clear that 'No international order which can be devised by human effort may be equated with the kingdom of God. Much of the disillusionment about international affairs to be found among Christians is due to the fact that the hopes vested in specific schemes for international betterment were of an almost religious quality, and it was forgotten that to all human institutions clings the taint of sin.' Nevertheless, 'it is erroneous to hold that our hope in the kingdom of God has no bearing upon the practical choices that men must make within the present order. The attitude of Christians toward specific proposals in the political sphere should be governed by their obedience to the living God and their understanding of his purpose in Christ.'[43] The moral responsibility of individuals, social groups, and states is upheld by a view that recognizes a difference in the quality of responsibility between such moral

---

[40]See W. A. Visser't Hooft and J. H. Oldham, *The Church and Its Function in Society* (London: George Allen and Unwin, 1937), 233-254.
[41]Section I; 2, a & b.
[42]Section V; 5. The Conditions of Peaceful Change.
[43]Section V; 3. The Kingdom of God and the International Order.

agents, but sees all as being 'under the judgment of God.'[44]

In its development of concepts and statements from a precise theological basis, and in its clear method of argumentation, the period represented by this document presents a very different approach from the prophetic style. It acknowledges tension between the ideal and the particularities of temporal life, and the difficulty, if not impossibility, of many individuals and groups arriving at the same moral prescriptions. Indeed, there is no possibility of a universal moral consciousness, since loyalties are divided and competitive. The method recognizes that the individual is the basic moral agent, but that the individual has membership in various groups, sometimes with competing interests. Nevertheless, the individual remains accountable to God for moral actions. Starting with theological categories and moving out to the world, asking the question, 'What is to be done?' reflects a realist view of moral truth, and a method that is essentially deontological. Without a doctrine of the church in relation to the world, however, there is a danger of slipping into a utilitarian ethic.

The close relationship of this approach to the position advocated by Niebuhr, and discussed previously, obviates the necessity to analyse in detail the theological and philosophical significance of the presuppositions of this ethical method. Suffice is to say that a view of humanity as sinful - a reality compounded in social life - had permeated the dominant attitude, and the dialectical tension of human existence was widely recognized. The desire to start ethical reflection with the revelation of God and move out to the world reflected a reassertion of God's transcendence, which reaffirmed the fact that all human efforts sat under his eschatological judgement.

Gustafson discerned that while the ethical type of discourse is very good at clarifying concepts and arguing logically with precision, 'in comparison with prophetic discourse it does not often locate the root of a problem or evoke a hopeful vision. Nor does its language have much motivating capacity.'[45] It would seem the matter of motivation entails a somewhat subjective judgement, but ethical moral discourse certainly lacks the exhortative quality of its prophetic cousin. At the same time, it avoids high platitudes and broad, baseless assertions. Considering its catholic method of debate and dialogue, it would seem that this approach managed a better balance of inclusiveness than its predecessor, which would account for its reputation as a most comprehensive and valuable statement of Christian social concern. In the words of Abrecht

> compared with the results of Stockholm, those of Oxford could be defined as a theological-ethical revolution, a challenge to the social-ethical misapprehensions of early forms of social idealism and the beginning of new Christian confidence in dealing with the intransigent problems of modern political and economic

---

[44]Ibid.
[45]Gustafson, 'An Analysis,' 270.

life....Thus Oxford marked the beginning of a new partnership between Christian theologians and ethicists on the one side and on the other side, social scientists, professions, working together to relate the faith to the world.[46]

This 'theological-ethical revolution' was to continue, and become enhanced in the next era of ecumenical cooperation on social ethics.

Policy Discourse and Realist Discontent

It is difficult not to choose a statement from the Amsterdam meeting in 1948 as representative of the next phase of ecumenical work in social ethics, described as policy discourse. However, all of the documents leading up to Amsterdam, and most resulting from the conference, reflected an extension of the method just examined.[47] But some of the questions and challenges that emerged from the conference built upon and enhanced the foundations laid at Oxford, so that a distinction between ethical and policy discourse could soon be made. The differences were well-entrenched by the 1950s, and the policy-style approach would dominate until the Fourth Assembly of the WCC at Uppsala in 1968, and would not completely disappear in the years following. Nor could the process itself be described as static. According to Abrecht, 'throughout this period the WCC was obliged to examine radically new propositions about economic justice and political order. The "policy discourse" thus constantly expanded.'[48]

Hence, the process of deliberation which led to the development of the Responsible Society documents broadened throughout the 1950s and 60s. By the time of the conference at Geneva in 1966, the method was widely inclusive, drew on the expertise of lay experts from around the world, and was far more oriented towards identifying policy specifics than highlighting competing views and tensions. As the method became more relevant to the world and its general social situation, the theological foundations of the system, though present, seem to have become more general in nature while the ethical policies became more specific.

The Reports that were presented at the World Conference on Church and Society at Geneva in 1966, included Sections I and II entitled, *Economic Development in a World Perspective* and *The Nature and Function of the State,* respectively. These reports will be considered here together with *The Report of the Working Group on Theological Issues and Social Ethics,* which provides an explicit statement of the theological reflections that fed and emerged from the conference. They are broadly representative of the policy approach, and reveal the difficulties of wrestling with a burgeoning revolutionary movement.

---

[46]Abrecht, 'Competing Forms of Discourse,' 37.

[47]Moreover, the Amsterdam conference was considered briefly in relation to Niebuhr's method in the previous chapter.

[48]Abrecht, 'Competing Forms of Discourse', 39.

The Report of Section I notes firstly that the discussions centred on 'the many and increasingly rapid advances in technology and economic organization which will continue to produce fundamental economic change with profound social and personal consequences in all countries, whatever their ideological and political forms.'[49] The desire to harness these advances for the 'common good' was the broader focus. The report thus called for further theological study to address the diverse understandings of 'the "human" as a criterion for judging economic and social change.'[50] Making reference to the development of this idea within the notion of Responsible Society, yet noting a contemporary diversity and disagreement on the issue, the report took into explicit account the nature of humanity in its personal, national, and universal expressions. This perspective was derived from a theological affirmation of the revelation of God in Jesus Christ, which points to the example and work of Christ, recognizing the image of God in each human, and bringing together a community of Christian fellowship. The report therefore calls for a wider representation of lay expertise to nurture the formation of national communities 'wider than family, clan or tribe, and conscious of regional and international ties.' In this respect, the church has a particular role to play: 'Enlightened self-interest has its part to play in serving the common good, but the task of the Church is to help to work out the common good, and constantly to stimulate the national and individual conscience.'[51] Here the church is seen as having an intermediary role, seeking to balance the interests of the individual and the broader collective.

In this document, the complexity of reaching solutions for the problems raised was acknowledged, and the ambiguity of the future for social ethics was indicated. Nevertheless, a note of optimism was sounded in the final paragraph, which confessed: 'We do not know how far the radical ethic of the kingdom of God can be realised on earth.' However, 'We do know that God appears to have set no limits to what may be achieved by our generation, if we understand our own problems aright and desire to obey in our circumstances.' The tension of competing approaches becomes almost tangible in the caveat of the final line: 'It is God who changelessly rules all change. The Church points to him and creates a stillness where his voice can be heard; when it is heard there is courage to encounter change, love to redeem knowledge, and patience to preserve order or to live responsibly in the midst of revolution.'[52]

The report of Section II goes into much greater detail regarding special issues of Christian participation. The contribution of social scientists and economists becomes quite apparent here, as concerns for constitutionality and revolution, violence, and minority rights are expressed. There is a real sense

---

[49]Section I, para 1.
[50]Section I, para 2.
[51]Section I, para 3.
[52]Section I, para 10.

that the participants started with a view of the world and attempted to work back to policy recommendations for churches and individuals who were involved directly and indirectly with what were admittedly complex issues. In relation to the call of Section I for the churches to foster a common consciousness, Section II affirmed this call, but balanced the integration of minorities into national life with an affirmation of cultural variety and individual freedom.[53] Despite the policy recommendations made, which seem marginally more specific than earlier 'middle axioms', the report was bound to generate controversy. Recognizing that 'These pragmatic decisions are difficult, and the varying conditions in different countries...will necessarily influence the decisions,' ongoing dialogue between differing groups was strongly encouraged 'for the sake of fuller integration of all' into the common life of nations.[54]

The theological reflection that supported these reports is more clearly stated in the *Report of the Working Group on Theological Issues and Social Ethics.* The document affirms early its relation to the questions posed by previous ecumenical groups regarding the relationship between God's salvation history and human activity in the world. But it immediately makes a break with the approach of Amsterdam and Evanston by claiming, 'Today however, the question has been posed anew, and must be answered anew in the rush of human events.'[55] Ideological developments on the world stage left the participants feeling that 'Previous religious and secular ideologies of social change and historical development have largely lost their comprehensive power to explain and guide the action of men.' Together with the rise of revolutionary impulses, participation of many world cultures, and acceleration of technological development, this change in thought led the participants to start with an assessment of what was happening in the world, akin to Gustafson's description of the primary question asked by policy-style discourse - 'What is going on?' There is no real verification that what the participants suggest is going on is, in fact, occurring. Still, they proceed to consider the context of faith in the light of what God is doing in the world.[56] In this respect, the focus is no longer simply on the word of God, but his activity in human existence. This renewed emphasis on God's immanence is accompanied by an interpretation of biblical categories in light of contemporary human experience. 'Christian theology is prophetic only in so far as it dares, in full reflection, to declare how, at a particular place and time, God is at work, and thus to show the Church where and when to participate in his work,' declares the report.[57] In this sense, the discourse reflects an essentially teleological ethic.

---

[53]Section II, para 86.
[54]Section II, para 87.
[55]*Report of the Working Group on Theological Issues and Social Ethics,* para 13.
[56]Ibid., para 18.
[57]Ibid, para 23.

But the approach attempts to maintain a distinct role for the church in society as it reminds participants that ethical action remains constantly under the judgement of God, and thus, 'there are only relative, secular structures subject to constant revision in the light of new human needs.' At the same time, God appears to be taking sides as his action 'is continually reshaping the order of human power, humiliating the proud and the rich and lifting up the oppressed.' The employment of contemporary jargon continues as the cross of Christ becomes 'the ultimate judgment on a self-protecting *status quo*,' and the Church emerges as 'the pilgrim people of God' whose calling 'is a continuing challenge to the securities of this world.'[58] Despite a move away from the attitude of humility that characterized earlier conferences, the report affirms that 'revolutions are also under the judgement when they make their cause absolute and promise final salvation.'[59] Further, there is a confirmation of eschatological hope in God's ultimate victory, just as God raised Christ 'from the death to which perverted human power put him,' thus 'Christians are called to work to transform human society at every point in the hope that God will use their work whether they succeed or fail.'[60] Ultimately, it is the task of theology to focus not on theories, but on action, and to interact with contemporary ideologies, offering support and correction.[61] The notion that it possibly could do both is not considered.

In general terms, the composition of the conference at Geneva was noted for its breadth of participation, and depth of expert reflection. It was the first ecumenical conference in which the 'third world', the Orthodox, Roman Catholic observers, and lay economists and social scientists were well represented.[62] This composition was reflected in the types of issues singled out for concern, and in the desire to confront and discuss issues of mutual importance with honest Christian reflection, drawing on the best resources possible to make the conclusions accurate and relevant. Thus the conference was prevented from 'taking refuge in theological abstractions.'[63]

Gustafson has noted the strengths and weaknesses of this type of approach. 'Policy discourse seeks to determine what is desirable within the constraints of what is possible,' he writes. 'At its best it is written from the standpoint of responsible agents and not external observers, i.e. it assumes the position of responsibility within enabling and limiting conditions. The range of necessary

---

[58]Ibid., para 19.

[59]Ibid., para 20.

[60]Ibid., para 21.

[61]Ibid., para 25.

[62]See, for example, Ronald Preston, 'A Breakthrough in Ecumenical Social Ethics?' in *Technology and Social Justice: An International Symposium on the Social and Economic Teaching of the World Council of Churches from Geneva 1966-Uppsala 1968,* ed. Ronald Preston (London: SCM Press, 1971), 15-40.

[63]Ibid., 16.

information and knowledge is broad; the assessment of power to affect change is crucial; the time frame for the achievement of ends is generally shorter and technical considerations are more prominent.' Yet, because it begins by asking what is going on in the world, this type of discourse 'necessarily works within limited visions, limited frames of reference. It accepts conditions which from prophetic and ethical perspectives might be judged to be morally wrong, or at least inadequate. The ethical informs but does not determine the choices of the policy-maker in most circumstances.' [64]

In specific terms, the report displays a certain degree of balance in its understanding of human individuals and collectives, though little direct discussion of the individual is present. In its method, it is inclusive of differing voices both in identifying and addressing issues of socio-ethical importance. But here we also see hints of possible difficulties that may arise when a method begins by looking at the world and asking what God is doing in it. It involves ruggedly subjective judgements, and magnifies, rather than harmonizes, differences in perspective and opinion. In this sense, moral truth is revealed through God's immanence, and the focus for human reflection is *praxis* rather than *doxa*. Asking what is going on may be a necessary question for an ethical method that seeks to be contemporary and relevant. But asking what God is doing in the world is quite another question, fraught with paralysing theological and philosophical ambiguities, or false certainties.

While acknowledging the reality of pluralism both in the composition of the meeting and in its method, the participants at Geneva were, for the time being, addressing areas of difference and recommending further study. At the same time, dissenters from both left and right expressed disappointment with the outcome of the conference. Not everyone was happy with what went on at Geneva. At least one participant took great exception to the attempt to speak not only *to* the churches, but *for* the churches on contentious political issues. Paul Ramsey elaborated his critique in a methodological way in a book following the conference, but there is no evidence his suggestions received great attention in subsequent WCC work on social ethics.[65]

On the other hand, the word *revolution* was very much in the air, both in sacred and secular realms, and 'Some of the new participants in ecumenical discussion of social issues, especially the youth and students were impatient with the deliberative style of ethical and policy discourse.'[66] Richard Schaull, a professor, missionary, and student leader wrote a paper which was widely circulated after Geneva, calling for theology to serve the revolutionary impulse by historicizing itself, and lending resources of transcendence to its temporal

---

[64]Gustafson, 'An Analysis,' 270.

[65]Paul Ramsey, *Who Speaks for the Church?* (Nashville: Abingdon, 1967). Ramsey's basic contention was that no body such as the WCC should or could presume to speak *for* the churches.

[66]Abrecht, 'Competing Forms of Discourse,' 39.

struggle, especially if utopianism is to be avoided. 'In recent years,' he wrote, 'there has been some discussion as to whether ecumenical social thought should give attention primarily to principles, values and middle axioms, or become contextual, or allow one to be a corrective to the other. The discussion in these terms will, I believe, produce very meagre results. Perhaps our task at this moment is to recognize this fact of the radical historicizing of all our thought, and work through the theological implications of it, allowing it to lead us where it will.'[67] The calls for revolution and liberation which were heard most loudly at Geneva for the first time, would lead to a method of action-reflection, which yielded similar forms of discourse as those that characterized the earlier idealist period at the beginning of the century.

Prophetic and Narrative Discourse and the Rejection of Realism

Our selection of texts brings us next to the *Larnaca Declaration,* which emerged from the WCC World Consultation on Diakonia in 1986. Though a more extensive meeting produced a report on the WCC Conference on Faith, Science, and the Future at MIT Boston in 1979, there was little new said in it, and it represented the last of weighty study documents produced by the WCC on issues of social ethics.[68] Many documents emerging before and after MIT had a particularly optimistic outlook regarding the transforming potential of revolutionary struggles. Larnaca, on the other hand is clearly representative of a shift toward a more prophetic-narrative style of discourse, which increasingly permeated WCC documents. It differs from earlier prophetic discourse, such as that which characterized the Stockholm meeting, in that it carries far more indictment than utopian thought, though an eschatological hope remains at the centre.

As a declaration, rather than a report, the statement does not provide a great deal of theological analysis, or specific practical direction. It speaks in broad and general terms, but even in this context, its theological statement is significant; at least as much for what it leaves out as what it includes. There is an affirmation of the unity of the human race: 'We are called to be neighbours to one and all;' a brief statement that Jesus Christ is Lord; and the acknowledgement that 'God's kingdom is one of Trinitarian sharing of love.' God is described as having 'ultimate ownership over matter and energy' but God's 'spiritual and material resources belong to all people and all must have a say in their use.' An increased association of God with nature is detectable, as God is described as 'manifest through all creation,' a trend which Ronald

---

[67]Richard Shaull, 'The Revolutionary Challenge to Church and Theology,' *PSB* 60 (1966): 25, 29-32, cited in Kinnamon and Cope, *Ecumenical Movement*, 299-303; 301-2.

[68]Preston, *Confusions,* 35ff; Abrecht, 'Competing Forms of Discourse,' 43.

Preston has consistently noted.[69] Further, there is a call to 'follow in the footsteps of the suffering servant, Christ our Lord.' Despite a confirmation of victory over death, the statement is decidedly not utopian, but is characterized by solidarity with the poor.

Statements of indictment against militarization, hunger, poverty, and oppression are general in nature, and there are neither theological justifications offered for statements made, nor descriptions of means by which the desired ends will be achieved. The call for solidarity means the declaration addresses sin in its collective forms, and attributes sin to structures and systems of churches and society, rather than to individuals. There is no acknowledgement of plurality, but a clearly implied sense of what constitutes sin, and what the Christian response should be. Any sense of tension arising from the difficulty of applying Christian truth to real situations is not present, only a bold call to action: 'As Christians, we must act, and act now, to ensure a decent life with dignity for all. Economic and social structures which perpetuate inequality and poverty must be replaced by a new international economic order and political structure,' which will ensure participation by all people.

The call for solidarity, while recognizing the collective element of human existence, ignores the moral tensions that can emerge between the conflicting interests of individuals and the various groups of which they claim membership. It affirms the unity of creation, but blurs the distinction between the church and other elements of society, identifying the kingdom of God perhaps too closely with activities which are not only ambiguous, but platitudinous and void of self-criticism. The renewed stress on the immanence of God renders truth as 'in-the-making'. As such, Christians participate in, rather than understand or bear witness to truth. These themes follow ecumenical deliberations on ethical issues through to the conclusion of the Justice, Peace and Integrity of Creation conciliar process, which issued a document of ten ethical affirmations, focusing particularly on the relationships inherent in creation, and the integrity of the natural order.

This document highlights some shifts in approach away from the more detailed policy-style discourse, but does not really reflect Gustafson's description of narrative discourse. Narrative discourse does not appear as frequently as other types in official reports and documents, but is widely seen in preparatory documents, studies, and publications of the WCC. One example of narrative discourse is seen in the address of Leslie Boseto, one of eight presidents of the WCC, to the assembly at the Fifth International Consultation of United and Uniting Churches at Potsdam, 1987.[70] In the paper entitled,

---

[69]Preston, *Confusions,* 37. Preston writes that even at MIT 'the question of our attitude to 'nature' was gaining ground. There is a reference to 'ecological liberation' and to the oppression of the earth. God links himself in solidarity with us; so must we do in solidarity with nature. Much more of this would be heard in the next decade.'

[70]Leslie Boseto, 'Address,' Kinnamon and Cope, eds., *Ecumenical Movement,* 454.

People are Security, he begins by sharing the experience of his Melanesian society, giving a personal account of family and village life. From this story, he makes a jump rather than a journey from the particular to the universal, using his experiences to draw conclusions and make assertions about socio-ethical life in general.

In his village, he says, people depend on people. Thus, 'when people arrive from outside a village they are freely given firewood and food, are loaned mats and are well accepted. There are no hotels or motels at the grassroots! There are no banks and life insurance schemes!' Since people depend on people in his experience, so must God depend on people. 'You may say that this is not theologically correct because God is always complete within us. But confessing the incarnation, that God became a human being in order to recreate and renew humanity means recognizing his dependence and security in people.' Previously significant themes such as God's transcendence, aseity, and the atonement are not present, as they are not accessed through his particular experience. Bringing his local context to the Scriptures allows him to reinterpret them according to his own story. From there, very broad assertions are made without justification, such as this: 'A new community which is grounded and rooted in Jesus Christ and his new commandment to love one another does not need nuclear weapons for its security. The main problem as far as I can see today is that people do not trust people. Hence our modern society's security is not rooted and grounded in people but in temporary, artificial systems and structures.' The discourse then merges with the prophetic style, as it proceeds to offer indictment against western churches and other human institutions, which by consequence of their geographical location, find their security 'in economic systems which continue to support a wealthy, powerful minority.'

In other documents, there may be found further examples of pure narrative being employed as stories are shared without broader implications being drawn out in specific ways. In Gustafson's view, 'The particular strength of narrative moral discourse is its specificity, concreteness, or absence of high-level distraction. It takes seriously the communal character and the historic traditional character of the Church. It gives continuity and shape to the moral ethos of the community.' Moreover, it sustains 'memory of the founding events of the church and of its continued life of both unfaithfulness and faithfulness.' But it 'is not as easy to move from the Christian story to answer the question of what ought to be done in issues of intervening into nature as some persons might think.'[71] Based on my contention in the present work, that these types of

---

[71]Gustafson, 'An Analysis,' 273. Stanley Hauerwas and L. Gregory Jones have taken exception to Gustafson's analysis on this point, suggesting that he oversimplifies and thus distorts the role of narrative in theology and ethics. They further criticise Gustafson for ignoring the epistemological implications and issues of personal identity in a narrative approach. However, since Gustafson's focus is on discourse rather than

discourse represent theological and philosophical presuppositions about the nature of ethics, I would suggest that it is not only difficult to move from narrative discourse to specific directions for ethical action, but impossible. This argument will be developed further in subsequent chapters.

From this particular document, however, we see that the narrative approach begins with a particular context, and an individual experience of that context, and universalizes the experience to the rest of humanity. It recognizes the importance of the church community and the local society as factors in moral formation, but does not allow for dialogue amongst people on matters that might cause division. It encourages only a telling of stories, which may be useful for exhortative or homiletical purposes, but precludes dialogue on specific issues, since one can only be true to one's own experience or context.[72] Implicit in this approach is a rejection of problem-solving approaches, which involve reason and debate in the ethical pursuit.[73] Moral truth is not revealed, demonstrated, or accessed, but formed in each local context. There are significant implications for the relationship between the church and the individual, and the church and the world, and the question of relativity rather than plurality moves to the fore. No tension within individuals as moral agents who embody competing interests and loyalties is acknowledged, nor is the complexity of relating faith to issues of common concern. Similarly, God as a transcendent reality ceases to exist, since God becomes realized as humans move in relationship to one another and the rest of creation.[74]

Turning to the questions we asked at the outset of this chapter, it remains to be considered which particular method represented by the types of discourse outlined here is best able to reconcile the variety of methods present. Gustafson may be right that the varieties of discourse do not necessarily conflict and that there is room in social ethics for each type, but this can be true only when their purpose is clear within a shared method. For as this study has revealed, the types of discourse used tend to reflect theological and philosophical assumptions which are difficult, if not impossible, to reconcile. Methods

---

philosophical method, it is difficult to see this as a sustainable critique of his observations. See Stanley Hauerwas and L. Gregory Jones, eds, *Why Narrative? Readings in Narrative Theology*, Grand Rapids: Eerdmans, 1989, 2-5.

[72]Any visitor to the WCC website in the latter part of the year 2000 was welcomed with the contemporary slogan, 'Your Story is Our Story,' reaffirming the methodological projection of the particular to the universal.

[73]Cf. Keith Clements, *Learning to Speak: The Church's Voice in Public Affairs* (Edinburgh: T&T Clark, 1995).

[74]Despite this criticism, much positive feedback has resulted from the 'Sikoni' process used during recent WCC meetings in Kenya. However, though broad participation, sense of inclusiveness, and sharing of stories may be therapeutic and cathartic, there is no evidence that any kind of decision for action acceptable by consensus or majority has been achieved through such a process. Gustafson's caveat that we need to be clear what we hope to achieve through each type of moral discourse is particularly relevant here.

require more than a clarification of language, since they embody a complex web of philosophical, theological, and practical considerations and influences. Nevertheless, when certain parameters for ethics are employed, we are able to distinguish between the potential of each method to have a unifying practical outcome based on the clarifying role of its philosophical presuppositions, and the verifying role of its theology.

Ethical Integrity

If we are to make any sense of the moral world as Christians, and not retreat from the challenge of social and political existence; if we are to maintain the centrality of Christian doctrine, while acknowledging the prevalence of post-modern challenges to the way the church thinks about and lives out its convictions, then there is need of a method which takes such challenges seriously, and meets them with confidence, if not perfection. Such a method, which does justice to the philosophical aspects of ethical existence, wrestles with its challenges, ideas, and ambiguities, and yet grounds moral philosophy firmly in historically and biblically conditioned theological categories. It would not necessarily revitalize the ethical pursuit, but at very least would provide a resting place on the way, and post a few directional arrows, offering the hope of a brighter future for Christian social ethics. Holding together various considerations, demonstrated to be of crucial importance to the present task, leads to the pursuit of a method of *integrity*.[75] Developed from the work of Alan P. F. Sell, integrity points towards the kind of method by which the work of social ethics may be undertaken with philosophical honesty, and theological wholeness.[76] As a means of drawing together the most important considerations of method highlighted thus far, an outline of what integrity entails will be helpful as we seek to move forward from here.

Sell acknowledges from the outset the ambiguous nature of the term 'integrity,' reinforcing its value for the present task, which is of necessity

---

[75]The requirement that ethics demonstrate integrity has been noted by various thinkers with only brief comment. The understanding of integrity offered here stands independent of Stanley Grenz's description in his surprisingly subtitled, *The Moral Quest: Foundations of Christian Ethics* (Leicester: Apollos, 1997), 230-2. Grenz puts forth briefly a rather more communitarian version of integrity than is here implied. Cf. Alisdair MacIntyre, *After Virtue*, 2nd ed. (London: Duckworth, 1985), 203. MacIntyre describes the 'virtue' of integrity as a quality within a given moral tradition. The plea for integrity in the present work is to be distinguished from other approaches to integrity that have been put forth in some related disciplines.

[76]This method is not put forth by Sell *per se*, but may be deduced from several of his works, including a consideration of his own method of approaching ethics, philosophy, and theology. It is most specifically developed from his work, *Aspects of Christian Integrity* (Louisville, KY: Westminster/John Knox Press, 1990), where he defines and engages the matter of methodological integrity directly.

ambiguous. Comprised of the 'principal meanings' of 'honesty and wholeness,' integrity is not regarded as 'a uniquely Christian virtue or characteristic.'[77] Nevertheless, when applied within and without the Christian task, integrity is able to provide a helpful framework for moving through the paralysing effects of ambiguity in Christian social ethics. Integrity is able to do justice to ambiguity by acknowledging its inevitability, and its effects, and also by clarifying ambiguity's limits. In our most honest moments, theologians must admit to a less-than-perfect appropriation of the truth of the gospel in attempting to apply it to real and complex situations. Yet, confessing that our moral apprehension is limited is not the same as saying there can be no apprehension at all. Integrity reminds us that the wholeness of Christian faith, doctrine, philosophy, and history, provides sufficient resources for renewing our confidence in the ethical task. Although Sell does not outline his approach to integrity in a systematic fashion, for the purposes of this study, the aspects of Christian integrity derived from his work will be grouped into three categories: theological verity; philosophical clarity; and practical unity.[78]

Theological Verity

A method of integrity challenges our subjectivity, and conditions our objectivity by holding together several distinctive parameters, reminding us to be honest to our Christian faith and heritage. As such, theological integrity calls us to uphold the truth of Christianity as worthy of inquiry and commitment.[79]

Integrity leads us to consider the Bible as a reliable account of revelation, calling us to take seriously its teaching, and upholding its authority in the life of the believing community, and in the lives of individual Christians. It guards against the use of the Bible in dishonest ways, through unbalanced use of proof-texts and dismissal of the historical nature of revelation. Further, the reminder of wholeness leads us to handle the Bible with care, taking account of scholarly insights, and holding all of its teaching, and resulting doctrines, in careful balance.[80]

Integrity also reminds us that we, as individuals, are part of a community of faith, which is not simply a community in one place and time. Our theology is conditioned by the fact that we theologize as part of a community that is global in composition, and historical in nature. The Christian family reaches around the world, even as it extends backward and forward in time, linking inexorably the saints of old and the contemporary context. Faithful consideration of the

---

[77]Ibid., ix.

[78]This is not to suggest that Sell is unsystematic in his thought, rather that this book as a collection of papers delivered in various locations does not have the purpose of being a systematic exposition of the concept of 'integrity'.

[79]Sell, *Aspects*, 112, 117.

[80]Ibid., 9-12.

historic faith, and our position within that broad context, guards against rugged individualism, blind subjectivism, and false claims of objectivity.[81] It will render dialogue a necessity, because no single person or group can assume to be able to survey the whole at one time.

Just as a method of integrity takes into consideration the context in which theology will be applied, so it will point consistently to the content of the inclusive gospel of grace, which in Christ brings reconciliation and points to a future of hope, even as it serves as transcendent judge of all our contexts.[82] This will remind us that Christianity is, at its very heart, a Way- more specifically a Way of life- which cannot be fully explained in words, but which is lived out by real people in a real place and in a real time in history.[83] There are aspects of the journey that cannot be put into words but are simply apprehended through faith. This recognizes that the Christian faith is characterized by mystery, but does not seek to hide behind mystery and make no claims to truth whatsoever. Rather, thought and experience must hold together in our theology, just as they must in our philosophy.[84]

Philosophical Clarity

The things we learn from theological integrity demonstrate why, for Christians, philosophy must always be filtered through our theology and not vice-versa. Yet it also reminds us that, as historical characters, we are ever under the influence of philosophy and must use its concepts as a means of expressing our theological convictions, most especially when seeking to express them in action. But a method of integrity will seek to understand the way Christians have been influenced by philosophy and the manner in which it may best be appropriated for use in theology and ethics. It will further challenge an ethical method to be aware of its use of philosophical language, and most significantly to clarify that use in every manner possible, in order to limit the rather reckless ambiguities which may arise.

Integrity calls us, therefore, to recognize the provisional nature of our knowledge of truth, and the tentative nature of our programmes of ethical application. As our theology reminds us of the noetic effects of sin, and our consequent ability to see only part of the picture, it challenges us to remember further that our philosophical conclusions are subject to self-critical revision.[85] We are capable of such revision because of anthropological considerations, confirmed by a theology that proposes the reasonableness of Christian theology and philosophy, and the subsequent requirement that our ethical methods be

---

[81]Ibid., 9, 12-14.
[82]Ibid., 118f.
[83]Ibid., 15.
[84]Ibid., 32-3.
[85]Ibid., 15-16.

rational.[86] According to Sell, this means rendering our methods sensible, consistent, and capable of interaction with philosophy, discussing ways our theological terms are both like and unlike those used by philosophy.[87] The task of philosophical clarity will also test our ethical methods for order and internal consistency.

Practical Unity

With these considerations in place, ethical methods may be evaluated according to their ability to uphold the unity of the Christian church, despite disagreements that may arise over particular issues. Holding together Spirit, Word, and fellowship, integrity leads us to acknowledge that we may have differences within the body of Christ, without surrendering the grace of unity that has been granted in Christ. Maintaining unity even in diversity, good ethical practice will hold together the demand of the gospel with its gift, not separating the love of God from his holiness.[88] It will mean leaders will be mindful of those at the grassroots level, together with who they form the people of God.

The theological and philosophical aspects of integrity will condition ethical method by guarding equally against platitudinous positions and the mistrust that may arise between contextual factions. They will confront the ambiguous nature of every ethical procedure with an assurance of the gift of grace, which allows us to be content with a less-than-perfect answer to our moral dilemmas. They will support methods that involve dialogue, study, and a search for common ethical ground between individuals and groups. They will seek to take as much direct action as unity will allow, and be willing to rest in ambiguity when unity is at stake. But integrity will not be content with the sort of ambiguity that attempts a cover-up of truth. Integrity will encourage participants in moral decision-making to at least make clear what positions are available for Christians, thus recognizing their diversity, while making specific actions optional where opinions divide. It will therefore encourage as much practical action as unity will allow. Moreover, integrity will remind those employing Christian ethical methods that they must clarify their intentions as to whether they seek to represent the church to the world, or the world to the church, and uphold the importance of doing both. Finally, a method of integrity

---

[86]Ibid., 16-17.

[87]Ibid., 18-19. Sell warns against jumping on every new philosophical 'ism' and attempting to translate it into theology. He is known to point to an appropriate observation of A. N. Prior, who stated in reference to A. J. Ayer that '[T]here's no one so completely and hopelessly out of date as the conductor of the bandwagon that's just gone past.' A. N. Prior, 'Contemporary British Philosophy,' *Phil* 33 (October 1958): 361.

[88]Sell, *Aspects*, 74.

will clarify and understand the individual and collective nature of moral agency, and seek as much as possible to confirm human responsibility for the ethical task.[89]

When applying this method in the ethical task, we discover that some statements examined here reveal a compromise of, or ignorance of, Christian theological integrity. Some confuse creation and Creator, human and non-human creation, and Christ, church and world. Some are optimistic, while some are cynical. A method of integrity offers guidance across the theological spectrum, challenging us to consider at what point we may be compromising truth for unity, and at what point we may be no longer guarding the truth and simply becoming sectarian. Further we discover that some approaches and statements reveal a lack of philosophical clarity: confusing concepts and moral agents; employing or undermining reason, prioritizing context over theology. Some display a blatant disregard for unity, preferring ruggedly contextual, experiential, or platitudinous positions, to ones that seek to draw together the various strands of the Christian church. The need for a method of integrity quickly becomes apparent in such an atmosphere of confusion.

Moreover, many of these aspects embody concerns raised from the examination of the first two methods examined in the present study - Rauschenbusch's social gospel, and the study-dialogue approach of Niebuhr's Christian realism. It should be immediately clear which of these methods best survives the test of integrity. But the story of ecumenical ethics did not end with the period dominated by Niebuhrian realism. In fact, there are several other approaches that have made a home within the WCC. The two most significant methods in the WCC since the 1960s are reflected similarly in the types of discourse discussed earlier and will be considered in the following two chapters, generally evaluated according to their measure as methods of integrity.

The *action-reflection* model has been hinted at in the present chapter, though not described in detail, as has the method of *moral formation*. Can our theological and philosophical reflections demonstrate one method to be preferable to another, in terms of practical outcome, and maintaining the unity of the faith, even in the face of moral ambiguity? Given the fundamental nature of differences between them, the only method which seems to offer some promise of moving past the present impasse is one which embodies integrity, insofar as it: recognizes plurality, though not sheer relativity of the ethical task; fosters an understanding of individual and collective expressions of moral agency in balance; perceives a capacity for human relations between individuals, groups and universal humanity; understands the provisional nature of ethical statements and actions; employs the unique resources of Christianity

---

[89]Ibid., 66-68. Sell suggests that ethical integrity is best maintained when talk of collective responsibility is not allowed to obliterate the moral responsibility of the individual agent.

in the ethical task. Whether the *action-reflection* or the *moral formation* method is able to achieve this better than the *study-dialogue* approach remains to be seen. To such considerations we now turn.

CHAPTER 8

Evolution Meets Revolution: Some Philosophical and Theological Impulses in an Action-Reflection Method

Christ is not a good man merely, whom God seized and made an example for all time; in his life, rather, the Love that is supreme has stooped down to suffer in behalf of men. This and nothing else has broken the world's heart.

H. R. Mackintosh

A study department is an ethical requirement rather than a tactical support of action.

Egbert de Vries

Introduction

T. W. Manson suggested that there is a basic philosophical tension in ethics, which represents the difference between the Hebrew and Greek approaches to morality.[1] While environment (*polis*) is the primary ethical category for the Greek mind, covenant relationship is the primary category for the Hebrew. One begins with the external conditions for justice, established through a complex system of rights and privileges guaranteed for citizens. The other view begins with a relationship, established through revelation-response, where individuals are always an integral part of their particular and general communities, yet possessing moral agency in their own right. Within the religious community, moral solidarity is expressed as a familial relationship, and within the social-political context it is expressed in a relationship of neighbours.[2] The difference between these two approaches to ethics is manifested quite plainly in ethical debate: 'One party or group says: "If you want people to live better, you must improve their living conditions"; the other says: "If you want to improve conditions, you must have better people".'[3] Manson acknowledged the impossibility of adjudicating between these two positions, and in a spirit of integrity, suggested that both views form a significant part of the way Christians approach ethics.

It would seem that an inability or unwillingness to balance these two

---

[1]T. W. Manson, *Ethics and the Gospel* (London: SCM Press, 1960), 11-12.
[2]Ibid., 17.
[3]Ibid., 12.

approaches is reflected in the methods of social ethics that have dominated the ecumenical scene since the 1960s. While the study-dialogue method has not by any means disappeared, it has found more prominent expression in the Faith and Order movement, and in certain study projects than in the social thought of the WCC as a whole.[4] With the ascendancy of a new method of action-reflection, submersion of the individual moral agent beneath the collective became the inevitable result, with the subsequent imbalance of internal and external ethical approaches.

Emergence of a Method

While the study-dialogue method produced a broad consensus in approach to social ethics throughout the 1950s, it was enhanced as professionals with a broad range of expertise brought their insights to bear on contemporary issues. The realist desire to match Christian teaching with what was going on in the world did not always yield practical results, but the study process presented options for Churches and individuals, and readied them for action when opinion coalesced on particular issues.[5] As the method developed, so did confidence amongst certain leaders that the Church ought to provide a more powerful voice for the oppressed and voiceless in society.

The issue of racism found a marked degree of consensus in the WCC, and as it moved to the fore as an issue of justice, it was accompanied by a commitment to move beyond study and dialogue to meaningful action.[6] The potential for

---

[4]Ronald Preston, for example, notes that Faith and Order does not stand accused of the same neglect of the study-dialogue method as the Units responsible for Church and Society. See 'On to Harare: Social Theology and Ethics in the World Council of Churches,' *EpRev* (October 1998): 26. Preston writes that the accusation of being a 'propagandist body for certain views...does not apply to Faith and Order which has always pursued the policy of getting different confessional views accurately stated and bringing them into dialogue for all to learn from each.' As an aside, he also points out that 'The slowness of the process has led to some impatience with the method; the remedy is renewed pressure on church governing structures, not abandoning the method.'

[5]Even the hotly debated report from the Geneva conference in 1966 offered detailed options for action by individuals, churches, and wider groups. It is also interesting to note that the two documents most often cited as ideal representations of broad if not universal agreement on social issues, were not issued by official church bodies. Both the *Kairos* and *Barmen* declarations were issued by informal groups of theologians rather than institutional ecumenical organisations, which calls to mind H. Richard Niebuhr's discussion on the idea that something ceases to be a movement when it becomes institutionalised. See H. Richard Niebuhr, *The Kingdom of God in America*, 165-170, and especially 168.

[6]Paul Abrecht has suggested that an increased participation in the WCC of African-Americans who endorsed a programme of study and action against racism led the

positive action was demonstrated as groups found agreement on a notoriously unambiguous issue, and so confronted the methods that sought to wrestle with issues of moral ambiguity.[7] Paul Abrecht suggests that it was 'this new dynamic concern for racial justice together with the urgent demand for Christian involvement in the struggle for freedom and justice in the Third World which more than any other factor accounts for the revolutionary spirit arising within the ecumenical movement in recent years.'[8]

In this climate, it was not long before the post-war consensus began to crumble

> The development of the World Council's concern for social change seemed at first to require no new theological-ethical categories. But inevitably it became necessary to think in terms of theological perspectives for radical change, and to find a Christian interpretation of the emancipation of the new nations and of their efforts at nation-building. In contrast with the familiar ecumenical emphasis on gradual social change and reform, the inquiries in the new nations pointed to the rapid breakdown of old social systems and traditions and the need for political and economic systems and supporting rapid development. In contrast with western Christian thought which despite all its preoccupation with secularization was based on assumptions of a society still greatly influenced by Christian values and institutions, Christian social thinking in the new nations tended to emphasize the Christian contribution to a pluralistic social ethic which would promote human values in a national perspective.[9]

This meant, among other things, a shift in attitude towards a positive view of nationalism for younger states, which sometimes linked together nationalist and revolutionary movements as collective agents for development and economic

---

revolutionary impulse. 'The Development of Ecumenical Social Thought and Action,' *A History of the Ecumenical Movement 1948-1968*, 244-7.

[7]This is to say, revolutionaries rejected methods that accepted a degree of moral ambiguity so long as it suited them. Following the WCC Assembly at Uppsala, a great furore erupted over the reference to the use of violence in revolution, and much discussion took place over the use of the phrase 'morally ambiguous' to gloss over if not justify revolutionary methods. See *The Report of Section III on World Economic and Social Development* as adopted by the Fourth Assembly of the World Council of Churches, Uppsala 1968, Sect. III 'Political Condition of World Development,' para. 15.

[8]Abrecht, 'The Development of Ecumenical Social Thought and Action,' 247. A tendency in days of rapid social change seemed to be an acquisition of amnesia - those seeking to address issues of rapid social change sought after the advice of experts with a zeal that would indicate they often forgot that they were first and foremost members of the Christian church. Technical expertise may lend credibility to a Christian point of view, but it may neglect the specific resources that the church may bring to bear on issues of social and political significance. In other words, technical expertise must be held together with theological expertise.

[9]Ibid., 249.

transformation. The predominant outlook contrasted sharply with the extremely critical attitude toward nationalism previously advocated within the WCC, and was reinforced by a view of collective consciousness that once again gave individual moral agency a derivative role.[10] This fact reinforces a previous suggestion that ethical methods have consistently reflected the dominant philosophical and historical issues of their contemporary world.

Some Philosophical Considerations

Commitment to revolution as a means of social change represented a rejection of methods that wrestled with the ambiguous nature of ecumenical ethics. Moreover, it was clearly connected to the philosophical influence of Marxist economic analysis, which was finding popularity in those areas of the world in urgent need of change. The increased involvement of Third World Church leaders fostered an increasingly broad pluralism of ideas that competed to dominate the social justice agenda of the WCC. Although this provided rich resources for new approaches, it also tended to favour a radical commitment to action which revolutionary methods provided.[11] In its earliest days, the focus on rapid social change demonstrated great potential for including diverse voices while maintaining open and productive dialogue. But soon it became apparent that patience for dialogue and study was limited. Ans van der Bent noted that while the study-dialogue method continued to lead into the 1960s, 'several "offsprings" of Church and Society...were born, taking "action-reflection" as their model...and advocacy as their approach. This was clearly an outcome of the widening "community" in the ecumenical family as more and more churches in the South voiced their commitment and their understanding of the gospel on the basis of their experience with human anguish.'[12]

The study-dialogue method, which sought to develop a middle axiom approach from Christian principles, as a means of bridging the gap between revelation and contemporary concerns, was rejected by many who felt the approach to be inadequate. On the one hand, middle axioms were considered

---

[10]Cf. Surjit Singh, 'Nation and Race,' *Biblical Authority for Today: A World Council of Churches Symposium on 'The Biblical Authority for the Churches' Social and Political Message Today,'* eds., Alan Richardson and W. Schweitzer (London: SCM Press, 1951). In this article from early in the WCC's history, Singh uses the consensus reached on biblical interpretation to apply the Bible to the specific issue of nationalism and race. In a very short time, the ecumenical attitude toward nationalism would be characterised by a dramatic shift in tone.

[11]While the study-dialogue method would welcome pluralism as a necessary element of power balance in ethics, when the field became so crowded, inevitably the loudest voices would be the ones most clearly heard. Moreover, in the midst of confusion, those with a definite program were more likely to draw attention than those which advocated a less clear-cut approach.

[12]Ans van der Bent, *Commitment to God's World*, 55.

too general to be of relevance in any specific context; on the other they were seen as so specific that they became quickly outdated, and so were of only temporary use. Though this was precisely the point of the middle axiom approach, such negative perceptions failed to appreciate the usefulness of the realist method itself, and judged its effectiveness on immediate results. Moreover, the study-dialogue method itself was seen by some to be based on rationalist Enlightenment principles, which advocated at least a relative degree of moral autonomy of the Kantian variety. By this time, however, ethicists were 'facing the objection (from both philosophy and theology) that the autonomous approach in ethics is too individualistic. True, moral judgment can be generalized and argued, and these operations are universal criteria of the individual human reason, but we cannot automatically assume the presence of transcendental reason and freedom in the empirical individual,' summarizes Dietmar Mieth. 'Observations such as these recall Hegel's criticism of Kant's moral philosophy and the criticisms applied by the theologies of "orthopraxis" to the individualism and "imperialism" of European middle-class Enlightenment.'[13] Consequently, the search for a method based on *praxis* led many on a path quite far removed from that traversed by the realists.

In the period between WCC Assemblies at Vancouver in 1983 and Canberra in 1991, one study group discussed and reported on the methodology of the Sub-unit on Church and Society. The importance of action is especially highlighted

> Church and Society's distinctive methodology has been described as interactive, that is, existing moral/theological insights, and the perception of contemporary concrete issues, illumine and deepen one another. Early meetings of the working group, noting Church and Society's limited resources, stressed that this should not mean avoidance of any practical orientation. One of the meetings affirmed: 'The ecumenical movement has always understood that working for justice, peace and the integrity of creation involves the perpetual interaction of theory and praxis in the context of human needs.'[14]

The report emphasizes that the scope of the Sub-unit's work should not be identified with any single element, but with the inter-relatedness of theology, ethics, scientific and social analysis and action at local, national and international levels.

Some have questioned the degree of balance that has, in fact, been struck between the various elements of the method as it has been manifested in ecumenical ethics, pointing out the tendency for action to take precedence over

---

[13]Dietmar Mieth, 'Autonomy or Liberation - Two Paradigms of Christian Ethics?' *Concilium* 172 *The Ethics of Liberation - The Liberation of Ethics* (Edinburgh: T&T Clark, 1984), 89.
[14]*Report of the Central Committee to the 7ᵗʰ Ass of the WCC, Vancouver to Canberra 1983-1990*, ed. Tom Best (Geneva: WCC, 1990), 119.

reason and reflection.[15] In any case, it is clear that the ideology borrowed to support the method places *praxis* at the centre, with philosophical reflection and theology providing supplementary roles.

The Influence of Marxism and Liberation

Though Marxism alone does not provide the basis for the sort of liberation theology that tends to characterize the action-reflection method, its categories are especially suited to the revolutionary thrust of action-reflection ethics.[16] Some theologians have employed a Marxist critique of economics, developed a type of historical materialism from Hegel, and highlighted the themes of action, crisis, and revolutionary change in their development of liberation ethics. Using ideology as a hermeneutical framework, theology was rewritten in the context of experiences of poverty and oppression. In this context, the subsequent methodological subservience of reflection to action is not surprising. Nor are its implications anything short of 'revolutionary' for Christian theology and ethics.

Marxism was present in WCC ethical circles long before it served as a dominant ideology there. Demonstrating the acumen of his prophetic foresight, Reinhold Niebuhr was among the first ecumenists to address the issues of ecumenical social ethics and Marxism directly. In a paper for the Amsterdam conference in 1948, he suggested

> There is even now no possibility of bringing social stability and a measure of justice to an impoverished world if this conflict between Christianity and marxism is not resolved. In the whole of Europe there are forms of socialism which dread and abhor the totalitarian consequences of a consistent communism. They do not always recognise that this totalitarianism may be, not so much a corruption of the original marxism as the inevitable consequence of consistent marxist principles.[17]

True to form, Niebuhr could understand the conflict only through an ambiguous tension, suggesting

> The problem of how to maintain freedom under the intense and complex forms of social cohesion in modern technical society and how to achieve justice when freedom is maintained cannot be solved by any neat principles. It must be approached pragmatically from case to case and point to point. We know that it is possible to buy security at too great a price of freedom; and to maintain freedom

---

[15]Ans van der Bent, 55. Cf. Ronald Preston, *Confusions in Christian Social Ethics.*

[16]Gordon Harland indicates that while some liberation theologians reject Marxism, and others embrace it wholesale, he agrees with Barr that the majority position would tend to favour a 'critical appropriation' of Marxist thought for liberation theology. *Christian Faith and Society* (Calgary: University of Calgary Press, 1988), 65-6.

[17]Reinhold Niebuhr, 'God's Design and the Present Disorder of Civilisation,' *Man's Disorder and God's Design*, vol. 3, First Assembly of the WCC, Amsterdam 1948 (New York: Harper, 1949), 21-2.

at too great a price of insecurity has no solution for this problem. It ought, however, to be possible for a vital Christian faith to help people to see that both freedom and order are facets of the love commandment to which we must approximate; and also that such approximations under conditions of sin and law are bound to be imperfect in all human history. The conflict between order and freedom is perfectly resolved only in the Kingdom of perfect love which cannot be perfectly realised in history.[18]

Niebuhr later became more definite in his pronouncements, indicating that Marx's 'polemical version of political realism obscured all the complex interactions between the rational and the vital impulses, and the double consequence of social creation and social confusion in both impulses.' Thus, Marxism 'created an apocalyptic vision of social redemption, rather than an empirical analysis of complex and intricate relations of human and social impulses.' Niebuhr concluded that 'Marxist utopianism…is really an old form of religious self-righteousness, and combines…realism and idealism. Thus, Marxism is realistic about the human nature and behaviour of the "sinners", the competitors, the bourgeoisie, but it is idealistic about the "redeemed" group, in this case not the church or the chosen nation, but the Messianic class.'[19] Niebuhr's realism reminded ethicists of the historical limits of any programme of liberation or justice. Hence, the realists maintained a healthy scepticism of ideologies in general, and their approach would preclude the adoption of any ideology in particular.[20]

However, by the time of the Geneva conference in 1966, WCC documents began to reveal the expression of a more positive understanding of ideology, and in 1968 the WCC sponsored a small Christian-Marxist dialogue.[21] In Uppsala, just two years later, the new approach was making itself most apparent, though not everyone was ready to accept the ideological framework. One Orthodox theologian noted of the report that

> not only is a Marxist understanding of the dynamics of the historical process adopted here without one single word of Christian qualification, but no attempt is made to elucidate, in Christian terms, the notions of 'masses', 'people', 'oppressed people', etc. Nowhere is the gospel of reconciliation and *love* mentioned, nowhere is to be found the hope that Christianity may transcend the divisions of the world….There can be no doubt therefore that the fundamental ideological presuppositions of the Report are overtly Marxist, and that this was

---

[18]Ibid., 22-3.

[19]Reinhold Niebuhr, *Man's Nature and His Communities: Essays on the Dynamics and Enigmas of Man's Personal and Social Existence* (London: Geoffrey Bles, 1966), 27.

[20]See Ans van der Bent, 96-106.

[21]See Ibid., 98-100. Ans van der Bent indicates that little progress was made after Uppsala. Even when the topic was raised at the Nairobi Assembly, participants were not sufficiently prepared to discuss such a complicated topic at the level required.

accepted as a self-evident basis for the approach to the socio-economic area as a
dialectical view of history centred on the notion of 'struggle'.[22]

At their meeting in Hanover in 1988, the central committee of the WCC
'noted with great interest the developments in many Marxist-led societies
which have profound and positive implications for the life and witness of the
churches in these societies and the ecumenical community.' Without
questioning what the primary role of the churches should be, the committee
asked the units responsible to study and examine 'the economic and political
changes, the fresh approaches to ideological and philosophical issues and the
contribution of the churches towards the restructuring of the society.'[23]
Throughout the period, ideology so influenced the agenda that at least one
participant would make the suggestion that 'theology is reduced to a vague
minimum of motto or slogans considered as sufficient to justify the ideological
option of the World Council of Churches.' Secular ideology became 'thus an
inner norm for theology. *Theologia ancilla ideologiae*.'[24] The influence of
Marxism was not embraced solely as an ideology, but often came to social
ethics filtered through the lens of liberation theology.

Many liberation theologians denied that their methods depend upon Marxist
ideology, insisting that, despite great affinity for Marxist doctrine, their
theology maintains a firm independence from it.[25] Nevertheless, since it became
so influential in the action-reflection method developing within the WCC, it is
illuminating to consider briefly how Marxism came to be used by liberation
theology in its approach to social ethics. Protestations aside, it may well be that
liberation theologians have relied more on Marxist dogma than they are
prepared to admit - a possibility which bears significant consequences for
ethical method.[26] The tendency to adopt ideological principles is not novel in

---

[22]Alexander Schmemann, 'Theology or Ideology?' *Technology and Social Justice,* ed.
Ronald Preston (London: SCM Press, 1971), 231-2.

[23]Minutes of the Central Committee of the WCC, Hanover, 1988, 93. Cf. van der Bent,
101.

[24]Schmemann, 'Theology or Ideology?' 228.

[25]The father of liberation theology, Gustavo Gutierrez has made this claim, as have
Leonardo and Clodovius Boff. Cited in Gordon Harland, *Christian Faith and Society,*
65. Nevertheless, in his most famous work, Gutierrez acknowledges the importance of
Marxism as a defining element of liberation theology. See Gustavo Gutierrez, *A
Theology of Liberation,* rev. ed., trans. and ed. Sister Caridad Inda and John Eagleson
(Maryknoll, NY: Orbis, 1988, [Originally published in Spanish in 1971]), 8.

[26]Most significant tensions over liberation theology in ecumenical circles have arisen
from the role of ideology in ethical and theological method, and so that aspect remains
the focus of discussion here. However, a fuller understanding of the development of
liberation theology may be found in the context of Catholic social teaching. See D. J.
O'Brien and T. A. Shannon eds., *Catholic Social Thought: The Documentary Heritage.*
(Maryknoll: Orbis, 1992); Michael Walsh and Brian Davies, eds., *Proclaiming Justice*

Christian social ethics in this period. Indeed, throughout the history of Christian thought, philosophy has been used to interpret and apply theology in various physical settings and intellectual contexts. As the present study continues to demonstrate, a problem for Christian ethics arises when philosophy serves not as a tool, but as the primary authority over the interpretation of revelation and the development of theology.

Alistair Kee, after tracing Marx's philosophical heritage through Hegel and Feuerbach, and looking towards the significance of his thought for liberation theology, suggested that

> the relevance of Marx for religion lies not in the specific remarks which he made on the subject, distributed throughout his works, but rather in the application of his general critical theories to the subject by experts in religion…it is possible to use Marx's general theory of alienation to expose the ways in which religion has contributed to oppression. More importantly it may be that Marx will also be suggestive when we ask how religion can contribute to the ending of alienation and the achievement of the truly human life.[27]

Though sympathetic, Kee reveals through his discussion that ideology serves as the key motif for the interpretation of human experience in liberation ethics.

Several aspects of Marx's thought in particular feed the liberation interpretation of human existence, bringing together both reason and experience. Critical of European Enlightenment thought, liberation theologians embrace Marx's belief that people are not 'puzzled by the world but oppressed in it.'[28] Their method does not abandon reason, for liberation too is a child of the Enlightenment.[29] But by turning to Marx rather than Kant for clues to understanding the world, liberationists embrace a critical reason which grows out of Marx's XIth Thesis on Feuerbach: 'The philosophers have only interpreted the world, in various ways, the point is to change it.'[30] Despite his disagreement with Feuerbach

---

and Peace: Documents from John XXIII to John Paul II. (London: Flame, 1991); Rodger Charles, S.J., *Christian Social Witness and Teaching: The Catholic Tradition from Genesis to Centesimus Anuus: Vol II: The Modern Social Contexts: Summaries: Analysis.* (Leominster: Gracewing, 1998); and George Weigel and Robert Royal eds., *Building the Free Society: Democracy, Capitalism and Catholic Social Teaching.* (Grand Rapids: Eerdmans and Washington, DC: Ethics and Public Policy Centre, 1993).

[27]Alistair Kee, *Domination or Liberation? The Place of Religion in Social Conflict* (London: SCM Press, 1986), 65.

[28]Ibid, 69.

[29]Ibid. Nevertheless, Gutierrez wants a theology of reflection on praxis to reinterpret the rational function of theology.

[30]Karl Marx, *Early Writings,* trans. and ed. T.B. Bottomore, (C.A. Watts & Co., 1963): 423, cit. Kee, *Domination or Liberation,* 69. This view is to be contrasted with the reason of critical realism that grows out of a doctrine of sin, and may only be considered in the context of sin.

Marx quite correctly observed that Feuerbach was actually presenting a very fruitful model for the understanding of the development of human consciousness and indeed societal life. It is a theory of a dialectical movement of externalization, objectification and internalization. Man has the capacity to conceive of ideals and to project them away from himself. They then take on objective form in the external world, in the form of institutions. Finally these institutions come to have an independent reality over against the individual. They act back and control man's life.[31]

The implications of this philosophy of structural existence influence various stages of the method's development, which conceives of moral consciousness, in its most basic and original form, as socially defined. Wrote Marx

In the social production of their life, men enter into definite relations that are indispensable and independent of their will, relations of production which correspond to a definite stage of development of their material productive forces. The sum total of these relations of production constitutes the economic structure of society, the real foundation, on which rises a legal and political superstructure and to which correspond definite forms of social consciousness. The mode of production of material life conditions the social, political and intellectual life processes in general. It is not the consciousness of men that determines their being, but on the contrary their social being that determines their consciousness.[32]

Marx's historical interpretation could not conceive of individuality as anything more than an evolutionary stage in the development of social consciousness.

In contrast with this view, the noted Peruvian Catholic Gustavo Gutierrez recognized the need to balance collective liberation with liberation of the individual, or at least to take both into consideration. The individual aspect was not seen as a 'spiritual' but a 'psychological' liberation, and Gutierrez felt it was not always included satisfactorily in the scope of liberation on collective and historical levels.[33] 'Psychological liberation includes dimensions which do not exist in or are not sufficiently integrated with collective, historical liberation. We are not speaking here, however, of facilely separating them or putting them in opposition to one another.' Gutierrez quotes David Cooper with approval

---

[31]Kee, *Domination or Liberation*, 63. One might be forgiven for wondering if this analysis might offer an explanation for what has happened in the organisation of the WCC in recent years.

[32]Karl Marx, preface to *A Contribution to the Critique of Political Economy* (Chicago: Charles H. Kerr, 1904), cit. in Charles C. West, 'Faith, Ideology, and Power: Toward and Ecumenical, Post-Marxist Method in Christian Ethics,' *Christian Ethics in Ecumenical Context: Theology, Culture and Politics in Dialogue,* ed. Shin Chiba, George R. Hunsberger, and Lester E. J. Ruiz (Grand Rapids, MI: Eerdmans, 1995), 40.

[33]Guttierrez, *Theology of Liberation*, 20.

It seems to me that a cardinal failure of all past revolutions has been the dissociation of liberation on the mass social level, i.e. liberation of whole classes in economic and political terms, and liberation on the level of the individual and the concrete groups in which he is directly engaged. If we are to talk of revolution today our talk will be meaningless unless we effect some union between the macro-social and micro-social, and between "inner reality" and "outer reality".[34]

Nevertheless, such liberation for the individual would come through a process whereby the oppressed are educated to understand their situation, and to conceive of historical possibilities beyond present realities. Thus, despite an explicit call for balance between individual and collective aspects of moral agency, the fulfilment of liberation is always found ultimately in the consciousness of the collective.

In this respect, the action-reflection model would seem to mirror the process of conscientization described by Paulo Friere in his well-known *Pedagogy of the Oppressed*. Friere insists on the balance of action and reflection for a method of true praxis, describing the two facets as mutually contingent. He writes

The insistence that the oppressed engage in reflection on their concrete situation is not a call to armchair revolution. On the contrary, reflection - true reflection - leads to action. On the other hand, when the situation calls for action, that action will constitute an authentic praxis only if its consequences become the object of critical reflection. In this sense, the praxis is the new *raison d'etre* of the oppressed; and the revolution, which inaugurates the historical moment of this *raison d'etre*, is not viable apart from their concomitant conscious involvement. Otherwise, action is pure activism.[35]

Overlooking the question of how conscientization could begin without an initial intervention of some educated elite to initiate the process for the oppressed, Friere emphasizes the importance of collective commitment, which arises through a rejection of moral ambiguity. For, 'as long as their ambiguity persists, the oppressed are reluctant to resist, and totally lack confidence in themselves.'[36]

Liberation, insofar as it is connected practically with this vision, is not regarded as a gift, or self-achievement, but a mutual process: 'At all stages of their liberation, the oppressed must see themselves as women and men engaged in the ontological and historical vocation of becoming more fully human. Reflection and action become imperative when one does not erroneously attempt to dichotomize the content of humanity from its historical forms.'[37]

---

[34]Ibid.
[35]Paulo Friere, *Pedagogy of the Oppressed,* rev. ed. (1970; reprint, New York: Continuum, 1993), 48.
[36]Ibid., 46.
[37]Ibid., 47-8.

Consequently, the action-reflection model for social ethics redefines Christian anthropology. People are not perceived as possessing ontologically inherent dignity as a result of bearing the image of God, which then makes doctrinal assertions about human needs, rights and responsibilities. Rather, people are invited to experience what it means to 'become' human by participating in the historical process, through a sort of collective existentialism. Echoing Heidegger, Volker Eid explains that in liberation ethics, 'Man does not have simply a ready-made nature which he need only put into effect. He must first create his own nature, and indeed do so as culture.'[38] Despite an oft-implied historical determinism, therefore, rationality remains - at least theoretically - at the fore. Such rationality is inseparable from human experience. History is certainly the primary category for this method, but history is directed by the imposition of collective reason. Friere confirms, 'To achieve...praxis, however, it is necessary to trust in the oppressed and their ability to reason.'[39]

In practice, however, reason itself is defined in collective terms. Noting the rejection of enlightenment rationalism of the Kantian variety which posits the relative autonomy of the moral agent, Dietmar Mieth writes of the liberationist ethical method: 'Here the individual aspect of personal values is moved from the centre of interest in favour of the dialogue aspect and in favour of the dialectical view of history. The starting point is not autonomy but the idea of a solidary and communicative freedom. Human reason is subject to the historical process; it too needs to be attained as a result of a process of liberation.'[40] Beyond this, and 'corresponding to this theology of collective liberation' he writes, 'there must be a practical ethos of liberation, an ethos of the people of God. This is why, in the perspective of liberation, the importance of basing moral judgments on human reason is replaced by the importance of the practical ethos.' Moreover, 'In Hegel's sense, ethos is more important than morality. But if this practical ethos is discovered in the liberating praxis of Christians, it owes its existence to God's liberating praxis as recognised by faith. The experience of contrasts which yields Christian ethos is determined by the faith of Christians in God's liberation.'[41] As ethics and reason are thus 'decentralised' in one universal sense, and 'universalised' in another, a

---

[38]Volker Eid, 'The Relevance of the Concept of Autonomy for Social Ethics,' *Concilium* 172, 24. Cf. Heidegger's *Sein und Zeit*, highlighting the obligation to fulfil the call to develop and realise the potential of our being. *Being and Time* (New York: Harper and Row, 1962).

[39]Friere, *Pedagogy*, 48. The deterministic aspects of the method would seem to be the result of marrying idealism with the Christian religion. Marx and Engels made it clear that history had no personality apart from the actions of humankind. Layering this humanistic conception of history with Christianity inevitably yields an ethical method that focuses on praxis. See Marx and Engels, *The Holy Family,* p. 93 cit. Antony Flew, *Thinking About Social Thinking,* 2nd ed., (London: Fontana Press, 1991), 61.

[40]Dietmar Mieth, 'Autonomy or Liberation', 89.

[41]Ibid., 90.

contextual hermeneutic of suspicion is introduced, whereby it may be said that 'those who champion universal reason always make it an instrument of domination....'.[42]

Considering that the 'psychological' liberation of the individual is necessitated by the collective - its historical demand for liberation - and is commandeered for its service, it is difficult to see how a balance between historical and spiritual, individual and collective aspects can be maintained. Indeed, despite his brief foray into aspects of the particular agent, Gutierrez himself does not take long to return to his historical exposition, emphasizing the role of revolution within a broader historical evolution

> To conceive of history as a process of human liberation is to consider freedom as a historical conquest; it is to understand that the step from an abstract to a real freedom is not taken without a struggle against all the forces that oppress humankind, a struggle full of pitfalls, detours, and temptations to run away. The goal is not only better living conditions, a radical change of structures, a social revolution; it is much more: the continuous creation, never ending, of a new way to be human, a *permanent cultural revolution.*[43]

Unlike even the social gospel, this line of thought moves outside of any traditional Christian concept of human nature, and rewrites anthropology in light of a new interpretation of history. Gutierrez explains

> In other words, what is at stake above all is a dynamic and historical conception of the human person, oriented definitively and creatively toward the future, acting in the present for the sake of tomorrow. Teilhard de Chardin has remarked that humankind has taken hold of the reins of evolution. History, contrary to essentialist and static thinking, is not the development of potentialities preexistent in human nature; it is rather the conquest of new, qualitatively different ways of being a human person in order to achieve an ever more total and complete fulfillment of the individual in solidarity with all humankind.[44]

A belief that they can and must participate in the process of hastening history towards its inevitable fulfilment lends liberationists the dogged determination to anticipate proleptically in social ethics the achievement of a single social consciousness. Such an interpretation renders the self-realisation of the collective as both the means and the goal of social ethics.

In Gutierrez's view, this politically-based expectation of eschatological realisation in uniformity of consciousness gives rise to new forms of ecumenical co-operation. On the one hand, contextual differences are emphasised, such as the concern in Latin America for practical rather than theoretical dialogue, where 'the oppressed and those who seek to identify with

---

[42]Ibid.
[43]Gutierrez, *Theoloogy of Liberation*, 21.
[44]Ibid., 21-2.

them face ever more resolutely a common adversary, and therefore, the relationship between Marxists and Christians takes on characteristics different from those in other places.' The break with traditional forms of dialogue is clear since

> on the other hand, meetings between Christians of different confessions but of the same political option are becoming more frequent. This gives rise to ecumenical groups, often marginal to their respective ecclesiastical authorities, in which Christians share their faith and struggle to create a more just society. The common struggle makes the *traditional* ecumenical programs seem obsolete (a 'marriage between senior citizens' as someone has said) and impels them to look for new paths toward unity.[45]

While the eradication of sectarian barriers is welcomed, one wonders how enduring an ecumenism can be, or if it may be called ecumenism at all, when it often appears to be based on a common political slogan rather than on a common faith or confession.

Ans van der Bent has further noted that with the action-reflection model, 'the whole approach became more conflictual; the world was seen as divided between oppressors and oppressed. Dealing with the North-South cleavage became more intricate than addressing the problem of the humanization of society in the West.' To support his assessment, van der Bent cites the final report of the *Humanum Studies*

> We may find ourselves freed to break community or unity in the search for truth, justice and the mutual correction and confrontation which will permit growth towards a mature and realistic love... We may well discover that Jesus Christ unites us in the confession of his name and so in the praise of God, Father, Son and Holy Spirit, and the freedom to repent, but on that basis we are liberated into all sorts of conflict, confrontation and anguish.[46]

Van der Bent concludes that, as a result, 'a dual approach to social ethics increasingly marked the ecumenical movement' with the study-dialogue approach on the one hand, and the action-reflection model on the other.[47] With the ready acceptance of militant action programmes on behalf of liberationists using the action-reflection method, divisions became even more pronounced. Marxist economic analysis and dependency theories of international relations became widely accepted as preferred frameworks for ethical thought and discussion.[48]

---

[45]Ibid., 60.

[46]Ans van der Bent, *Commitment*, 56.

[47]Ibid.

[48]This is confirmed by J. Andrew Kirk in Appendix A of 'The World Council of Churches: Programme to Combat Reactionaries?,' *Theology Encounters Revolution* (Leicester: IVP, 1980). Philip Wogaman suggests that there are no facts to confirm the

Indeed, according to liberation methodology, theology itself must be rewritten in the light of Marxist ideology. Kee concludes that

> the new method and its critique of the old method are deeply indebted to the perspectives provided by the early Marx. The most obvious point of contact is with the XIth Thesis on Feuerbach, but the difference between the two methods might also be seen as an illustration of Marx's fundamental point about the reversal of reality...Marx exposed a tendency to false consciousness which characterizes the individual's relationship to social institutions. The institution, although socially constructed, appears to the individual to be part of the natural order of things. Its existence is taken for granted and its form of existence controls the consciousness and the life of the individual within the sphere of influence.[49]

Similarly, then, theology 'would be something man-made which now assumes independent existence and acts back to control both thought and behaviour.'[50]

For liberationists, theology no longer can be given priority of place in ethical method. In its place, a new ideology offers a contextual interpretation of theology, reality, and God's action in the world. Hence the initial question of the action-reflection model is not that of its predecessors, asking 'What are we to say and do?' or even 'What is going on?,' but 'What is God doing in the world?' Theology then serves only 'as an *a posteriori* justification of positions and attitudes agreed upon without any serious theological search and analysis.'[51] Alexander Schmemann confirmed, 'It is the whole point indeed that if the Uppsala Report subordinates in fact theology to something else, this 'something else' is precisely an ideology.'[52]

According to a model of Marxism described by Charles West, an ideology has five characteristics

> First, it is the reflection of the life and struggle of a particular group in society. Second, it is an analysis of both the history and the structure of reality from the perspective of that group. Third, it is a guide to the group in bending powers of the world to its social purposes in the search for peace, prosperity, and justice.

WCC ever sponsored revolution. See his *Christian Perspectives on Politics*, rev. ed., (Louisville, KY: Westminster/John Knox Press, 2000), 271. Nevertheless, Wogaman cannot deny that significant sectors within the WCC supported revolutionary activity. Without indicating any direct involvement with revolutionary movements, the WCC Assembly at Canberra noted with pride their role in the movement towards liberation, justice and peace. While giving thanks to God, they nevertheless affirm that, 'the WCC's share in inspiring some of these changes has not been insignificant.' See Minutes of WCC Seventh Assembly Canberra, 7-20 Feb. 91, Doc PL 20.3 Sect IIIB Box 361.003, WCC Archives.

[49]Kee, *Domination or Liberation*, 71.
[50]Ibid., 72.
[51]Schmemann, 'Theology or Ideology,' 226.
[52]Ibid., 228.

Fourth, it claims to be true not only for the group but for all people; it claims to be a universal expression of reality and justice. Finally, it offers hope to all of society at the end of the process and the struggle.[53]

West's summary points to the characteristics of liberation that distinguish its ethics from the study-dialogue approach. In common, the methods have a correspondence view of reality, but for liberationists, reality is accessed and understood through human experience in a particular context, and is always in-the-making. The desire for change is manifested in a method of praxis, which, similar to the social gospel method, projects moral truth from the particular to the universal. It is an eschatological system, and in that respect, the very foundation of the method looks forward to a future, teleological realization in utopia.

Yet, the 'here and now' are crucially important, as the present anticipates the kingdom, and as the kingdom is made manifest in the midst of a humanity which has reached a certain ethical and ontological maturity.[54] Though God is attributed with the task of inaugurating the kingdom, it is human effort in history, based on certain anthropological assumptions, which anticipates its fulfilment.[55] Juan Bonino believes that 'an eschatological faith makes it possible for the Christian to invest his life historically in the building of a temporary and imperfect order with the certainty that neither he nor his effort is meaningless or lost.'[56] Borrowing heavily from Jürgen Moltmann's *Theology of Hope*, many liberationists embraced the apparent contradictions between history and hope. Boff wrote, 'Total liberation, generated by full freedom, constitutes the essence of the Reign of the eschatological goodness of God. History is en route to this goal. Our task is to hasten that process. The Reign of God has an essentially future dimension, one unattainable by human practices; it is the object of eschatological hope.'[57] The end result is almost a world-spirit dualism, where action in the world is justified by an eschatological hope which is largely undefined, and whose reality is unnecessary. Support for revolutionary movements grows out of an eschatology that anticipates a realization of the kingdom in temporal political and social categories.[58]

---

[53]West, 'Faith, Ideology and Power,' 41.

[54]Gustavo Guteirrez, *The Poor and the Church in Latin America* (London: Catholic Institute for International Relations, 1984), 26. Gutierrez was evidently influenced by theologians such as Dietrich Bonhoeffer and J. A. T. Robinson, who similarly and sometimes controversially posited the developing 'adulthood' of the human race.

[55]See, for example, Leonardo Boff, *Faith on the Edge,* trans. Robert Barr (San Francisco: Harper and Row, 1989), 146f.

[56]Juan Bonino, *Revolutionary Theology Comes of Age* (London: SPCK, 1975), 152.

[57]Boff, *Faith on the Edge,* 133.

[58]Bonino criticises Western theologians such as Moltmann and Metz for allowing an eschatological 'anticipation' of the Kingdom, rather than insisting on its historical 'realisation.' Bonino, *Revolutionary Theology,* 140.

Some Theological Considerations

As discovered previously in discussions of other methods, the theological implications of the shift toward the action-reflection model become most apparent in the understanding of the collective and individual aspects of human existence. Throughout the seventies and eighties, the theology of revolution, which was developed into a theology of liberation in the words of Abrecht, 'became increasingly influential as the theological-ethical inspiration for most ecumenical thought and action about political and social justice.'[59] The movement sought to re-define Christianity to meet a new challenge of a new humanity in a new age, and its understanding of structural sin and repentance, though not necessarily homogeneous in its composition, nevertheless came to dominate the ecumenical understanding of these concepts.

Sin

Generally speaking, in liberation theology, sin and salvation are to be understood equally in personal and social dimensions, though sin itself as a term seemed to fall into disfavour, being traded for words like 'oppression', 'demonic structures', and 'guilt'.[60] In the Uppsala report, the utopianism of Marxism was evidenced in the 'rejection by secular thought of the Christian notion of evil and sin.' As these concepts became equated with structures, the possibility of changing structures and gaining some type of utopian fulfilment became possible, at least in theory. After an initial reference to sin, the Uppsala report substitutes the impersonal and objective word, 'structures.' One theologian reflected that 'What is implicitly and explicitly absent is thus the soteriological dimension and content of the Christian faith, its insistence on *salvation*, and not only on improvement and 'the solution of problems.'[61] By 1973, much social thought in the WCC could be found equating personal and group sin, in qualitative if not quantitative terms. Structural sin, for the liberationists, was that force which maintained the centre-periphery relationship of wealthy and poor countries, and was something which needed to be 'overthrown', or people 'liberated' from, rather than something from which people might repent. In true idealist fashion, the tendency to submerge the individual in the collective conscience became apparent once again.

Nevertheless, liberationists such as Gutierrez saw the collective interpretation as a deeper understanding of sin than more traditional approaches, and it was against such an individualistic rendering that Gutierrez

---

[59]Paul Abrecht, 'The Predicament of Christian Social Thought After the Cold War,' *ER* 43 (July 1991): 322.

[60]This is attributable in part to an anthropocentric interpretation of the cross that focuses on Jesus' suffering more than God's holiness. Such a focus may be largely inspired by dire social conditions that understandably obscure vision beyond immediate context.

[61]Schmemann, 'Theology or Ideology,' 229.

reacted.[62] In 'the liberation approach,' he wrote

> sin is not considered as an individual, private, or merely interior reality - asserted
> just enough to necessitate 'spiritual' redemption which does not challenge the
> order in which we live. Sin is regarded as a social, historical fact, the absence of
> fellowship and love in relationships among persons, the breach of friendship with
> God and other persons, and, therefore, an interior, personal fracture. When it is
> considered in this way, the collective dimensions of sin are rediscovered.[63]

Accordingly, individuals and groups could join in the struggle against sin by
renouncing the materialism of the world, and identifying with the poor and
oppressed. '...Jesus' intrinsic relationship to the kingdom means that our
contact with him will not come primarily through cultic acclamation or
adoration but through following Jesus in the service of God's kingdom.'[64]
Labouring on behalf of the poor becomes an act of worship, and the attempt to
negate sin by introducing love into social structures was considered Christ-like
and salvific wherever it was engaged, whether in the name of Christ or in the
name of humanity. In a sense, this was the only repentance available, and was
made possible by love. Hence, the notion of God's 'preferential option for the
poor' became a central motif of ecumenical ethics.

For the liberationist, love is immediately applicable and relevant to society.
There is generally no moral patience for the models of ethics that desire and
seek means of achieving proximate justice, through intermediary principles,
rather than a direct application of Christian love. Instead of seeking consensus
on some practical middle ground, this approach sought to translate love directly
into structures of society, 'for love is not so much an emotion as a
determination of the will,' according to the WCC Conference on Faith, Science
and the Future at MIT Boston, 1979.[65]

It is clear that advocates of this strand of ecumenical thought believed in the
possibility of structural transformation, understood as a participatory salvation
and holistically defined. This is illustrated in a discussion of salvation in the
report of the WCC Commission on World Mission and Evangelism, in
Bangkok, 1973

---

[62]It must be noted that Catholic religious observance has usually placed a greater
emphasis on particular 'sins' than 'sin' as a condition, which accounts, in part, for
Gutierrez's view.

[63]Gutierrez,, *A Theology of Liberation,* 102-103.

[64]Jon Sobrino, *Jesus in Latin America* (Maryknoll: Orbis, 1987), 50. Cf. Raymond Fung,
'Good News to the Poor - A Case for a Missionary Movement,' *Your Kingdom Come:
Mission Perspectives: Report on the World Conference on Mission and Evangelism,
Melbourne, Australia 12-25 May 1980* (Geneva: WCC, 1980), 83ff.

[65]Reprinted in ibid., 312.

The salvation which Christ brought, and in which we participate offers a comprehensive wholeness in this divided life. We understand salvation as newness of life - the unfolding of true humanity in the fullness of God. It is salvation of the souls and the body, of the individual and society, mankind and 'the roaming creation.' As evil works both in personal life and in exploitative social structures which humiliate mankind, so God's justice manifests itself both in the justification of the sinner, and in social and political justice.[66]

At first, a balance is sought between these two important aspects of moral existence. The report continues: 'As guilt is both individual and corporate so God's liberating power changes both persons and structures. We have to overcome the dichotomies in our thinking between soul and body, persons and society, human kind and creation.'[67] The advocacy of blurred lines between these aspects of moral agency paves the way for the next suggestion of the report, which argues that in the process of salvation, there are three modes of reform: economic; political; and personal. Which aspect takes precedence over the others is a matter of historical and situational context. The argument that ultimately came to dominate the ecumenical social agenda was the one that posited the determined historical necessity of dealing with the political and economic structures of society as the priority over individual aspects of salvation.

If a good deal of this approach sounds remarkably reminiscent of the social gospel, we should not be surprised. The philosophical influences underlying both approaches are quite similar, and combined with the apparent lack of clarity in defining terms and desired outcomes, wide frustration resulted in ecumenical social ethics. In the words of Paul Abrecht, 'the proponents of the proposed new order were more explicit about what they opposed in the present system than about the character of the new one which they envisaged.... Their views represented a mixture of Marxist economic doctrine and elements of the kind of Christian social idealism well known in the heyday of the Social Gospel.'[68] Gutierrez himself, during a teaching stint at Union Theological Seminary in New York, 'read Rauschenbusch for the first time and exhorted his North American students to resume Rauschenbusch's work.'[69]

For ecumenical participants, there was a sense that some lessons had been learned from the previous decades, and from the experience of the social gospel. Despite a utopian promise, the manifestation of eschatological hope evolved so that many considered it more as Moltmann's 'hope against hope' than a persistently optimistic outlook in the face of deep and broad suffering. In

---

[66] Report on Section II, in Bankok Assembly 1973: Minutes and Report of the Assembly of the Commission on World Mission and Evangelism, Geveva: WCC, 1973, 88-90.

[67] Reprinted in ibid., 323.

[68] Abrecht, 'The Predicament of Christian Social Thought After the Cold War,' 323.

[69] Gary Dorrien, *Soul in Society: The Making and Renewal of Social Christianity* (Minneapolis: Fortress Press, 1995), 360.

the mid 1960s, John Bennett noted that 'the emphasis upon Christian social responsibility is as strong as it was in the "Social Gospel," but it is not accompanied by the same optimistic view of history or the same confidence that Christian solutions of social problems are available.' Though the mood was more hopeful than it had been in the 'realist' period, there was 'no tendency to identify the kingdom of God with any social developments in history. There remain the warnings of Christian realism concerning the finiteness and the sin of man, and the precariousness of all human schemes.'[70] The eschatological dimension, which was then highlighted as a source of judgement and fulfilment, in later years gave way to the notion of eschatology as judgement for the oppressor, and fulfilment for the oppressed.

Within the liberation-revolution paradigm, sin and responsibility were interpreted collectively to such an extent that they became identified absolutely with impersonal structures rather than human beings. Sin was structural, so were the solutions. Where methods previously focused on the individual, liberationists felt not enough account had been taken of the 'world's sin', factors in social structures which limited 'concrete freedom'.[71] The personal involvement and response of the moral person was absent altogether, leaving room for moral agency only possibly at some abstract collective level, as sin was divorced from any direct, individual, human responsibility. With respect to the Uppsala Report, Alexander Schmemann made several observations and posed several relevant questions. A lengthy quotation is appropriate

> The document deals abundantly with 'masses', 'nations', 'peoples' and 'societies' and very little with 'persons'.... One could argue, of course, that the areas of the economic and the social are *par excellence* areas of collective, supra-personal interests and realities and that therefore the personalism of Christian experience, being not explicitly denied, has no reason to be stressed in this particular document. But is it so? Is not a radical reduction of man to the economic and social the very essence of those secular ideologies whose basic categories, vocabulary and 'world-view' the Uppsala Report seems so obviously to endorse? And if it is so, is it not a self-evident duty for Christians at least to make some reservations as to that reduction? Granted that Christian personalism was much too often identified with non-Christian individualism, was it not urgent to clear that matter? Is not the Christian vision in which, on the one hand, the whole world exists for one man and, on the other hand, man fulfils himself only by becoming in Christ man-for-others, the specifically and uniquely Christian response to the tragic reduction of human existence to either demonic selfishness or ant-like collectivism? Not only do all these questions remain unanswered, they are not even mentioned, such is the blind surrender of the drafters of the Report to an

---

[70]John C. Bennett, *Christian Social Ethics in a Changing World* (New York: Association Press & London: SCM, 1966), 371. Comparing the present widespread belief in humanity's essential goodness, one might be forgiven for thinking that Bennett is here the optimist.

[71]Deitmar Mieth, 'Autonomy or Liberation,' 89.

ideology in which there is simply no room for the personal and their fear of not being sufficiently 'social'.[72]

Schmemann's questions have yet to receive adequate reply from within the WCC. He recalls the roots of the study-dialogue method as he continues

> And yet, how can we speak of a 'responsible' society without founding it, first of all, on the responsible human being, and thus on his transcendent freedom and spiritual nature? How can one speak of 'development' without even mentioning that for Christians the goal of all development is not 'society' but man in his unique and eternal *hypostasis*, and that only because of the experience of that uniqueness can the 'economic' and the 'social' become themselves problems of a spiritual and human order.[73]

Despite calls to repentance, and confessions of guilt often present in WCC reports, it is difficult indeed for potential agents to take responsibility for actions which are so far removed from their personal will and conscience that they are attributed to 'structures'. This is further complicated when structures are divorced from their human creators, and described as 'demonic', thus extending the possibility of rejection of responsibility on the basis of moral abdication in a collective form of, 'the devil made me do it!' The difficulty is to maintain a sense of personal responsibility for the structures which humans construct, and which, it must be conceded, are more than the sum of their parts. In the words of Karl Popper, 'The social group is *more* than the mere sum total of the merely personal relationships existing at any moment between any of its members.'[74] Yet it is possible for this analysis to be pushed farther than is warranted.

For liberationists, although individuals are called to repent of their role in supporting sinful structures, atonement comes through participation in a collective revolution, allowing self-righteous messianism to thrive on the left, and the right. In an environment where human action is perceived as a continuation of the incarnation, moral responsibility for oppressive structures is not only difficult to maintain, but from the perspective of the oppressed, a structure may be very difficult to forgive, even when the revolution is over.[75] This raises a spectre of issues regarding the responsibility of the individual in

---

[72]Schmemann, 'Theology or Ideology,' 234.

[73]Ibid.

[74]Karl Popper, 1957, 17, cit. Flew, *Thinking About Social Thinking*, 63.

[75]In a lecture at a conference on forgiveness and reconciliation at St. Antony's College, Oxford, September 1998, Donald Shriver indicated, that as a human being, 'I find it very difficult to forgive a structure. I need to forgive a person.' Those involved in the Truth and Reconciliation Commission in South Africa affirmed this sentiment. The importance of face-to-face confrontations between individuals was seen as a crucial aspect of the healing process, which needed to be addressed at a level that was quite separate from politics and structures.

the face of political change and public apologies, and individual responses to such structural issues.

Antony Flew has highlighted some philosophical difficulties encountered in discussions about collective identity, arguing that there is no need to draw a firm line between the positions of the methodological collectivist and the methodological individualist. 'There is no need, for instance...either to deny any sort of reality at all to social wholes; or to maintain that all statements embracing social notions are by logical analysis reducible to statements referring only to single individuals.'[76] By the same token, if individual moral agency is to be maintained, we must 'refuse to treat any of the most numerous outcomes of various social arrangements...as if they were...the planned and intended consequences of the actions of some super-agent, or of some committee of super-agents.'[77] The need for ethics to be clarified in both language and method becomes evident when we are challenged by Flew to consider that not every outcome in society is the result of a direct action or intention. Without clarification of this reality, 'Any society...thus becomes one in which all the ills to which flesh is heir are inflicted intentionally. It is manifest that such a society can be redeemed, if at all, only by the most totally revolutionary transformation.'[78] Disparity expressed in the language of conflict may too easily lead to actions that misapprehend the true relationship between individuals and various groups that comprise global economic and social systems.

Some of the problems with a solely collective interpretation of sin were early documented in the 1979 central committee minutes of the WCC, which clarifies several difficulties inherent in the use of the terms 'sin' and 'repentance' in discussions of social ethics: 'Taken together,' the minutes reported

> the reactions to and the comments on the JPSS report were varied, diverse and in some cases even contradictory. Where criticisms, reservations or hesitations were expressed, the following reasons were given: the distinction between the human and the divine, history and eschatology was not made clearly enough; there was a tendency at times towards an unexamined messianism; the elements of 'sin', 'humility', 'repentance', 'sacrificial servant', etc. were not given sufficient consideration; the use of biblical materials should be more carefully treated; a great deal more work needs to be done in order to move from theological categories to political categories.[79]

Even at this relatively early stage, it was becoming evident that terms like 'sin'

---

[76]Flew, *Thinking About Social Thinking*, 63.

[77]Ibid., 66.

[78]Ibid., 74.

[79]Minutes of the Central Committee of the WCC, 1979, reprinted in *The Ecumenical Movement: An Anthology of Key Texts and Voices*, 67.

and 'repentance' were being used in very different ways and were crying out for clarification, a task that still requires attention.

Christology

When soteriology is understood solely or even primarily in terms of social structures, there are obvious and serious implications for Christology. Liberation views of soteriology and Christology grow out of an understanding of theological statements as doxological rather than realistic affirmations of truth. Such an understanding of dogma facilitates the process whereby theology is reinterpreted in the light of ideology.

As an example, liberation theologian Jon Sobrino states that his theological starting point is the historical Jesus, since he views dogma as doxological rather than historical. 'To reach the point of making a doxological statement, the one making it must experience a rupture, must take a leap' from a historical statement to one which surrenders self to God.[80] This interpretation of separation between faith and history encourages Sobrino to seek after the Jesus of history rather than of traditional credal formulation, which has the effect of overlooking two thousand years of Christian historical witness. When doxological statements are thus re-ordered, Sobrino can assert that Jesus 'became' the Son of God, and revealed the process by which others participate in the same process. Sobrino was aware that he might be accused of adoptionism at this point but maintained that he was working from an ethical not metaphysical understanding, since metaphysical affirmations could only be doxological and not historical statements. Liberation thus sets christology in light of soteriology, where Jesus does not merely set a pattern; rather, 'Christ the liberator means that the incarnational process has not come to an end; it passes over into the eschatological process: history is seen as the decision in favour of the full incarnation, hominisation of man.'[81]

Describing such a rupture between the Christ of faith and the Jesus of history has serious implications for a Christian understanding of truth, and of the historical witness of the faith. P. T. Forsyth lamented the result for the Christian faith when social aims replace theology and cause the church to lose an appreciation of historic dogma. For those who place ideology before theology, the truth 'is not found in a great and final liberating Word for the moral Soul.' To such as these, dogma rooted in historical truth is abhorrent 'because a historic redemption is so, or a final revelation, or an absolute Gospel. The growth of such freedom is only the growth of human nature turned religious.' God 'is a Liberator rather than a Redeemer. It is natural freedom

---

[80]Jon Sobrino, *Christology at the Crossroads*, trans. John Drury (Maryknoll: Orbis, 1978), 324.
[81]Dietmar Mieth, 'Autonomy or Liberation,' 90.

rarefied and refined. It is not regeneration.'[82] On this matter and indeed many others, Forsyth was irrepressible

> The essential thing about dogma is not its length, breadth nor thickness but its finality. And the fundamental difference between a dogmatic and an undogmatic Christianity is that for the former Christ has done the final thing for the human soul while for the latter He has but won the highest height. The one prizes Christ for His grace, the other for His excellency. The one calls Him Saviour in the new creative sense (and nothing is so final as creation); the other calls Him hero - the soul's hero no doubt but still its *beau ideal* and not its Redeemer.[83]

In the revelation of the cross of Christ, sin and liberation are seen in the stark context of God's judgement. Forgiveness replaces conflict, as it has come 'in the presence of Jesus Christ and very specially in the presence of his Cross. For there we confront the full expression of God's mind both to sinners and to sin.'[84] Revelation of God's holy love confronts all humanity everywhere with the severity of sin, and its universality. This is not simply an abstract, theoretical or even doxological concept. The cross 'is not simply a visual aid. We do not just see love there in an abstract sort of way. We see love in action. We see love *doing* something - for us.' Therefore, 'Christ is our representative in the sense that he, as the Man, makes the requisite offering of obedience and love to the Father which we could never make. He, the sinless one, vanquishes sin as we never could, for at the Cross God-in-Christ meets the full horror of sin in head-on collision, and triumphs.'[85] At this defining moment of history we see something new; 'Never was sin so exposed, and by exposure, so doomed, reprobated, sentenced, as by his treatment of it from the beginning to the end. When Christ had done with sin, it stood there a beaten, powerless thing; paralysed, vanquished, dethroned, stripped of every covering, every mask, flung out in utter degradation.'[86] The sway of sin is replaced by a new covenant, the cost of which can never give way to sentimental optimism, or be substituted by human effort, no matter how self-sacrificing. Rather

> the doctrine of justification by faith sounds a note of sombre realism, places a question mark against the confident declarations of the visionaries, and raises doubts about the fundamental perfectibility of human nature. It is, however, a critical, not a negative approach to ethics, whether personal or social. It warns us

---

[82]Peter Taylor Forsyth, *Theology in Church and State* (London: Hodder & Stoughton, 1915), 114.

[83]Ibid., 115.

[84]Hugh Ross Mackintosh, *The Person of Jesus Christ*, ed. T. F. Torrence, (1912; reprint, Edinburgh: T&T Clark, 2000), 38.

[85]Alan P. F. Sell, *Christ Our Saviour* (Shippensburg, PA: Ragged Edge Press, 2000), 42.

[86]H. R. Mackintosh, *Person*, 39.

of the false prophets of naïve moral optimism, insisting that human nature in its totality - from the highest to the lowest of human faculties - is permeated by sin.[87]

This does not render human effort meaningless. In the context of the cross of Christ, we are faced with the seriousness of sin, and with both individual and collective aspects of redemption. In this light, the practical consequences for Christian, theological ethics may be held in proper balance. For the cross represents 'love in the first instance directed upon the world, but directed upon the world in such a way that it should be taken home in every individual experience.'[88] Thus, the Christian community

> Having been brought into being by the cross…continues to live by and under the cross. The cross now governs our perspective and behaviour. All our relationships have been radically transformed by it. The cross is not just a badge to identify us, and the banner under which we march; it is also the compass which gives us our bearings in a disoriented world. In particular, the cross revolutionizes our attitudes to God, to ourselves, to other people both inside and outside the Christian fellowship, and to the grave problems of violence and suffering.[89]

In other words, Christian moral agents, as individuals and in community expression, are responsible agents: 'The *gift* of our justification lays upon us the *obligation* to live in accordance with our new status.' But the individual Christian, and the redeemed fellowship do not rely on their own capabilities for success: 'Our justification brings about a new obedience - an obedience that would not be conceivable before our justification and that ultimately rests on the grace of God.'[90] And God's grace is required if the church is to live out the love commandment with any measure of integrity. For the command is the self-sacrificing challenge to love 'as I have loved you.'[91] Once again, we are faced with Niebuhr's impossible possibility, compounded by the problem of group existence, where self-interest is not easily disposed.

W. A. Visser't Hooft indicated the necessary relationship between doctrine and ethics when he referred to his oft-quoted remark from Uppsala in 1968 that 'church members who deny in fact their responsibility for the needy in any part of the world are just as much guilty of heresy as those who deny this or that article of faith.'[92] He writes

---

[87]Alister McGrath, *Justification by Faith* (Basingstoke, Hants: Marshall Pickering, 1988), 124.

[88]Peter Taylor Forsyth, *The Work of Christ* (1910; reprint, London: Independent Press, 1948), 116.

[89]John Stott, *The Cross of Christ* (Downers Grove, IL: IVP, 1986), 256.

[90]McGrath, *Justification*, 117.

[91]T. W. Manson also indicates that the law may be summed up in Jesus' words 'Be perfect as your heavenly Father is perfect.' *Ethics and the Gospel*, 60.

[92]In fact, this was quoted as recently in a report of the Central Committee of the WCC.

If I had known beforehand that this sentence would become so popular, I would have added a complimentary phrase such as: 'And church members who deny that God has reconciled men to himself in Christ are just as much guilty of heresy as those who refuse to be involved in the struggle for justice and freedom for all men and who do nothing to help their brethren in need.' For it seems to me that the health of the ecumenical movement depends on our readiness to stand with equal firmness for these two convictions at the same time.[93]

Such a statement may not solve easily the matter for ecumenical social ethics, but it does recall the balance between two important aspects of Christian ethics suggested at the opening of this chapter.

When seeking to balance human responsibility with the grace of God in ecumenical social ethics, it is difficult to avoid a realist approach, which is more clearly expressed in the study-dialogue method, than in the action-reflection model. Alister McGrath echoes Niebuhr when he reflects on Luther's method, which focused on the justification of the sinner. He concludes

Although it is often suggested that human social problems are a consequence of human *society* rather than human *nature*, the realist approach to ethics suggests that the fallenness of human nature infects the society in which we live. Individual self-interest becomes the corporate egoism of contending groups. These insights suggest that a 'perfect society' is impossible in history, simply because of the individuals who compose such a society. Thus the goal of Christian social moral action is not the *perfection* of society, but its *amelioration* - to make society better in the realization that it cannot be perfect because of human fallenness. If such insights are right, Christians who wish to be involved in politics and social action must realize that they, like everyone else, must operate within the context of the fallen system of human groups.[94]

As Niebuhr affirmed, the amount of progress any society can make is limited by sin, but may be open to creative possibilities because of God's grace.

Contextual Theology

Over recent decades, the fragmentation of the liberation theology movement, and the dogged application of the action-reflection method of social ethics, have resulted in the development of numerous 'contextual' theologies. Though perhaps an inevitable outcome of liberation philosophy, the situation nevertheless poses the problem of reconciling increasingly diverse interpretations of important terms, and begs the subsequent question of how a theology that has retreated into a specific context can make any reference to the wider socio-political situation of which we are part as a common humanity. This is not to say that theology is somehow independent of context - to the

---

[93]W. A. Visser't Hooft, *Memoirs* (Geneva: WCC, 1987), 363.
[94]McGrath, *Justification*, 125-6.

contrary, theology and ethics are always done in a context, for as historical beings, we cannot approach them any other way. But even those 'deeply committed to contextuality in Christian theology and Christian life' must 'cultivate an awareness of the dangers of contextuality.'

Douglas John Hall noted some of the dangers of contextualization in his critical appraisal of the JPIC process. 'To say it in a sentence,' he wrote, ' the real danger of contextualism is that it will devolve into the kind of regionalism or localism that threatens both the unity of the church and the unity of truth. With the reduction or demise of earnest attempts at global theology, we might see the emergence of a theological tower of Babel where, in contrast to Pentecost, the various provinces of "Christendom" could no longer communicate with one another.'[95] Hall explains how the dangers of contextuality must be confronted if the ecumenical movement is to hold together against forces of fragmentation

> Precisely *because* we have begun to think contextually, we are all the more in need of an ecumenical dialogue that can be a forum for testimony and interchange among many differing contexts. The old ecumenism asked how the separated *churches* might rediscover unity in Christ. The ecumenism that is called for now is one that asks how distinctive *worldly contexts*, evoking the need for distinctive articulations of the Christian message, may yet contribute to a Christian witness that is expansive enough to have global implications. To achieve such a new ecumenism, however, we shall have to learn not only how to be forthright about *our own* contexts and their quite explicit demands upon the faith; we shall have also to learn how to listen intelligently to the testimonies of those who speak out of socio-historical contexts very different from our own.[96]

Hall's remarks may raise many questions about what, if anything, Christians across different contexts may actually have in common, and may subsequently reveal him to be more comfortable with deeper levels of contextualization of the Gospel than some others. Nevertheless, he points to an important criticism of the WCC in the contemporary period, namely, the need for ecumenical groups to acknowledge and address diversity rather than gloss over differences in a superficial manner, manifesting a lack of deeper theological reflection and dialogue, and issuing in statements which are reflective only of the most outspoken group.[97]

---

[95]Douglas John Hall, 'The State of the Ark: Lessons from Seoul,' *Between the Flood and the Rainbow: Interpreting the Conciliar Process of Mutual Commitment (Covenant) to Justice, Peace, and the Integrity of Creation*, compiled by D. Preman Niles (Geneva: WCC, 1992), 37. It should come as no surprise that like Paul Abrecht, Hall was a student of Niebuhr.

[96] Ibid.

[97]Ibid., 37-8. Contextual aspects may enrich and positively challenge theology when it does not slide into sectarianism, a tendency that may easily overtake the ability of Christians to share across contexts. Cf. Alan P. F. Sell, *Commemorations: Studies in*

The relatively recent tendency for ecumenical social ethics to slide into contextual fragmentation is not entirely unrelated to the liberation focus on ideological action-reflection as an ethical method. For although 'Marxism was also paradoxical in its view of human knowledge and human nature,' supporters avoided its logical conclusion 'because they trusted that the materially determined laws of history would lead humanity through class struggle and revolution to the total emancipation of humankind.' However, as Charles West has pointed out, 'If one takes its doctrine of ideology with final seriousness, the result is complete relativism both moral and metaphysical.'[98] The importance of a theological rather than ideological starting point in ethics becomes particularly acute when it is recognized that 'a sustained interpretation and critique of society is required from the perspective of the community that acknowledges there is no authority except from God.'[99]

The conflictual nature of liberation encouraged participants in ecumenical ethics to declare their allegiances and so make it plain to all whether they found themselves on the side of the oppressed or the oppressor. Those on the side of the oppressed claimed a certain validity for their position, based on the fact of their political context. Coupled with the thrust toward a more positive view of nationalism, which emerged when revolutionary concerns were expressed politically, the matter of historical context took on primary significance. It became the norm for such declarations of identity to be made at the outset of contributions to conferences and meetings, and for the contextual experience to be universalized to the rest of the world. This is evidenced in one paper which began, 'I come from Latin America. Above all, I am a Latin American. I insist on this aspect of my personal identity in order to stress, from the beginning, the multiform nature of the reality existing under the name Latin America.' The author proceeds to analyse the global economic situation based on his local experience, and without technical or outside input, save for a neo-Marxist theory of international systems which focuses on a centre-periphery analysis supported by a negative reading of Weber's thesis. This leads to the author's bold conclusion that, 'If human rights are violated in Latin America, it happens primarily to maintain a social order that benefits especially the nations of the centre who are concerned with protecting their markets and private investments of their citizens.' It is therefore necessary for churches to repent, and take the

---

Christian Thought and History (Calgary: University of Calgary Press and Cardiff: University of Wales Press, 1993), 51-55.

[98]West, 'Faith, Ideology and Power,' 45.

[99]James Gustafson, *Can Ethics Be Christian?* (Chicago and London: University of Chicago Press, 1975), 61. Despite general affinity for N. H. G. Robinson's position regarding the commonalities between Christian ethics, and ethics in general, it is difficult at this point not to feel at least a little sympathy for those narrative approaches which struggle to assert the uniqueness of the Christian story, and its formative ethic. Cf. N. H. G. Robinson, *The Groundwork of Christian Ethics* (London: Collins, 1971).

side of the poor, to 'remove themselves from the historical compromise of the wealth of the North' so they no longer share responsibility in the domination and exploitation of the South. Further, they must 'change the social context of their exegesis and their theological reflection to a perspective that reflects the concrete historical situation and aspirations of the people in the periphery.'[100] Not only does this reflect a one-sided analysis, without any room for constructive dialogue, but it lacks any distinctively Christian framework. Beyond that, it lets off too easily those who are considered to be part of the 'rich' Churches: History has demonstrated that it may be much easier to renounce wealth than to propose solutions for its redistribution.

The matter of applying love directly to society and structures, when the individual agent is drowned in collective mind and action, becomes especially acute for social ethics that seek to be ecumenical and not purely contextual. Just as supporters of the action-reflection model have shunned general principles, so have they been unable or unwilling to answer those objections raised against attempts to translate love directly into society only from their subjective and limited perspective. Early in the development of the method, Bennett noted that

> in the writing of some contextualists two conceptions take the place of principles: the discernment of what God is doing to humanize man in a situation, and the idea of the *koinonia*. The first raises questions as to how we know what God is doing in the very ambiguous situations which we continually confront unless we have in our minds some criteria - drawn, it may be, from the very idea of humanization. Such criteria would be necessary protection against aberration, such as in the case of many churchmen who saw God at work positively in Hitler. The *koinonia* also raises questions that point beyond itself. If the *koinonia* is a kind of cell group of Christians working together in a revolutionary crisis…it may be necessary to choose between such groups. This would involve some criteria. If the *koinonia* is the larger church, it is in continual need of reformation in the light of some criteria.[101]

Bennett demonstrates that, despite the call for contextualization and direct applications of love to structures, there are intermediary principles at work in action-reflection ethics whether they are recognized or not. After all, 'Love unguided by any tested considerations can be very blind and often very wrong.'[102] In contrast to the conflictual and suspicious nature of the action-reflection model, the study-dialogue approach calls together a common humanity, reminding us that God has been at work throughout the history of human experience. Bennett concluded

---

[100]Joaquim Beato, 'Good News to the Poor - Its Implications for the Mission of the Church in Latin America Today,' *Your Kingdom Come*, 102.
[101]Bennett, *Christian Ethics in a Changing World*, 376-7.
[102]Ibid., 376.

The experience of nations in which there has been a continuous development of institutions of political participation of all the people and of institutions which protect the rights of persons surely has meaning for the political goals of the rapidly changing societies. The churches in their desire to be open to the new should not cast off what can still be found good in the old. Though the concept of the responsible society as expressed in the ecumenical literature is a source of judgment upon all achievements, it grows out of the experience of partially won human rights and freedoms that are the deposit of previous revolutions and that are as much the work of God as anything that can be seen in the struggles and the partial victories of the present.[103]

Bennett's caveat continues to bear striking relevance to the scene of ecumenical ethics in the present day.

For social ethics that seek to be truly ecumenical, there is an inherent difficulty in employing the reflection-action method. While certain universalities of human existence are highlighted, such as political and social dynamics and conflicts, the method does not allow for diversity of approaches or opinions. Since it is a basic premise of the method itself that there must be a universal moral consciousness, then there can be only one right way of looking at the world. Hence, toleration for various points of view is severely limited, as the liberation struggle is advanced through conflict.[104] God is seen to be always favouring the side of the oppressed, and praxis growing out of a reflection-action model will lead his chosen people to a universal understanding of what is to be done, based on what God is already doing through history, in the world.[105] Study and dialogue are thus considered obsolete and irrelevant. The contrast is clear, as

reflection about praxis is replaced by reflection arising out of praxis. This means, for instance, that it is very hard to draw up general solutions to problems in advance, before they have been worked on practically. On the one hand, we are striving for concrete utopias; on the other, we are concerned only about the steps immediately ahead of us. This provides a better basis for an ethos of change than by trying to shape praxis according to predetermined ethical judgments. From the point of view of theological ethics, what we have is diagnosis rather than integration. Whereas autonomous ethics in a Christian context is heavily dependent on analytical reason, striving to analyse scientifically the various

---

[103]Ibid., 381.

[104]True to the Hegelian dialectic that characterises this conflict, one author asserts: '...only those who dare to live daily this conflict, who nail their own interests to the cross,' will attain the kingdom of God. Julia Esquivel, 'The Crucified Lord: A Latin American Perspective,' *Your Kingdom Come,* 60.

[105]God's immanence is paramount in an approach that believes 'The cry "Your Kingdom Come" can only come from the perspective of the poor who have this hope as a community.' See Ibid. Such a conviction rests on a liberation hermeneutic of the Exodus story.

experiences, here we have an analysis of faith which shows 'reasonable' solutions to be in fact subservient to extrinsic interests.[106]

Ans van der Bent confirms that in the WCC, 'the superiority of the socialist liberation perspective over against the older liberal capitalist approach was widely affirmed. The liberation alternative was clearly considered the valid model for all the developing countries - with inescapable consequences for the entire world.' As for all idealist approaches, there can be no mechanism incorporated for mediating disputes, or even confronting the different approaches of various Christians representing a variety of viewpoints. Moreover, despite its call for a universal consciousness to be manifested in history, it actually fosters a rugged contextualization, where any notion of individual responsibility for sinful structures, or accountability to the revelation of the cross of Christ is modified, if not obliterated in collective interpretation. The rewriting of theology renders doctrine ultimately subservient to an ideology, which leads subsequently to a relativistic ethical fragmentation that exchanges any notions of a universal collective moral consciousness for messianic and parochial collective allegiances.

Addressing the issue of a fragmented moral consciousness will not be easy for ecumenical groups, and many issues surrounding the nature of social and individual moral agency remain unresolved. Along with a post-modern fragmentation, the strands represented by the heirs of Rauschenbusch's idealism and Niebuhr's realism have remained present and at odds within the WCC, and other denominational and ecumenical groups. An effort to recover the theological nature of Christian social ethics within a relativistic contextual philosophical environment has led to the more recent development of yet another method of social ethics within the WCC. The idea of moral formation represents both a reaction to and manifestation of contextual relativism. It recalls the slogan of Amsterdam and Evanston - 'let the church be the church' - but it relies on dubious non-foundational assertions rooted in a more rugged contextualism than liberation theology. Despite challenges to the direction in which the churches appeared to be headed, few have heeded the warnings of those who feel that the churches 'cannot live in their many situations with an absolute law from which can be deduced all that is required of the Christian who seeks to be obedient, or with a moral and political relativism that knows no criteria for the human, and no conflicts of conscience in the choice of political means, and no goals for political change with moral claims.'[107] Instead, many have chosen to embrace ethical relativism, while others retreat into narrative, or surrender to deconstructionism, and reject any 'advocacy of the antique.'[108] It

---

[106]Deitmar Mieth, 'Autonomy or Liberation,' 90.

[107]Bennett, *Christian Social Ethics in a Changing World*, 381.

[108]Milbank uses this as a disparaging critique not only of the old realist and idealist schools, but also of those who have rejected foundationalism in contemporary ethics,

will be seen in the following chapter if their proposals offered an effective method for Christian social ethics near the end of the twentieth century.

---

such as Alasdair MacIntyre. See John Milbank, *Theology and Social Theory* (Oxford: Blackwell, 1990), 326.

CHAPTER 9

An Uncommon Community: Some Philosophical and Theological Impulses in a Moral Formation Method

If, for Christianity, 'philosophy' is finished and surpassed, then there can be no more 'truth and falsity'. Because no positive non-being is posited, as by Platonism, and no pure material potency, as in Aristotelianism, nothing that is, can be in any sense wrong. There can be no more illusions, and no unmaskings: instead, there are deficiencies. To be 'wrong' is now to do evil, and to do evil is rather not to do the good, for something 'to be lacking'. Neither ignorance nor sin make 'mistakes'; instead they somehow do not do enough.

Salvation is only in common: it is only the peace of the altera civitas.

John Milbank

Introduction

In *An Experiment in Criticism*, C. S. Lewis expressed an appropriate apologetic sentiment for the church when he wrote: 'Christian evangelism should by its very means convey the gospel which heals the wounds of individuality without undermining the privilege of it.'[1] Holding together the individual and the collective, his statement serves as a helpful reminder for social ethics as well as evangelism. We have seen thus far that a balanced view of social ethics will consider both collective and individual aspects of human existence and moral agency, in both theoretical and practical forms. Such balance will remind churches, as intermediary groups between the levels of individual and universal humanity, that they are not only comprised of individuals but are themselves inextricably related to a much broader collective of human existence.

In this chapter I shall explore a further, newer ethical method which has found a home in ecumenical circles, namely, that which we will refer to as 'moral formation.' With the influences of philosophical deconstructionism in

---

[1] C. S. Lewis, *An Experiment in Criticism*, 1961, 140.

the air, and in light of the contextual fragmentation, which was perhaps an inevitable result of the action-reflection method, ecumenical ethics has been faced with a post-modern challenge. The proliferation of information technology and the globalization of culture have combined with other social and philosophical influences to initiate significant changes in most societies of the world. The resulting shift from modern to post-modern conditions has raised important issues for theological debate and ethical praxis, especially in ecumenical contexts.

The response of many ethicists to this social, cultural, and philosophical *milieu* has been to abandon methods that rest on reason and some degree of moral autonomy, and seek a new approach, which focuses on the community of faith, and the narrative upon which its existence depends. The result is a more thoroughly theological core for ethics, and a rejection of methods of dialogue both within and without the church. But while many of these responses to post-modernity attempt to heal the wounds of individuality, they also possess a general undercurrent that tends to undermine its privilege.

Ecclesiology and Ethics

The development of the narrative approach to ethics has been nurtured in ecumenical circles by the Ecclesiology and Ethics project of the WCC, and was affirmed most recently at the 1998 Assembly at Harare.[2] Ecclesiology and Ethics was a joint study of the Faith and Order Unit and the Justice, Peace and Creation Unit of the WCC, seeking to heal a long-standing breach between the two, which have tended to follow different methods in their approaches to ecumenical issues. According to Tom Best and Martin Robra, Ecclesiology and Ethics 'sought to explore the link between what the church *is* and what the church *does*. It explored the ethical dimension not as a separate "department" of the church's life, but as integrally related to its worship, its confession of faith, its witness and service in the world.' Moreover, it attempted to integrate the distinctive language and thought-forms of theology and ecclesiology with those of contemporary Christian ethical reflection, leading to the formation of an

---

[2]In the unpublished Report of the Policy Reference Committee II, WCC Assembly, 1998, 'story' received a prominent endorsement as a method for social ethics, as the committee made broad claims for what it might achieve: 'People's stories show and reflect the longing and desire for sustenance of life through fulfilling the essential needs of all people, for the protection of life through peace-building and peace making in situations of violence and war, for the enhancement of life through the strengthening of accountability in a truly democratic society and the improving of people's economic welfare by broadening opportunities and solidarity linkages, and for the enrichment of life through the deepening of people's spirituality and cultural activities as well as the up-building of just and sustainable communities.' How stories are capable of revealing all of this, much less achieving it, is not discussed.

inclusive new vocabulary.[3] As a result, the Ecclesiology and Ethics programme focused on the church as a community of moral formation. It borrowed a slogan from Stanley Hauerwas - the church doesn't *have* a social ethic, the church *is* a social ethic - and its published studies largely reflect similar theological and philosophical influences.[4] Therefore, the basic question was no longer 'What is going on?' or 'What is God doing?', still less 'What are we to do?', but rather, 'Who are we?'[5]

The published studies of Ecclesiology and Ethics largely reflect post-modern theological and philosophical influences. Hauerwas and others, including Hans Frei, George Lindbeck, and John Milbank, have been described as leaders in a new movement of theology and ethical discourse, completely lacking homogeneity, and variously referred to as 'radical orthodox,' 'post-liberal,' or even 'post-evangelical.' Regardless of the label affixed to their methods, they share one thing in common, and that is a commitment to post-foundationalist epistemology, as a response to the work of philosophers who have called into question the legitimacy of ethics that are separated from narrative and language.[6]

Some Initial Philosophical Considerations

At the outset, it is important to introduce several observations about the contemporary intellectual climate in theology and ethics. Though the term post-modern is used, it must be recognized that there is wide debate about the use of

---

[3]See Thomas F. Best and Martin Robra, eds., *Ecclesiology and Ethics: Ecumenical Ethical Engagement, Moral Formation and the Nature of the Church* (Geneva: WCC, 1997), especially vii-ix and 72-87.

[4]Hauerwas's influence has permeated Christian social ethics with the idea of moral formation. See for example Stanley Hauerwas, *After Christendom?* (Nashville, TN: Abingdon, 1991), and *In Good Company: The Church as Polis* (Notre Dame, IN: University of Notre Dame Press, 1995). See also George Lindbeck, *The Nature of Doctrine: Religion and Theology in a Postliberal Age* (Philadelphia, PA: Westminster, 1984); Hans Frei, *Types of Christian Theology*, ed. George Hunsinger and William Placher (London and New Haven, CT: Yale University Press, 1992); Stanley Fish, *Is There a Text in this Class? The Authority of Interpretive Communities* (London and Cambridge, MA: Harvard University Press, 1980).

[5]It would seem that the struggle for identity as individuals, and as church communities, is a significant post-modern issue, recently moving a debate about personhood to the fore of theology, at least in some circles. We should not be surprised to see this trend reflected in ecumenical ethics.

[6]Alasdair MacIntyre has been one of the most significant figures in this field, his work assumed or expressly described as the catalyst for making more explicit the connection between narrative, community and ethics. See Alasdair MacIntyre, *After Virtue: a study in moral theory*, 2nd ed. (London: Duckworth, 1985); and *Whose Justice? Which Rationality?* (London: Duckworth, 1988).

the term itself, let alone what it signifies. There is, therefore, a great diversity of method from one scholar to another, so any comments made here will reflect either broad generalizations or specific observations of ethical method. For this reason, the focus will be on common strands, or most influential ideas, which seem to have given rise to the moral formation method in ecumenical ethics, rather than on specific differences between individual scholars.

Moreover, the concerns of these scholars are to be taken seriously, even though a full embrace of their methods may be rejected. Important questions of epistemology and hermeneutics raised in the post-modern situation deserve disciplined attention, though not at the expense of constructive theology and ethics. The critique of rationalism, individualism and communalism from various quarters has much to challenge us and teach us, whilst we may eschew the relativism of some. Many of these considerations have much to do with the form and function of language and epistemology. Therefore, an understanding of the moral formation method must begin with a glance at the reason for the importance of language to the post-modern scene.[7]

With the failure of the logical positivists to find any significant measure of success in their task early in the last century, Ludwig Wittgenstein drew certain conclusions regarding the role of language in forming reality. His ideas have since found particular resonance amongst contemporary philosophers who embrace the idea that language games form, structure, or otherwise determine reality.[8] Declaring the 'failure of the Enlightenment project,' ethicists find meaning for existence only within a particular 'narrative,' where individuals are formed by a story shared with others whose reality is constructed by the same language, and hence similar thought patterns and experiences.[9]

Meaningful dialogue with those from other language games may be more or

---

[7]Some themes mentioned here are explored most thoroughly in Alan Sell *Confessing and Commending the Faith*, (Cardiff: UWP, 2002). See especially Chapter 4, which considers 'The Meaning, Use and Reference of Religious Language,' and which was published since this chapter was originally written.

[8]At least one contemporary philosopher stated explicitly that Wittgenstein made these ideas necessary. See Jean-Francois Lyotard, *The Postmodern Condition: A Report on Knowledge,* trans. Geoff Bennington and Brian Massumi (Manchester: Manchester University Press, 1984).

[9]Cf. Alasdair MacIntyre, *AfterVirtue.* Although MacIntyre offers a clear statement about the nature of rational inquiry and truth at the end of the Enlightenment era, some ethicists have developed his thought in ways he did not necessarily intend. For an examination of some of the individual and community tensions in MacIntyre's work see Stuart Rosenbaum, 'MacIntyre or Dewey,' *AJTP* 19 (January 1998): 35-59; Cf. Jeffrey Bloechl, 'The virtue of history: Alasdair MacIntyre and the rationality of Narrative,' *PSC* 24 (1998): 43-61.

less precluded, dismissed as irrelevant or deemed impossible.[10] In a technological society, where no individual self 'not even the least privileged among us, is ever entirely powerless over the messages that traverse and position him at the post of sender, addressee, or referent' there is a need for an organizing principle to legitimate society, though any notion of totalizing narratives is rejected outright.[11] Narratives thus have their own authority since 'the people are only that which actualizes the narratives...not only by recounting them, but also by listening to them and recounted themselves through them...'.[12] According to Michel Foucault, language is more a 'producer of subjectivity than a meaningful product of autonomous subjects.'[13] In this view, language, not the moral agent, is seen to be autonomous. Narrative knowledge thus requires 'no instituting deliberation, no cumulative progression, no pretension to universality...'.[14] Not only is a common ground denied, but moral life does not even have to make rational sense, since reason itself is jettisoned - 'The postmodern subject does not need a coherent world.'[15]

In his forward to Jean-Francois Lyotard's *The Postmodern Condition: A Report on Knowledge*, Frederic Jameson notes the emergence of deconstructionist and postmodern thought from the ferment of Marxism and revolutionary modes of thinking. In this sense, postmodernism may be seen as replacing Marxist class analysis with new categories that make up contemporary society. Thus

> although he has polemically endorsed the slogan of a "postmodernism" and has been involved in the defense of some of its more controversial productions, Lyotard is in reality quite unwilling to posit a postmodernist stage radically different from the period of high modernism and involving a fundamental historical and cultural break with the last. Rather, seeing postmodernism as a discontent with an [*sic*] disintegration of this or that high modernist style - a moment in the perpetual "revolution" and innovation of high modernism, to be succeeded by a fresh burst of formal invention - in a striking formula he has characterized postmodernism, not as that which follows modernism but rather as a

---

[10]Unlike many who have fed upon his thought, MacIntyre offers suggestions of how dialogue might continue to be engaged across traditions. See *Whose Justice? Which Rationality?*, chapter 19.

[11]Lyotard, *Postmodern*, 15.

[12]Ibid., 23.

[13]Cited in J. Middleton and G. Walsh, *Truth is Stranger than it Used to Be* (London: SPCK, 1995), 50.

[14]Lyotard, *Postmodern*, 30.

[15]Middleton and Walsh, *Truth is Stranger*, 55. Ronald Preston continues to argue for the existence of a common good. See 'The Common Good,' *EpRev* 24 (January 1997), 12-20.

cyclical moment that returns before the emergence of ever *new* modernisms in the stricter sense.[16]

With Foucault, Lyotard 'passionately denounces' the rhetoric of liberation as a totalizing metanarrative, which, along with all totalizing metanarratives such as modernity, the Enlightenment, and even Christianity, must be deconstructed after the approach of Jacques Derrida. Only when such systems of thought are deconstructed are they stripped of the violence they wreak over society and individuals by seeking to suppress all people and thought under a single explanatory narrative.

Post-modernism is therefore critical rather than utopian, and it rejects the possibility or desirability of any form of universality, even by consensus, declaring that in such situations, the self is dissolved 'into a host of networks and relations, of contradictory codes and interfering messages.' Notions of utopia aside, the post-modern philosopher distrusts the notion that there can or ought to be any reasonable agreement between members of society. They undermine authority and legitimacy in society, arguing that institutions are not content until they legislate by formulating prescriptions 'that have the status of norms' producing 'denotative utterances concerning what is true' and 'prescriptive utterances with pretensions to justice.'[17]

Lyotard thus rejects both methods described by T. W. Manson at the beginning of the previous chapter, which begin with either internal or external approaches to ethics, and consider their individual and collective aspects. 'The principle of consensus as a criterion of validation seems to be inadequate,' he writes. In the first place, 'consensus is an agreement between men, defined as knowing intellects and free wills, and is obtained through dialogue,' which is rejected as an impossible approach. Secondly, 'consensus is a component of the system which manipulates it in order to maintain and improve its performance.'[18] Believing there to be 'no reason to think that it would be possible to determine metaprescriptives common to all...[language games], it seems neither possible, nor even prudent,' to seek after social consensus through dialogue.[19] To the contrary, Lyotard's ultimate vision of science and knowledge is as a search 'not for consensus, but very precisely for "instabilities," as a practice of *paralogism*, in which the point is not to reach agreement but to undermine from within the very framework in which the previous "normal science" had been conducted. The rhetoric in which all this is conveyed is to be one of struggle' and conflict.[20]

The implications of the proliferation of such philosophy for ecumenical

---

[16]Frederic Jameson, in Lyotard, *Postmodern*, xvi.

[17]Lyotard, *Postmodern*, 31.

[18]Ibid., 60.

[19]Ibid., 65.

[20]Jameson in Lyotard, *Postmodern*, xix.

ethics become disturbingly apparent through the questions that may be raised against it. Is the legitimacy of narrative sufficient to sustain morality when metanarratives and metaphysics are rejected outright, and when the notion of consensus achieved through discussion is dismissed as doing 'violence to the heterogeneity of language games'? Is there a future for ecumenical ethics in the climate of post-modern philosophy whose 'principle is not the expert's homology, but the inventor's paralogy'?[21] Post-modern thought would seek to avoid answering such questions. And yet those who would wish to answer 'yes' find themselves adapting to the new categories of thought with little examination of their origins and premises. Laying aside critical faculties of reason and their accompanying historical perspective, it would seem the church is left to conform to post-modern categories, however unwitting, or to intentionally reject them and risk becoming a voice crying in the wilderness.[22] Though the origins and development of post-modern philosophy may seem to lie more in the ferment of Marxism, hermeneutical suspicion, and the failure of dialectical revolution than in modernity as a whole, the effects of deconstructionism on epistemology have been felt far and wide.

In general terms, the post-modern thrust in philosophy has contributed to a rejection of old patterns of thought which were based on correspondence theories of reality and reason, attributed to the secular impulses of the Enlightenment. Perpetual 'newness' is exalted while the 'old' is dismissed as antique and irrelevant. Universality of consciousness is denied, both in an idealistic sense, and in a realistic one that incorporates reason into its method in a central role. Consequently, any notion of there being unwarranted first principles, which serve as a foundation for philosophy, theology, or ethics, is rejected, and epistemology is left floundering. This summary dismissal of 'the Enlightenment project' has serious consequences for doing Christian ethics ecumenically, most especially in reaching an understanding of collective moral consciousness, both inside and outside of the church. Arguments positing the social construction of religion reinforce the notion of community as found in the doctrine of the Christian church, but fail to preserve the individuality of the church's members, who seek refuge from moral autonomy as part of a nurturing and nurtured fellowship.[23]

---

[21]Ibid., xxiv.

[22]It is acknowledged that this may be an acceptable and noble mission, if the voice crying in the wilderness is speaking the truth.

[23]Sociologists such as Emile Durkheim have influenced Christian theology in some circles, describing religion as a mere social self-reflection. Sociologists seem to have been the quickest to adopt post-modern categories and apply them to religion in general or the Church in particular. See for example, David Lyon, *Jesus in Disneyland* (Cambridge and Oxford: Polity Press, 2000); and works by Zygmunt Bauman.

Theological Adaptation of Philosophical Influences

Christians have responded to and been influenced by post-modern thinking in various ways, many choosing to accept the premise that we live in an irreversibly post-foundationalist world. For those working primarily in Christian ethics, such as Stanley Hauerwas, the 'end' of foundationalist epistemology resulting from assumptions about the reification role of language, has led in distinct directions, some of which are helpful, and some which are less cheering for the task before us. On the one hand, the call for ethics to be more theological must be received with enthusiasm. But as with most things philosophical, the post-modern Christian ethicists are often right in what they affirm, but wrong in what they deny.

In Stanley Hauerwas's view, for example, reality for the Christian is formed through membership in the community called the church. Through baptism, worship, and celebration of the eucharist, Christians become part of God's story, or narrative, and through their actions of worship, reality is structured.[24] Theology, therefore, cannot 'transcend particularistic communities', as it, along with ethics, is understood as an activity of worship.[25] Consequently, there can be no 'strong overlap between the church and the world.'[26] Ethics, indeed social ethics, is a matter of the church witnessing to the truth it embodies as the church, through a life of worship.

In his book *In Good Company: The Church as Polis*, Hauerwas indicates his rejection of individualism in light of his understanding of the community of faith

> I should not hide the fact that informing this account of the church is quite a different understanding of salvation than is assumed by many Christians today. I have little use for the current fascination with individual salvation in either its conservative or liberal guises. Such accounts of salvation assume that God has done something for each person which may find expression in the church. I do not assume that salvation is first or foremost about my life having "meaning" or ensuring "my" eternal destiny. Rather, salvation is being engrafted into practices that save us from those powers that would rule our lives making it impossible for us to truly worship God.[27]

---

[24]Expressions of worship are described by George Lindbeck as first-order statements. If all of life is conceived of as worship, then all of life takes place as a first-order statement whose truth cannot be logically challenged. See George A. Lindbeck, *The Nature of Doctrine: Religion and Theology in a Postliberal Age* (Philadelphia: Westminster, 1984).

[25]Hauerwas, *After Christianity?* 89.

[26]Hauerwas, *In Good Company: The Church as Polis*, 88. Cf. Hauerwas and William Willamon, *Resident Aliens: Life in a Christian Colony* (Nashville, TN: Abingdon, 1989).

[27]Hauerwas, *In Good Company*, 8.

We will overlook the communal works-salvation implicit in this statement for now, but it is clear that in his high view of the church, Hauerwas highlights - contrary to Niebuhr - the perfection-potential rather than the sinfulness of the community that is the church.[28] The church is defined much more distinctly than simply as one group amongst competing groups in society.

Hauerwas refuses to see this view as strictly communitarian, because the very word implies a plurality of communities, which he does not wish to acknowledge. 'Community is far too weak a description for that body we call church,' he writes. 'As Alasdair MacIntyre has pointed out, contemporary communitarians usually advance their proposals as a contribution to the politics of the nation-state. Liberals want governments to remain neutral between rival conceptions of the human good. Communitarians want government to give expression to some shared vision of the human good that will define some type of community.'[29] Hauerwas believes that when a Romantic notion of common good is married with the Aristotelian version of the *polis,* the community as nation-state is prone to dangerous forms of self-realisation. The challenge for the church in rejecting this type of communitarianism, is to resist the temptation to use the nation-state for the furthering of its own goals

> I seek, therefore, not for the church to be a community, but rather to be a body constituted by disciplines that create the capacity to resist the disciplines of the body associated with the modern nation-state and, in particular, the economic habits that support that state. For the church to *be* a social ethic, rather than to *have* a social ethic, means the church must be (is) a body polity. The crucial question is how the church can be such without resorting to mirroring the nation-state and/or being tempted to use the nation-state for the disciplining it so desires and needs. The latter temptation is almost irresistible in modernity once the church has been forced to become a 'voluntary association'.[30]

The desire to uphold the nature of the church as God's gift is recognized, and welcomed, as is the call to be more theological in our ethical thought, allowing Christian concepts to determine the content of our action. But the contention that the church lifts people beyond their common interest as sinners with the rest of humanity raises a flag of caution, especially in light of a proper doctrine of creation. A doctrinal suggestion that 'the community of reference for all people is the inclusive, universal community,' inevitably 'has political consequences,' since 'no people can be understood as total aliens....'[31] Maintaining a focus on the universality of the human race within Creation precludes the post-modern interpretation of what it means for the church to be

---

[28]Ibid., 11. In fact, despite being taught by Niebuhrians, Hauerwas is openly and stridently critical of (what some might say is a misinterpretation of) Niebuhr's method.
[29]Ibid., 25.
[30]Ibid., 26.
[31]Phillip Wogaman, *Christian Perspectives on Politics,* 117.

comprised of potentially sectarian 'resident aliens.' When the formative narrative defines the Christian community, barriers of ethical disunity may be too quickly erected, since such a limited community of reference permits its members to treat non-members as creatures of lesser value and to regard its adversaries as enemies of God.[32] It may well be true that in a pluralistic society 'a sustained interpretation and critique of society is required from the perspective of the community that acknowledges that there is no authority except from God,' but it is not clear that such a critique will be forthcoming from a community which sets itself above the rest of society, and refuses to acknowledge the moral dilemmas faced by its individual members on a daily basis.

Nevertheless, Hauerwas vehemently denies charges of sectarianism, and in some theoretical senses, rightly so. He simply does not want to address issues of social and political ethics at all. What he wants to address are those things that cause the community of the people of God to be ethically formed, and their lives to be ethically lived. We may find sympathy with his efforts, but less so when we consider the alternative vision of Milbank who pushes these ideas to an extreme when he suggests that the 'Church is first and foremost neither a programme, nor a "real" society, but instead an enacted, serious fiction.'[33] Despite his sympathy with Milbank, Hauerwas wishes to maintain the physicality of the church, but he is unable to avoid a dangerous position when he sympathizes enthusiastically with an exclusivist state church model.[34] Once again, we see individual and collective aspects of theology and ethics confused and without a promising outcome.

The End of Foundationalism?

It may be that we welcome recent post-modern admissions that the day of 'Christendom' is over.[35] It is largely true that unlike the times in which Rauschenbusch, and even Niebuhr were living, Christianity is no longer the sole arbiter of truth and ethics in western society, or even the predominant influence upon the individual or collective conscience. It is also true that in an era of intense globalization, the desire to seek differentiation through culture and nationalism has found a resurgence, which demands further exploration.[36] But it does not follow from such admissions that the structures of the

---

[32]Ibid.

[33]Milbank cited in Hauerwas, *In Good Company,* 29.

[34]Ibid., 31.

[35]This has been the declaration of many theologians in the past two decades. It is not a particularly shocking declaration from the perspective of those who have never considered 'Constantinian' Christianity to be either desirable or the norm.

[36]The Faith and Order department of the WCC is currently studying the relationship between Christian Churches and nationalism.

Enlightenment have been, or should be dismissed altogether. It is perhaps too readily forgotten that the progress of the Enlightenment in Europe and the west was inexorably tied up with the relationship of Christianity to the state and society, and with the development of Christianity itself. 'Christendom' as expressed through the nation-state may have had its best (and worst) day, but that is not to say that its effects are no longer present, or should no longer be present in the social realm.

At the same time, it is far from evident that the post-modern response gives us sufficient tools for understanding some of the more complex features of the individual relationship to the collective, both within and without the church. We may indeed be part of a story, an inclusive narrative, one that positively reinforces the unity of the church. But we are not *merely* part of a story, even a morally deterministic one, where affirmations of the complexities involved in moral individuality and collectivity are too easily overlooked. We may not be able to 'look to civilisation to satisfy nature's claim,' much less the church's claim, but it does not follow that we are unable 'to restate' for post-modern, post-liberal society (and for the church, for that matter) 'the theological truths which long since gave the Western political tradition its rationale.'[37]

A strong impetus for the rejection of foundationalism emerges from a scepticism regarding texts. The hermeneutic of suspicion that fed action-reflection models of social ethics is easily pushed to its inevitable fragmentary conclusion. In an atmosphere where reality is created, either by the individual, or by community as some ethicists contend, the notion that the original intention of an author may be accessed by a reader, is rejected as impossible. Texts, therefore, have many interpretations - as many interpretations as readers - and each one is considered as valid as any other.[38]

The implication for the use of the Bible in ethics becomes obvious. If there is no inherent meaning in any scriptural text, and no means of accessing it if there were, then the Bible is irrelevant, even for Christian ethics. Irrelevant that is, apart from a narrative framework, where the telling of the story forms those who will continue living the story, which is considered true in the context of the community made real by its telling. The temptation is to criticize the approach for being relativist, as biblical truth is regarded from a traditional point of view as being true only for a select group of people. But from the point of view of the community, there is no such claim as 'true for us,' since reality is created by

---

[37]Oliver O'Donovan *Resurrection and Moral Order: An Outline for Evangelical Ethics* 2nd ed., (Leicester: Apollos, 1994), 74. O'Donovan here refers to what Niebuhr accomplished in a modern, liberal society, something Hauerwas declares to be impossible now.

[38]Such scepticism often emerges out of discomfort with ambiguity. As Kevin Vanhoozer describes the deconstructionist work of Jacques Derrida, he writes, 'If he can't have perfect knowledge, he won't have any of it.' *Is there a meaning in this text?: The Bible, the reader and the morality of literary knowledge* (Leicester: Apollos, 1998), 300.

narrative. There is no other truth because there is no other reality that may be considered. This ignores the fact that reality of individuals may, in fact, be formed by several, sometimes competing narratives, and the notion that many different kinds of communities seem to be formed by the telling of the same story. This has serious implications not only for Christian ethics, but also for Christian unity. Moreover, some recent work has served to offer a strong case for a rejection of textual scepticism.[39]

Despite its strengths, a strictly ecclesial approach to ethics neglects the fact that humans are members of various collectives in society. And, as Niebuhr pointed out, sometimes they have conflicting interests. Though Hauerwas is correct that it is our membership in the church that ought largely to define the form of our ethical interests, it is not readily apparent that this is in fact always the case. Nor is it apparent that because the church ought to suggest the content of our ethic, it therefore operates from an 'independent position *au dessus de la melee.*'[40] Nicholas Wolterstorff offers a much more helpful post-foundationalist approach when he admits

> Rare will be the Christian scholar all of whose control beliefs are contained within his actual Christian commitment. This is justifiably the case. The reasons why a medical researcher rejects the theory lying behind the Chinese practice of acupuncture as not even the sort of theory he will entertain will most likely have little if anything to do with his religion. Rather, it will have to do with his being imbued with a whole orientation to disease developed in the Western world within the last century. In general, no one is *just* a Christian. He is also, say, an American, a Caucasian, a member of the middle class, of somewhat paranoid personality. All of these appellations suggest characteristic sets of beliefs which, in the appropriate circumstances, may function as control within his theory-devising and theory-weighing.[41]

Therefore, even post-foundationalist Christian social ethics will of necessity involve some sort of reason, competition and weighing of interests; will seek to draw upon the expertise of a wide range of specialists; and will yield more than a degree of ambiguity with which we must learn to be comfortable, and be willing to challenge.[42]

---

[39]Ibid. In response to thinkers such as Jacques Derrida, and Stanley Fish, Vanhoozer's volume offers a helpful rebuttal. See also Nicholas Wolterstorff, *Divine Discourse: Philosophical Reflections on the Claim that God Speaks* (Cambridge: Cambridge University Press, 1995).

[40]Ronald Preston, 'The Common Good,' 14.

[41]Nicholas Wolterstorff, *Reason within the Bounds of Religion*, 2nd ed. (1984; reprint, Grand Rapids, MI: Eerdmans, 1999), 83.

[42]Niebuhr referred often to the 'web of belief' in his work - an idea borrowed more recently by Stanley Grenz from Quine, and translated into the very Canadian term, 'mosaic' of belief. See W. V. O. Quine and J. S. Ullian, *The Web of Belief* (New York: Random House, 1970); Stanley Grenz, *Renewing the Center: Evangelical Theory in a*

Certainly not all post-foundationalists are so eager to dismiss the past three hundred years of western history as a failed 'Enlightenment project.' While declaring the death of foundationalism, Nicholas Wolterstorff suggests that even such a death (if we are willing to accept it as such) does not leave us floundering or groundless. Rather, it leaves us free on good philosophical ground to make faith claims and, as the Church, declare as our one foundation the Holy Love of God revealed in the reconciling cross of Jesus Christ.[43]

Wolterstorff points out that despite the demise of foundationalism, there is still much that may be said and believed with good reason within the theological and ethical task. He writes

> On all fronts foundationalism is in bad shape. It seems to me that there is nothing to do but give it up for mortally ill and learn to live in its absence. Theorizing is without a foundation of indubitables. In saying this I do not at all mean to deny that there is an objective reality with a nature independent of what we all conceive and believe...Nor do I mean to deny that you and I can attain true belief concerning that objective reality...Nor do I mean to deny that you and I can attain knowledge of that objective reality...Nor do I mean to deny that we are warranted in accepting some from among the thicket of human beliefs and in rejecting others...I mean just to affirm that the proposed rule for warranted theory acceptance is untenable. It is not the case that one is warranted in accepting some theory if and only if one is warranted in believing that it is justified by propositions knowable noninferentially and with certitude. From this it does not follow that there is no structured reality independent of our conceivings and believings - though the difficulties of foundationalism have led many to this position. Nor does it follow that we must give up truth as the goal of theoretical inquiry - though the difficulties of foundationalism have made this view particularly attractive to many. Nor does it follow that we can never know the truth - though the difficulties of foundationalism have led to a wave of agnosticism. Nor does it follow that one belief is as warranted for me as another. All that follows is that theorizing is without a foundation of indubitables.

Post-Theological Era (Grand Rapids: Baker, 2000); Stanley Grenz and John R. Franke, *Beyond Foundationalism: Shaping Theology in a Postmodern Context* (Louisville, KY: Westminster/John Knox Press, 2001). Cf. Wolfhart Pannenberg, *Anthropology in Theological Perspective*, 361ff.

[43]Even Hauerwas applauds the Baptist James McClendon for offering an alternative to traditional approaches to the problems of foundationalism. Hauerwas wonders if it is McClendon's philosophical astuteness or denominational affiliation which leads him to his helpful conclusions, locating his foundation in Christ: 'The baptist tradition never sought a "worldly" foundation since it knew there is no foundation other than Jesus Christ,' Hauerwas writes approvingly. It would seem that to describe Jesus Christ as the foundation of the church, of life, or of ethics, is acknowledgement of an ethical foundation, but Hauerwas and his sympathisers do not wish to view it as such, certainly not in a universal sense. See Hauerwas, *In Good Company*, 33. Cf. James McClendon Jr., and James M. Smith, *Systematic Theology: Ethics* (Nashville: Abingdon, 1986).

Our future theories of theorizing will have to be nonfoundationalist ones.[44]

We may be uncomfortable surrendering even this much ground to post-modernism, especially with the retreat to 'faith' claims rather than 'truth' claims, which is what faith claims must ultimately be.[45] Yet here we see that even within a 'narrative' approach, reason and common ground may not be categorically denied. Philosophy sometimes affirms what theology has long held to be true, and will hold to be true long after the next philosophical tide has come in and gone out again.

Despite some helpful aspects, it is still not entirely clear that post-foundationalist methods are reflecting the contemporary situation in their initial presuppositions. In rejecting what they describe as 'Enlightenment foundationalism,' philosophers have identified a difficulty of determining a starting-point for epistemology, which has repercussions for ethics. Rationalism is dead, they say, because there are no universal first principles upon which it may be based. But if this were as serious a challenge as some philosophers and theologians make it out to be, it is a conclusion that should have unnerved scientists more than theologians. The fact that science has replaced religion as a voice of authority in society, carrying on with its 'Enlightenment' presuppositions without acknowledging the end of the modernist 'project' demonstrates relatively how quick theology is to march to the beat of the philosophical drum.[46] The fact is that scientists could not wholly embrace this suggestion without surrendering the scientific enterprise altogether.[47] Similarly,

---

[44]Wolterstorff, *Reason*, 56-57.

[45]Those who have found in Christ an enduring ethical foundation may be especially disturbed by this choice of words. Yet, even they must confess that they cannot demonstrate God -in-Christ empirically to universal satisfaction. That is the mystery of faith, but it doesn't make it any less true, or any less a foundation for me, the Church, or the cosmos. This admission is not so far removed from the experience of the confessing Church throughout the ages, for whom the foundation of life has been known universally and with good reason. Cf. Wolfhart Pannenberg, *An Introduction to Christian Anthropology*, 15f. Pannenberg suggests: 'Without a sound claim to universal validity Christians cannot maintain a conviction of the truth of their faith and message. For a "truth" that would be simply my truth and would not at least claim to be universal and valid for every human being could not remain true even for me. This explains why Christians cannot but try to defend the claim of their faith to be true.'

[46]We are reminded of Alan Sell's warning, recorded earlier, against being too eager to wed a philosophy of religion to any philosophical 'ism'. It cannot be denied that post-modernism, and anti-foundationalism are to be included in this caveat.

[47]To be fair, Milbank allows that scientists may legitimately retain their methods if their observations are confined to the isolation of repeatable patterns, which relate to closed formal systems, and do not seek to relate to the general or universal. Unlike science, human behaviour cannot be so defined nor confined, and thus social science cannot demonstrate anything, but merely be narrated. The fact that scientists rarely, if ever, confine their theories and methods to closed systems without general application seems

those who make a case for moving 'beyond' the Enlightenment would be more true to their cause if they stopped writing and talking and thinking about it. Having said that, the post-modern challenge is real and is before us, and so must be held in view as we proceed in a consideration of ecumenical ethics. The way that post-moderns perceive of collective and individual moral consciousness is important to consider if ecumenical ethics are to move forward with any kind of conversation at all. We may or may not need to establish ethics on the basis of reason, or some universally valid principles, but we certainly cannot do without them altogether.

The post-modern challenge reinforces the argument that ethics will necessarily be characterized by ambiguity, a fact acknowledged by Rauschenbusch and embraced by Niebuhr. But it does not necessarily follow that ambiguity is the end of the road for social ethics, or that the only alternative is certainty within a narrow band of narrative existence.[48] Rather, as Wolterstorff has demonstrated, the post-foundationalist challenge in no way precludes the use of parameters for defining a reasonable course of action, based on a reasonable, if not unwarranted foundation. He calls such parameters 'control beliefs' for authentic commitment, or, those particular beliefs that condition how Christians live out their lives in particular places and times. Moreover, such beliefs ought to exercise control over the devising of theories about how Christian life ought to be lived

> The Christian scholar ought to allow the belief-content of his authentic Christian commitment to function as control within his devising and weighing of theories. For he like everyone else ought to seek consistency, wholeness, and integrity in the body of his beliefs and commitments. Since his fundamental commitment to Christ ought to be decisively ultimate in his life, the rest of his life ought to be brought into harmony with it. As control, the belief-content of his authentic commitment ought to function both negatively and positively. Negatively, the Christian scholar ought to reject certain theories on the ground that they conflict

---

to suggest that they do not share Milbank's interpretation. See Milbank, *Theology and Social Theory* (Oxford: Blackwell, 1990), 259-277. Science has not been immune from philosophical scrutiny that its methods also represent worldview commitments rather than pure truth claims. See, for example, Michael Polanyi, *Personal Knowledge: Towards a Post-Critical Philosophy* (Chicago: University of Chicago Press, 1958), and Thomas Kuhn, *The Structure of Scientific Revolutions* (Chicago: University of Chicago Press, 1970). Cf. David Naugle, *Worldview: The History of a Concept* (Grand Rapids, MI: Eerdmans, 2002).

[48]Cf. P. T. Forsyth, *The Principle of Authority* (London: Hodder and Stoughton, 1912), 52ff. Forsyth suggested in *Positive Preaching and the Modern Mind* (London: Hodder and Stoughton, 1917), 179-183, that uncertainty was a particular threat to the church of his day. In *The Principle of Authority*, Forsyth argued that the authority of certainty lay beyond faith experience, and challenges the problem of ethical relativity: 'The real ground of our certitude, therefore, is the nature of the thing of which we are sure, rather than the nature of the experience in which we are sure.'

or do not comport well with the belief-content of his authentic commitment. And positively he ought to devise theories which comport as well as possible with, or are at least consistent with, the belief-content of his authentic commitment.[49]

Although Wolterstorff here illustrates the impossibility of building a non-foundationalist approach without foundations, his point is appreciated.[50] A Christian approach to social ethics needs at least, to demonstrate integrity and elaborate its 'control beliefs' in a coherent and internally consistent manner.

Moreover, it would be well to keep in mind that just as the post-foundationalists are correct to remind us of the pre-eminent role theology ought to have over philosophy, their very existence demonstrates the responsive role theology often has to philosophy, expressed well in the development of twentieth-century social ethics. To be true to our theological heritage, the philosophical presuppositions that we have reached the end of reason, and that the Enlightenment is 'over', deserve to be challenged by Christian thought. We need not accept so readily the dismissal of helpful philosophical categories, especially when we consider some of the theological implications.

For example, some significant implications for Christology emerge from Hans Frei's 'identity descriptions' of Jesus in the Gospels. In Frei's understanding, Jesus' identity *is* that which is depicted in the biblical narratives.[51] When traced to its logical conclusion, such an assertion demands the entire theological task to be deconstructed, and reconstructed in a completely new fashion. If 'Jesus and his story are one,' then Jesus is removed from the possibility of historical investigation. A separation of Jesus from history eliminates from an ethical method some elements that we have argued to be crucial for maintaining ethical integrity. Not only that, but individuality and community, creature and Creator become confused at the level of the church, if not in the Godhead. In such an atmosphere, moral formation is the only possible method of approach since ethical discussion in any other context is precluded. It is difficult to see any way through this confusion without rejecting the method entirely.

On the other hand, those valid concerns raised by the post-modern challenge must be addressed and incorporated into a method which is broadly inclusive, and which takes account of realists and idealists alike who have formed and will continue to form, part of the landscape in social ethics. Scholars like

---

[49]Wolterstorff, *Reason,* 76. Wolterstorff later defines his desire for the subject of such theorising to be in the area of ethics, a suggestion particularly appropriate to the present task.

[50]In a reference to J.H. Yoder in his review of *Christian Theism and Moral Philosophy,* Alan Sell suggests that despite 'opposition to certain kinds of allegedly exclusive methodological foundations,' such an ethicist is 'not utterly bereft of somewhere to plant his feet.' *SCE* 13 2000, 111.

[51]This is a point identified by Richard C. Allen, 'When Narrative Fails,' *JRE* (Spring 1993): 34.

Hauerwas cannot be dismissed simply as cantankerous surrealists who prefer a narrative retreat into relativism to direct social engagement on a reasonable foundation. For example, the 'suggestion that some sorts of neo-orthodox theology are but variants of liberal Protestantism, insofar as the revealed word of God speaks only for itself without penetrating human construction' points to a real epistemological concern for ethics, but one which need not drive too firm a wedge between faith and reason, as Niebuhr illustrated.[52] At the same time, post-foundationalist questioning of Enlightenment methods challenges us to recognize a ruggedly dogmatic orientation towards problem-solving in social ethics, often seeking out a single moral principle which is sufficient for all people at all times and everywhere, and finding it an impossible task. Equally, the fact that we have found it so difficult to live with ambiguity has been reflected in messianic ethical programs of many sorts. On the left, radical political movements seek the establishment of their version of the kingdom of God through violent intervention; on the right, particular interpretations of Christian ethics are used to justify sectarianism and murder. In both cases, ambiguity is a word that does not enter the picture, except as justification of violence, and coercion becomes the means to establish a parochial version of the 'gospel' of Christ. While moral community rather than moral ambiguity has been the watchword of ecclesial ethics, their epistemological questioning at least opens the door for an ethic that seeks to move beyond a 'problem-solving' method that actually fails to solve any problems. If theology is to have the determinative say in ethical method, then idealists, realists, and post-modernists may well have to learn to live together in an atmosphere of ambiguity, albeit one with parameters which limit ambiguity when it compromises truth, and stretch ambiguity when it becomes tired and static.[53]

Ecclesiology and Ethics in the WCC

Despite our various levels of intellectual comfort with post-modern ideas, they reflect some of the influences that have found expression in the Ecclesiology and Ethics programme of the WCC. Though Hauerwas was not physically present at the table of participants for the Ecclesiology and Ethics programme, his ideas and those of other ethicists and philosophers dealing with post-modernism in various ways, found influence through several who did attend and guide the direction of the consultation meetings. Duncan Forrester, who served as co-moderator of the study, and Lewis Mudge who was a participant, both acknowledge a debt to Hauerwas, and Forrester finds Alasdair MacIntyre's 'analysis of the modern predicament as breakdown of community

---

[52]Hauerwas, *In Good Company*, n.228.
[53]Cf. O'Donovan, *Resurrection and Moral Order*, 257-262.

and ethical fragmentation compellingly attractive.'[54] 'MacIntyre discerns a massive crisis of community and of morality in the modern world, so that we are in a new Dark Ages, whether we recognize it as such or not,' Forrester writes. His description of MacIntyre's thought on this point reveals how it captured his imagination

> In the famous conclusion to *After Virtue* he draws a comparison with the old Dark Ages, when men and women of intelligence, faith and good will ceased to identify the continuance of civility and moral community with the propping up of the Roman imperium. Instead, they explored the tradition and established communities of shared faith in which they could "live in truth" and offer an alternative understanding of life and of community and of morality. He goes on to suggest that modern morality is only fragments wrested from a tradition which has been rejected or forgotten. It lacks coherence, and fails to attract the degree of support it needs if it is to provide a basis for healthy community life together.[55]

Rather than question whether MacIntyre's assessment is accurate, Forrester opts to respond to the challenge he poses. He insists

> If there is anything to be said for MacIntyre's diagnosis, the Christian response should be twofold: on the one hand, commending Christian ethical "fragments" in the hope that some of them may be recognized as public truth, and that then people may enquire as to the quarry from which they came. This is, in a way, ethical evangelism, or at least a recognition that law and gospel cannot be separated. On the other hand, it is essential that the church…should present a kind of working model of community and of virtue, the gospel manifested in the life of a community, the church. Modern secular ethics claims to be independent both of theology and of metaphysics. Commonly now it seeks a fragile grounding in consensus. We face a new situation, which is also a new opportunity. And we can only grasp that opportunity with the church in its varied manifestations providing a hermeneutic for law and gospel.[56]

But it is hardly clear that a single hermeneutic is possible from the many perspectives of the communities that presently comprise the global church.

Another aspect which Forrester, and indeed MacIntyre and Hauerwas seem to overlook in their analyses is that the contemporary church, as a global phenomenon, can hardly be equated with the tradition which 'propped up' the

---

[54]Duncan Forrester, 'Living in Truth and Unity,' in *Ecclesiology and Ethics*, Best and Robra, eds., 102. Hauerwas's influence is acknowledged on page 94. Forrester's 'communitarian' approach is made clear also in *Beliefs, Values and Policies: Conviction Politics in a Secular Age* (Oxford: Clarendon, 1989). Cf. Lewis S. Mudge, *The Church as Moral Community: Ecclesiology and Ethics in Ecumenical Debate* (Geneva: WCC, 1998).
[55]Forrester, 'Living in Truth and Unity,' 102.
[56]Ibid.

Roman imperium. Various church traditions have been defining what it means to live out the reality of faith community for generations, witnessing to the truth through supporting and resisting public policy, as the case may have required throughout history. Perhaps the ages would not have to be quite so dark if the faith community and its 'men and women of intelligence, faith and good will' were more ready to protect and bear witness to the Light in the midst of society, by pointing to knowledge learned and advantages gained, even in the face of rejection (or perhaps more so in the face of rejection), than to hasten its demise by voluntarily and only-too-willingly jumping out of the way, or standing curiously on the sidelines.

Tom Best and Martin Robra agreed that there were at least two positive things to emerge from the Ecclesiology and Ethics study - the recovery of the church as the locus of ethics, and the recovery of portions of the ecumenical memory 'including some earlier blueprints for bridges.'[57] This may be well and good, but the major themes of the study offer little promise of advance in ethical methodology. For example, two overarching themes or convictions were present throughout the study, 'that ethical reflection and action - indeed, *ecumenical* ethical reflection and action - are intrinsic to the nature and life of the church. Thus ecclesiological and ethical reflection are inseparable: Christian ethical engagement is an expression of our deepest ecclesiological convictions, and our ecclesiology must be informed by our experience of ethical engagement, by our living out of the gospel in the complex situations of the world. For what we do follows from who we understand ourselves to be, and where we understand ourselves to be at home.' Acknowledgement of contextuality is important. But the difficulties raised by this first statement are compounded in light of the second: 'The second conviction is closely related: that ecclesiology and Christian ethics must stay in close dialogue, each honouring and learning from the distinctive language and thought-forms of the other.'[58] Given the substance of the first conviction, how is the second possible in any constructive manner? If communities are formed by narratives, and geography and culture confirm the parochial nature of such narratives, then no reality outside of each community can be conceived, and no dialogue is possible across realities constructed by mutually exclusive language. Though a common narrative as the 'church universal' might be accessed, it is not clear from these definitions, or from recent history, that even this degree of universality is encouraged or possible. Thus, the approach lends too much credence to the value of language theories and contextuality, and reflects the true divide that exists between the two major programmes of the WCC.[59]

---

[57]*Ecclesiology and Ethics*, viii.

[58]Ibid., ix.

[59]In a conversation on November 24, 1999, Dr. Tom Best admitted to the unconventional method of the study, particularly its rapid advancement to print - a process uncommon to the usual practices of Faith and Order.

The theological basis of Ecclesiology and Ethics is laid out thinly and early in the first report of the series of three consultations, entitled *Costly Unity*. Here, an early effort to confirm unity in a common narrative is contained in the suggestion that it is 'the memory of Jesus Christ' which is 'formative of the church itself,' where the 'Trinity is experienced as an image for human community and the basis for social doctrine and ecclesial reality. The theological conclusion is exactly Hauerwas's point: 'the church not only has, but is, a social ethic.'[60] The study affirms that fellowship and shared witness extend beyond the boundaries of the Church, but refrains from the ecclesiastical imperialism of referring to those outside the Church as anonymous or crypto-Christians. It further confirms that the Church 'is not *constituted* by or dependent for its ongoing existence upon the moral activities of its members,' rather, 'its origins and ongoing life rest in the lavish grace and patience of God.'[61] The implications of the reality of moral existence encourages the study to acknowledge the ambiguity and complexity of concrete moral challenges, where 'it is not to be expected that all the members of a particular church, or all church organizations in a particular region, will arrive at the same moral decision in each particular situation. Christian freedom encompasses sincere and serious differences of moral judgment.'[62] The participants recognized this freedom as distinct from 'wholesale moral relativism,' stating, 'There are boundaries, and it will always be the case that certain decisions and actions are in contradiction to the nature and purpose of the church and the central teaching of the gospel.'[63] Such clear-cut cases include those addressed by the Barmen declaration and Kairos documents, which are frequently upheld as models of ecumenical theological agreement.[64] Quoting Visser't Hooft's comment on moral heresy, the study affirmed that there are certain moral issues that can arise that place at stake the very identity of the church.[65]

Thus, the study begins and continues with some most helpful and corrective affirmations, though it fails to provide any further theological or philosophical reflection to validate its statements. It is not long before the documents begin to reflect a preponderance of narrative interpretation, influenced by the response to post-modernist epistemology. True though affirmations of the nature of the church community experience of worship and fellowship may be, and corrective though they are of approaches that neglect ecclesiology and theology seriously if not altogether, it cannot be denied that they reflect a broader

---

[60]*Ecclesiology and Ethics*, 5.

[61]Ibid.

[62]Ibid.

[63]Ibid.

[64]Though, as noted previously, both documents were born outside of formal ecumenical institutional machinery.

[65]The approach to ethical issues as *status confessionis* will be addressed more directly in chapter nine.

acceptance of philosophical principles, which are assimilated without critical debate and reflection.

The influence of contemporary philosophy is most clear in the development of the methodological approach of *moral formation*, where the church is understood to be constructed by its own narrative, despite early statements to the contrary. The second stage of the report entitled *Costly Commitment* describes the process of moral formation as taking place 'within the ethos or environment of a particular society, community or church. The songs we sing, the stories we tell, the issues we debate, the instruction we offer, the persons thought worth emulating, the common habits and practices of a culture - these are the sources and "signatures" of "our" ethos. And the "moral environment" is marked not least by the way a community, society or church is ordered - who does what, by what means, and with what kind of authority. Thus it is the whole *way of life* which morally forms and educates (or malforms and miseducates), and this way of life both creates and reflects a particular moral ethos.'[66] The final study, entitled *Costly Obedience*, confirms that it is the worship practices of the church that form the church, and its moral life, freeing the Church to seek 'new vocabularies' and 'new patterns'.[67]

Suddenly, the influence of post-modern categories of thought has become most apparent. When a brand of faith contextualisation is combined with the necessary conviction of humility that 'almost every view is at least partially true,' and 'none can claim the whole truth,' there seems to be no real space for dialogue and debate as to which views are more true than others. The study thus acknowledges the fragmentation of ethical consensus in society and retreats to consider its own position, while affirming that Christians have something distinctive to say in sharing with secular ethicists in the public realm.[68] The inconsistency of these various lines of argument is not acknowledged, and perhaps not recognized. Moreover, a commitment to reconstruction implies an acceptance of some sort of imposed deconstruction.[69] Though the post-modern challenge to the very concept of *oikoumene* is recognized in the study, its theological response is most disappointing, discussing the church in relation to the 'resonance' of Christ, generated by the 'energy-field' of the Holy Spirit.[70]

The moral formation approach may help remind us of who the church is as a moral community, and this is perhaps the best material to emerge from the

---

[66] *Ecclesiology and Ethics,* 42.

[67] Ibid., 72-3.

[68] Ibid., 54.

[69] Though it is possible that in the spirit of paralogism, the inconsistency is recognised and welcomed!

[70] A doctrine of the Holy Spirit is not the only possible area for grounding an understanding of unity in the contemporary intellectual context, and it is less so when described in terms which reflect more science fiction than Christian tradition. *Ecclesiology and Ethics,* 76-81.

study. Lewis Mudge warned that 'If the church is not fully the church, in the sense of being a theologically-principled way of life in its own right, then any moral engagement with the world outside, any engaged concern for general human well-being, is going to end with distinctiveness in the faith being swallowed up in platitudes.'[71] Though it may seem self-evident to some, Konrad Raiser suggested that 'such direct linking of ethics and ecclesiology is new to the tradition of most churches.'[72] Regardless of its novelty, it does not bring us any nearer to knowing what we should do, and how we should do it, which has been a perennial dilemma of ecumenical ethics. Although the church may have something distinctive to share with the world, it is not clear from this study that there is any way we might define what that distinctive something actually is, nor how it might be communicated. Obsessive self-reflection becomes an inevitable by-product of the approach.

Some Implications for Individual and Community Agency

In his response to the Ecclesiology and Ethics study, participant and co-moderator Duncan Forrester issued an important caveat by suggesting that 'it is of greatest importance that Christians are not trapped into the individualism characteristic of post-enlightenment ethics.'[73] Stating that 'one cannot be a Christian in isolation, only in relationship,' Forrester follows Hauerwas's lead in equating Christian ethics and church ethics. Ethics will always, therefore, be communitarian, though he is keen to point out that 'Christian ethics is not the in-house discourse of an enclosed community leading a ghetto-like existence, without accepting responsibility for the "world". It makes universal claims about the good as such, not simply about the good that happens to be chosen by Christians. Christian understandings of forgiveness, reconciliation, and justice...have urgent relevance to the public realm.'[74] Forrester also wishes to clarify the kind of communitarian ethic he is pointing towards

> Just as Christian ecclesial ethics is opposed to individualism, so it cannot accept a free-floating communitarianism or regard collectivist ethics resting on socialist or other understandings of community as adequate. The church gives a special shape to the understanding of community, a shape which has become specially relevant

---

[71]Lewis Mudge, 'Ecclesiology and Ethics in Current Ecumenical Debate,' *ER* 48 (January 1996): 11.

[72]Konrad Raiser, 'Ecumenical Discussion of Ethics and Ecclesiology,' *ER* 48 (January 1996): 4.

[73]Duncan Forrester, 'Living in Truth and Unity,' *Ecclesiology and Ethics*, 97.

[74]Ibid., 98. Forrester and several other leading theologians of the present generation are greatly indebted to the Enlightenment and the moral critique of theology which enabled individuals to take a conscientious stand against untoward authorities, both biblicist and ecclesial. In this context, it would be helpful if individualism and individuality were more clearly distinguished amongst those offering a post-Enlightenment critique.

in an age when on the one hand there is much fragmentation and breakdown of community, and on the other hand still powerful forms of collectivism which diminish human beings and human freedom through a coercive uniformity. The challenge of today is to discover what it is to be the church of Jesus Christ for the sake of the world. And this is a costly quest.[75]

At face value, we may readily and heartily agree with the sentiments of this statement. But when we understand the philosophy that has influenced at least some adherents of the approach, perhaps the most costly thing about it is being asked to surrender our common humanity, and our connection with the rest of the created world, for whom Christ came, and for who he died. It is difficult to see how this method leads beyond introspection. In Ronald Preston's reaction to the study, he remarks,

> The chief point made is that moral commitment is the *esse* of the Church. But who ever denied that? There is no disagreement that rooted in the biblical witness is the belief in Yahweh, and that membership of his people is no way of avoiding basic moral demands. On the contrary, God's people are not chosen for privileges or moral exemptions but to follow his inescapable moral demands. Joint Consultations are hardly needed to establish this.[76]

Though we may, in fact, wish to uphold the work of Christ as the true *esse* of the Church, we cannot deny that moral commitment is a clear implication of that *esse*. In Preston's view, and many others, there is much more to be done in working toward a method that can bring some clarity to the way churches make ethical decisions together. The ecclesial approach gives rise to questions to which its proponents have failed to offer satisfactory answers: If we are morally formed by the same narrative, how is it that we can so often arrive at different ethical conclusions, and how do we resolve our conflicts within the body, let alone outside of it? What might characterize the relationship between the church and the 'rest of the world' in the moral formation approach? Once again, these issues are clarified in a brief examination of the relationship between the individual, group and universal expressions of moral agency.

We will remember that Rauschenbusch's negative experience of individualism in the church led him to submerge the church beneath the wider kingdom ideal, which found expression in collective human endeavours of many kinds. A slow but determined evolution would bring the kingdom to realization in human society, of which the church was but a part. By contrast, Niebuhr was concerned so much for the facts of the situation, and the impossibility of the possible, that the role of the church was submerged often beneath general political reflection. His Reformed view could not allow him to perceive of any significant disjunction between the church and the world, and

---

[75]Ibid.
[76]Preston, 'On to Harare,' 28.

his Lutheranism saw both as permeated by sin. Because of this, only a pragmatic study-dialogue process could produce any ethical fruit on a collective level, and even then it would rarely be a victorious exercise. Hauerwas is right to point out that under the influence of Niebuhr and others, 'Christians can lose any sense that the way they think about the world is different than how others may think about the world.'[77] Recovery of this sense is among the most positive contributions of the moral formation approach. But while participation in the church is crucial for Christians, as it *informs*, *transforms*, and *reforms* our understanding of reality and ethics, it alone does not *form* it, and the difference is of crucial significance.

Oliver O'Donovan has noted the methodological significance of Hauerwas's starting point in contrast with his own: '...where I turn to the Christ-event and to the apostolic witness, he turns first to the practices of the church.'[78] He explains that Hauerwas has 'strong reservations about...a theology not determined by tradition, a theology that can transcend particularistic communities.'[79] According to such a view, salvation is not only found in and through the church, but the church becomes the salvation for the world. Hauerwas says that in the eucharist, 'we - that is, the church - have been made part of God's sacrifice, God's life, for the world.' In this view, 'the great good news is that by making us participants in God's sacrifice of Jesus we become the salvation of the world.'[80] Subsequently, the church is seen itself as a polis, a political community, or rather *the* political community. One might not be faulted for suggesting this approach seems at least as triumphalistic as 'Constantinian Christianity', whose demise has been widely welcomed and heralded.

Although Christians are saved as individuals, we are saved into, but not by, membership in a community. In agreement with the post-modern theologians we acknowledge that '...we may not appeal to the invisibility of the church as a means of avoiding pain - or the challenge of fellowship - in this world.' In opposition to the post-modern theologians, we recognize 'The opposite danger is that if we think only of the visible Church conceived as an institution, people may wrongly come to believe that they are saved not by grace but by enrolment: a doctrine of works if ever there was one! And the Church may come to believe, equally wrongly, that it, and not the Cross, opens the way of salvation; that its sacraments are the prerequisites of eternal life. In fact, the opposite is the case: "The Christian rites grew out of the Good News; they were not incantations to conjure it up from a void".'[81]

---

[77]Hauerwas, *The Church as Polis*, 157.

[78]O'Donovan, *Resurrection and Moral Order*, xv.

[79]Hauerwas, *After Christendom?* 89.

[80]Hauerwas, *In Good Company*, 167.

[81]Bernard Lord Manning, cited in Alan P. F. Sell, *The Spirit Our Life* (Shippensburg, PA: Ragged Edge Press, 2000), 57.

Moreover, as Bonhoeffer reminded us, 'The death and the life of the Christian is not determined by his own resources; rather he finds both only in God's Word to him. The Reformers expressed it this way: Our righteousness is an "alien righteousness" a righteousness that comes from outside of us (*extra nos*).' With this, Hauerwas might readily agree, stressing that righteousness is external to the individual, but embodied in the community that is the church. But Bonhoeffer makes it clear that even to point to ourselves – even as the church - as the source of such righteousness, is misdirected. The Reformers 'were saying that the Christian is dependent on the Word of God spoken to him. He is pointed outward, to the Word that comes to him. The Christian lives wholly by the truth of God's Word in Jesus Christ. If somebody asks him, Where is your salvation, your righteousness? he can never point to himself. He points to the Word of God in Jesus Christ, which assures him salvation and righteousness.'[82] Bonhoeffer is intent to express that assurance and encouragement can come only to individual believers in fellowship where 'God permits them to meet together and gives them community. Their fellowship is founded solely upon Jesus Christ and this "alien righteousness". All we can say, therefore, is: "the community of Christians springs solely from the biblical and Reformation message of the justification of man through grace alone; this alone is the basis of the longing of Christians for one another".'[83]

Insights about the nature of Christian community may be best appreciated when balanced with a dynamic of individuality. Again, Bonhoeffer offers a challenge

> Let him who cannot be alone beware of community. He will only do harm to himself and to the community. Alone you stood before God when he called you; alone you had to answer that call; alone you had to struggle and pray; and alone you will die and give an account to God. You cannot escape from yourself; for God has singled you out. If you refuse to be alone you are rejecting Christ's call to you, and you can have no part in the community of those who are called.[84]

He continues, 'We recognize, then, that only as we are within the fellowship can we be alone, and only he that is alone can live in fellowship. Only in the fellowship do we learn to be rightly alone, and only in aloneness do we learn to live rightly in the fellowship. It is not as though the one preceded the other; both begin at the same time, namely, with the call of Jesus Christ.'[85] Once again, finding a balance between individual and collective aspects of moral agency is crucial to resolving the impasse, remembering that Christ, and not the Church, is the centre and source of our salvation.

---

[82]Bonhoeffer, *Life Together*, 11.

[83]Ibid., 12. Hauerwas wants to deny that even God has an objective ethic. See Samuel Wells, *Transforming Fate Into Destiny* (Carlisle: Paternoster, 1998), 13ff.

[84]Bonhoeffer, *Life Together*, 57-8.

[85]Ibid., 58.

Such salvation comes to individuals, grafting them into a community by the atonement of their Lord, thereby healing the wounds of individuality by granting solace in a racial salvation, without eliminating the privilege of self as created in the image of God and responsible to Him. Sell suggests a serious flaw in the high Church attitude of some post-modernist responses when he writes

> In an extreme form the doctrine that the Church is the continuation of the Incarnation is tantamount to the belief that the Church as an institution is not the witness to, but the substitute for, Christ. But this is completely to overlook the Church's creaturely status. It also cuts at the foundation of Christian discipleship, which is not membership in an institution but union with a risen Saviour: "The Christian Church on earth was designed and fitted to be the home where Christian might meet with Christian, and hold fellowship together; it was neither designed nor fitted to be a substitute for the union and fellowship of the sinner with his Saviour" (James Bannerman).[86]

Seeking balance between individual and collective aspects of salvation, and recalling the Trinitarian source of our theology, prevents our ethics as church communities and church members from becoming either too ghettoized, or drowned in indifference.

But is there a sense in which our uniqueness as a community of faith indwelt by the Holy Spirit means we must stress our 'difference' from the rest of the world? While views which draw a firm line between church and society must be rejected, such scholars as Milbank, Hauerwas, and J. H. Yoder remind us that we must also be wary of those which seek to turn the church into a political messianic community, whose sole interest is the 'Christianizing' of society and culture through means of conflict and power. This is a lesson to be learned by Christians occupying opposite ends of the theological and political spectrum. Responding to J. H. Oldham's description of the role of the worshipping community in the concept of the 'Responsible Society,' Yoder applauded the fact that 'this centrality of the church continued to be affirmed in the basic documents of ecumenical social strategy in succeeding years.' But he also observed that such centrality 'did not remain equally clear when studies on specific problems came into view.' Yoder acknowledged the complexity of the post-war ecumenical scene where 'concrete studies were necessary to relate to problems of social organization concerning which often it appeared that there would not be such a thing as a specifically *Christian* point of view. It seemed that in such cases there would exist only the *correct* point of view of the expert - the economist, the agronomist, the sociologist, who could not necessarily be found within the church.' 'Furthermore,' noted Yoder, 'it seemed that the basis of social cooperation between Christians and non-Christians would have to be something other than a specifically Christian standard. We cannot be sure that

---

[86]Sell, *Spirit*, 55.

in all this process of study, the central importance of the Christian community as a new humanity was kept in view, not only as a verbal affirmation, but also as an instrument of social change.'[87] This conclusion seems more than fair, considering the inattention of Niebuhr and his colleagues to matters of ecclesiology, and more recent developments in ecumenical ethics seem to confirm Yoder's other criticism

> In the published documents arising from the ecumenical conversation on social ethics since 1948 there has been a degree of success in avoiding the temptations of which Christians accuse the Pharisees. There is little tendency to seek to resolve these problems by trusting in some kind of immutable law or a loophole-free casuistry. But one cannot be so sure that there has been equal success in discerning and avoiding the temptation of the Sadducees, which is also a form of servitude to the Powers. By this we mean the assumption that the forces which really determine the march of history are in the hands of the leaders of the armies and the markets, in such measure that if Christians are to contribute to the renewal of society they will need to seek, like everyone else - in fact in competition with everyone else - to become in their turn the lords of the state and of the economy, so as to use that power toward the ends they consider desirable.[88]

The case may be overstated, but although time does not permit a foray into the eschatological dimensions of this statement, it is clear that it serves as a caveat both to those who would seek messianic justification of violence in overcoming oppression, and the domination of a Christian society established through culture wars. Yoder thus affirms 'that the biblical understanding of the powers in history can give us a more adequate intellectual framework of the task of *social* discernment to which we are especially called in our age. This discernment is not simply a way of helping the needy with their social problems, a kind of updated philanthropy, nor does it mean simply to guide individual Christians by helping them to do good deeds or to avoid sin.' Rather, it is 'a part of Christians' proclamation that the church is under orders to make known to the Powers, as no other proclaimer can do, the fulfilment of the mysterious purposes of God (Eph. 3:10) by means of that Man in whom their rebellion has been broken and the pretensions they had raised have been demolished.' Unlike many of his sympathizers, Yoder does not want to

---

[87]John Howard Yoder, *The Politics of Jesus*, 2nd ed. (Carlisle: Paternoster and Grand Rapids: Eerdmans, 1994, 152-3. We will recall Niebuhr's suggestion that in-group activity, ethics would reflect the lowest common denominator. This is challenged by scholars who have done work on stages of moral reasoning, such as Piaget and Kohlberg, who argued that one way moral agents progress to a higher stage of moral reasoning is by participating in ethical discussions with people who occupy a higher level. See for example, Kohlberg's *Selected Papers on Moral Development and Moral Education*, 1973; Cf. Craig Dykstra, *Vision and Character: A Christian Educator's Alternative to Kohlberg* (New York: Paulist Press, 1981).
[88]Yoder, *Politics*, 153.

diminish the role of the individual

> the proclamation of the lordship of Christ is not a substitute for nor a prerequisite to the gospel call directed to individuals. Nor is it the mere consequence within society of the conversion of individuals one by one. Nor does it dispense with, or guarantee, or always necessarily facilitate such conversions.... That Christ is Lord, a proclamation to which only individuals can respond, is nonetheless a social, political, *structural* fact which constitutes a challenge to the Powers. It thus follows that the claims which such proclamation makes are not limited to those who have accepted it, nor is the significance of its judgment limited to those who have decided to listen to it.[89]

In putting forth this argument, Yoder affirms the role of the church, while making Christ central to all ethical thought and work. He confirms the convictions of H. R. Mackintosh, who wrote that if we regard Jesus Christ as Saviour, 'we must see him at the centre of all things. We must behold him as the pivotal and cardinal reality, round which all life and history have moved. That is a place out of which his Person simply cannot be kept.' Accordingly, 'we dare not permanently live in two mental worlds, dividing the mind hopelessly against itself. We cannot indulge one day the believing view of things, for which Christ is all and in all, and the next a view of philosophy or science for which he is little or nothing or in any case ranks as quite subordinate and negligible.' 'After all,' Mackintosh affirms, 'we have but one mind, which is at work both in our religion and our science; and if Christ is veritably supreme *for faith*, he is of necessity supreme altogether and everywhere. Growingly it becomes impossible to revert to a scientific or philosophical attitude in which the insight into his central greatness which we attain in moments of religious vision is resolutely and relentlessly suppressed.'[90] It matters that we are Christians when we do social ethics, and it matters that we understand ourselves to share a common humanity with those outside of the church.[91]

Such arguments, regarding the relevance of faith to the rest of life, have surfaced time and again throughout the ages of Christian history, manifested perhaps most famously in the theologies of Luther and Calvin. Though Luther's vision of 'two kingdoms' did not envision a compartmentalisation of the Christian and secular life, in his view 'love' had 'no more place in secular

---

[89]Ibid., 156-7.

[90]Mackintosh , *The Person of Jesus Christ,* 50-1.

[91]Cf. H.R. Niebuhr, *Christ and Culture* (London: Faber and Faber, [1952]); Cf. Ernst Troeltsch, *The Social Teaching of the Christian Churches,* trans. Olive Wyon (London: George Allen and Unwin, 1931). Niebuhr described the various relationships between Church and world as understood from Christian history, while Troeltsch famously linked Church and culture to such an extent that he believed them to be inseparable.

politics than punitive justice has place in the church.'[92] Nevertheless, when 'he spoke of "two kingdoms", he was as sure as Augustine had been that both belonged to an overarching Kingdom of God,' argues Donald Shriver. In this sense, Luther had much in common with Calvin's approach to social ethics, and Shriver accuses later generations of Lutherans of dissolving the dialectic into a forced dualism. This contrasts with the Calvinist view, which did not force any deep, divide between church and world. In Shriver's words: 'The divine judgment and forgiveness that Christians shared around the communion table had unique depths of spirit and truth; but the duty to repent of sin and to offer forgiveness to the repentant could not in principle be confined to the church pew.'[93] The difference between this approach and that of Luther is subtle, but significant: 'Calvin conceived religion and politics as related neither in the "two-level" medieval Catholic hierarchical scheme nor in the "two kingdom" paradoxes of Lutheranism. Calvin's God was sovereign over the whole of reality, and the increasing divine activity in the whole world implied not passive acceptance by believers but engagement in the same whole world in obedience to the divine will.' For Calvin, 'in this vision, between the realm of the church and the realm of the state there were no qualitative differences of ethical norm or ethical responsibility. "The good of the whole community," as Ernst Troeltsch put it, was the constant theme of Calvinist ethics, which forever called its adherents - whether government officials, ordinary citizens, or church leaders - to the same criticism and reform of sin-beset but redeemable human institutions.'[94]

This positive strain is evident to varying degrees in both Rauschenbusch's thought and Niebuhr's work, and perhaps accounts for the best of Christian social ethics in past centuries. For whatever its weaknesses in approaching issues of church and state relations, such a Reformed understanding perhaps takes better account than most of the theological themes of creation, covenant, and the sovereignty of God. Yet, regardless of the approach favoured by various scholars, the present point is to highlight the fact that the current debate regarding the relationship of the church to the world, and the nature of competing moral allegiances for individuals and churches is not at all new. Integrity calls us to take account of the historical witness as well as the biblical one, and invites us to use all of the tools at human disposal to understand and interpret the Christian faith. When we recognize the deep historical nature of this debate, we are confronted with the fact that to jettison the foundations which underlie it may reflect more an avoidance of its inherent tension than a

---

[92]Donald Shriver, *An Ethic for Enemies: Forgiveness in Politics* (Oxford: Oxford University Press, 1995), 53.
[93]Ibid., 57.
[94]Ibid., 55. Cf. Troeltsch, vol II, 652.

revelation of helpful new insights.[95]

And so, we have come to see that theological and philosophical considerations in the development of ethical method are, in many ways, virtually inseparable. The ethical method that tends to dominate in any given period of time is largely a reflection of the contemporary philosophical influences that are very much 'in the air' and finding expression in the surrounding theological debate. Yet, despite the fact that we are only ever creatures of our time, there is reason to believe that the ethical task may be undertaken with confidence and clarity, and the resources of philosophy and theology brought to bear on methodological aspects of social ethics. The task is no simple or straightforward one. How are we to move from the particular to the general, and how are we to apply principles of redemption and justification to a broader world, which awaits with 'groaning' the fulfilment of these doctrines? It may well be that 'the church experiences in faith the forgiveness of all her sins and a new beginning through grace,' while 'for the nations there is only a healing of the wound, a cicatrization of guilt, in the return to order, to justice, to peace and to the granting of free passage to the church's proclamation of Jesus Christ.'[96] Is this the best the church can hope for, and if so or not, how do we bring the resources of the church to bear on the quest for justice in the wider world of which we are an inextricable part?

As it happens, we may well agree with Hauerwas and others who demand that Christian ethics be more theological, and who insist that ethics that are Christian can only be done from the perspective of the church. The demand is particularly acute when it is seen as a response to the ideological captivity of ethics that characterized much of the ecumenical scene in previous decades. In this desire at least, foundationalists and non-foundationalists may find common ground, despite the latter's protestations. For regardless of whether 'reason can lead us to a knowledge of that which exists,' most agree that it alone 'cannot give us knowledge of where our moral commitments should lie, nor can it provide us with the passion necessary to make those commitments.'[97] Such statements ring true, not primarily because Christians have nothing in common with the 'rest of the world,' but because they possess and are possessed by unique resources which inform the understanding and living of ethics, and which define their inexorable relationship within the faith community, and as individuals and faith communities to the 'rest of the world' ontologically, ethically, and apologetically. James Gustafson explains that

---

[95]Wolterstorff describes it as a matter of learning how to say both yes and no to the world. See Nicholas Wolterstorff, 'Christian Political Reflection: Diognetian or Augustinian,' *PSB* 20 (1999).

[96]Bonheoffer, *Ethics*, 117.

[97]Kenneth W. M. Wozniak, *Ethics in the Thought of Edward John Carnell* (Lanham, NY and London, University Press of America, 1983), ix.

the Church proclaims the reality, the existence of the living Lord, who has brought all things into being, and whose provident care sustains and preserves life from human self-destruction. It proclaims that all human communities stand under the divine authority and are judged by it, that they are finite and corrupted, and not worthy of final loyalty and trust. It proclaims God's care for every single one, as well as his ordination of social existence, and thus provides the ground of faith and hope and love out of which pluralism can be tolerated, and indeed, become a fruitful historical mode of common life. It proclaims that all men are responsible *to God, for* the neighbour, near and distant.[98]

In contrast to such an inclusive application of theology, an emphasis on a theology of 'difference' along with strident contextualization and the post-modern tendency to speak epistemologically only from and to a particular interest group may lead ecumenical social ethics into a perpetual state of paralysis. Yet Milbank suggests that there is, for him, 'no method, no mode of argument that charts us smoothly past the Scylla of foundationalism and the Charybdis of difference.'[99] Is this forced dichotomy appropriate? Must we really choose between the six-headed monster in 'advocacy of the antique' (if such advocacy can indeed be described as monstrous) and the disorienting, destructive whirlpool of difference? Or do the doctrines of the Christian faith suggest a more universal and inclusive understanding of general principles that may be applied in social ethics? Is the gospel, even across differences of philosophy, theology, geography, and experience, able to provide the churches with sufficient resources to recover a common interest apart from, or at least in addition to, individual and parochial group interests? I believe that it can, especially if theological doctrines broadly conceived within a paradigm of integrity are given first consideration in a method of social ethics, and the philosophical and historical conditions that give them rise are not ignored. After all, if Odysseus could elicit a safe sailing route from Circe, who was responsible for setting the dilemma, might not we also express hope in the possibility that our Creator God might give clues for navigating similarly treacherous waters?

By now it should be clear that the WCC has no single method for addressing issues in social ethics.[100] In fact, it entertains a plurality of methods, and tends to be dominated by the approach that most closely reflects the prevailing philosophical winds. This has meant that the WCC has not had an effective, unifying method which has offered leadership in social ethics for more than two decades, though there are scattered calls within and without the WCC for a

---

[98]James Gustafson, *Can Ethics be Christian?* (Chicago and London: University of Chicago Press, 1975), 60.
[99]Milbank, *Theology and Social Theory*, 327-8.
[100]This was confirmed to me as a fact of the WCC's existence by Dr. Thomas Best, Executive Secretary for the WCC's Faith and Order Unit, in a conversation November 24, 1999.

return to methods of dialogue, study, and theological reflection, to support ecumenical work in ethics.[101] How do we learn to balance harmony and holiness, popularity and principle, a desire for unanimous resolutions with the Word of God? Considering the varied approaches to understanding the relationship of the individual to the collective, and the relationship between collectives, determining how we get 'there' from 'here' is at least as important as understanding how we got 'here' from 'there'.

---

[101]See, for example, 'The Report of the Programme Guidelines Committee' in 'Documents Adopted by the WCC Eighth Assembly, Harare 3-14 December 1998'. The report indicates that 'In every stream in the hearings there was a call for taking seriously the need to build theological and biblical foundations for programmes. This will require close working relationships and shared responsibilities across teams, with Faith and Order particularly involved with others.' 20. The present task is validated by the recommendation that the WCC 'should also engage in self-study and analysis of its own work styles and methodologies.' 21. Cf. Ronald Preston, 'On to Harare: Social Theology and Ethics in the World Council of Churches,' 24-33. Preston does not see the closer working relationship between Faith and Order and the other sections of the WCC as an excuse for other sections to neglect theology, study, and dialogue, simply because these have been strengths of Faith and Order.

CHAPTER 10

In Advocacy of the Antique: Recovering the Best of a Study-Dialogue Method

We have always had our internal dissent and our perplexities. In many ways we have surpassed our forerunners - in our openness to new currents in the world's cultures and in our ecological sensitivities. But I wish we could emulate the best wisdom of our past as we break new ground.

Roger Shinn

It is only the raw procacity of the hour that speaks of theological science as a disease of the Church. But quackery is the worst heresy.

P. T. Forsyth

Introduction

Thus far, I have suggested that a study-dialogue method of social ethics is an approach that is best able to recognize collective and individual aspects of moral agency, without drowning one in the other. It takes seriously the differences that may arise between groups seeking to debate ethical issues, and allows for discussion to continue even when agreement seems unlikely. Moreover, it highlights the tensions and necessities of reason and revelation, maintaining the idea that there may be better or worse ethical positions on various issues, while upholding at least the possibility of rational agreement on ethical matters. As a method, it is able to embody ethical integrity. But what is to be done with this method if, as with all methods, the study-dialogue approach is a child of the intellectual impulses of the time? If this method rests on philosophical premises that have been rejected by many, and on a theological approach that no longer enjoys the degree of consensus it once did, is there any point in pursuing it within ecumenical social ethics? If there is such a point, how is the study-dialogue method to be applied in an ethos quite different in character from the one in which it flourished several decades ago? Or would it be wise to heed the advice of the post-modernist response and reject the value of this antique, in pursuit of an ethical design that is ever new, and ever elusive? Perhaps heeding this advice would be simpler than the alternative, but the easier way is not necessarily the better way.[1]

A Critique from the Antique

An advocacy of past method has been undertaken by a group of sympathetic ecumenists, themselves dismissed as antiques by some ecumenical leaders, who have issued a severe critique of the present state of affairs in ecumenical social ethics. In the last decade, a searching examination of ecumenical ethical method was informally launched by several 'friends' of the WCC, who were concerned for the direction social ethics were taking in the period leading up to and following the World Convocation on Justice, Peace and the Integrity of Creation held at Seoul in March, 1990.[2] Meeting together for the first time in July 1990 at Vancouver, the group gathered from five continents to reflect upon, discuss, and attempt 'to understand what is happening at present in ecumenical social thought, as developed in the programs and processes of the WCC.'[3] The group described their composition: 'Most of us have been directly involved in one or another aspect of the social thinking of the World Council. Some of us have been so involved over a period of many years; others are students or local pastors.'[4] As a result of their experience and deliberations, they concluded, 'We are convinced that ecumenical social thought is at a moment of great challenge and opportunity. It is also, we believe, in a state of some confusion and disarray. Hence we propose a careful review of the ways in which the churches, through the WCC, should be developing their understanding of Christian responsibility amidst the hopes, fears and perplexities of our time.'[5]

In their initial report, sent as an open letter to Emilio Castro, the General Secretary of the WCC at the time, they organized their criticisms around four concerns. The first of these was a concern about the relation between faith and social ethics in an ecumenical context. This issue was brought to the fore by the JPIC process, which left many discouraged and frustrated by the lack of tangible ethical results and the hollow, platitudinous statements which seemed

---

[1]In this chapter, I hint at some of the current debates surrounding authority, personhood, diversity and dialogue in ethics. I also point towards some of the possible directions for discussion on the issue of dialogue with contemporary postmodern philosophy and ethics, particularly in the work of Emmanuel Levinas, Paul Ricoeur and Mikhil Bakhtin. I encourage the reader to seek to make relevant intellectual connections, and I intend to pursue these themes in work elsewhere. This leaves the focus of the chapter as primarily practical in nature, while highlighting the centrality of theology and philosophy for good practice.

[2]The organizing secretary for these meetings was Paul Abrecht.

[3]Terence Anderson, Moderator of the Group, 'An Open Letter to Dr. Emilio Castro, The General Secretary of the World Council of Churches,' Vancouver, July 27, 1990, 1.

[4]Ibid.

[5]Ibid., 2.

to take their place. After JPIC, many felt that ecumenical ethics had reached a crucial watershed, where something had to be done if they were to survive long into a new century. 'The absolutist style of many formulations in the JPIC Report gives the impression of insisting on one ethical norm to the exclusion of others,' the report declared. The churches 'have diverse experiences, diverse encounters with the power structures of the world, diverse ministries. Yet they share a divine gift, a Scripture, a history, a ministry, and a hope. The WCC is possible because we appreciate one another in our diversities as well as in our shared faith. We celebrate our varieties of experience. We need each other most of all when we differ, when we irritate each other, when we disagree.'[6] Diversity in the midst of social ethical challenges means churches must learn to combine courage and modesty. Absolutist claims are challenged by the Scriptures, which 'illustrate both irenic and polemic qualities in Christian life. The churches need to remember that there are times to act as conciliators, helping antagonistic parties to communicate and share understandings. There are other times to act as advocates, siding with the poor and oppressed, as the Bible tells us God does, while never forgetting that we all need God's forgiveness.' To that end, the 'WCC will betray its mission if it cries peace when there is no peace, if it lets reconciliation become a slogan to mute cries against injustice. It will also betray its mission if it become a contender in an arena of partisans, all claiming God's endorsement for their acts and opinions.' Thus the group concluded: 'We believe that Christians always - never more than in the WCC today - need the divine gift that empowers us to speak the truth in love and to listen to the truths that others speak.'[7]

   The second issue concerned the process of social ethics in an ecumenical context. Confirming some conclusions of the present study, the group further expressed its belief 'that ecumenical social ethics has lost the quality of dialogue, analysis and study which brings together differing, even opposing, experiences and perspectives, and aims at deeper understanding both of one another and of the word of God.' The group described the loss of the study-dialogue method as resulting in a 'poor understanding of social problems, imprecise guidance of the conscience, and violation of the rights and just demands of parts of humanity not adequately defended in ecumenical debate.' They suggested that general exhortations are not only insufficient, but may be counter-productive. The need for greater investigation and understanding of the facts of the world around us is apparent, and undertaking the task 'may result in fewer resolutions and declarations than in recent years, but more solid analysis; less ideological rigidity, but more substantive understanding of differing convictions; deeper agreement, where agreement is reached, in policy and action.' Moreover, 'Dialogue and openness need not lessen the force of moral action against injustice. It places that action in the context of continuing

---

[6] Ibid.
[7] Ibid., 3.

relations with the neighbour, with the enemy, and with God.'[8] Such a dialogical process depends for its integrity upon an inclusive discussion involving those who are directly affected or involved, and experts with special knowledge, theologians and ethicists, and those Churches and councils of Churches 'who seek to bear corporate witness to the Gospel in the world.'[9] Priority amongst these participants ought to be determined by the nature of the problem that requires confrontation.

Thirdly, in the report, the group identified a concern about the role of ecumenical agencies in methods of social ethics. 'A council of churches and its staff cannot think *for* the churches. A conciliar structure cannot be papal. If it goes too far beyond the churches, its declarations, however true, will not be heard.'[10] Addressing issues is 'first an educational and consultative activity, and only then an act of proclamation and a call to common action.' Though this process may be too slow 'to meet every emergency,' it is essential 'if the church is to have integrity to witness with moral and spiritual authority to the powers and self-interests of the world.' Only a process such as this is able to help bring 'the mind of the whole church, of which the activist group is one part, to an encounter with the word of God and the human situation that compels it to speak and commits it to act together.' Thus, continual dialogue encourages churches to see resolutions as 'episodes' in the process, 'not its climax.'[11] It invites more dialogue and reflection that may lead to refinement of resolutions, and even better approaches to problems of social ethics.

Fourthly, the group sought to express a concern about the authority of ecumenical statements. 'Wherever Christians come together, as in ecumenical conference or assembly, they are called to witness. But formulating the specifics of that witness is always an exacting task, gathering in the presence of God, expecting that the Holy Spirit will be at work through these human deliberations.' Critical of recent processes, they continued

> Where moral positions are determined beforehand and serious conflicts of moral conviction are avoided or suppressed, a human authority takes over from God and the meeting becomes a propaganda instrument. If on the other hand, an ecumenical meeting dissolves controversy in pious generalizations, the word of God is equally misused and misdirected. A resolution of a council of churches differs from that of a particular denomination because it cannot commit the discipline and structure of a church. Its authority, rather, is intrinsic, stemming

---

[8]Ibid.

[9]Ibid., 4.

[10]Ibid. Cf. Ronald Preston, *Confusions in Christian Social Ethics,* 167. Preston believes the WCC may run a little ahead of the Churches, but only a little. Its primary task is not to be a frontier movement but to illuminate the frontier.

[11]'An Open Letter,' 5.

from its perceived faithfulness to the Gospel and the weight it carries by its own truth and wisdom.[12]

The criticisms of the group reflect, in large part, some practical concerns related to those philosophical and theological ones raised throughout this dissertation.

Following the Canberra Assembly in 1991, the concerns of the group were reinforced by an increasing dismay at the way ethical issues were being approached. A report by British Anglicans largely reflected concerns about a perceived staff-driven agenda which confronted a poorly-prepared gathering, and engendered little debate, while introducing forms of Christianity which left many uncomfortable and struggling to understand the relationship between gospel and culture.[13] Furthermore, some perceived that the diversity inherent in a world council had become overshadowed by 'a firm ideology,' which 'has largely succeeded in dominating this pluralism.'[14] Perhaps much of this provides further evidence that superficial agreement may be an inevitable result when moral fragmentation precludes serious dialogue, and dissension of individual and intermediary group agents is viewed as selfish or narrow-minded. In such an atmosphere, both a spirit of honest conviction and liberal dialogue are undermined, if not eliminated. At Canberra, broader interests had become so marginalized, including those of Orthodox and Evangelical Christians, that sympathetic Anglicans found themselves actually contemplating, though rejecting, the possibility of disassociation with the WCC.[15] These sentiments were echoed at the next meeting of those ecumenists who were informally but actively engaged in social ethical critique.

The concerns expressed in an initial open letter from Vancouver were refined and further defined at a consultation in Berlin, May-June 1992, chaired by the Archbishop of York, John Habgood.[16] In true study-dialogue approach, the participants had prepared and received twelve study papers in advance of the conference, allowing the discussion to take place at a more advanced level than would have been possible otherwise. They intended their critique to be a positive one, and focused on six themes including: the need to recognize diversity (against an orthopraxis that excludes honest dissent); ecumenical selectivity (against programme plans which tend to be immodest and pretentious); the need to test 'prophecy' against serious intellectual criticism; technical competence (against a distrust of scientific methodology and

---

[12]Ibid., 5-6.

[13]Bishop of Bristol; 'Meeting the WCC,' *After Canberra*, a collection of reflections from Church of England delegates at the Canberra Assembly in 1991, 4.

[14]David L. Edwards, 'How Canberra Feels,' in ibid., 8.

[15]See ibid., and George Austin, 'Do we Need the WCC?' in ibid.

[16]Their report was issued as *A Statement to the World Council of Churches on The Future of Ecumenical Social Thought: Report of an informal discussion of church leaders, theologians, social ethicists and laity. Berlin, May 29-June 3, 1992.*

rationality); theological foundations which had become seriously eroded; and staff interests which they believed had formed an elite which staff themselves claimed to deplore.[17] The report acknowledged that in addition to doctrinal and ecclesiastical differences, another type of disagreement had arisen in the search for an ecumenical social ethic. 'This has to do with the various ideological assumptions and convictions that are informing ethical judgments in the social, economic, and political spheres, and consequently shaping WCC policies.' The question was posed, 'Are ideological partisans as prepared for the discipline of registering their disagreements as they are enthusiastic about proclaiming their agreements?'[18] However, the registration of disagreements is no easy task when participants hardly recognize the influences that have informed their own position.

The report of what was now coined 'the Berlin group' was not well received by WCC officials. General Secretary Emilio Castro wrote to Habgood, largely dismissing the group's concerns as Western patriarchy at worst, and the nostalgia of the 'Club of retired Ecumenists' at best.[19] Paul Abrecht took stock of the responses to the Berlin Statement on the Future of Ecumenical Social Thought just before the group's next meeting at Manchester in July 1993. He suggested that the staff response by the WCC was 'on the whole negative.' Emilio Castro further refused to send the report to members of the Central Committee, agreeing instead to refer it internally to the Units concerned. Abrecht notes that 'the staff of Unit III were for the most part angered by our criticisms, and refused to accept that our judgments had any merit.'[20] Considering the poor reception of their work by the WCC, the group began to circulate its report externally. Despite the appointment of a new General Secretary to the WCC, the general attitude did not change. Abrecht reported that 'on April 27, (1993) I had a long talk with Konrad (Raiser). He repeated that he wanted dialogue on the issues we had raised and proposed that this be carried on' through consultations. 'Despite these encouraging statements,' Abrecht wrote, 'it is my impression that Konrad regards our views as passé - a hangover from an earlier theological ethical period (1938-1948).'[21] Raiser may

---

[17]Ibid., 6-8.

[18]Ibid., 17.

[19]Emilio Castro, General Secretary, WCC in a letter to John Habgood, Geneva, 28 August, 1992.

[20]Paul Abrecht, unpublished personal paper, 'One Year After Berlin: Responses to the Statement on 'The Future of Ecumenical Social Thought.'

[21]Ibid. Abrecht points out further of Raiser that, 'He is personally committed to the support of contemporary Christian action groups, including extra-ecclesial groups, and their new ways of doing theology and ethics. He has reiterated this point in many statements in recent months. He is confident that the JPIC conciliar process will prevail. When I said that Professor Douglas John Hall's account of the Soeul Convocation's failure to address the fundamental theological problem seemed to confirm our criticisms of JPIC's lack of theological substance, he dismissed Hall's article, saying, "If Hall has

have offered a marginally more congenial, if somewhat patronizing response to the group, but Abrecht concludes, 'it is not certain, despite the expressed readiness for dialogue, that the WCC and Unit III in particular will readily alter its theological-ethical approach. They seem wedded to "eschatological realism" and to praxis ethics.'[22] The general assessment of the Berlin group was that 'from a theological-ethical point of view,' recent programmes and documents such as JPIC and Ecclesiology and Ethics 'over-simplified formulations of ecumenical concerns and methodology.'[23] Thus the group continued with its own critical dialogue, and by 1994 had refined and summarized its critique concisely into three issues: the problems of diversity; biblical hermeneutics; and expert advice.[24]

These three issues confronted by the group point to, but fall short of fully addressing some of the philosophical, theological and practical issues raised in the present study. In the contemporary intellectual ethos, compared with that in which the study-dialogue method first took root, the possibility for success may appear significantly limited. The matters of expert advice and biblical hermeneutics raise numerous issues that are not easily resolved, even amongst Christians sharing similar ecclesiologies, let alone within an ecumenical context. Post-modernism has pushed aside notions of foundationalism and realism which were once taken for granted, most particularly by the Niebuhrian school which is largely represented by the Berlin group. In response to the Berlin critique, some contemporary ethicists might ask: 'Which experts? Whose advice? Which facts? Whose text?' Therefore, some philosophical issues must be tackled by ecumenical ethicists before the concerns of the Berlin group may be addressed adequately. In this respect, it would be interesting and helpful for members of the Berlin group themselves to address contemporary philosophical debates with their wisdom, and experience. Their critique might bear more effectiveness overall if they were to recognize and acknowledge the importance of philosophical aspects of ethical method. Such insight is needed.

---

any answers let him present them". Konrad appears confident that the Seoul position has widespread ecumenical support particularly in the churches of the South. In his letter to John Habgood he emphasizes that the way in which the study document on "Christian Faith and the World Economy Today" links theology with social analysis, is "an approach which I fully support".

[22] It is not surprising that Abrecht anticipated the most summary rejection of their views to come from the Youth Department. It is interesting to note further that the churches of the South which are supposedly supportive of the present method of the WCC, are generally not representative of the masses of southern Christians who are now members in Pentecostal and other evangelical churches, which have been courted for membership, but without wide success by the WCC. Cf. page 6 of Abrecht's report.

[23] Report on the Meeting with the World Council of Churches on the Future of Ecumenical Social Thought, at the Ecumenical Institute, Bossey, Switzerland, February 18-19, 1994, 3.

[24] Ibid., 4. Cf. Roger Shinn, 'Friendly Dialogue,' *OW,* (April 1994): 13.

We cannot simply turn the clock back and in a call for a return to *status quo ante* pick up the ethical task where Niebuhr and his colleagues left off. How can we make real in the present the past effectiveness of the study-dialogue method?

In an attempt to examine the alternatives for applying the study-dialogue method in a contemporary context, the framework of integrity, which has served as the backbone of this project, again provides encouragement for the task at hand. The threefold task of finding an application which provides philosophical clarity, offers theological verity, and yields practical unity cannot rest in an unfounded commitment to the study-dialogue process, but must seek to mediate between the various forms of expression the study-dialogue approach may manifest under present intellectual and practical conditions. The problems defined by the Berlin Group as issues of biblical hermeneutics, diversity, and expert advice may be clarified briefly in the light of this framework. It may be fair to say that the three issues raised by the Berlin group embody perennial problems of ecumenical ethical method. That is, they give philosophical, theological, and practical form to the difficulty of expressing a collective ethical voice without undermining the ethical integrity of individuals and intermediary groups.

Recovery of an Antique Critique

We will consider the three main concerns raised by the Berlin group in reverse order, with Paul Ramsey as a primary guide. Over thirty years ago, Ramsey wrestled with these issues directly at a time when he perceived ecumenical ethics to be moving in a destructive direction. Writing in critical response to the state of Christian social ethics following the Geneva conference, Ramsey sailed against the prevailing winds, and time has proved his as a prophetic voice.[25] As such, he calls us back to Oxford and Amsterdam, from a time when he recognized the received wisdom being seriously eroded in ecumenical social ethics. We turn to consider what insights Ramsey offers into the three key issues raised by the Berlin group, with respect to philosophical clarity, theological verity and practical unity. We will further consider how each aspect nurtures a study-dialogue approach in light of the contemporary intellectual and practical climate.

Experts and Integrity: A Matter of Philosophical Clarity

The first matter to be considered is that of expert advice. It would seem that the Berlin group, as confirmed by some of Ronald Preston's work, overlooks the philosophical ethos which raises objections against the appeal for external expert advice to direct social ethical deliberations which are to be distinctively

---

[25]Paul Ramsey, *Who Speaks for the Church?* Nashville and New York: Abingdon, 1967.

Christian. A suspicion of expertise is overshadowed by an inability to agree on how experts are identified and defined, as many participants acknowledge that in the contemporary world, conflicting expert 'advice' may be solicited to support any number of issues. The epistemological crisis, and an inability to overcome philosophical barriers of language and reference leave the matter of defining experts, and comprehending the truth of their claims in doubt. Does the postmodern reluctance to speak from any position of expertise, save from a theological one, seem justified?

The notion of expert advice is one direction taken at Geneva that drew criticism from Ramsey. His words are remarkably relevant as he emphasizes the importance of Christian ethics to be primarily theological, refraining from offering specific and binding advice in the public realm. He writes

> In order for the church to regain *its* voice and for the churches or Christians in council to speak for the churches to the world today, we must resist the temptation to believe that what needs to be done is to improve the church's use of "experts." It is the aim of specificity in the church's resolutions and proclamations that should be radically called in question. The better use of political and other experts to improve *that* might only make matters worse.[26]

'The notion that laymen who are experts, for example, in the political and economic sciences can enable the church to speak a relevant Christian word to today's world and at the same time to point out the particular policy to be followed is simply an illusion,' Ramsey states provocatively. But in a word particularly relevant to the present situation, he continues

> It takes an expert to pick an expert. Or rather the experts disagree; and if there is any reason at all and not just an accident why one set of experts and not another comes to council, the decision concerning which ones are to be picked to inform church councils will inevitably be made by some *curia* or persons in control of setting up such councils in terms of the particular interests, positions, or trends of thought the experts are already reputed for. This is not exactly the way basically to improve deliberation.... Selection from among available political analysts will be an arbitrary one so long as particularity is in view. And when the church's goals in social ethics, its deliberations, and its procedures for deliberation are corrected, the movement will not be any longer in the direction of presuming to give specific prudential advice to political leaders, but rather in the direction of regaining the church's own voice relevant to today's problems.[27]

Experts, then, need to be as much from the theological realm as anywhere. Procedural reforms 'will be of no avail unless and until we in the older ecumenical movement regain the understanding that it is the Christian life and Christian action we are trying to clarify, and help one another clarify, in today's

---

[26]Ibid., 138.
[27]Ibid., 138-9.

world.'[28]

To these sentiments, we might hear shouts of 'Amen!' from the congregation of narrative theologians who have embraced a post-foundationalist epistemology. This challenges the expressed view of some members of the Berlin group, who would like to see a return to developing specific policy statements in addition to ethical principles. It stands against those who might like to see the church return to a place of significance on the international political stage. Moreover, it affirms those points raised by the moral formation method that remind Christian ethicists that the context for ethics is firstly the church, and that our ethics must be theological if we are to have anything distinctive to say at all. Appreciating the primacy of theology enables the church to call experts into service in a manner which might best employ their intellectual and practical resources for Christian ethics.

Ramsey noted perceptively that, 'It has been easier to arrive at specific recommendations and condemnations after inadequate deliberation than to penetrate to a deeper and deeper level the meaning of Christian responsibility - leaving the conscience of individuals and groups of individuals both the task and the freedom to arrive at specific conclusions through untrammelled debate about particular social policies.' He continued, 'Radical steps need to be taken in ecumenical ethics if ever we are to correct the pretense that we are makers of political policy and get on with our proper task of nourishing, judging, and repairing the moral and political *ethos* of our time.'[29] While Ramsey sought the development and application of a method that would prevent policies from being too specific, his approach would similarly prevent them from being too general.

Despite a concern that the issues he raises may quickly become dated, at times Ramsey sounds a remarkable note of sympathy with our contemporary post-modern critics, though his basic assumptions remain distinct. 'There is urgent need, and now is the time,' writes Ramsey, 'for those of us who love the church, and who share in striving for an ecumenical ethics in the world of today, to engage in a probing examination of what we are doing (and consequently failing to do) in formulating the church's address to the world.' He continues

> My thesis is that, if such an examination is undertaken, we will no longer be able
> to speak and act as if there is a closer identification between Christian social
> ethics and the policy making of the Secular City than was asserted even in the
> Middle Ages. In the *contents* of ecumenical ethics there needs to be some way to
> tell some difference between the spiritual and the temporal power. Yet I fear that
> to propound this thesis even in an age that is assertedly post-Christian will only

---

[28]Ibid., 141.
[29]Ibid., 15.

brand the author as one who believes the church to be a spiritual cult with no pertinent social outlook.[30]

Criticizing the approaches which take their ethical cues from 'what God is doing in the world,' that is, those we have described as following the 'action-reflection' method, Ramsey sounds as contemporary as any Christian ethicist writing today when he argues that the task of Christians 'should be the nurture of a Christian ethos within the autonomies of the modern world, and not by manifold thought and action to attenuate that ethos still more my eliding it into worldly wisdom. One cannot have it both ways,' he insists, 'by declaring we have taken our exodus from "Christendom" while continuing to fashion Christian social ethics in the manner of the great cultural churches of the past.'[31] Though we might deny the view that the two cities are distinct in any final or absolute sense, Ramsey brings back to the fore the issue of the uniqueness of the church, and the necessity for it to be theological before it can consider how it might be political. Such insights attest to the relevance of his comments and approach, in the face of those who would dismiss ethics and ethicists from a previous era. Ramsey recognized the perennial relevance of the deeper issues he was tackling.

However, regardless of the similarities between Ramsey's expressed sympathies and those who would pioneer a method of 'moral formation', there is an important difference. Whereas advocates of moral formation do not wish to speak of political policies as such, or in any sense to participate in the world outside of the church, Ramsey believed it was important for Christian ethicists to consider how best to share a pluralistic society. From his perspective, Christianity needs to inform the moral ethos of the Church and the nations, much as Rauschenbusch believed they should. But beyond that, Ramsey felt that the churches have a role to play in clarifying the possible positions individuals and groups could take on political issues, without prescribing a particular course and risk speaking out with little support or authority. Couched in post-modern language, this would mean that Ramsey did not wish to 'do violence' to the consciences of individuals and groups by having the churches insist on singular courses of ethical action. Yet he wanted the church, through unified efforts, to equip its people for social participation. What we need, he argued, is 'to sort out what may be action-oriented or policy-oriented statements that fall within the *de jure* competence of the churches and churchmen to enunciate to anyone who has the ears to hear.' In true Niebuhrian style, he would add the following qualification: 'However relevant, these will be distinct from public policy formation in which we with all men engage as citizens - inspired by our faith and ethics no doubt, but with no special guidance that should either bind or ease the consciences of men in venturing the actions

---

[30]Ibid., 19-20.
[31]Ibid., 20.

that shape our common future.'[32]

Perhaps surprisingly, and despite many similarities, it is at this juncture that Ramsey also differs significantly from the Berlin group, as its members express a belief in the need for churches to formulate statements which will be authoritative, and address the public realm, though they urge selectivity in this task.[33] Without pushing too far, he recalls that the main purpose of Christian social ethics is to serve and equip the church, which may or may not lead to transformation of public policy at a political level. This reinforces the importance of dialogue at two levels.

First, if the main social-ethical call of the church is to equip the church for service and action, rather than to change public policy, the various members of the global church will need to dialogue together and face their diverse understandings of doctrine and the accompanying ethical implications. As Niebuhr recognized, dialogue is essential if the church is to find both the theologically self-critical voice and the conviction to undertake actions that are both truly just, and sustainable. From the action of engaging internal dialogue, a potential for wider dialogue emerges. If a dialogue of integrity achieves any measure of agreement, the church may extend the dialogue beyond its own concerns, to the wider world, bringing the resources of experts and others to bear on the discussion. Christian social ethics may subsequently make a contribution beyond the walls of the church.

Second, if the church wishes to remain faithful to its particular concerns, and also promote them in the public realm, then it is worth recognizing the limits of its contribution. The church does not need to have the definitive word on every issue. But it does carry the responsibility to offer a distinctly theological reflection on matters of internal and external relevance. In order to do this well, the church must be willing to learn to dialogue with others who do not necessarily share their same presuppositions or 'language'. To be true to its gospel witness, the church must be prepared to represent and express a distinctively Christian worldview in contexts which seem sometimes strange or hostile, and to persist even when understanding seems distant and unlikely. Dialogue helps to maintain a commitment to the concept of theological 'truth', while acknowledging the philosophical challenges cross-disciplinary communication. It does not capitulate to the philosophical ethos which says we cannot speak except within our own language game, and thus manifests the unity of the church as it works together to overcome divisions between theologians, and those who have particular gifts of learning and experience to bear on issues concerning the whole of human life, for the benefit of Christians and non-Christians.

But how can dialogue help when members of the church are often so far apart on what the narrative of scripture has to say on a given issue? This

---

[32]Ibid., 19.
[33]The Berlin Group, *The Future of Ecumenical Social Ethics,* 6.

immediately raises the next issue raised by the Berlin group - the matter of hermeneutics. In what sense does a gathering of experts in theology, let alone other disciplines, offer any measure of clarification on what should be done or said on ethical matters, if there is little chance of agreement on biblical interpretation and subsequent application? By emphasizing the thoroughly theological nature of Christian ethics, does the church simply retreat into a distinctive narrative that cannot be shared by others outside of its story? And what happens when even a shared commitment to the narrative yields varied results as to its meaning and the action it inspires?

Hermeneutics and Integrity: A Matter of Theological Verity

The matter of hermeneutics comes to the fore when theological warrants for ethical statements are considered. The Berlin group identified as a significant problem the degree of superficial agreement that takes place in social ethics, without any discussion of how ethical statements are related to scripture and doctrine. Referring to Ramsey's reluctance to step from scripture into the public realm, Keith Clements accuses him of compartmentalizing the public voice of the church, arguing that public concern is far more tied into the entire life of the church than he allowed.[34] Clements points to work by Mark Ellingsen to argue that ecumenical dialogue involves more than theological agreement. Yet Ellingsen actually demonstrates the lack of scriptural or doctrinal warrant displayed in many, if not most, ecumenical statements, highlighting exactly Ramsey's motivation for writing. A common pronouncement that means nothing because its words can be interpreted as meaning anything, should not be the goal of ecumenical ethical dialogue.

In his study of ecumenical statements on social issues, Mark Ellingsen concludes that 'the churches disagree theologically insofar as they employ different kinds of theological arguments in arriving at the same conclusions concerning ethics.'[35] Conceding that 'virtually every logically conceivable theological mode of argumentation is employed by at least one church statement' which he studied, he believes that, nevertheless, 'the churches' treatment of social justice may point a way to another avenue for overcoming the present divisions of the churches. Their theological disagreements do not preclude common action or a common praxis, at least with regard to social justice.'[36] Ellingsen defers more than once to the slogan of Stockholm, adjusting it to indicate that neither service nor doctrine cause divisions in the churches. Though we may be inclined to agree with sentiments behind such

---

[34]Keith Clements, *Learning to Speak: The Church's Voice in Public Affairs* (Edinburgh: T&T Clark, 1995), 21.
[35]Mark Ellingsen, *The Cutting Edge: How Churches Speak On Social Issues* (Grand Rapids and Geneva: Eerdmans and WCC, 1993, 111.
[36]Ibid., 115

unifying proclamations, ecumenical history has challenged his conclusions. Indeed, perhaps neither service nor doctrine needs *necessarily* to divide; but we cannot deny that the variety of theological arguments and methods employed have, in fact, produced, or reflected divisions.[37]

As the present study has demonstrated, and in contrast to Ellingsen's conclusion, the types of theological arguments employed were recognized as a source of disagreement on social issues from the earliest ecumenical meetings at Stockholm. Though from time to time, efforts have been made since to gloss them over, or pretend they don't exist, the period dominated by Niebuhrian realism demonstrated that nothing short of confronting them will assist in moving beyond the impasse. History has shown that by confronting differences, churches are able to enjoy a greater degree of unity than is possible when differences are ignored.

To this end, Ellingsen's study provides some helpful insights. Examining church statements on social issues from various confessional traditions, and representing several ecumenical bodies, he notes the nature of the theological appeal of each statement. Appeal is made variously to christology, gospel, creation, anthropology, redemption, pneumatology, or creed. The WCC documents included in the study similarly reflected an appeal to various Christian doctrines, but the majority related in one way or another to creation and anthropology, or christology, gospel, and redemption. One sought explicitly to reflect the 'biblical vision.' Most surprising is the large number of statements on various social issues that offered no clear theological warrant for the position taken. In Ellingsen's estimation, these included the final reports of Uppsala, and JPIC, and amongst the documents adopted by the WCC Assembly at Harare, few make any direct appeal to theology as a basis or support for claims about a variety of social issues. Ellingsen's study confirms that further reflection on the theological and biblical basis of methods and statements is needful.[38]

Ramsey identified this need thirty years earlier, however. Observing the slide into contextualism, arising from the preponderance of a singular hermeneutic of suspicion, he recognized the importance of considering theology as determinative for ethical method. He noted that, 'Since the method of doing ethics was set up to be contextual, it is not at all surprising that the theology and ethics resulting from this were contextual in the extreme. No stream rises higher than its source.'[39] Considering issues of interpretation of Scripture, theology, and context, Ramsey understood the danger of focusing

---

[37]Moreover, it suggests that doing the right things for the wrong reasons may be an acceptable form of ecumenical ethics, something which would require moral justification in itself.

[38]This apparent neglect of theological issues may be partly responsible for the reaction against the secularization of ethics which gave rise to the moral formation method.

[39]Ramsey, *Who Speaks?* 74.

hermeneutics first on the immediate situation

> It is not surprising that a narrowly contextual ethic can be the only insight to come from (by methodological pre-arrangement) doing Christian ethics contextually and by induction from perspectives needed in the solution of problems. So also if the Christian analysis of world political and economic problems is set up to be without primary attention to Christian theology and ethics, then it is not at all surprising that the resulting reports and conclusions on these questions read for so much of the way as if they could have issued from many another world gathering of concerned liberals. It was advertently or inadvertently designed to be that way: in other than Christian *terms*.[40]

The matter which is highlighted in the final analysis is determined largely by the location of the launch. Ramsey would thus wish to emphasize first in ethical method, those elements of theology, scripture, and Christian tradition which condition a particularly Christian approach to social ethics. He would confirm the Berlin group's contention that 'we must acknowledge a wide hermeneutic arc from scripture to our present economic order,' but he would be quite definite as to which point of the arc would serve as a most adequate starting point.

This issue is highlighted in Ramsey's discussion of one particular incident at Geneva, which relates the issue of hermeneutic to a particular understanding of the human person as individual and in community. His discussion offers further evidence of the methodological basis that undermines either individual or collective moral agency. Referring particularly to a change in wording from 'person' to 'persons-in-community', Ramsey insisted that the change precluded various understandings of the meaning of 'person', forcing an interpretation that supported the monist tendencies of the revolutionaries. One participant, 'called the section's attention to the fact that the person transcends his communities and that ecumenical Christian thought would be beating retreat if it did not say so.'[41] Nevertheless, the hermeneutical pre-eminence of ideology could not take account of conflicting interpretations of the identity of the human person.

One way that a biblical hermeneutic may enhance the process of ecumenical ethics is highlighted in a document published in 1951, the result of an ecumenical study conference held at Oxford in 1949.[42] The conference represented the desire of the churches to discover common ground on biblical interpretation, to enable them 'to make a common witness to our faith, even in

---

[40]Ibid.

[41]Ramsey identified this participant as Professor Michael Fogarthy of the University College of South Wales, 79.

[42]Alan Richardson and W. Schweitzer, eds., *Biblical Authority for Today: A World Council of Churches Symposium on 'The Biblical Authority for the Churches' Social and Political Message Today* (London: SCM Press, 1951).

the social and political realm.'[43] The fact of common ground in the church and specifically in the reading of the bible is assumed

> In this book, we, as members of different Christian confessions and denominations, living in different parts of the world, have made an attempt to read and interpret Holy Scripture together. We could not have done so unless our common starting point had been the Bible, which bound us together even before we knew each other personally. In all our churches around the world, the Bible is read and its message proclaimed in preaching, in liturgy, in fellowship and in service; the message of man's salvation through Jesus Christ, our Lord.[44]

The participants agreed that it 'has always been the task of the Church to unfold the message of the Bible and to defend it against misinterpretations. This is, in fact, the root of all Christian theology.' True to their method, the participants did not intend to gloss over differences, but readily acknowledged that the bible was the source of many divisions among them. By demonstrating and confronting the differences of approach and interpretation, they managed to produce a document entitled, 'Guiding Principles for the Interpretation of the Bible,' believing together that 'To look for guidance in the Word of God is, it seems to us, especially urgent in a time like ours when the Church has to face so many difficult questions in all realms of human life.'[45] All agreed that the 'Christian's authority lies in the will of God. It is agreed that the Bible stands in a unique position in mediating that will to us.' As the conference 'endeavoured, on the basis of the work of earlier conferences, to develop specific principles of interpretation, for the use of the Bible in relation to social and political questions,' the participants discovered 'a measure of agreement that surprised us all.'[46]

Despite the fact that the participants were largely of 'Western' backgrounds, the diversity of the 1949 Oxford conference should not be underestimated, lending significance to what remains an important document.[47] The conference not only revealed a common starting point in God's Word which 'confronts us' in the bible, but participants agreed that the objective word was able to produce humility among its hearers, 'so that they are more ready to listen and to discuss

---

[43]'Guiding Principles for the Interpretation of the Bible,' as accepted by the Ecumenical Study Conference, held at Wadham College, Oxford, from June 29th to July 5th, 1949 cited in ibid., 240-244.

[44]Richardson and Schweitzer eds., *Biblical Authority*, 7.

[45]'Guiding Principles,' Section I.

[46]Ibid., opening paragraph.

[47]In fact, one participant was from India, and a student representative was from Nigeria. Also participating were Americans, British, Germans, Swedes, Swiss, Japanese, and French representing at least 7 Christian traditions. Out of 16 full participants, and 4 youth delegates, in 1951, this was a broadly representative group.

than they are to assert their own opinions.'[48] In the objectivity of scripture, they found a common authority. They agreed that 'the primary message of the Bible concerns God's gracious and redemptive activity for the saving of sinful man that he might create in Jesus Christ a people for himself. In this, the Bible's central concern, an authoritative claim is placed upon man and he is called upon to respond in faith and obedience throughout the whole of his life and work.' Though acknowledging the different roles played by tradition, reason, and natural law in the approaches of various confessions, there was significant theological agreement that 'the centre and goal of the whole Bible is Jesus Christ,' who is seen through both Old and New Testaments as 'the fulfillment and the end of the Law.'[49] Moreover

> It is agreed that the unity of the Old and New Testaments is not to be found in any naturalistic development, or in any static identity, but in the ongoing redemptive activity of God in the history of one people, reaching its fulfillment in Christ. Accordingly it is of decisive importance for hermeneutical method to interpret the Old Testament in the light of the total revelation in the person of Jesus Christ, the Incarnate Word of God, from which arises the full Trinitarian faith of the Church.'[50]

Subsequently, the document outlines a method for interpreting scripture, taking into account context, history, literary meaning, and textual reliability. In an attempt to discover the biblical teaching on particular social or political issues, the document argues that a direct study of relevant texts is imperative, since any general principles established may quickly become dated, reflecting 'more the presuppositions of our own time than the message of the Bible. Only then may we safely deduce applications for our own situation.'[51] Treating the canon with balance is suggested as the key, beginning with the New Testament, and taking Old Testament texts into account in light of the total revelation. Overemphasis on any single passage which obscures wider biblical perspective is discouraged. Further, 'it is agreed that the Biblical teaching on social and political issues must be viewed in the light of the tension between life in the kingdoms of this world and participation in the Kingdom of God.'[52]

In order to make actual application of the teachings of scripture to the world, the document highlights the fact that no situation may be absolutely identical to one in the bible, and therefore the problem of adaptation is particularly acute: there can be no ethical restorationism.[53] Nevertheless, in each situation, the

---

[48]'Guiding Principles,' section I a.

[49]Ibid., section I d.

[50]Ibid., section I e.

[51]Ibid., section III a.

[52]Ibid., section III c.

[53]This recalls the social gospel approach which asked, 'What would Jesus do?' Of course, in reality, we can only surmise what Jesus might do, especially when we

bible is able to offer guidance orienting ethics towards the word of God. The bible speaks both to and through the church, most effectively as the church is remade by the word of God. Despite wide agreement, the document recognizes significant differences in doctrine and approach between ecumenical participants. However, the goal is not to give up efforts to reach agreement on biblical teachings for ethics, but to forge onward in the struggle for understanding, since it is an actual experience of the Ecumenical Movement that 'when we meet together, with presuppositions of which we may be largely unconscious, and bring these presuppositions to the judgment of Scripture, some of the very difficulties are removed which prevent the Gospel from being heard. Thus the Bible itself leads us back to the living Word of God.'[54] In this way, the document highlights some of the best aspects of the study-dialogue method of doing social ethics.

It is clear from this document that for the study-dialogue method, the locus of authority for social ethics is the will of God revealed in the word of God, accessed provisionally, and with humility through the bible, under the guidance of the Holy Spirit.[55] The role of theology is primary as it seeks to mediate human understanding of God's will to particular situations. Although an awareness of contextual limitations is present, there is a real belief that humans can have knowledge of God's will, and are able to apply it to greater and lesser degrees in church and society. The ethical foundation for Christians is love, since 'the law of love has always a binding and compelling hold upon us, and in it we encounter the inescapable will of God.'[56]

When theology was considered primary, all contexts did not disappear, but became relativized in light of the word of God. What this would mean for individual and collective approaches to ethics becomes clear. The individual is responsible before God, as a moral agent, but reaches moral decisions as part of a particular faith community, which in turn has fellowship with other Christian faith communities. While churches and their members share society with the rest of human creation, there is an on-going tension between the reality of the

---

consider that Jesus rarely did what people expected. Cf. The famous social gospel book by Charles Sheldon, *In His Steps* (Toronto, 1897) - and its present manifestation as the WWJD movement/marketing scheme.

[54]'Guiding Principles', section IV c.

[55]Cf. Philip L. Quinn, 'The Primacy of God's Will in Christian Ethics,' *Christian Theism and Moral Philosophy,* eds. Michael Beaty, et. al., 261-86. Quinn highlights an understanding of God's will as the locus of Christian ethics.

[56]'Guiding Principles,' section I b. A commitment to Christ, and to the Word of God led participants to seek earnestly after moral truth, and a belief in the ontological gift of unity led them to continue searching together despite significant philosophical differences, especially regarding the roles of tradition, reason and law, in applying the requirements of love to society. This may be described as a triumph of philosophical and moral realism, or a manifestation of 'enlightenment project' ethics, but it was only made possible by a commitment to Christian truth, revealed and not made.

Kingdom of God and the reality of temporal social and political life. These conclusions are theologically conditioned. They do not simply represent a pooling of opinion.

Along with recognition that there could be no universal agreement emerging from a single perspective, the study-dialogue method acknowledged the diversity amongst the churches represented and committed to work together exploring the sources of difference, and possibilities for agreement.[57] Solutions reached would always be provisional, and incremental, requiring revision and new work with each issue confronted. Principles devised were not intended to wreak violence by taking on independent existence, or by lasting for all time, but through continual discussion, their development and application would be a continual process. Unity was manifested in the very commitment to struggle together despite comprehending the limits of human efforts in social ethics.

One scholar demonstrated successfully the application of the agreed hermeneutic to the problem of racism.[58] In his example, hermeneutics takes into account the authority of scripture and the determinative role of theology, while acknowledging the importance of contextual application. Efforts of individuals and churches to respond to ethical issues are regarded as significant, as is the contention that the kingdom may not be brought to fruition by mere human striving. Moral agents are free and reasonable individuals, who may extend their egoistic impulses beyond themselves to expression on a group level (nationalism), but they are ultimately accountable and therefore responsible to an external authority revealed in the word of God. Society's ills are addressed through individuals, and through individuals representing Churches, but group identities of all kinds are ultimately derivative of single moral agents. Since basic moral agency rests with the individual, societal change must involve addressing both the individual, and the surrounding environment that restrains the extension of individual ego through groups and nations.[59] Yet the church has a special role as a unique society, founded to demonstrate, and not simply communicate, truth. Though it will be prone to sinful assertions as well as other groups in society, it is called to bear witness to the One who judges all moral efforts. That such a level of helpful, practical agreement was possible is challenging to our contemporary philosophical quandaries.

In the intervening years, much attention in the realm of theology has been given over to matters of hermeneutics. Contemporary scholars may well laugh at the apparent simplicity of such an approach to the text. The linguistic turn in

---

[57]Cf. Edward Duff, *The Social Thought of the World Council of Churches* (London: Longmans, 1956), 95. Duff indicates the impossibility of *full* agreement.

[58]Surjit Singh, 'Nation and Race,' in Richardson and Schweitzer, eds., *Biblical Authority*, 310-322.

[59]Cf. C. Stephen Evans, 'A Kierkegaardian View of the Foundations of Morality,' in Beaty et.al. eds., 73-76. Evans explains that ethical individuality is not opposed to a relational view of the self, for it sees the self as formed by relationship with others.

theology has thrown up more problems for hermeneutics and theology than could have been imagined in Niebuhr's day. Many scholars would turn such an analysis of scripture on its contextual head. Nevertheless, despite the diversity present, and the philosophical and theological difficulties of resolving the meaning of texts, there is an increasing commitment to the bible as the recognized narrative that feeds the life of the church. With such new resources within the life of the church, there should be ample frameworks and guidance available for fresh dialogue on the issue of hermeneutics. Overcoming the challenges will require the church to face the barriers of rugged contextuality, and allow the narrative to speak to the whole church, challenging our presuppositions of culture and pretensions to collective power and individual authority. Entering a dialogue with one another will also entail entering a dialogue with the text, and through the text, with The Author, who invites us to dialogue.[60]

Yet, even if agreement through dialogue on hermeneutics is not an readily achievable goal, it is possible to further solidify our socio-ethical commitments nonetheless. It is perhaps a result of Ramsey's appreciation of the hermeneutical problem in ethics that he believed social ethics needed to refrain from offering specific solutions for every issue, and he argued instead for a method that could embrace a broad interpretive community. He would most likely affirm the sentiment that although 'the WCC is not likely in the near future to agree on a single hermeneutic pleasing to all its members.... what we can do is to acknowledge the hermeneutic issues and refrain from hurling selected biblical texts at those who differ from us.'[61] Diversity could not be used as an excuse for doing ethics rapidly and poorly, but it would necessarily condition the method employed in ecumenical deliberation, especially one that takes biblical hermeneutics seriously.

Diversity and Integrity: A Matter of Practical Unity

Ramsey recognized that there are often 'a number of moral choices that may sincerely be accepted even by persons who view political questions in the light of the same ethical perspectives. For us to pronounce upon them in our conferences would be to try to lead decision one way, and beyond any good reason or Christian warrant for doing so.'[62] He suggested that one way to avoid introducing factions into ethical deliberations is for participants to 'take along with us in our minds a "counterpart" - a fellow Christian we know who disagrees with us on specific economic, social, and political conclusions, whose particular "scruples" are different from ours, but who (we cannot deny) thinks

---

[60]This idea is developed most helpfully by Esther Reed, in *The Genesis of Ethics*, (London: Darton, Longman and Todd), 2000.
[61]Shinn, *OW*, 13.
[62]Ramsey, *Who Speaks*, 54.

about his life and his responsibilities upon the same basis that we do.'[63] Wrestling with this 'friend' during deliberations would prevent participants from attempting to control the agenda and drive it in sectarian directions.

It was not that Ramsey did not believe the church had anything to say on issues of social and political importance. Indeed, he suggested that if we wait until we arrive at the gates of Auschwitz to make any declarations, we will have waited too long and neglected our Christian responsibility. But too often, the self-imposed pressure to speak would mean issuing statements that reflect a false unity on issues that are too complex for rapid agreement. 'It is often said in defense of specific recommendations or condemnations that churchmen can agree on these without being in agreement on the theological, the ethical, or even the political *reasons* for them; and that the important thing is the agreement on policy,' he wrote.[64]

The deterioration of social ethics after Stockholm demonstrated that theology is far more closely related to the level of ethical agreement and policy formation than some social gospel advocates thought. The realists took this challenge seriously and pursued dialogue at every level in an attempt to underscore and inform any agreements reached. And yet, the neglect of method yielded only a superficiality of agreement that masked real fragmentation, and an inability to confront diversity: 'We have been calling for decades for responsible society, responsible government. It is high time for this judgment to be called upon ourselves. We should be resolved to say no more about responsibility in society until we have done something about responsible deliberation, and the procedures necessary for this to be made possible, at conferences sponsored by the churches, the NCC and the WCC.'[65]

The post-modern tendency for image to be divorced from substance is a danger that faces us in the task of social ethics.[66] Ecumenical ethics cannot be a simple matter of persuasion of the majority at a large international gathering, giving the appearance of unity while neglecting its substance. Unity for the church, even in ethics, must be real unity, based as far as possible on real facts, real theology, and real discussion, even if it reveals seemingly irreconcilable differences.[67] Unity depends on an acknowledgement of diversity on philosophical, theological, and practical levels, which may come through a commitment to ongoing dialogue, rather than easy agreements on dubious theological grounds.[68]

---

[63]Ibid., 56.

[64]Ibid., 137.

[65]Ibid., 60-1.

[66]Oliver O'Donovan, 'The Concept of Publicity,' *SCE*, 13 2000, 18-32.

[67]See Ramsey's summary of Gollwitzer's critique on this point, Ramsey, *Who Speaks?* 113-4.

[68]This must be real diversity which acknowledges the individuality of persons, and yet their inevitable inter-relatedness. If we cannot conceive of our individuality apart from

Despite the lessons of Stockholm and later conferences, some still pursue the line of producing statements independently of their various theological and philosophical implications. In a contemporary context where the meaning of language is constantly called into question, it seems especially wise to advocate discussion of what various participants actually mean by the words they use, or how various groups interpret and apply the words used in ecumenical discourse. To agree on a policy statement in word only, on the condition that the words may be applied in any way at all in differing contexts, hardly seems like agreement at all. Ramsey argued that unlike a political enterprise, the church does not form a 'continuing community of political policy formation and execution in which we live by agreements that submerge many fundamental differences and live with the results of the execution of such agreements.'[69] To the contrary, differences between Christians meeting together to issue statements on ethical policy matter very much, because 'faulty theology,' and an 'inadequate understanding of Christian social ethics' may too easily help sustain a specific decision which enjoys popular support.

In this regard, Ramsey's suggestion to 'bring a friend in mind' to the deliberation table might help diversity to be confronted and addressed in creative ways. If nothing else, 'to take such a counterpart along with us would enliven the self-denying ordinance that we need to impose on ourselves when we gather and presume to speak as churchmen. Then we might not so often call evil what we know may be good in the particular conscientious judgments of others with whom we should not break faith or break the life - the one body of Christ.'[70] So far, as the friend we have brought along as a dialogue partner in this chapter, Ramsey has demonstrated a continuing relevance, which supports the need for a study-dialogue approach. But where, in a practical sense, can the church go from here? Is there a way of demonstrating unity while maintaining diversity? In light of the historical and philosophical evidence, there would seem to be sufficient reason to return to a realist approach to see if there are aspects that may be applicable to the contemporary context, in order that it may be nudged beyond the present state of confusion and impasse.

Developing Integrity Principles

Not everyone sees the value in recovering the legacy of the past. Duncan Forrester expresses frustration with approaches that neglect the identification of the church with particular needs of society. And yet he wants to embrace a

---

our relationships with others, and God, then philosophies that suggest the self is found *only* in others become problematic for a truly relational personal ontology. Cf. Paul Ricoeur, *Oneself as Another*, trans. Kathleen Blamey, Chicago and London: University of Chicago Press, 1992.

[69]Ramsey, *Who Speaks*, 137.

[70]Ibid., 57.

method that focuses on the formation of the moral agent rather than the decision-making process. Forrester critiques the suggestion that

> The prime Christian contribution to social ethics is in the indicative rather than the imperative mood...It is Christian belief about the kind of place the world is, about the depth of human sinfulness and the possibilities of divine grace, about judgment and hope, incarnation and salvation, God's concern for all and his care for each, about human freedom and divine purpose - it is beliefs such as these which make the difference, and provide the context within which the intractable realities of social and political life can be tackled with wisdom and integrity.[71]

For Forrester 'the argument needs to be pushed further. These indicatives can best be seen coming together in a story rather than a theoretical system, a story which is the irreducible core of the Christian faith. Any great tradition, as Alasdair MacIntyre shows, rests upon a canon which is largely in narrative form - Homer and the Bible to name but the two most obvious examples.'[72] Furthermore, 'Dogmas, principles, and ethical systems are time-bound endeavours to give an account of the significance of the story in terms of a particular culture and age.'[73] It is the story, rather than principles, which give guidance.[74] As Lesslie Newbigin states, principles can too easily become demonic, or once the principles are distilled from the story, the story itself is too easily jettisoned.[75]

Valid though his concerns for the preservation of Christian character may be, Forrester's objection ignores concerns about how members of the story may be best informed and equipped for ethical participation - can it only be through a telling of the story, or do people need real help to meet the dilemmas of real situations with their real faith? A study-dialogue method meets Forrester's most important objections, and yet moves beyond the moral formation method by seeking to clarify not only who Christians are, but what they should do, or at least clarify their options for moral action.

A study-dialogue method attempts to manage a precarious balance between broad affirmations and specific policy actions. It allows us to chart a course between pious generalities and particular policy conclusions. In a study dialogue method it is possible to maintain the right of difference for individuals and churches, while acknowledging a unity in Christ that supersedes our differences, and allows the possibility for continuing dialogue, consensus, and collective action on some issues. This can to be achieved in an atmosphere of

---

[71]John Habgood, cited in Duncan Forrester, *Beliefs, Values and Policies: Conviction Politics in a Secular Age,* Oxford: Clarendon, 1989, 28.
[72]Ibid., 28. Cf. Alasdair MacIntyre, *Whose Justice? Which Rationality?* London, Duckworth, 1988, 11.
[73]Forrester, *Beliefs, Values and Policies,* 28.
[74]Ibid., 29.
[75]Lesslie Newbigin cited in ibid., 28-9.

integrity, where some access to the Real is acknowledged so that as the church, we address ethical paralogisms in attempts to understand and apply The Logos, rather than succumb to a mere ethic of hyper-reality.[76] The 'old' realist school, which includes Niebuhr and Ramsey, still has much that is valuable to say even if we cannot simply turn the clock back on post-modernity.[77] The integrity of the antique suggests certain things that are instructive in finding a *via media* which many rightly argued was necessary if the WCC was to avoid irreconcilable polarization of differing views. The guidance they offer, insofar as it represents a broader impetus towards an effective method for contemporary social ethics, deserves fresh attention in light of the contemporary situation.

Middle Axioms

Following after Niebuhr, Ramsey was distressed that, at Geneva, certain discourses and official utterances were formulated, which represented a political stance many found to be unacceptable. These were inappropriate, since the specific statements had no real authority to speak for the churches if large numbers disagreed with their formulations. Moreover, he did not think it was the church's role to instruct political leaders regarding the actions they must take in the political realm. By no means was he advocating the post-modern approach of more recent ethicists, but he did address their important concern that Christian ethics be theologically consistent. In fact, he stated strongly that 'The church has a proper role in addressing itself to the problems of political morality and the common life. We ought not to yield to those who say that the church should stay out of politics.'[78] Yet, he did not believe it was instructive for churches to merely agree at some superficial level in order to present the appearance of unity. The church should no less overstep than understep its boundaries on such matters. Like Nicholas Wolterstorff encouraging the church to learn to say both 'yes' and 'no' to the prevailing culture and political authorities, Ramsey argued that 'Christian political ethics cannot say what should or must be done but only what may be done.'[79] Such an approach would prevent totalising narratives from wreaking havoc over decades of ecumenical dialogue, and at the same time not only instruct the consciences of particular church members or bodies, but 'inform the ethos and conscience' of nations

---

[76]Cf. Berlin Group cited in *One World*, 14; David Lyon, *Jesus in Disneyland* (Oxford and Cambridge: Polity, 2000).

[77]Cf. Stanley Grenz, 'Beyond Foundationalism: Is a Nonfoundationalist Evangelical Theology Possible?' *JCTR*, [http://apu.edu/¬CTRF/papers/ctrfpapers.html], 1998.

[78]Ramsey, *Who Speaks*, 27.

[79]Ibid., 152. Cf. Nicholas Wolterstorff, 'Christian Political Reflection: Diognetian or Augustinian,' *PSB*, 20 2 1999, 168.

and political leaders.[80]

Ramsey turned to his esteemed colleague John Bennett to plead again the case for the so-called 'middle axiom' approach. In his 1961 presidential address to the American Society of Christian Ethics, Bennett related his struggle as a teacher of potential ministers, in attempting to discern what kind of ethical guidance is appropriate for them to give to their congregations. The same difficulty existed at an ecumenical level, he suggested

> It is important to have some designation of objectives or judgments which have a particular reference to our concrete situation, which are determiners of policy and yet which are not identical with the most concrete policy which is the immediate guide to action....The corporate teaching of the church on controversial social issues is seldom more specific than the projection of so-called 'middle-axioms' but if these do become a part of the mind of the church it becomes possible for it more effectively to encourage its members and many voluntary groups to experiment with the support of specific policies.[81]

Despite the reluctance to identify the church with any single particular policy, the principles debated and derived through the approach would be seen as action-oriented.

Like many others, Ramsey had little support to give the use of 'middle axiom' as a term. In his view, expressions such as 'middle axiom' and 'responsible society' simply 'summarize an ecumenical consensus that once existed. They mark the point at which in ecumenical ethics we ceased to press on in fundamental analysis of the Christian understanding of the social good (lest disagreement break out), and instead leaped over to policy-making pronouncements on which, it was found, churchmen could reach some sort of agreement.'[82] It seems in such debates that the disdain for the term often precedes or even precludes their discussion. Nevertheless, such middle axioms offer a practical approach to, and application of, the study-dialogue process. They not only recognize and maintain the tension between the individual and the collective, but they represent potential manifestations of an approach of integrity to ethics in general. Moreover, they seek to reflect equally upon the truth of Christian doctrine, and the reality of the situation in which such doctrine or story is lived out, and they dissuade the church from claiming more expertise than it has. In order to avoid the pejorative dismissal of the approach based on a simple term, we will refer to 'middle axioms' as 'ethical integrity principles.'

Ramsey believed that rather than issue a single policy line, the church needs

---

[80]Ramsey, *Who Speaks*, 154.

[81]Bennett, cited in ibid., 14-15. See the middle axiom approach also discussed in Ronald Preston, 'Middle Axioms in Christian Social Ethics,' *Church and Society in the Late Twentieth-Century: The Economic and Political Task* (London: SCM, 1983), 141-156.

[82]Ramsey, *Who Speaks*, 169, n.4.

to elaborate alternatives, especially when speaking for the church as a whole body. In a day of increased diversity, it may be said that this is appropriate when ecumenical bodies are speaking *to* the church as well. While the church goes on continually with the business of moral formation, informing the ethos of church and society as it lives its life in the world, there are times when a public word is needed. In such cases, Ramsey insisted, it is more appropriate to affirm that Christian opinion will not abandon magistrates if particular actions are taken, than to suggest which actions ought to be taken.[83]

The discussion may be taken further in light of a study-dialogue method. Agreement on statements and actions could progress as far as consensus allows. When consensus breaks down, it would be the task of participants to study and elaborate the reasons for their differences. At least in this activity, dialogue could continue, even though participants may find they encounter strong disagreement. Various groups could then outline the options they believe may be taken by Christians, along with the reasons why they support these positions. It would be left to the churches and individuals within them to discuss them further and apply them in their respective contexts. In the other direction, if an issue arises from a particular context and is brought to the table for debate, it ought to be pursued toward as much agreement as possible. This approach not only prevents ecumenical bodies from being too outspoken on issues that enjoy only a small measure of agreement, but also balances the development of gospel principles with the necessities of context. In such situations, consensus is recognized as the goal and ideal, but is usually considered a rare possibility. Most times, debate, discussion and dialogue about possible alternatives, and their accompanying theological and philosophical arguments will be expected. Thus the integrity of constituents and the collective body will be maintained.

Though in sympathy with some of Ramsey's stated objectives, Duncan Forrester believes such an approach does not go far enough.[84] Forrester suggests that 'it also requires to be recognized that a lot of men and women do not find statements of such generality as speaking for them, or addressing their condition. They look for some word that is more specific and concrete.' Moreover

> there are still multitudes of problems about how to relate the measured theological statements that are intended to give guidance in a variety of situations and the responses to particular crises and problems which take full account of the experiences, emotions, and sufferings involved. The ecumenical movement is today constraining us to move beyond the older ways of contributing to the public realm without, one hopes, losing the notable insights that that work produced.[85]

---

[83]Ramsey builds this on the affirmation made by the Archbishop of Canterbury on the situation in Rhodesia. Ibid., 120.
[84]Forrester, *Beliefs, Values and Policies*, 57.
[85]Ibid., 57-8.

It is difficult to see how Forrester's concerns are to be addressed without the church speaking an official word on every specific situation that affects the lives of its members within their various contexts. Yet it is just this 'leapfrogging' from issue to issue that Ramsey suggested the church should avoid. There is nothing in a study-dialogue method that prevents contextualization of ethical principles on the local level, by the people most directly concerned. On the contrary, various integrity principles outlined at the conference level may encourage and empower local Christians to translate and apply them in a manner appropriate to their context. This would seem to be true contextualization, while avoiding the danger of confusing principle and precept.[86] Here Forrester seems to caricature Ramsey's argument by saying he *never* permits a specific word.[87] It does not seem that Ramsey precludes a specific word, but rather insists that it should be clarified when and why a specific word should be given, and that in most instances, specificity is more properly addressed at the local level than at the inter-denominational level of ecumenical dialogue.

Forrester communicates a valid and passionate concern for the needs of people and churches at the grassroots, facing complex political and social situations. When a study-dialogue method is developed more fully, it offers the potential for devising stronger authoritative statements, of the kind he seems to seek. When there is consensus on an issue - the possibility of which is acknowledged by this method - then a specific statement may be formulated and issued. Because of its rarity and unanimity it will speak with authority, and draw much more attention, thus being far more effective than issuing a word on every concern that might arise.

This approach will facilitate an improved discussion of biblical hermeneutics, and foster theological understanding. By discussing which principles are possible, and justifying divergent positions to one another, differences in interpretation of scripture, and the roles scripture and theology should play in ethics will be visibly highlighted. This will encourage increased dialogue and study on various approaches to scripture and theology, and the relevance of theology and scripture for application in ethics.

This is not to say that theology is everything that must be considered in ethical deliberation. Some have made the 'mistake' of thinking that if we are to be more theological then every issue of ethical importance must be treated as a matter of *status confessionis*.[88] There has been a desire amongst some

---

[86] The distinction between principle and precept in ethics is highlighted by P. T. Forsyth in *Socialism, the Church and the Poor* (London: Hodder and Stoughton, 1908), 59.

[87] Forrester, *Beliefs, Values and Policies*, 58.

[88] This tendency in some recent ecumenical ethics has been attributed largely to the work of Ulrich Duchrow. Though an effective means of dealing with certain issues, it is rarely the case that Churches are guilty of intentionally using the Gospel to justify sin. See the document 'Racism and South Africa,' issued by the General Council of the World

ecumenical ethicists to address matters of social ethics universally as such. According to this approach, issues of injustice are considered sufficiently serious to exclude from fellowship any churches that refuse to renounce their participation in particular oppressive structures. Many who advocate this position point to the *Kairos* declaration and beyond that to a possible misunderstanding of the WARC document which addressed the issue of apartheid in South Africa. The WARC document suspended from membership in the World Alliance those Reformed Churches in South Africa which employed the gospel in providing a defence of apartheid. Condemning the theological justification of sin as heresy, the WARC document suspended the churches on grounds of *status confessionis*, outlining steps to future reconciliation. The *Kairos* document took this a step further and declared not only theological justification of apartheid as heresy, but also the very political structure itself. From this lead, some have developed an approach to ecumenical social ethics that would seek to treat all matters of the churches' participation in oppressive structures and the perpetuation of poverty and injustice as a matter of *status confessionis*.

The problems such an approach raises are made obvious from the perspective of the Berlin critique, and a study-dialogue method, as they threaten to unbalance the moral agency of communities and individuals. Firstly, it should be recognized that in a study-dialogue approach which takes diversity seriously, very few occasions will arise which produce the kind of unanimity that characterized the WARC and *Kairos* documents. Secondly, consultation of experts, at least in theology, would remind ethicists of the complexities that characterize politics and economics which render simple answers regarding poverty and liberation impossible. In reality, few churches can be seen to be intentionally using the Gospel to justify their government's oppression of poor or otherwise marginalized people. Thirdly, various hermeneutical approaches to the Bible do not make it universally clear that the basic presuppositions of this approach are indeed correct. Many debates rage about the primacy of God's preferential option for the poor over and against God's preferential option for sinners, independently of their socio-economic category. On this front and many others, the Berlin group's call for discussion regarding biblical interpretation becomes especially pertinent.

All of this serves to reinforce the suggestion that a contemporary adaptation of a middle axiom approach, conditioned by realist impulses, and manifested in a study-dialogue method offers most promise for the future of Christian social

---

Alliance of Reformed Churches, Ottawa, 1982. The document reads, 'We declare, with Black Reformed Christians of South Africa, that apartheid ("Separate Development") is a sin, and that the moral and theological justification of it is a travesty of the Gospel, and in its persistent disobedience to the Word of God, a theological heresy.' In this respect, the situation constituted a *status confessionis*. This is not the same as making every sin of the Church a matter of *status confessionis*, as some are inclined to do.

ethics. The development of integrity principles, based on the love command, with as much agreement toward consensus as possible, demonstrates an approach that is conditioned by theological, philosophical, and practical integrity. The result is that freedom and authority are recognized and balanced in the life of the moral agent, at individual and various collective levels. In this way, theology is given a pre-eminent role in ethical method, and the integrity of the gospel is maintained.

Conclusion

Twilight and Shadow: Methods of Christian Social Ethics in a New Era

In the spiritual journey we travel through the night towards the day. We walk not in the bright sunshine of total certainty but through the darkness of ignorance, error, muddle and uncertainty. We make progress in the journey as we grow in faith.

Christopher Bryant

Knowledge is proud that he has learned so much; Wisdom is humble that he knows no more.

William Cowper

Christian action in the world will not sustained or carried out in an intelligent and effective manner unless it is supported by doctrinal convictions that have achieved some degree of clarity.

John Macquarrie

One could say that we have now reached the twilight of this study. Does that imply we are none the wiser regarding the matter of method in Christian social ethics, since we are left in the dim light which is neither day nor night? Paul Ramsey believed that social ethical method was exactly the concern of the twilight - the twilight between day and night, which represents the space between generalities and particularities in ethical practice.[1] A method which was able to thrive in the muted shades of twilight was one that would be most successful. This was not to say that we are unable to distinguish between night and day, but rather that the best and worst aspects of both may be seen clearly from the perspective of the twilight, especially when Christ's light comes to shine there, and the judgment of God hovers over like a shadow. Light and dark; night and day; generalities and particularities; individuals and collectives - in the space between these extremes is found adequate light to integrate

---

[1] Paul Ramsey, *Who Speaks for the Church?* Nashville: Abingdon, 1967, 46. Several contemporary scholars have described the current theological climate as one of 'twilight' – between the decline of modernity and the rise of postmodernity.

various strands of ethical argument, and diverse perspectives of ethical participants. In the twilight, extremes are mitigated and mediated, and garishness muted. In the twilight, the advantages and weaknesses of light and dark are best appreciated. In the balanced view of the twilight, Christ's light of hope and shadow of judgment bring integrity to the ethical task, as they illumine human striving, and remind us of our limits.

We have seen that the ability to prolong the twilight, or to spend any time there at all, differs between methods that represent diverse philosophies, theologies, and practicalities. For Rauschenbusch and the social gospel, there was a definite recognition of the difficulty in finding middle ground between general suggestions and detailed ethical policy. But patience to linger in the twilight was absent. Rauschenbusch was not willing to spend time in the twilight when he believed so strongly in the ability of the all-embracing light of Christ to shine in human social existence. This meant that a balanced view was lost. Focusing on the light of Christ to the exclusion of the shadow of judgment blurred the Creator-creature distinction, and drowned the individual agent in the sea of collective sin and salvation. In the midst, the church surrendered its distinctive voice, and encountered insurmountable difficulties in attempting to offer solutions to concrete problems when the broader social movement began to falter. Superficial agreements were insufficient for ethics which sought to be ecumenical by turning a blind eye to significant theological and philosophical differences.

Niebuhr and the post-war realists were far more prepared to linger in the twilight and even to set up camp there. This led Niebuhr to achieve a measure of balance between those extreme aspects which compromised the social gospel method. Accordingly, he reasserted the importance of individuals and groups in ethical life, and managed to hold the two in creative tension, acknowledging the unique dynamics of community existence, but preserving the moral agency of the individual. Spending time in the twilight meant that he would see the value of philosophy, but preserve the integrity of theology in ethical method. His appreciation of Christ's light and shadow would lead him to recapture a sense of sin and grace in ethics. But perhaps, for Niebuhr, Christ's light was not perceived to be bright enough, or the shadow of judgment was too strong. For although he believed Christians should have a voice in the public realm, it was not evident how that voice could be distinguished from any others around it, revealing a neglected ecclesiology. Nor was it clear what that voice should say, or even could say, pointing to a neglected pneumatology. Nevertheless, the willingness to embrace the twilight as a dwelling-place for ecumenical ethics yielded the most effective study-dialogue method for social ethics in the twentieth century, achieving broad consensus from Oxford to Amsterdam and beyond.

It was not long before ecumenical participants in social ethics developed an impatience with the twilight, and sought to drive into the blinding light of day, convinced that humanity could focus its beams for social advancement.

Mistaking the extreme of human striving for the light of Christ, revolutionaries sought through an action-reflection method to liberate humanity from the twilight of moral existence. While the focus of ethics narrowed into fragmented context, individuals again were smothered - this time beneath the idealism of revolution. Doctrine was also relegated a subordinate place to the priority of political action, being rewritten in ways that suited the immediate context of revolution. When the revolution failed, the Church was left with little to say.

Convinced of the need to restore the uniqueness of the Christian church in social ethics, some recent ecumenical participants have succumbed to post-modern pressures to contextualize themselves to a narrow band of twilight, outside of which they do not perceive of any existence. This ecclesiological idealism has restored the church's unique voice, but also led advocates of a moral formation method to imagine that it is the only voice. An interpretation of the Christian community as formed solely by narrative again compromises the integrity of the individual, while denying a wider reality that offers the challenge of dialogue and growth. For in a narrow band of twilight, not only are other views excluded but only a small part of Christ's light and shadow may be perceived. The limits are not worth the risk of excluding crucial elements of theological and philosophical truth in ethics, possibly discernible in a broader and more open view.[2]

A method of integrity, however, seeks to prolong the twilight and reflect upon various aspects of life within it. It takes into balanced consideration aspects of philosophy and practical context, while allowing theology to retain a place of methodological pre-eminence. It seeks to bring those dwelling in the twilight together in dialogue, grasping after the day but mindful of the night, allowing Christ's light and shadow to challenge and correct in flexible ways which find relevant expression in every local context, situating that context within a vision of the whole church. It maintains the tensions of individual and collective existence, and allows the excesses of one view to be corrective of the other. It allows the development of principles insofar as there is agreement, and encourages dialogue when consensus seems elusive. Moreover, it allows philosophy to clarify, theology to verify, and ethical practice to unify the social ethics of the Church, as an attempt is made to mediate between certainties of belief and ambiguities of ethics.

Even these methodological suggestions reveal shortcomings. It will be far from universally accepted that there is room for both certainty in faith and ambiguity in ethics. Although the participants in a study-dialogue method

---

[2]This is not to suggest that there are no boundaries, only that boundaries of truth encompass all of humanity as bearers of the imago dei and the whole of creation as the object of God's redemption. To focus solely on the voice of the Church is to risk neglecting God's interest in the rest of the world, and his activity of grace and general revelation within it. We will recall N. H. G. Robinson's suggestion that Christian ethics extends that degree of natural morality which exists in even the unsanctified. See N. H. G. Robinson, *The Groundwork of Christian Ethics* (London: Collins, 1971), 305.

sometimes need to accept the limited potential for agreement, much work needs to be done to convince theologians and ethicists that recovery of the dialogue table is desirable, or even possible. Increased engagement with philosophy and competing philosophical presuppositions is needful if ecumenical ethics are to move forward in a constructive manner. And it is far easier said than done to encourage real people in real situations to be patient in the twilight rather than push the ethical agenda toward the full light of day, which is impossible to achieve fully on this side of eternity. On the other hand, it is maintenance of a delicate balance which is required if we are to prevent Christian ethics from slipping into utter darkness.[3] To hold together the strands of individual and collective humanity, and individual and collective Christianity in the contemporary world requires insight and skill beyond any method practiced in the twentieth century, while learning from their mistakes and building upon their successes.

There are few alternatives if the church hopes to retain a critical or prophetic dialogue with the powers and principalities of this world, let alone maintain any degree of internal integrity. The unity of the church is not rooted in ethics, but it is expressed there. If the present state of confusion in Christian social ethics is a symptom of a much bigger problem, then those who are concerned for the unity and integrity of the church cannot afford to ignore it.

On the other hand, the present crisis offers an opportunity to churches in local contexts to confront ethical issues together in grassroots communities, rather than seek a top-down resolution of the problem. This approach may be more suited to the present philosophical climate, and may contribute to the unity of the church in some very practical ways. But even here, tools are needed to equip churches of different traditions to meet together, discuss, and understand perspectives and approaches which are quite unfamiliar to their own. The method of study-dialogue suggested in the previous chapter may be helpful not only at structural levels, but in local contexts as well, as church members meet to discuss potential means of prophetic witness in local communities. But methodological limitations must be confronted, addressed, and accepted at the outset.[4]

At least this work has demonstrated that some issues may be clarified through dialogue, recalling history, and wrestling with philosophical and

---

[3] Cf. Duncan Forrester, *Beliefs, Values and Policies*, 3. Forrester recounts a parable of G. K. Chesterton regarding the fate of a lamp-post whose value and relevance was so criticised and undermined that intellectual dialogue was forced to carry on in darkness. Alasdair MacIntyre suggests that a new dark age is already upon us, in which the only survivors will be moral communities. See *After Virtue: a study in moral theory*, 263.

[4] The practical implications of the methodological question are being pursued beyond the boundaries of the research presented in this work. See Anna Robbins, 'Ethical Models for the Twilight Zone of Church and Culture,' *Movement for Change: Evangelical Perspectives on Social Transformation*, ed. David Hilborn, (Carlisle: Paternoster Press, 2004), 70-94.

theological concepts as they are employed in ethics. And yet, there is much more to discover. Even if the study-dialogue method were universally employed, there are still myriad issues to sort out regarding how actual statements are devised on behalf of churches, what authority may be accorded to them, and how concrete actions may be taken on those occasions when agreement is reached. Moreover, the dynamic of the relationship between word and action must be addressed, since statements tend to reflect group agency, whereas Christian praxis must inevitably be carried out by individuals who are in some way existentially committed to the task. From this, issues of coercion, discipline, freedom and obedience inevitably spring. Also, while the study-dialogue method preserves the unity of the church by acknowledging its diversity, are there times when an ethical stance by sub-groups warrants a breach of fellowship? In such cases, how can the principle of consensus be maintained over and against that of democracy? These are only a few of an endless array of questions which require further examination. From the perspective of the twilight, this thesis has succeeded in serving up more questions than it has answered, though it may be suggested that raising good questions is better than offering answers to poor ones.

Nevertheless, at the conclusion of this work, several affirmations may be made regarding method in twentieth century Christian ethics. First, there is an ongoing methodological task.[5] We have seen how, in the last century, the effectiveness of Christian social ethics has depended largely on aspects of method. Whether participants have wished to affirm or deny it, the way that theology, philosophy and aspects of context are pieced together matter for the final outcome of ethical practice and ethical decision-making. Unlike those early meetings at Stockholm, ecumenical gatherings can no longer afford to deny that service may equally divide and unite, just as doctrine may do, and the two are not unrelated. Future methods will need to remember this hard-learned lesson, and seek to hold doctrine and service together. Ignoring theological issues may offer the gloss of superficial agreement but in the long run little can be achieved if the difference of competing visions is not acknowledged.

Second, future methods will need to be aware of philosophical influences in theology and ethics. Agreement sometimes may be precluded on seemingly theological grounds, when what is really at issue is competition of contemporary philosophical worldviews which cause participants to interpret scripture and doctrines in diverse ways. With little appreciation of philosophical influences and the role they play in ethical development and decision-making, success in the task of Christian ethics will be severely limited. Overcoming such a problem will require astute self-awareness and a

---

[5]This suggestion refutes the position of many narrative and anabaptist ethicists regarding the value of methodology, including John Howard Yoder in 'Walk and Word: The Alternative to Methodologism,' *Christian Theism and Moral Philosophy*, eds. Michael Beaty, et. al., 181-198.

willingness of participants to become vulnerable to examination in areas often taken for granted, and little understood. This will require the development and nurture of mutual trust, and will be related intimately to the issue of Christian unity.

Third, participants and theorists in social ethics must be constantly and consistently aware of the dynamics of individual and collective moral agency. This thesis has merely served to highlight and clarify the problem. A more complete examination of aspects of each type of agency could yet be done, since it is evident that ethicists assume too readily the characteristics of agency without considering the complexities involved. Not only do ethical methods need to consider aspects of individual and collective action, but also examine the relationships which exist between the two, and between various groups within the broader collective. Mere structuralism cannot suffice, just as a simplified individualism which pays scant attention to the dynamics of group behaviour is inadequate. This problem is particularly acute in an age that is torn ideologically between disturbing visions of pure individualism and totalizing collectivism. The Church has particular resources to bring to bear on this subject, if it will resist the trend to retreat into its own cosseted narrative to the neglect of a whole humanity inhabiting a shared space.

Whether contemporary ethicists like it or not, ethical decision-making will always be a part of the Christian life. Neither history, nor philosophy, nor theology, nor scripture is able to affirm the contention that Christians will always 'do the right thing' in accordance with their virtuous nature, especially when they are considered together in all of their diversity as the body of Christ.[6] Now, more than ever, Christians live in a world full of complexities and contradictions which forces decisions upon them if they lack the courage or conviction to make decisions for themselves. Equipping the saints for the ministry of the church as individuals, acting together for the good of the whole community, speaking and acting with conviction when required, and remaining silent when there is nothing helpful to be said requires diligence and discipline. Yet this hard work is necessary if the church is to continue to provide a foundation for belief, and a means of speaking and acting prophetically and authoritatively in the midst of particular situations.[7]

---

[6]Samuel Wells suggests that although Stanley Hauerwas initially intended to address the issue of character in Christian ethics, this aspect was neglected in light of other concerns, especially the effort to counter ethical 'decisionism'. See Samuel Wells, *Transforming Fate into Destiny: The Theological Ethics of Stanley Hauerwas*, (Carlisle: Paternoster, 1998), 13-23.

[7]Cf. John de Gruchy, *Liberating Reformed Theology* (Grand Rapids: Eerdmans, 1991). The integrity of this task depends on a commitment to the whole gospel. This will yield not only 'a commitment to the evangelical doctrines as affirmed in early catholic tradition and retrieved by the Reformation but also a commitment to the biblical prophetic witness to God's purposes of justice and equity within society.' Thus, 'while a tradition can wither and die - or worse, become an albatross around or necks - it can also

Ethical integrity will mean that 'Christian ethical reflection will be theological reflection; and Christian praxis will be devotional praxis - it will flow from gratitude to God. In Christian ethical theory, gift and demand will be held together as an indissoluble whole; in Christian praxis there will be a constant concern - a striving - to ensure that the actions performed are consistent with the gospel proclaimed.'[8] To this end, it will be an ongoing task to keep the tendency towards madness at bay. Through rigorous study and patient dialogue may the church receive the wisdom and grace to thrive in the twilight, so that whether night descends or a new day dawns, we will find the necessary resources to live together well, and for the good of all.

---

be retrieved as a source of empowerment in the present, providing the symbols not only for its own revitalisation and renewal, but for society at large.' 39-40.

[8] Alan P. F. Sell, *Aspects of Christian Integrity* (Louisville, KY: Westminster/John Knox Press, 1990), 61.

Select Bibliography

Published Works: Books

Audi, R. and N. Wolterstorff, *Religion in the Public Square: The Place of Religious Convictions in Political Debate* (Lanham/Boulder/New York/London: Rowman & Littlefield, 1997).

Barbour, R. (ed.), *The Kingdom of God and Human Society* (Edinburgh: T & T Clark, 1993).

Barth, K., *Dogmatics in Outline*, G.T. Thomson (tr.), (London: SCM, 1949).

— *Evangelical Theology: An Introduction*, G. Foley (tr.), (Grand Rapids: Eerdmans, 1963).

— *The Christian Life: Church Dogmatics IV, 4: Lecture Fragments*, G. Bromiley (tr.), (Edinburgh: T & T Clark, 1981).

Bauckham, R., *The Bible in Politics: How to Read the Bible Politically* (Louisville: Westminster/John Knows Press, 1989).

Beasley-Murray, G.R., *Jesus and the Kingdom of God* (Grand Rapids: Eerdmans/ Exeter: Paternoster, 1986).

Beaty, M., C. Fisher and M. Nelson (eds.), *Christian Theism and Moral Philosophy* (Macon: Mercer University Press, 1998).

Bebbington, D., *Evangelicalism in Modern Britain* (Grand Rapids: Baker Book House, 1989).

Beckley, H., *Passion for Justice: Retrieving the Legacies of Walter Rauschenbusch, John A. Ryan and Reinhold Niebuhr* (Louisville: Westminster/John Knox Press, 1992).

Bell, G.K.A. (ed.), *The Stockholm Conference 1925: Official Report* (London: Oxford Univeristy Press, 1926).

Bennett, J.C., *Christian Realism* (London: SCM, 1941).

— *Christians and the State* (New York: Scribner's, 1958).

— (ed.), *Christian Social Ethics in A Changing World: An Ecumenical Theological Inquiry* (New York: Association Press/London: SCM, 1966).

Bent, A.J. van der, *Commitment to God's World: A Concise Critical Survey of Ecumenical Social Thought* (Geneva: WCC, 1995).

Best, T.F. (ed.), *Beyond Unity-In-Tension* (Geneva: WCC, 1988).

— (ed.), *Report of the Central Committee to the 7th Assembly of the WCC, Vancouver to Canberra 1983-1990* (Geneva: WCC, 1990).

— and M. Robra (eds.), *Ecclesiology and Ethics: Ecumenical Ethical Engagement, Moral Formation and the Nature of the Church* (Geneva: WCC, 1997).

Beyerhaus, P., *God's Kingdom and the Utopian Error* (Wheaton: Crossway Books, 1992).

Bingham, J., *Courage to Change: An Introduction to the Life and Thought of Reinhold Niebuhr* (New York: Charles Scribner's Sons, 1972).

Bland, S., *The New Christianity* (Toronto: Toronto University Press, 1973).

Block, W. and I. Hexham (eds.), *Religion, Economics and Social Thought* (Vancouver: Fraser Institute, 1982).

Bloesch, D.G., *Freedom for Obedience: Evangelical Ethics for Contemporary Times* (San Francisco: Harper and Row, 1987).

Boff, L., *Faith on the Edge*, R. Barr (tr.), (San Francisco: Harper and Row, 1989).

Bonhoeffer, D., *The Cost of Discipleship*, R.H. Fuller (tr.), (1937; reprint London: SCM, 1959).

— *Life Together*, J. Doberstein (tr.), (London: SCM, 1954).

— *Ethics*, N.H. Smith (tr.), (London: SCM, 1955).

Bonino, J., *Revolutionary Theology Comes of Age* (London: SPCK, 1975).

Brown, C., *Niebuhr and His Age* (Philadelphia: Trinity Press International, 1992).

Brown, R.M. (ed.), *The Essential Reinhold Niebuhr: Selected Essays and Addresses* (New Haven: Yale University Press, 1986).

Brunner, E., *The Divine Imperative*, O. Wyon (tr.), (London: Lutterworth, 1937^2).

— *Justice and the Social Order*, M. Hottinger (tr.), (London/Redhill: Lutterworth, 1945)

— *Revelation and Reason*, O. Wyon (tr.), (Philadelphia: The Westminster Press, 1946).

Bryan, G. (ed.), *Communities of Faith and Radical Discipleship* (Macon: Mercer University Press, 1986).

Bultmann, R., *Jesus Christ and Mythology* (New York: Scribner, 1958).

Carnell, E.J., *The Theology of Reinhold Niebuhr* (Grand Rapids: Eerdmans, 1951).

— *The Case for Biblical Christianity*, R.H. Nash (ed.), (Grand Rapids: Eerdmans, 1969).

Carter, P.A., *Decline and Revival of the Social Gospel 1920-1940* (Ithaca: Cornell University Press, 1956).

Charles, R., *Christian Social Witness and Teaching: The Catholic Tradition from Genesis to Centesimus Annus, Vol. II: The Modern Social Teaching: Contexts: Summaries: Analysis* (Leominster: Gracewing, 1998).

Chiba, S. et. al. (eds.), *Christian Ethics in Ecumenical Context: Theology, Culture, and Politics in Dialogue* (Grand Rapids: Eerdmans, 1995).

Chilton, B. and J.I.H. MacDonald, *Jesus and the Ethics of the Kingdom* (Grand Rapids: Eerdmans, 1987).

Clements, K., *Learning to Speak: The Church's Voice in Public Affairs* (Edinburgh: T & T Clark, 1995).

Clow, W.M., *Christ in the Social Order* (New York: George H. Doran, 1913).

Davies, B. and M. Walsh (eds.), *Proclaiming Justice and Peace: Documents from John XXIII to John Paul II.* (London: Flame, 1991).

Davies, D.R., *Reinhold Niebuhr: Prophet from America* (London: James Clarke & Co., 1945).

Dorrin, G., *Soul in Society: The Making and Renewal of Social Christianity* (Minneapolis: Fortress Press, 1995).

Duchrow, U., *Global Economy: A Confessional Issue for Churches?* (Geneva: WCC, 1987).

Duff, E., *The Social Thought of the World Council of Churches* (London: Longmans. Green & Co., 1956).

Durkin, K., *Reinhold Niebuhr* (London: Geoffrey Chapman, 1989).

Dykstra, C., *Vision and Character: A Christian Educator's Alternative to Kohlberg* (New York: Paulist Press, 1981).

Edwards, D.M., *Christianity and Philosophy* (Edinburgh: T & T Clark 1932).

Eliot, T.S., *The Idea of a Christian Society* (London: Faber, 1942).

Ellingson, M., *The Cutting Edge: How Churches Speak on Social Issues* (Grand Rapids: Eerdmans/Geneva: WCC, 1995).

Elliott, C. et. al. (eds.), *Christian Faith and Political Hopes* (London: Epworth Press, 1979).

Elliott, C., *Comfortable Compassion? Poverty, Power and the Church* (London: Hodder and Stoughton, 1987).

Ellul, J., *The Presence of the Kingdom*, O. Wyon (tr.), (New York: Seabury Press, 1948 and 1967).

Fackre, G., *The Promise of Reinhold Niebuhr* (Philadelphia: Lippincott, 1970).

Federal Council of the Churches of Christ in America, *Twenty-Five Eventful Years* (New York: FCC, 1933).

Fey, H.E. (ed.), *A History of the Ecumenical Movement, 1948-1968* (Geneva: WCC, 1993³).

Fish, S., *Is There a Text in This Class? The Authority of Interpretive Communities* (London/Cambridge: Harvard University Press, 1980).

Fishburn, J.F., *The Fatherhood of God and the Victorian Family: The Social Gospel in America* (Philadelphia: Fortress Press, 1981).

Flew, A.G.N., *Evolutionary Ethics* (London: Macmillan, 1967).

— *Thinking About Social Thinking* (London: Fontana Press, 1991²).

Foster, D. and P. Mojzes (eds.), *Society and Original Sin: Ecumenical Essays on the Impact of the Fall* (New York: Paragon House, 1985).

Fox, R., *Reinhold Niebuhr: A Biography* (New York: Pantheon Books, 1985).

Forrester, D., *Beliefs, Values and Policies: Conviction Politics in a Secular Age* (Oxford: Clarendon Press, 1989).

— *The True Church and Morality: Reflections on Ecclesiology and Ethics* (Geneva: WCC, 1997).

Forsyth, P.T., *Positive Preaching and the Modern Mind* (London: Hodder & Stoughton, 1907).

— *Socialism, the Church and the Poor* (London: Hodder & Stoughton, 1908).

— *The Person and Place of Jesus Christ* (London: Hodder & Stoughton, 1909).

— *The Work of Christ* (London: Hodder & Stoughton, 1910).

— *The Principle of Authority* (London: Hodder & Stoughton, 1912).

— *Theology in Church and State* (London: Hodder & Stoughton, 1915).

Fowler, R.B., *A New Engagement: Evangelical Political Thought, 1966-1976* (Grand Rapids: Eerdmans, 1982).

Frei, H., *Types of Christian Theology*, G. Hunsinger and W. Placher (eds.), (London/ New Haven: Yale University Press, 1992).

Friere, P., *Pedagogy of the Oppressed*, Rev. Ed. (New York: Continuum, 1993).

Gardner, E.C., *Christocentrism in Christian Social Ethics: A Depth Study of Eight Modern Protestants* (Lanham: University Press of America, 1983).

Garvie, A.E., *The Ritschlian Theology* (Edinburgh: T & T Clark, 1899).

Gay, C.M., *With Liberty and Justice for Whom?* (Grand Rapids: Eerdmans, 1991).

Gill, R., *The Social Context of Theology* (London/Oxford: Mowbrays, 1975).

— *A Textbook of Christian Ethics* (Edinburgh: T & T Clark, 1985).

Gladden, W., *Ruling Ideas and the Present Age* (London: James Clarke & Co., 1895).

— *The Church and Modern Life* (London: James Clarke & Co., 1908).

Green, T.H., *Prolegomena to Ethics* (Oxford: University Press, 1883).

Grenz, S., *The Moral Quest: Foundations of Christian Ethics* (Leicester: Apollos, 1997).

— *Renewing the Center: Evangelical Theory in a Post-Theological Era* (Grand Rapids: Baker, 2000).

— and R. Olson, *20ᵗʰ Century Theology* (Downers Grove: IVP, 1992).

— and J.R. Franke, *Beyond Foundationalism: Shaping Theology in a Postmodern Context* (Louisville: Westminster/John Knox Press, 2001).

Gruchy, J. de, *Liberating Reformed Theology* (Grand Rapids: Eerdmans, 1991).

Gustafson, J., *The Church as Moral Decision-Maker* (Philadelphia/Boston: The Pilgrim

Press, 1970).

— *Theology and Christian Ethics* (Philadelphia: The Pilgrim Press, 1974).

— *Can Ethics Be Christian?* (Chicago/London: University of Chicago Press, 1975).

— *Theology and Ethics* (Oxford: Basil Blackwell, 1981).

— *Ethics From a Theological Perspective, Vol. II: Ethics and Theology* (Chicago: University of Chicago Press, 1984).

Gutierrez, G., *A Theology of Liberation*, Rev. Ed., Sister C. Inda/J. Eagleson (trs. and eds.), (Maryknoll: Orbis, 1988).

— *The Poor and the Church in Latin America* (London: Catholic Institute for International Relations, 1984).

Hamilton, K., *Earthly Good* (Grand Rapids: Eerdmans, 1990).

Handy, R.T. (ed.), *The Social Gospel in America, 1870-1920* (New York: Oxford University Press, 1966).

— *A Christian America: Protestant Hopes and Historical Realities*, Rev. Ed. (New York/Oxford: Oxford University Press, 1960).

Harland, G., *The Thought of Reinhold Niebuhr* (New York: Oxford University Press, 1960).

— *Christian Faith and Society* (Calgary: University of Calgary Press, 1988).

Harnack, A., *What is Christianity?* B. Saunders (tr.), (London: Williams and Norgate, 1901).

— and W. Herrmann, *Essays on the Social Gospel*, G.M. Craik (tr.), M.A. Canney (ed.), (London: Williams and Norgate, 1907).

Harries, R. (ed.), *Reinhold Niebuhr and the Issues of Our Time* (London/Oxford: Mowbray, 1986).

Harrison, B.W., R.L. Stivers and R.H. Stone (eds.), *The Public Vocation of Christian Ethics* (New York: The Pilgrim Press, 1986).

Hart, T. (ed.), *Justice the True and Only Mercy: Essays on the Life and Theology of Peter Taylor Forsyth* (Edinburgh: T & T Clark, 1995).

Hauerwas, S., *After Christendom?* (Nashville: Abingdon, 1991).

— *In Good Company: The Church as Polis* (Notre Dame: University of Notre Dame Press, 1995).

— and A. MacIntyre (eds.), *Revisions: Changing Perspectives in Moral Philosophy* (London/Notre Dame: University of Notre Dame Press, 1983).

— and W. Willamon, *Resident Aliens: Life in a Christian Colony* (Nashville: Abingdon, 1989).

Hay, D.A., *Economics Today: A Christian Critique* (Grand Rapids: Eerdmans, 1989).

Henry, C., *Aspects of Christian Social Ethics* (Grand Rapids: Eerdmans, 1964).

Heidegger, M., *Being and Time* (New York: Harper and Row, 1962).

Hofmann, H., *The Theology of Reinhold Niebuhr*, L.P. Smith (tr.), (New York: Charles Scribner's Sons, 1956).

Hopkins, C.H., *The Rise of the Social Gospel in American Protestantism 1865-1915* (New Haven: Yale University Press, 1940).

Hudson, W. (ed.), *Walter Rauschenbusch: Selected Writings* (New York: Paulist Press, 1984).

Huxley, T.H., *Evolution and Ethics and Other Essays*. Collected Essays Vol. IX (London: Macmillan & Co., 1894).

James, W., *The Varieties of Religious Experience*. Gifford Lectures 1901-1902. Mentor Edition (New York: New American Library, 1958).

Kant, I., *A Critique of Pure Reason*, N.K. Smith (tr.), (London: Macmillan, 1929).

— *Fundamental Principles of the Metaphysic of Ethics*, T.K. Abbott (tr.), (London: Longmans Green & Co., 1949[10])

— *Religion within the Limits of Reason Alone*, T.M. Greene and H.H. Hudson (trs.), New York: Harper & Row, 1960).

Kee, A., *Domination or Liberation: The Place of Religion in Social Conflict* (London: SCM, 1986).

Kegley, C. (ed.), *Reinhold Niebuhr: His Religious, Social and Political Thought*, Rev. Ed. (New York: The Pilgrim Press, 1984).

Kierkegaard, S., *The Sickness Unto Death*, W. Lowrie (intro. and tr.), (Princeton: Princeton University Press, 1941).

— *Concluding Unscientific Postscript*, D. Swenson (tr.), (Princeton: Princeton University Press, 1944).

Kinnamon, M. and B.E. Cope (eds.), *The Ecumenical Movement: An Anthology of Key Texts and Voices* (Geneva: WCC/Grand Rapids: Eerdmans, 1997).

Kirk, J.A., *Theology Encounters Revolution* (Leicester: IVP, 1980).

Kroeker, P.T., *Christian Ethics and Political Economy in North America: A Critical Analysis* (Montreal/Kingston: McGill-Queen's University Press, 1995).

Landis, B., compiler, *A Rauschenbusch Reader: The Kingdom of God and the Social Gospel* (New York: Harper and Bros., 1957).

Landon, H.R. (ed.), *Reinhold Niebuhr: A Prophetic Voice in Our Time* (Greenwich: Seabury Press, 1962).

Lefever, E.W., *Amsterdam to Nairobi: The World Council of Churches and the Third World* (Washington: Ethics and Public Policy Center, 1979).

— *Nairobi to Vancouver: The World Council of Churches and the World, 1975-87* (Washington: Ethics and Public Policy Center, 1987).

Lewis, C.S., *An Experiment in Criticism* (Cambridge: Cambridge University Press, 1961).

Lewis, G. and B. Demarest, *Challenges to Inerrancy* (Chicago: Moody Press, 1984).

Lindbeck, G., *The Nature of Doctrine: Religion and Theology in a Postliberal Age* (Philadelphia: Westminster, 1984).

Lochman, J.M., *The Faith We Confess: An Ecumenical Dogmatics*, D. Lewis (tr.), (Edinburgh: T & T Clark, 1984).

Lovin, R., *Reinhold Niebuhr and Christian Realism* (Cambridge: Cambridge University Press, 1995).

Lyon, D., *Jesus In Disneyland* (Cambridge/Oxford: Polity Press, 2000).

Lyotard, J.-F., *The Postmodern Condition: A Report on Knowledge*, G. Bennington and B. Massumi (trs.), (Manchester: Manchester University Press, 1984).

MacGregor, G.H.C., *The Relevance of the Impossible: A Reply to Reinhold Niebuhr* (London: Fellowship of Reconciliation, 1941).

MacIntyre, A., *After Virtue: A Study in Moral Theory* (London: Duckworth, 1985²).

— *Whose Justice? Which Rationality?* (London: Duckworth, 1988).

Mackie, R.C. and C.C. West (eds.), *The Sufficiency of God* (Philadelphia: The Westminster Press, 1963).

Mackintosh, H.R., *The Person of Jesus Christ*, T.F. Torrence (ed.), originally published 1912 (Edinburgh: T & T Clark, 2000).

Mackintosh, R., *Christian Ethics* (London: TC & EC Jack, 1909).

Macintosh, D.C. (ed.), *Religious Realism* (Cambridge: Cambridge University Press, 1931).

Macquarrie, J., *20ᵗʰ Century Religious Thought* (Philadelphia: Trinity Press International, 1988).

Manson, T.W., *Ethics and the Gospel* (London: SCM, 1960).

Maritain, J., *Man and the State* (London: Hollis and Carter, 1954).

Marx, K., *Early Writings*, T.B. Bottomore (tr. and ed.), (London: C.A. Watts & Co.,

1963).
— and F. Engels, *The Communist Manifesto*, Intro. A.J.P. Taylor (Middlesex: Penguin, 1967).
Mascall, E.L., *The Importance of Being Human* (London: Oxford University Press, 1959).
Maurice, F.D., *Social Morality* (London: Macmillan, 1872).
Mazzini, J., *The Duties of Man* (London: Chapman & Hall, 1862).
— *Essays: Selected From the Writings, Literary, Political, and Religious of Joseph Mazzini*, W. Clarke (intro. and ed.), (London: Walter Scott, 1892).
McClendon, J. Jr. and J.M. Smith, *Systematic Theology: Ethics* (Nashville: Abingdon, 1986).
McGrath, A., *Justification by Faith* (Basingstoke: Marshall Pickering, 1988).
Meyer, D., *The Protestant Search for Political Realism 1919-1941* (Westport: Greenwood Press Publishers, 1960).
Middleton, J. and G. Walsh, *Truth is Stranger than It Used to Be* (London: SPCK, 1995).
Milbank, J., *Theology and Social Theory: Beyond Secular Reason* (Cambridge: Basil Blackwell, 1990).
Minus, P., *Walter Rauschenbusch: American Reformer* (New York/London: Macmillan, 1988).
Moberg, D.O., *The Great Reversal* (Philadelphia: Lippincott, 1972).
Moltmann, J., *Jesus Christ for Today's World*, M. Kohl (tr.), (Minneapolis: Fortress Press, 1994).
— Nicholas Wolterstorff and E.T. Charry, *A Passion for God's Reign*, M. Volf (ed.), (Grand Rapids/Cambridge: Eerdmans, 1998).
Moore, G.E., *Principia Ethica* (Cambridge: University Press, 1903).
— *Ethics* (London: Thornton Butterworth, 1912).
Mott, S.C., *Biblical Ethics and Social Change* (New York/Oxford: Oxford University Press, 1982).
Mudge, L.S., *The Church as Moral Community: Ecclesiology and Ethics in Ecumenical Debate* (New York: Continuum, 1998).
Neill, S., *The Christian Society* (London: Nisbet, 1952).
Niebuhr, H. Richard, *The Kingdom of God in America* (New York: Harper and Bros., 1937).
— *Christ and Culture* (New York: Harper and Bros., 1951).
— *The Responsible Self: An Essay in Christian Moral Philosophy* (San Francisco: Harper, 1963).
Niebuhr, Reinhold, *Leaves from the Notebook of a Tamed Cynic*, (1929; reprint New York: DeCapo, 1976).
— *Moral Man and Immoral Society* (New York: Charles Scribner's Sons, 1932).
— *Reflections on the End of an Era* (New York: Charles Scribner's Sons, 1934).
— *An Interpretation of Christian Ethics* (reprint New York/London: Harper, 1935).
— *Beyond Tragedy* (New York: Charles Scribner's Sons, 1937).
— *Christianity and Power Politics* (New York: Charles Scribner's Sons, 1940).
— *The Nature and Destiny of Man: A Christian Interpretation, Vol. I: Human Nature* (New York: Charles Scribner's Sons, 1941).
— *The Nature and Destiny of Man: A Christian Interpretation, Vol. II: Human Destiny* (New York: Charles' Scribner's Sons, 1943).
— *The Children of Light and the Children of Darkness* (New York: Charles Scribner's Sons, 1944).
— *Faith and History* (London: Misbet, 1949).

— *Christian Realism and Political Problems* (New York: Charles Scribner's Sons, 1953).

—*The Self and the Dramas of History* (London: Faber and Faber, 1956).

— *Love and Justice*, B. Robertson (ed.)., Louisville: Westminster/Knox University Press, 1957).

— *Man's Nature and His Communities* (New York: Charles Scribner's Sons, 1965).

— *Faith and Politics*, R. Stone (ed.), (New York: George Braziller, 1968).

— and P. Sigmund, *The Democratic Experience* (New York: Frederick A. Praeger, 1969).

— *Reinhold Niebuhr: Theologian of Public Life*, L. Rasmussen (ed.), (London: Collins Liturgical Publications, 1988).

Niebuhr, U., *Remembering Reinhold Niebuhr* (San Francisco: Harper, 1991).

Niles, D.P., compiler, *Between the Flood and the Rainbow* (Geneva: WCC, 1992).

Novak, M., *The Spirit of Democratic Capitalism* (New York: Simon and Schuster, 1982).

O'Brien, D. and T.A. Shannon, *Catholic Social Thought: The Documentary Heritage* (Maryknoll: Orbis, 1992).

O'Donovan, O., *Resurrection and Moral Order: An Outline for Evangelical Ethics* (Leicester: Apollos, 1994).

— *The Desire of the Nations: Rediscovering the Roots of Political Theology* (Cambridge: Cambridge University Press, 1996).

Oldham, J.H. and W.A. Visser't Hooft, *The Church and Its Function in Society, Vol. I: Church, Community and State* (London: George Allen and Unwin, 1937).

Orr, J., *Theology and the Evangelical Faith* (London: Hodder and Stoughton, 1898).

Padilla, R. and C. Sugden (eds.), *Texts on Evangelical Social Ethics 1974-1983*, Grove Series on Ethics No. 58 (Nottingham: Grove Books, 1985).

— *How Evangelicals Endorsed Social Responsibility*, Grove Series on Ethics No. 59 (Nottingham: Grove Books, 1985).

Pannenberg, W., *Anthropology in Theological Perspective*, M.J. O'Connell (tr.), Edinburgh: T & T Clark, 1985).

Patterson, B.E., *Reinhold Niebuhr* (Peabody: Hendrickson, 1977).

Philips, P.T., *A Kingdom on Earth: Anglo-American Social Christianity 1880-1940* (University Park: The Pennsylvania State University Press, 1996).

Pietz, D., *Solidarity as Hermeneutic: A Revisionist Reading of the Theology of Walter Rauschenbusch* (New York: Peter Lang, 1992).

Preston, R. (ed.), *Technology and Social Justice: An International Symposium on the Social and Economic Teaching of the World Council of Churches from Geneva 1966 to Uppsala 1968* (London: SCM, 1971).

— *Religion and the Persistence of Capitalism: The Maurice Lectures for 1977 and other studies in Christianity and Social Change* (London: SCM, 1979).

— *Church and Society in the Late Twentieth Century: The Economic and Political Task* (London: SCM, 1983).

— *The Future of Christian Social Ethics* (London: SCM, 1987).

— *Confusions in Christian Social Ethics* (London: SCM, 1994).

Quine, W.V.O. and J.S. Ullian, *The Web of Belief* (New York: Random House, 1970).

Ramsey, P., *Basic Christian Ethics* (London: SCM, 1950).

— *Who Speaks for the Church?* (Nashville/ New York: Abingdon, 1967).

Rashdall, H., *Conscience and Christ* (London: Duckworth, 1916).

— *The Idea of Atonement in Christian Theology* (London: MacMillan, 1919).

Rasmussen, A.T., *Christian Responsibility in Economic Life* (Philadelphia: Westminster, 1965).

Rauschenbusch, W., *Christianity and the Social Crisis* (London: Macmillan, 1907).
— *Prayers of the Social Awakening*, (Boston: The Pilgrim Press, 1910).
— *Christianizing the Social Order* (London: Macmillan, 1912).
— *Unto Me* (Boston/New York/Chicago: The Pilgrim Press, 1912).
— *Dare We Be Christians?* (1914; reprint Cleveland: The Pilgrim Press, 1993).
—*The Social Principles of Jesus* (New York: Grosset and Dunlap, 1916).
— *A Theology for the Social Gospel* (1917; reprint Louisville: Westmisnter/John Knox Press, 1997).
— *The Righteousness of the Kingdom*, M. Stackhouse (ed. and intro.), (Nashville: Abingdon Press, 1968).
Reed, Esther, *The Genesis of Ethics*, (London: DLT, 2000).
Richardson, A. and W. Schweitzer (eds.), *Biblical Authority for Today: A World Council of Churches Symposium on 'The Biblical Authority for the Churches' Social and Political Message Today* (London: SCM, 1951).
Richmond, J., *Ritschl: A Reappraisal. A Study in Systematic Theology* (London: Collins, 1978).
Ritschl, A., *The Christian Doctrine of Justification and Reconciliation*, H.R. Mackintosh and A.B. Macaulay (eds.), (Edinburgh: T & T Clark, 1902).
Robinson, N.H.G., *Christ and Conscience* (London: James Nisbet & Co., 1956).
— *The Groundwork of Christian Ethics* (London: Collins, 1971).
Rouse, R. and S. Neill (eds.), *A History of the Ecumenical Movement 1517-1948* (Geneva: WCC, 1993[4]).
Royce, J., *The Spirit of Modern Philosophy* (Boston/New York: Houghton Mifflin Col, 1892).
— The Religious Aspect of Philosophy (Boston/New York: Houghton Mifflin Col, 1892).
— The World and the Individual (New York/London: Macmillan, 1901).
— *The Problem of Christianity, Vol. I: The Christian Doctrine of Life* (New York: Macmillan, 1914).
Schleiermacher, F., *On Religion: Speeches to Its Cultured Despisers*, J. Oman (tr.), (New York: Harper & Brothers, 1958).
— *The Christian Faith*, H.R. Mackintosh and J.S. Stewart (eds.), (Edinburgh: T & T Clark, 1928).
Schweitzer, A., *The Quest of the Historical Jesus* (London: SCM, 1981).
— *The Mystery of the Kingdom of God*, W. Lowrie (tr.), (London: Black, 1925).
Scott, N.A. Jr. (ed.), *The Legacy of Reinhold Niebuhr* (Chicago: University of Chicago Press, 1975).
Scriven, C., *The Transformation of Culture: Christian Social Ethics after H. Richard Niebuhr* (Kitchener/Scottsdale: Herald Press, 1988).
Seeley, J.S., *Ecce Homo* (London/Cambridge: Macmillan, 1866[2]).
Sell, A.P.F., *Theology in Turmoil: The Roots, Course and Significance of the Conservative-Liberal Debate in Modern Theology* (Grand Rapids: Baker, 1986).
— *The Philosophy of Religion 1875-1980* (London: Routledge, 1988).
— *Aspects of Christian Integrity* (Louisville: Westminster/John Knox Press, 1990.)
— *Commemorations: Studies in Christian Thought and History* (Calgary: University of Calgary Press/Cardiff: University of Wales Press, 1993).
— *Philosophical Idealism and Christian Belief* (Cardiff: University of Wales Press, 1995).
— *The Spirit Our Life* (Shippensburg: Ragged Edge Press, 2000).
— *Confessing and Commending the Faith* (Cardiff: University of Wales Press, 2002).
Sharpe, D., *Walter Rauschenbusch* (New York: Macmillan, 1942).

Sheldon, C., *In His Steps* (London: Frederick Warne & Co.; Chicago: Advance Publishing Co., 1897).

Shriver, D., *An Ethic for Enemies: Forgiveness in Politics* (Oxford: Oxford University Press, 1995).

Silone, I., pres., *The Living Thoughts of Mazzini* (London: Cassell, 1939).

Smith, T.L., *Revivalism and Social Reform* (New York/Nashville: Abingdon, 1957).

Smucker, D.E., *The Origins of Walter Rauschenbusch's Social Ethics* (Montreal/Kingston: McGill-Queen's University Press, 1994).

Sobrino, J., *Christology at the Crossroads*, J. Drury (tr.), (Maryknoll: Orbis, 1978).

— *Jesus in Latin America* (Maryknoll: Orbis, 1987).

Spencer, H., *The Data of Ethics* (New York: John Alden, 1891).

Stassen, G.H., D.M. Yeager and J.H. Yoder, *Authentic Transformation: A New Vision of Christ and Culture* (Nashville: Abingdon, 1996).

Stone, R., *Reinhold Niebuhr: Prophet to Politicians* (Nashville: Abingdon, 1972).

— *Professor Reinhold Niebuhr: A Mentor to the 20th Century* (Louisville: Westminster/John Knox Press, 1992).

Stott, J., *The Cross of Christ* (Downers Grove: IVP, 1986).

Streeter, B.H. et. al., *Foundations* (London: Macmillan, 1913).

Sullivan, R., *Immanuel Kant's Moral Theory* (Cambridge: Cambridge Univeristy Press, 1989).

Temple, W., *Christianity and Social Order* (Harmondsworth: Penguin Books, 1942).

Thomas, J.H., *Subjectivity and Paradox* (Oxford: Blackwell, 1957).

Troeltsch, E., *The Social Teaching of the Christian Churches*, 2 vols. (London: George Allen and Unwin, 1931).

Ucko, H. (ed.), *The Jubilee Challenge: Utopia or Possibility?* (Geneva: WCC, 1997).

Vanhoozer, K.J., *Is There a Meaning in this Text?: The Bible, the Reader and the Morality of Literary Knowledge* (Leicester: Apollos, 1998).

Visser't Hooft, W.A., *The Background of the Social Gospel in America* (1928; reprint St. Louis: The Bethany Press, 1963).

— *Memoirs* (Geneva: WCC, 1987).

Warnock, M., *Ethics Since 1900* (London: Oxford University Press, 1966²).

Warren, H., *Theologians of a New World Order: Reinhold Niebuhr and the Christian Realists 1920-1948* (Oxford: Oxford University Press, 1997).

Weber, M., *The Protestant Ethic and the Spirit of Capitalism*, T. Parsons (tr.), (New York: Charles Scribner's Sons, 1958).

Weigel, G. and R. Royal (eds.), *Building the Free Society: Democracy, Capitalism and Catholic Social Teaching* (Grand Rapids: Eerdmans/Washington, DC: Ethics and Public Policy Center, 1993).

Wells, D. (ed.), *Reformed Theology in America* (Grand Rapids: Eerdmans, 1985).

Wells, S., *Transforming Fate into Destiny: The Theological Ethics of Stanley Hauerwas* (Carlisle: Paternoster, 1998).

White Jr., R.C. and C.H. Hopkins (eds.), *The Social Gospel: Religion and Reform in Changing America* (Philadelphia: Temple University Press, 1976).

Wilder, A., *Eschatology and Ethics* (Westport: Greenwood Press, 1978).

Wogaman, P., *Christian Perspectives on Politics*, Rev. Ed. (Louisville: Westminster/John Knox Press, 2000).

Wolterstorff, N., *Until Justice and Peace Embrace* (Grand Rapids: Eerdmans, 1982).

— *Reason Within the Bounds of Religion* (Grand Rapids: Eerdmans, 1984²).

— *Divine Discourse: Philosophical Reflections on the Claim that God Speaks* (Cambridge: Cambridge University Press, 1995).

World Council of Churches, *Man's Disorder and God's Design, Vol. III: The Church and the Disorder of Society, Vol. IV: The Church and the International* (London: SCM, 1948).

— *Church and State: Opening a New Ecumenical Discussion*, Faith and Order Paper NO. 85 (Geneva: WCC, 1978).

— *Challenge to the Church: A Theological Comment on the Political Crisis in South Africa: The Kairos Document and Commentaries*, Programme Unit on Justice and Service: Commission on the Programme to Combat Racism (Geneva: WCC, 1985).

— *The Role of the World Council of Churches in International Relations* (Geneva: WCC, 1986).

— *Report and Background Papers of the Meeting of the Working Group, Potsdam, GDR, July 1986*, Church and Society (Geneva: WCC, 1986).

— *Church and World*, Faith and Order Study Document (Geneva: WCC, 1990).

Wozniak, K.W.M., *Ethics in the Thought of Edward John Carnell* (Lanham/London: University Press of America, 1983).

Wundt, W., *Ethics, Vol. I: The Facts of the Moral Life*, J. Gulliver and E. Titchener (trs.), (1886; reprint London: Swan Sonneschein & Co., 1908).

Wurth, G.B., *Niebuhr*, D.H. Freeman (tr.), (Philadelphia: Presbyterian and Reformed Publishing Col, 1960).

Yoder, J.H., *The Politics of Jesus* (Carlisle: Paternoster/Grand Rapids: Eerdmans, 1994^2).

Published Works: Articles

Aagaard, A.M, 'Ethics on the Joint Working Group Agenda', *ER* 48 (April, 1996), 139-142.

Abrecht, P., 'From Oxford to Vancouver: Lessons from Fifty Years of Ecumenical Work for Economic and Social Justice', *ER* 40 (April, 1988), 147-168.

— 'The Predicament of Christian Social Thought After the Cold War', *ER* 43 (July, 1991).

— 'Competing Forms of Discourse in Ecumenical Social Thought or Ecumenical Experience with Different Forms of Ethical Discourse', *Towards a New Humanity: Essays in Honour of Dr. Paulos Mar Gregorios*, K.M. George and K.J. Gabriel (eds.), (Delhi: SPCK, 1992), 30-45.

Allen, R.C., 'When Narrative Fails', *JRE* 21.1 (Spring, 1993), 27-67.

Aulen, G., 'Criticism, Claim, and Confidence: The Realism of the Christian Conception of Man', *Int* 3 (April, 1949), 131-141.

Ayers, R.H., 'Methodological, Epistemological, and Ontological Motifs in the Thought of Reinhold Niebuhr', *MT* 7 (January, 1991), 153-173.

— 'The Ecumenical Perspective in the thought of Reinhold Niebuhr', *USQR* 48 http://www.cc/columbia.edu

Beato, J., 'Good News to the Poor – Its Implications for the Mission of the Church in Latin America Today', *Your Kingdom Come: Mission Perspectives: Report on the World Conference on Mission and Evangelism, Melbourne, Australia 12-25 May 1980* (Geneva: WCC, 1980).

Bediako, K., 'New Paradigms on Ecumenical Cooperation: An African Perspective', *IRM* LXXXI (July, 12), 375-380.

Bennett, J.C., 'Theologians of our Time: Reinhold Niebuhr', *ExpTim* LXXV (May, 1964), 237-40.

— 'The Greatness of Reinhold Niebuhr', *USQR* XXVII (Fall, 1971), 3-8.

— 'Breakthrough in Christian Social Ethics', *ER* 40 (April, 1988), 132-146.

Bent, A.J. van der, Precious Unity and Vulnerable Ethics', *JES* 33 (Summer, 1996), 315-329.

Best, T.F., 'Introduction to the Papers from the Meeting on "Ecclesiology and Ethics", *ER* 47 (April, 1995), 127.

Bettis, J., 'Theology and Politics: Karl Barth and Reinhold Niebuhr on Social Ethics after Liberalism', *RL* XLVIII (Spring, 1979), 53-62.

Bloechl, J., 'The Virtue of History: Alasdair MacIntyre and the Rationality of Narrative', *Philosophy and Social Criticism* 24.1 (1998), 43-61.

Boff, C., 'The Social Teaching of the Church and the Theology of Liberation: Opposing Social Practices?', *Concilium* No. 150, *Christian Ethics: Uniformity, Universality, Pluralism*, J. Pohrier and D. Mieth (eds.), (Edinburgh: T & T Clark, 1981), 17-22.

Bosch, D.J., 'Ecumenicals and Evangelicals: A Growing Relationship?', *ER* 40 (July-October, 1988), 458-472.

Brakemeier, G., 'Justification by Grace and Liberation Theology: A Comparison', *ER* 40 (April, 1988), 215-222.

Brown, R.M, 'Reinhold Niebuhr: A Study in Humanity and Humility', *JR* 54 (October, 1974), 325-331.

Bryant, M.D., 'Sin and Society', *Society and Original Sin: Ecumenical Essays on the Impact of the Fall*, D. Foster and P. Mojzes (eds.), (New York: Paragon, 1985), 149-163.

Butselaar, J. van, 'Thinking Locally, Acting Globally: The Ecumenical Movement in the New Era', *IRM* LXXXI (July, 1992), 363-374.

Carnell, E.J., 'Reinhold Niebuhr's View of Scripture', *Inspiration and Interpretation*, J.W. Walvoord (ed.), (Grand Rapids: Eerdmans, 1957).

— 'Conservatives and Liberals Do Not Need Each Other', *CT* (May, 1965), 39.

Castro, E., 'Ethical Reflections Among the Churches', *ER* 47 (April, 1995), 170-180.

Clapsis E., 'Ecclesiology and Ethics: Reflections by an Orthodox Theologian', *ER* 47 (April, 1995), 155-169.

Cocks, H.F.L., 'The Gospel and the Church', *Congregationalism Today*, J. Marsh (ed.), (London: Independent Press, 1943).

Corner, M.A., 'The Umbilical Cord: A View of Man and Nature in Light of Darwin', *SJRS* 4.2 (Autumn, 1983), 121-137.

Dickinson, R., 'Rauschenbusch and Niebuhr: Brothers Under the Skin?' *RL* XXVII.2 (Spring, 1958), 163-171.

— 'Changing Perspectives on Economic Development: A Contribution to the On-Going Discussion', *Development Assessed: Ecumenical Reflections and Actions on Development*, WCC Unit III Justice, Peace and Creation (Geneva, 9-12 January 1995).

Dunfee, S.N., 'The Sin of Hiding: A Feminist Critique of Reinhold Niebuhr's Account of the Sin of Pride', *Soundings* 65 (Fall, 1982), 316-327.

Dyck, A.J., 'Rethinking Rights, Preserving Community: How My Mind Has Changed', *JRE* 25.1 (Spring, 1997), 3-14.

Eid, V., 'The Relevance of the Concept of Autonomy for Social Ethics', *Concilium* No. 172, *Christian Ethics: Uniformity, Universality, Pluralism*, J. Pohrier and D. Mieth (eds.), (Edinburgh: T & T Clark, 1981), 24-34.

Espy, E. (ed.), *Can You Still Say* Christus Victor?, *JES* 16.1 (Winter, 1979).

Esquivel, J., 'The Crucified Lord: A Latin American Perspective', *Your Kingdom Come: Mission Perspectives: Report on the World Conference on Mission and Evangelism, Melbourne, Australia, 12-25 May 1980* (Geneva: WCC, 1980).

Feenstra, R., 'Reassessing the Thought of Reinhold Niebuhr', *CTJ* 23 (November,

1988), 142-160.

Fenn, W.W., 'Modern Liberalism', *AJT* XVII (October, 1913), 509-519.

Fisher, C.W., 'Toward a Christian Social Ethic and Action', *RL* XXVII.2 (Spring, 1958), 199-207.

Forrester, D., 'Ecclesiology and Ethics: A Reformed Perspective', *ER* 47 (April, 1995), 148-154.

Forsyth, P.T., 'Orthodoxy, Heterodoxy, Heresy and Freedom', *Hibbert Journal* 8 (January, 1910), 321-329.

Fox, R.W., 'The Niebuhr Brothers and the Liberal Protestant Heritage', *Religion and Twentieth Century American Intellectual Life*, M.J. Lacey (ed.), (Cambridge: Woodrow Wilson International Center for Scholars/Cambridge University Press, 1989).

Fung, R., 'Good News to the Poor – A Case for a Missionary Movement', *Your Kingdom Come: Mission Perspectives: Report on the World Conference on Mission and Evangelism, Melbourne, Australia 12-25 May 1980* (Geneva: WCC, 1980).

Gamwell, F.I., 'Religion and the Justification of Moral Claims', *JRE* 11.1 (Spring, 1983), 35-61.

— G. Barden and R. Green, 'On Recovering Moral Philosophy: An Exchange', *JRE* 24.1 (Spring, 1996), 193-204.

Garvie, A., 'The Danger of Reaction, Theological and Ethical', *AJT* XXI (July, 1917), 325-357.

Geest, W. van, 'The Relationship Between Development and Religion', *ERT* 22.1 (January 10998), 61-77.

Gilkey, C.W., 'The Function of the Church in Modern Society', *AJT* XVIII (January, 1914), 1-23.

Gerrish, B.A. et. al. (eds.), 'Reinhold Niebuhr', *JR* 54 (October, 1974), 325-434.

Gill, R., 'Moral Communities and Christian Ethics', *SCE* 8 (1995), 20-32.

Goodchild, P., 'Christian Ethics in the Postmodern Condition', *Studies in Christian Ethics* 8 (1995), 367-385.

— 'Probing the Depths of Practical Reason: Looking Back Over Twenty-five Years', *JRE* 25.1 (Spring, 1997), 15-23.

Green, T.M. et. al., 'Reinhold Niebuhr: A Symposium', *USQR* XI (May 1956), 3-22.

Greenlaw, W.A., 'Nature of Christian Truth: Another Look at Reinhold Niebuhr and Mythology', *Saint Luke's Journal of Theology* 19 (June, 1976), 195-202.

— 'Second Look at Reinhold Niebuhr's Biblical Dramatic Worldview', *Encounter* 37 (Autumn, 1976), 344-355.

Grenz, S., 'Beyond Foundationalism: Is a Nonfoundational Evangelical Theology Possible?' *JCTR* (1998): http://apu.edu/¬CTRF/papers/ctrfpapers.html

Guroian, V., 'The Possibilities and Limits of Politics: A Comparative Study of the Thought of Reinhold Niebuhr and Edmund Burke', *USQR* XIV (May, 1959), 44-49.

Harland, H.G., 'Theology and Social Action: The Contemporary Debate', *Touchstone* 1 (January, 1983), 5-14.

Harries, R., 'Re-review: Reinhold Niebuhr's Moral Man and Immoral Society', *MC* XXV (1982), 53-57.

Hart, T.A., 'Sinlessness and Moral Responsibility: A Problem in Christology', *SJT* 48.1 (1995), 37-54.

Hauerwas, S., 'When the Politics of Jesus Makes a Difference', *CC* 110 (October 13, 1993), 982-987.

Hay, D., 'What Does the Lord Require? Three Statements on Christian Faith and Economic Life', *Transformation* (January, 1993), 10-15.

Henn, W., 'Reactions and Responses...to *Costly Unity* and to the Discussion in Santiago: A Roman Catholic Perspective', *ER* 47 (April, 1995), 140-147.

Herman, S.W., 'Luther, Law, and Social Covenants: Cooperative Self-Obligation in the Reconstruction of Lutheran and Social Ethics', *JRE* 25.2 (Fall, 1997), 257-275.

Hershberger, G.F., 'The Modern Social Gospel and the Way of the Cross', *MQR* XXX.1 (January, 1956), 83-103.

Heuvel, A. van den, 'The Honest to God Debate in Ecumenical Perspective', *ER* 16 (April, 1964).

Hickin, R.A., 'Niebuhr on Progress and Sin', *ET* 60 (October, 1948), 4-7.

Hutchinson, R.C., 'Reinhold Niebuhr and "Contextual Connections"', *This World* 6 (Fall, 1983), 102-109.

Hopkins, C.H., 'Review of R.T. Handy *The Social Gospel in America*', *USQR* XXII (May, 1967), 367-369.

— 'Review of Walter Rauschenbusch *The Righteousness of the Kingdom*', *USQR* XXIV (Winter, 1969), 211-213.

Hütter, R.L., 'The Church: Midwife of History or Witness of the Eschaton', *JRE* 18.1 (Spring, 1990), 27-54.

Jordon, E., 'The Meaning of Charity', *AJT* XX (October, 1916), 549-562.

Kerr, F., 'Moral Theology after MacIntyre re: modern ethics, tragedy and Thomism', *SCE* 8 (1995), 33-44.

Komonchak, J., 'Moral Pluralism and the Unity of the Church', *Concilium* No. 150, *Christian Ethics: Uniformity, Universality, Pluralism*, J. Pohrier and D. Mieth (eds.), (Edinburgh: T & T Clark, 1981), 89-94.

Korff, W., 'Nature or Reason as the Criterion for the Universality of Moral Judgments?' *Concilium* No. 150, *Christian Ethics: Uniformity, Universality, Pluralism*, J. Pohrier and D. Mieth (eds.), (Edinburgh: T & T Clark, 1981), 82-88.

Lasch, C., 'Religious Contributions to Social Movements: Walter Rauschenbusch, the Social Gospel, and its Critics', *JRE* 18.1 (Spring, 1990), 7-26.

Lash, N., 'Theologies at the Service of a Common Tradition', *Concilium* No. 171, *Different Theologies, Common Responsibility: Babel or Pentecost?* (Edinburgh: T & T Clark, 1984), 74-83.

Lebacqz, K., 'Change, as in "How I've..." or They Don't Make Pants the Way they Used to', *JRE* 25.1 (Spring, 1997), 25-32.

Lindberg, C., 'Luther's Critique of the ecumenical assumption that doctrine divides but service unites', *JES* 27 (Fall, 1990), 679-696.

Lindley, S., 'Neglected Voices and *Praxis* in the Social Gospel', *JRE* 18.1 (Spring, 1990), 75-102.

Lochman, J.M., 'The Problem of Realism in R. Niebuhr's Christology', *SJT* 11 (1958), 253-264.

Lodberg, P., 'The History of Ecumenical Work on Ecclesiology and Ethics', *ER* 47 (April, 1995), 128-139.

— 'Apartheid as a Church-Dividing Ethical Issue', *ER* 48 (April, 1996), 173-177.

Longwood, M., 'Niebuhr and a Theory of Justice', *Dialog* 14 (Fall, 1975), 253-262.

Lovin, R., 'Theology and Society in the '80s', *Criterion* 22 (Spring, 1983), 10-15.

Lyman, E., 'Social Idealism and the Changing Theology', *AJT* XVII (October, 1913), 639-645.

MacFarland, C.S., 'The Progress of Federation Among the Churches', *AJT* XXI (July, 1917), 392-410.

Macquarrie, J., 'How Is Theology Possible?' *USQR* XVIII (March, 1963), 295-305.

Marney, C., 'The Significance of Walter Rauschenbusch for Today', *Foundations* II (January, 1959), 13-26.

McCann, D.P., 'Hermeneutics and Ethics: The Example of Reinhold Niebuhr', *JRE* 8.1 (Spring, 1980), 27-53.

— 'Political Ideologies and Practical Theology: Is There a Difference?' *USQR* XXXVI (Summer, 1981), 243-257.

McCormack, T., 'The Protestant Ethic and the Spirit of Socialism', *BJT* XX 3 (September, 1969), ???

Mehl, P.J., 'Kierkegaard and the relativist challenge to practical philosophy', *JRE* 14.2 (Fall, 1986), 247-278.

— 'In the Twilight of Modernity: MacIntyre and Mitchell on Moral Traditions and Their Assessment', *JRE* 19.1 (Spring, 1991), 21-54.

Middleton, R.G., 'Social Christianity Yesterday and Today', *RL* 16.1 (Spring, 1947), 186-197.

Mieth, D., 'Autonomy or Liberation – Two Paradigms of Christian Ethics?' *Concilium* No. 172, *The Ethics of Liberation – The Liberation of Ethics* (Edinburgh: T & T Clark, 1984).

Milbank, J., 'Can Morality Be Christian?' *SCE* 8 (1995), 45-59.

Miller, R.C., 'William James and the American Scene', *AJTP* 15.1 (January, 1994), 3-14.

Mode, P., 'Aims and Methods of Contemporary Church-union Movements in America', *AJT* XXIV (April, 1920), 224-257.

Mott, S.C., 'The Use of the New Testament for Social Ethics', *JRE* 15.2 (Fall, 1987), 225-260.

Mudge, L.S., 'Ecclesiology and Ethics in Current Ecumenical Debate', *ER* 48 (January, 1996), 11-27.

— 'Veritatus Splendor and Today's Ecumenical Conversation', *ER* 48 (April, 1996), 158-163.

Myers, B.L., 'A Funny Thing Happened on the way to Evangelical-Ecumenical Cooperation', *IRM* LXXXI (July, 1992), 387-407.

Newbigin, L, 'Whose Justice?' *ER* 44 (July, 1992), 308-311.

New Mexico Conference of Churches, 'Ethical/Moral Differences within and Ecumenical Covenant', *ER* 48 (April, 1996), 181-184.

Nichol, I.G., 'Church and State in the Calvinist Reformed Tradition', *Baptism, Peace and the State in the Reformed and Mennonite Traditions*, R.T. Bender and A.P.F. Sell (eds.), (Waterloo: Wilfried Laurier University Press, 1991).

Niebuhr, H.Richard, 'The Social Gospel and the mind of Jesus', D. Yeager (ed.), *JRE* 16.1 (Spring, 1988), 109-127.

Niebuhr, Reinhold, 'Ten Years That Shook My World', *CC* 56 (April 26, 1939).

— 'Validation of the Christian View of Life and History', *TToday* 6 (April, 1949), 31-48.

— 'False Defense of Christianity', *C&C* 10 (1950), 73-74.

— 'Coherence, Incoherence, and Christian Faith', *USQR* VII (January, 1952), 11-24.

— 'Law and Love in Protestantism and Catholicism', *JRT* 9.2 (1952), 95-111.

— 'Significance of the Growth of "Christian Action"', *C&C* 14.4. (1954), 30-32.

— 'Our Dependence is Upon God', *CQ* 33 (January, 1955), 29-36.

— 'Law and Grace in Christianity and Secularism', *C&C* 15.11 (1955), 81-82.

— 'Christian Life and an Economy of Abundance', *USQR* XI (January 1956), 25-31.

—'Lessons from the Detroit Experience', *CC* 82 (April 21, 1965), 487-490.

— 'Faith as the Sense of Meaning in Human Existence', *C&C* 26 (June 13, 1966), 127-131.

— 'A View of Life from the Sidelines', *CC* 101 (December 19-26, 1984), 1195-1198.

Novak, M., 'Democratic Capitalism: A North American Liberation Theology',

Transformation 2 (January/March, 1985), 18-23.

O'Donovan, O., 'The Concept of Publicity', *SCE* 13 (2000), 18-32.

Padilla, R.C., 'Wholistic Mission: Evangelical and Ecumenical', *IRM* LXXXI (July, 1992), 381-382.

Pickering, G.W., 'Theology as Social Ethics', *AJTP* 17.1 (January, 1996), 7-28.

Post, S., 'The Purpose of Neighbour-Love', *JRE* 18.1 (Spring, 1990), 181-194.

Preston, R., 'Christian Faith and Capitalism', *ER* 40 (April, 1988), 279-286.

— 'The Common Good', *EpRev* 24 (January, 1997), 12-20.

— 'On to Harare: Social Theology and Ethics in the World Council of Churches', *Epworth Review* (25) (October, 1998), 24-33.

Prior, A.N., 'Contemporary British Philosophy', *Phil* XXXIII (October, 1958).

Raines, J.C., 'Eccentric Man: The Idea of Sin Revisited and Revised', *Encounter* 32 (Autumn, 1971), 257-277.

— 'Sin as Pride and Sin as Sloth: Reinhold Niebuhr and Karl Marx on the Predicament of Man', *C&C* 29 (February 3, 1969), 4-8.

Raiser, K., 'Ecumenical Discussion of Ethics and Ecclesiology', *ER* 48 (January, 1996), 3-10.

Rasmussion, L., 'Moral Community and Moral Formation', *ER* 47 (April, 1995), 181-188.

Robeck, C.M., 'A Pentecostal Looks at the World Council of Churches', *ER* 47 (January, 1995), 60-69.

Robbins, A., 'After Honesty: *The Honest to God* Debate Revisited', *Full of the Holy Spirit and Faith*, S.A. Dunham (ed.), (Wolfville: Gaspereau Press, 1997), 22-40.

— 'Forsyth on Gospel and Society: A Matter of Principle', *P.T. Forsyth: Theologian for a New Millennium*, A.P.F. Sell (ed.), (London: URC, 2000), 209-236.

— 'Ethical Models for the Twilight Zone of Church and Culture,' *Movement for Change: Evangelical Perspectives on Social Transformation*, David Hilborn, (ed.), Carlisle: Paternoster Press, 2004.

Robeck, C.M., 'A Pentecostal Looks at the World Council of Churches', *ER* 47 (January, 1995), 60-69.

Robra, M., 'Theology of Life – Justice, Peace, Creation: An Ecumenical Study', *ER* 48 (January, 1996), 28-37.

Rosenbaum, S., 'MacIntyre or Dewey?' *AJTP* 19.1 (January, 1998), 35-59.

Schenck, D. Jr., 'Recasting the "Ethics of Virtue/Ethics of Duty" Debate', *JRE* 4 (Fall, 1976).

Sell, A.P.F., Review of 'Christian Theism and Moral Philosophy', by M. Beaty et. al. (eds.), *SCE* 13 (2000), 108-112.

— 'A Renewed Plea for "Impractical" Divinity', *SCE* 8 (1995), 68-91.

Shaull, R., 'The Revolutionary Challenge to Church and Theology', *PSB* 60 (1966), 25-32.

Shinn, R.L., 'Faith and Politics: The Mission to Speak', *C&C* 43 (March 21, 1983), 85-88.

— 'Christian Social Ethics in North America', *ER* 40 (April, 1988), 223-232.

Shippey, F.A., 'The Church's Responsibility for Society: Sociological Forms of Religious Expression in Western Christianity', *RL* XXVII.2 (Spring, 1958), 172-184.

Smith, G.B., Review of 'The Problem of Christianity', by J. Royce, *AJT* XVII (October, 1913), 638.

— Review of 'A Theology for the Social Gospel', by W. Rauschenbusch, *AJT* XXII (October, 1918), 583-588.

Smucker, D.E., 'The Rauschenbusch Story', *Foundations* II.1 (January, 1959), 4-12.

Sockness, B.W., 'Luther's Two Kingdoms Revisited: A Response to Reinhold

Niebuhr's Criticism of Luther', *JREd* 20 (Spring, 1992), 93-110.

Soskice, J.M., 'Community and Morality "After Modernity": A response to Robin Gill', *SCE* 8 (1995), 14-19.

Sugden, C., 'Called to Full Humanity – a perspective from Western Europe', *Transformation* 15.1 (January-March, 1998), 28-30.

Thomas, G.F., 'Political Realism and Christian Faith', *TToday* XVI (July, 1959).

Thompson, D.L., 'Basic Doctrines and Concepts of Reinhold Niebuhr's Political Thought', *JChSt* 17 (Spring, 1975), 275-299.

Turner, P., 'Social Advocacy as a Moral Issue in Itself', *JRE* 19.2 (Fall, 1991), 157-181.

Vandervelde, G., 'Costly Communion: Mission Between Ecclesiology and Ethics', *ER* 49 (January 1997), 46-60.

VanElderen, M., 'Friendly Dialogue: A Positive, Outspoken Critique', *OW* (April 1994), 11-14.

Vanhoozer, K., 'Mapping Evangelical Theology in a Post-modern World', *Trinity Journal* 16 (1995); reprinted in *ERT* 22.1 (January, 1998).

Votaw, C.W., 'Primitive Christianity An Idealistic Social Movement', *AJT* XXII (January, 1918), 54-71.

Wallis, L., 'Theology and the Social Problem', *AJT* XVII (October, 1913), 645-648.

Wasserman, L., 'Reinhold Niebuhr: An Analysis of Man and Groups', *JSP* 11 (January, 1980), 1-5.

Watts, C.M., 'The Problem of Universal Love in the Thought of Reinhold Niebuhr', *JrelS* 17 (1991), 44-55.

Williams, B., 'Ethical Disagreements as an Obstacle to Ecclesial Communion', *ER* 48 (April, 1996), 178-180.

Williams, L., *The Reign of the New Humanity*, Amity Tract No. 11 (August, 1907).

Williams, P., 'Christian Realism and the Ephesian Suggestion', *JRE* 25.2 (Fall, 1997), 233-240.

Williamson, G. Jr., 'Niebuhrian Critique of Niebuhrian Thought', *Andover Newton Quarterly* 15 (January, 1975), 182-195.

Woelfel, J., 'Victorian Agnosticism and Liberal Theology: T.H. Huxley and Matthew Arnold', *AJTP* 19.1 (January, 1998), 61-76.

Wolterstorff, N., 'Christian Political Reflection: Diognetian or Augustinian', *The PSB* XX (1999), 150-168.

World Council of Churches, 'The Ecumenical Dialogue on Moral Issues: Potential Sources of Common Witness or of Divisions', *ER* 48 (April, 1996), 143-154.

Yoder, J.H., 'The Hermeneutics of Peoplehood: A Protestant Perspective on Practical Moral Reasoning', *JRE* 10.1 (Spring, 1982), 40-67.

Unpublished Works

'Berlin Group' Documents

Anderson, T., Secretary, Report of First Meeting, Vancouver, July 16-27, 1990; in the form of 'An Open Letter To Dr. Emilio Castro, The General Secretary of the World Council of Churches, July 27, 1990' (Personal papers of Paul Abrecht).

'The Future of Ecumenical Social Thought: Report of an informal discussion of church leaders, theologians, and social ethicists and laity', Berlin, May 29 - June 3, 1992 (WCC Archives, Br 280.916 F9890).

Castro, E., Secretary General of the WCC, Letter to J. Habgood, Archbishop of York, August 28, 1992 (Personal papers of Paul Abrecht).
Raiser, K., Secretary General of the WCC, Letter to J. Habgood, November 2, 1992 (Personal papers of Paul Abrecht).
Albrecht, P., Berlin Group Convenor, Summary of Responses to the Statement on 'The Future of Ecumenical Social Ethics', in preparation for meetings July 1993 Manchester, Geneva, July 15, 1993 (Personal papers of Paul Abrecht).
Report on the Meeting with the World Council of Churches on the Future of Ecumenical Social Thought at the Ecumenical Institute, Bossey Switzerland, February 18-19, 1993. Includes appendices of letters exchanged between J. Habgood and K. Raiser; a paper by R. Shinn, 'A Few Reflections on Social Thought in the World Council of Churches'; and the Theology of Life Programme Proposal, as published in the Report of Unit III Commission, Justice, Peace and Creation, meeting in Larnaca, Cyprus, October 18-22, 1993 (Personal papers of Paul Abrecht).
Abrecht, P., Personal and Confidential Memo to Members of the Vancouver-Berlin-Manchester Group Concerning the Continuing Discussion of the Future of Ecumenical Social Thought; Geneva, August 1995 (Personal papers of Paul Abrecht).

Rauschenbusch Papers

Rauschenbusch, W., 'The Corporate Life of Humanity', unpublished lecture, 1896 (Rauschenbusch Family Papers, Record Group 1003, Box 17, American Baptist Archives, Rochester).
— 'How Can the Aims of the Social Movement Be Realized?' unpublished paper (Rauschenbusch Family Papers, Record Group 1003, Box 19.2, American Baptist Archives, Rochester).
— 'The Contributions of Socialism to the New Social Feeling' (Record Group 1003, Box 22, American Baptist Archives, Rochester).
— 'Justice, 1916', Companions of the Holy Cross; Byfield, August 1916 (Record Group 1003, Box 20, American Baptist Archives, Rochester).

World Council of Churches Documents

World Council of Churches, Biofiles 280.99.99 (WCC Archives, Geneva).
— 'Report and Background Papers', Church and Society: Meeting of the Working Group on Social Ethics, Glion Switzerland, September 1987 (WCC Archives, Geneva).
— 'Minutes of the Central Committee', Hanover 1988 (WCC Archives, Geneva).
— 'Minutes of the Central Committee', Geneva, March 25-30, 1990 (WCC Archives, Geneva)
— 'Minutes of WCC 7th Assembly', Canberra, February 7-20, 1991 (WCC Archives, Geneva).
— 'Minutes of the Central Committee', Geneva, September 11-19, 1997 (WCC Archives, Geneva).
— 'Documents Adopted by the WCC Eighth Assembly', Harare, December 3-14, 1998 (WCC Archives, Geneva).
— 'Report of the Policy Reference Committee II', WCC Assembly, Harare 1998 (WCC Archives, Geneva).
— 'Report of the Programme Guidelines Committee', WCC Assembly, Harare, 1998

(WCC Archives, Geneva).
— Faith and Order Department papers relating to the Study Programme 'Ethnic Idenity, National Identity, and the Unity of the Church', Papers prepared by T.F. Best, August 1998, for a meeting at Cartigny, June, 1998 (Personal papers of T.F. Best).

Dissertations

Berke, M.B., 'Political Philosophy and the Tragic Sense of Life: A Study of Reinhold Niebuhr', PhD dissertation, Yale University, 1990.

Keeling, J.K., 'The Transcendence of Grace: A Study of the Theology of Reinhold Niebuhr', PhD dissertation, University Chicago, 1974.

Lane, G.L., 'Historicality and Repentance: A Philosophical Reconstruction of Reinhold Niebuhr's Christian Anthropology', PhD dissertation, University of Chicago, 1989.

McClintock, D.A., 'Walter Rauschenbusch: The Kingdom of God and the American Experience', PhD dissertation, Case Western Reserve University, 1975.

Nordberg, T.G., 'The Centrality of the Cross in Reinhold Niebuhr's Christian Theology and Ethics', PhD dissertation, McGill University, 1988.

Wortham, G.M., 'A Study of the Theme of Justice in the Theology of Reinhold Niebuhr in Critical Comparison with the Theology of the Selected Latin American Theologians', PhD dissertation, University of Edinburgh, 1989.

Person Index

Subject Index

Paternoster Biblical Monographs
(All titles uniform with this volume)
Dates in bold are of projected publication

Joseph Abraham
Eve: Accused or Acquitted?
A Reconsideration of Feminist Readings of the Creation Narrative Texts in Genesis 1–3
Two contrary views dominate contemporary feminist biblical scholarship. One finds in the Bible an unequivocal equality between the sexes from the very creation of humanity, whilst the other sees the biblical text as irredeemably patriarchal and androcentric. Dr Abraham enters into dialogue with both camps as well as introducing his own method of approach. An invaluable tool for any one who is interested in this contemporary debate.
2002 / 0-85364-971-5 / xxiv + 272pp

Octavian D. Baban
Mimesis and Luke's on the Road Encounters in Luke-Acts
Luke's Theology of the Way and its Literary Representation
The book argues on theological and literary (mimetic) grounds that Luke's on-the-road encounters, especially those belonging to the post-Easter period, are part of his complex theology of the Way. Jesus' teaching and that of the apostles is presented by Luke as a challenging answer to the Hellenistic reader's thirst for adventure, good literature, and existential paradigms.
2005 */ 1-84227-253-5 / approx. 374pp*

Paul Barker
The Triumph of Grace in Deuteronomy
This book is a textual and theological analysis of the interaction between the sin and faithlessness of Israel and the grace of Yahweh in response, looking especially at Deuteronomy chapters 1–3, 8–10 and 29–30. The author argues that the grace of Yahweh is determinative for the ongoing relationship between Yahweh and Israel and that Deuteronomy anticipates and fully expects Israel to be faithless.
2004 / 1-84227-226-8 / xxii + 270pp

Jonathan F. Bayes
The Weakness of the Law
God's Law and the Christian in New Testament Perspective
A study of the four New Testament books which refer to the law as weak (Acts, Romans, Galatians, Hebrews) leads to a defence of the third use in the Reformed debate about the law in the life of the believer.
2000 / 0-85364-957-X / xii + 244pp

Mark Bonnington
The Antioch Episode of Galatians 2:11-14 in Historical and Cultural Context

The Galatians 2 'incident' in Antioch over table-fellowship suggests significant disagreement between the leading apostles. This book analyses the background to the disagreement by locating the incident within the dynamics of social interaction between Jews and Gentiles. It proposes a new way of understanding the relationship between the individuals and issues involved.

2005 / 1-84227-050-8 / approx. 350pp

David Bostock
A Portrayal of Trust
The Theme of Faith in the Hezekiah Narratives

This study provides detailed and sensitive readings of the Hezekiah narratives (2 Kings 18–20 and Isaiah 36–39) from a theological perspective. It concentrates on the theme of faith, using narrative criticism as its methodology. Attention is paid especially to setting, plot, point of view and characterization within the narratives. A largely positive portrayal of Hezekiah emerges that underlines the importance and relevance of scripture.

2005 / 1-84227-314-0 / approx. 300pp

Mark Bredin
Jesus, Revolutionary of Peace
A Non-violent Christology in the Book of Revelation

This book aims to demonstrate that the figure of Jesus in the Book of Revelation can best be understood as an active non-violent revolutionary.

2003 / 1-84227-153-9 / xviii + 262pp

Robinson Butarbutar
Paul and Conflict Resolution
An Exegetical Study of Paul's Apostolic Paradigm in 1 Corinthians 9

The author sees the apostolic paradigm in 1 Corinthians 9 as part of Paul's unified arguments in 1 Corinthians 8–10 in which he seeks to mediate in the dispute over the issue of food offered to idols. The book also sees its relevance for dispute-resolution today, taking the conflict within the author's church as an example.

2006 / 1-84227-315-9 / approx. 280pp

Daniel J-S Chae
Paul as Apostle to the Gentiles
His Apostolic Self-awareness and its Influence on the Soteriological Argument
in Romans
Opposing 'the post-Holocaust interpretation of Romans', Daniel Chae competently demonstrates that Paul argues for the equality of Jew and Gentile in Romans. Chae's fresh exegetical interpretation is academically outstanding and spiritually encouraging.
1997 / 0-85364-829-8 / xiv + 378pp

Luke L. Cheung
The Genre, Composition and Hermeneutics of the Epistle of James
The present work examines the employment of the wisdom genre with a certain compositional structure and the interpretation of the law through the Jesus tradition of the double love command by the author of the Epistle of James to serve his purpose in promoting perfection and warning against doubleness among the eschatologically renewed people of God in the Diaspora.
2003 / 1-84227-062-1 / xvi + 372pp

Youngmo Cho
Spirit and Kingdom in the Writings of Luke and Paul
The relationship between Spirit and Kingdom is a relatively unexplored area in Lukan and Pauline studies. This book offers a fresh perspective of two biblical writers on the subject. It explores the difference between Luke's and Paul's understanding of the Spirit by examining the specific question of the relationship of the concept of the Spirit to the concept of the Kingdom of God in each writer.
2005 / 1-84227-316-7 / approx. 270pp

Andrew C. Clark
Parallel Lives
The Relation of Paul to the Apostles in the Lucan Perspective
This study of the Peter-Paul parallels in Acts argues that their purpose was to emphasize the themes of continuity in salvation history and the unity of the Jewish and Gentile missions. New light is shed on Luke's literary techniques, partly through a comparison with Plutarch.
2001 / 1-84227-035-4 / xviii + 386pp

Andrew D. Clarke
Secular and Christian Leadership in Corinth
A Socio-Historical and Exegetical Study of 1 Corinthians 1–6
This volume is an investigation into the leadership structures and dynamics of first-century Roman Corinth. These are compared with the practice of leadership in the Corinthian Christian community which are reflected in 1 Corinthians 1–6, and contrasted with Paul's own principles of Christian leadership.
2005 / 1-84227-229-2 / 200pp

Stephen Finamore
God, Order and Chaos
René Girard and the Apocalypse
Readers are often disturbed by the images of destruction in the book of Revelation and unsure why they are unleashed after the exaltation of Jesus. This book examines past approaches to these texts and uses René Girard's theories to revive some old ideas and propose some new ones.
2005 / 1-84227-197-0 / approx. 344pp

David G. Firth
Surrendering Retribution in the Psalms
Responses to Violence in the Individual Complaints
In *Surrendering Retribution in the Psalms*, David Firth examines the ways in which the book of Psalms inculcates a model response to violence through the repetition of standard patterns of prayer. Rather than seeking justification for retributive violence, Psalms encourages not only a surrender of the right of retribution to Yahweh, but also sets limits on the retribution that can be sought in imprecations. Arising initially from the author's experience in South Africa, the possibilities of this model to a particular context of violence is then briefly explored.
2005 / 1-84227-337-X / xviii + 154pp

Scott J. Hafemann
Suffering and Ministry in the Spirit
Paul's Defence of His Ministry in II Corinthians 2:14–3:3
Shedding new light on the way Paul defended his apostleship, the author offers a careful, detailed study of 2 Corinthians 2:14–3:3 linked with other key passages throughout 1 and 2 Corinthians. Demonstrating the unity and coherence of Paul's argument in this passage, the author shows that Paul's suffering served as the vehicle for revealing God's power and glory through the Spirit.
2000 / 0-85364-967-7 / xiv + 262pp

Scott J. Hafemann
Paul, Moses and the History of Israel
The Letter/Spirit Contrast and the Argument from Scripture in 2 Corinthians 3
An exegetical study of the call of Moses, the second giving of the Law (Exodus 32–34), the new covenant, and the prophetic understanding of the history of Israel in 2 Corinthians 3. Hafemann's work demonstrates Paul's contextual use of the Old Testament and the essential unity between the Law and the Gospel within the context of the distinctive ministries of Moses and Paul.
2005 / 1-84227-317-5 / xii + 498pp

Douglas S. McComiskey
Lukan Theology in the Light of the Gospel's Literary Structure
Luke's Gospel was purposefully written with theology embedded in its patterned literary structure. A critical analysis of this cyclical structure provides new windows into Luke's interpretation of the individual pericopes comprising the Gospel and illuminates several of his theological interests.
2004 / 1-84227-148-2 / xviii + 388pp

Stephen Motyer
Your Father the Devil?
A New Approach to John and 'The Jews'
Who are 'the Jews' in John's Gospel? Defending John against the charge of antisemitism, Motyer argues that, far from demonising the Jews, the Gospel seeks to present Jesus as 'Good News for Jews' in a late first century setting.
1997 / 0-85364-832-8 / xiv + 260pp

Esther Ng
Reconstructing Christian Origins?
The Feminist Theology of Elizabeth Schüssler Fiorenza: An Evaluation
In a detailed evaluation, the author challenges Elizabeth Schüssler Fiorenza's reconstruction of early Christian origins and her underlying presuppositions. The author also presents her own views on women's roles both then and now.
2002 / 1-84227-055-9 / xxiv + 468pp

Robin Parry
Old Testament Story and Christian Ethics
The Rape of Dinah as a Case Study

What is the role of story in ethics and, more particularly, what is the role of Old Testament story in Christian ethics? This book, drawing on the work of contemporary philosophers, argues that narrative is crucial in the ethical shaping of people and, drawing on the work of contemporary Old Testament scholars, that story plays a key role in Old Testament ethics. Parry then argues that when situated in canonical context Old Testament stories can be reappropriated by Christian readers in their own ethical formation. The shocking story of the rape of Dinah and the massacre of the Shechemites provides a fascinating case study for exploring the parameters within which Christian ethical appropriations of Old Testament stories can live.

2004 / 1-84227-210-1 / xx + 350pp

Ian Paul
Power to See the World Anew
The Value of Paul Ricoeur's Hermeneutic of Metaphor in Interpreting the Symbolism of Revelation 12 and 13

This book is a study of the hermeneutics of metaphor of Paul Ricoeur, one of the most important writers on hermeneutics and metaphor of the last century. It sets out the key points of his theory, important criticisms of his work, and how his approach, modified in the light of these criticisms, offers a methodological framework for reading apocalyptic texts.

2006 / 1-84227-056-7 / approx. 350pp

Robert L. Plummer
Paul's Understanding of the Church's Mission
Did the Apostle Paul Expect the Early Christian Communities to Evangelize?

This book engages in a careful study of Paul's letters to determine if the apostle expected the communities to which he wrote to engage in missionary activity. It helpfully summarizes the discussion on this debated issue, judiciously handling contested texts, and provides a way forward in addressing this critical question. While admitting that Paul rarely explicitly commands the communities he founded to evangelize, Plummer amasses significant incidental data to provide a convincing case that Paul did indeed expect his churches to engage in mission activity. Throughout the study, Plummer progressively builds a theological basis for the church's mission that is both distinctively Pauline and compelling.

2006 / 1-84227-333-7 / approx. 324pp

David Powys
'Hell': A Hard Look at a Hard Question
The Fate of the Unrighteous in New Testament Thought
This comprehensive treatment seeks to unlock the original meaning of terms and phrases long thought to support the traditional doctrine of hell. It concludes that there is an alternative—one which is more biblical, and which can positively revive the rationale for Christian mission.
1997 / 0-85364-831-X / xxii + 478pp

Sorin Sabou
Between Horror and Hope
Paul's Metaphorical Language of Death in Romans 6.1-11
This book argues that Paul's metaphorical language of death in Romans 6.1-11 conveys two aspects: horror and hope. The 'horror' aspect is conveyed by the 'crucifixion' language, and the 'hope' aspect by 'burial' language. The life of the Christian believer is understood, as relationship with sin is concerned ('death to sin'), between these two realities: horror and hope.
2005 / 1-84227-322-1 / approx. 224pp

Rosalind Selby
The Comical Doctrine
The Epistemology of New Testament Hermeneutics
This book argues that the gospel breaks through postmodernity's critique of truth and the referential possibilities of textuality with its gift of grace. With a rigorous, philosophical challenge to modernist and postmodernist assumptions, Selby offers an alternative epistemology to all who would still read with faith *and* with academic credibility.
2005 / 1-84227-212-8 / approx. 350pp

Kiwoong Son
Zion Symbolism in Hebrews
Hebrews 12.18-24 as a Hermeneutical Key to the Epistle
This book challenges the general tendency of understanding the Epistle to the Hebrews against a Hellenistic background and suggests that the Epistle should be understood in the light of the Jewish apocalyptic tradition. The author especially argues for the importance of the theological symbolism of Sinai and Zion (Heb. 12:18-24) as it provides the Epistle's theological background as well as the rhetorical basis of the superiority motif of Jesus throughout the Epistle.
2005 / 1-84227-368-X / approx. 280pp

Kevin Walton
Thou Traveller Unknown
The Presence and Absence of God in the Jacob Narrative
The author offers a fresh reading of the story of Jacob in the book of Genesis through the paradox of divine presence and absence. The work also seeks to make a contribution to Pentateuchal studies by bringing together a close reading of the final text with historical critical insights, doing justice to the text's historical depth, final form and canonical status.
2003 / 1-84227-059-1 / xvi + 238pp

George M. Wieland
The Significance of Salvation
A Study of Salvation Language in the Pastoral Epistles
The language and ideas of salvation pervade the three Pastoral Epistles. This study offers a close examination of their soteriological statements. In all three letters the idea of salvation is found to play a vital paraenetic role, but each also exhibits distinctive soteriological emphases. The results challenge common assumptions about the Pastoral Epistles as a corpus.
2005 / 1-84227-257-8 / approx. 324pp

Alistair Wilson
When Will These Things Happen?
A Study of Jesus as Judge in Matthew 21–25
This study seeks to allow Matthew's carefully constructed presentation of Jesus to be given full weight in the modern evaluation of Jesus' eschatology. Careful analysis of the text of Matthew 21–25 reveals Jesus to be standing firmly in the Jewish prophetic and wisdom traditions as he proclaims and enacts imminent judgement on the Jewish authorities then boldly claims the central role in the final and universal judgement.
2004 / 1-84227-146-6 / xxii + 272pp

Lindsay Wilson
Joseph Wise and Otherwise
The Intersection of Covenant and Wisdom in Genesis 37–50
This book offers a careful literary reading of Genesis 37–50 that argues that the Joseph story contains both strong covenant themes and many wisdom-like elements. The connections between the two helps to explore how covenant and wisdom might intersect in an integrated biblical theology.
2004 / 1-84227-140-7 / xvi + 340pp

Stephen I. Wright
The Voice of Jesus
Studies in the Interpretation of Six Gospel Parables
This literary study considers how the 'voice' of Jesus has been heard in different
periods of parable interpretation, and how the categories of figure and trope may
help us towards a sensitive reading of the parables today.
2000 / 0-85364-975-8 / xiv + 280pp

Paternoster
9 Holdom Avenue,
Bletchley,
Milton Keynes MK1 1QR,
United Kingdom
Web: www.authenticmedia.co.uk/paternoster

July 2005

Paternoster Theological Monographs
(All titles uniform with this volume)
Dates in bold are of projected publication

Emil Bartos
Deification in Eastern Orthodox Theology
An Evaluation and Critique of the Theology of Dumitru Staniloae
Bartos studies a fundamental yet neglected aspect of Orthodox theology: deification. By examining the doctrines of anthropology, christology, soteriology and ecclesiology as they relate to deification, he provides an important contribution to contemporary dialogue between Eastern and Western theologians.
1999 / 0-85364-956-1 / xii + 370pp

Graham Buxton
The Trinity, Creation and Pastoral Ministry
Imaging the Perichoretic God
In this book the author proposes a three-way conversation between theology, science and pastoral ministry. His approach draws on a Trinitarian understanding of God as a relational being of love, whose life 'spills over' into all created reality, human and non-human. By locating human meaning and purpose within God's 'creation-community' this book offers the possibility of a transforming engagement between those in pastoral ministry and the scientific community.
2005 / 1-84227-369-8 / approx. 380 pp

Iain D. Campbell
Fixing the Indemnity
The Life and Work of George Adam Smith
When Old Testament scholar George Adam Smith (1856–1942) delivered the Lyman Beecher lectures at Yale University in 1899, he confidently declared that 'modern criticism has won its war against traditional theories. It only remains to fix the amount of the indemnity.' In this biography, Iain D. Campbell assesses Smith's critical approach to the Old Testament and evaluates its consequences, showing that Smith's life and work still raises questions about the relationship between biblical scholarship and evangelical faith.
2004 / 1-84227-228-4 / xx + 256pp

Tim Chester
Mission and the Coming of God
Eschatology, the Trinity and Mission in the Theology of Jürgen Moltmann
This book explores the theology and missiology of the influential contemporary theologian, Jürgen Moltmann. It highlights the important contribution Moltmann has made while offering a critique of his thought from an evangelical perspective. In so doing, it touches on pertinent issues for evangelical missiology. The conclusion takes Calvin as a starting point, proposing 'an eschatology of the cross' which offers a critique of the over-realised eschatologies in liberation theology and certain forms of evangelicalism.
2006 / 1-84227-320-5 / approx. 224pp

Sylvia Wilkey Collinson
Making Disciples
The Significance of Jesus' Educational Strategy for Today's Church
This study examines the biblical practice of discipling, formulates a definition, and makes comparisons with modern models of education. A recommendation is made for greater attention to its practice today.
2004 / 1-84227-116-4 / xiv + 278pp

Darrell Cosden
A Theology of Work
Work and the New Creation
Through dialogue with Moltmann, Pope John Paul II and others, this book develops a genitive 'theology of work', presenting a theological definition of work and a model for a theological ethics of work that shows work's nature, value and meaning now and eschatologically. Work is shown to be a transformative activity consisting of three dynamically inter-related dimensions: the instrumental, relational and ontological.
2005 / 1-84227-332-9 / xvi + 208pp

Stephen M. Dunning
The Crisis and the Quest
A Kierkegaardian Reading of Charles Williams
Employing Kierkegaardian categories and analysis, this study investigates both the central crisis in Charles Williams's authorship between hermetism and Christianity (Kierkegaard's Religions A and B), and the quest to resolve this crisis, a quest that ultimately presses the bounds of orthodoxy.
2000 / 0-85364-985-5 / xxiv + 254pp

Keith Ferdinando
The Triumph of Christ in African Perspective
A Study of Demonology and Redemption in the African Context
The book explores the implications of the gospel for traditional African fears of occult aggression. It analyses such traditional approaches to suffering and biblical responses to fears of demonic evil, concluding with an evaluation of African beliefs from the perspective of the gospel.
1999 / 0-85364-830-1 / xviii + 450pp

Andrew Goddard
Living the Word, Resisting the World
The Life and Thought of Jacques Ellul
This work offers a definitive study of both the life and thought of the French Reformed thinker Jacques Ellul (1912-1994). It will prove an indispensable resource for those interested in this influential theologian and sociologist and for Christian ethics and political thought generally.
2002 / 1-84227-053-2 / xxiv + 378pp

David Hilborn
The Words of our Lips
Language-Use in Free Church Worship
Studies of liturgical language have tended to focus on the written canons of Roman Catholic and Anglican communities. By contrast, David Hilborn analyses the more extemporary approach of English Nonconformity. Drawing on recent developments in linguistic pragmatics, he explores similarities and differences between 'fixed' and 'free' worship, and argues for the interdependence of each.
2006 / 0-85364-977-4 / approx. 350pp

Roger Hitching
The Church and Deaf People
A Study of Identity, Communication and Relationships with Special Reference to the Ecclesiology of Jürgen Moltmann
In *The Church and Deaf People* Roger Hitching sensitively examines the history and present experience of deaf people and finds similarities between aspects of sign language and Moltmann's theological method that 'open up' new ways of understanding theological concepts.
2003 / 1-84227-222-5 / xxii + 236pp

John G. Kelly
One God, One People
The Differentiated Unity of the People of God in the Theology of
Jürgen Moltmann
The author expounds and critiques Moltmann's doctrine of God and highlights the systematic connections between it and Moltmann's influential discussion of Israel. He then proposes a fresh approach to Jewish–Christian relations building on Moltmann's work using insights from Habermas and Rawls.
2005 / 0-85346-969-3 / approx. 350pp

Mark F.W. Lovatt
Confronting the Will-to-Power
A Reconsideration of the Theology of Reinhold Niebuhr
Confronting the Will-to-Power is an analysis of the theology of Reinhold Niebuhr, arguing that his work is an attempt to identify, and provide a practical theological answer to, the existence and nature of human evil.
2001 / 1-84227-054-0 / xviii + 216pp

Neil B. MacDonald
Karl Barth and the Strange New World within the Bible
Barth, Wittgenstein, and the Metadilemmas of the Enlightenment
Barth's discovery of the strange new world within the Bible is examined in the context of Kant, Hume, Overbeck, and, most importantly, Wittgenstein. MacDonald covers some fundamental issues in theology today: epistemology, the final form of the text and biblical truth-claims.
2000 / 0-85364-970-7 / xxvi + 374pp

Keith A. Mascord
Alvin Plantinga and Christian Apologetics
This book draws together the contributions of the philosopher Alvin Plantinga to the major contemporary challenges to Christian belief, highlighting in particular his ground-breaking work in epistemology and the problem of evil. Plantinga's theory that both theistic and Christian belief is warrantedly basic is explored and critiqued, and an assessment offered as to the significance of his work for apologetic theory and practice.
2005 / 1-84227-256-X / approx. 304pp

Gillian McCulloch
The Deconstruction of Dualism in Theology
With Reference to Ecofeminist Theology and New Age Spirituality
This book challenges eco-theological anti-dualism in Christian theology, arguing that dualism has a twofold function in Christian religious discourse. Firstly, it enables us to express the discontinuities and divisions that are part of the process of reality. Secondly, dualistic language allows us to express the mysteries of divine transcendence/immanence and the survival of the soul without collapsing into monism and materialism, both of which are problematic for Christian epistemology.
2002 / 1-84227-044-3 / xii + 282pp

Leslie McCurdy
Attributes and Atonement
The Holy Love of God in the Theology of P.T. Forsyth
Attributes and Atonement is an intriguing full-length study of P.T. Forsyth's doctrine of the cross as it relates particularly to God's holy love. It includes an unparalleled bibliography of both primary and secondary material relating to Forsyth.
1999 / 0-85364-833-6 / xiv + 328pp

Nozomu Miyahira
Towards a Theology of the Concord of God
A Japanese Perspective on the Trinity
This book introduces a new Japanese theology and a unique Trinitarian formula based on the Japanese intellectual climate: three betweennesses and one concord. It also presents a new interpretation of the Trinity, a co-subordinationism, which is in line with orthodox Trinitarianism; each single person of the Trinity is eternally and equally subordinate (or serviceable) to the other persons, so that they retain the mutual dynamic equality.
2000 / 0-85364-863-8 / xiv + 256pp

Eddy José Muskus
The Origins and Early Development of Liberation Theology in Latin America
With Particular Reference to Gustavo Gutiérrez
This work challenges the fundamental premise of Liberation Theology, 'opting for the poor', and its claim that Christ is found in them. It also argues that Liberation Theology emerged as a direct result of the failure of the Roman Catholic Church in Latin America.
2002 / 0-85364-974-X / xiv + 296pp

Jim Purves
The Triune God and the Charismatic Movement
A Critical Appraisal from a Scottish Perspective
All emotion and no theology? Or a fundamental challenge to reappraise and realign our trinitarian theology in the light of Christian experience? This study of charismatic renewal as it found expression within Scotland at the end of the twentieth century evaluates the use of Patristic, Reformed and contemporary models of the Trinity in explaining the workings of the Holy Spirit.

2004 / 1-84227-321-3 / xxiv + 246pp

Anna Robbins
Methods in the Madness
Diversity in Twentieth-Century Christian Social Ethics
The author compares the ethical methods of Walter Rauschenbusch, Reinhold Niebuhr and others. She argues that unless Christians are clear about the ways that theology and philosophy are expressed practically they may lose the ability to discuss social ethics across contexts, let alone reach effective agreements.

2004 / 1-84227-211-X / xx + 294pp

Ed Rybarczyk
Beyond Salvation
Eastern Orthodoxy and Classical Pentecostalism on Becoming Like Christ
At first glance eastern Orthodoxy and classical Pentecostalism seem quite distinct. This ground-breaking study shows they share much in common, especially as it concerns the experiential elements of following Christ. Both traditions assert that authentic Christianity transcends the wooden categories of modernism.

2004 / 1-84227-144-X / xii + 356pp

Signe Sandsmark
Is World View Neutral Education Possible and Desirable?
A Christian Response to Liberal Arguments
(Published jointly with The Stapleford Centre)
This book discusses reasons for belief in world view neutrality, and argues that 'neutral' education will have a hidden, but strong world view influence. It discusses the place for Christian education in the common school.

2000 / 0-85364-973-1 / xiv + 182pp

Hazel Sherman
Reading Zechariah
The Allegorical Tradition of Biblical Interpretation through the Commentary of
Didymus the Blind and Theodore of Mopsuestia
A close reading of the commentary on Zechariah by Didymus the Blind
alongside that of Theodore of Mopsuestia suggests that popular categorising of
Antiochene and Alexandrian biblical exegesis as 'historical' or 'allegorical' is
inadequate and misleading.
2005 / 1-84227-213-6 / approx. 280pp

Andrew Sloane
On Being a Christian in the Academy
Nicholas Wolterstorff and the Practice of Christian Scholarship
An exposition and critical appraisal of Nicholas Wolterstorff's epistemology in
the light of the philosophy of science, and an application of his thought to the
practice of Christian scholarship.
2003 / 1-84227-058-3 / xvi + 274pp

Damon W.K. So
Jesus' Revelation of His Father
A Narrative-Conceptual Study of the Trinity with Special Reference to
Karl Barth
This book explores the trinitarian dynamics in the context of Jesus' revelation of
his Father in his earthly ministry with references to key passages in Matthew's
Gospel. It develops from the exegeses of these passages a non-linear concept of
revelation which links Jesus' communion with his Father to his revelatory words
and actions through a nuanced understanding of the Holy Spirit, with references
to K. Barth, G.W.H. Lampe, J.D.G. Dunn and E. Irving.
2005 / 1-84227-323-X / approx. 380pp

Daniel Strange
The Possibility of Salvation Among the Unevangelised
An Analysis of Inclusivism in Recent Evangelical Theology
For evangelical theologians the 'fate of the unevangelised' impinges upon
fundamental tenets of evangelical identity. The position known as 'inclusivism',
defined by the belief that the unevangelised can be ontologically saved by Christ
whilst being epistemologically unaware of him, has been defended most
vigorously by the Canadian evangelical Clark H. Pinnock. Through a detailed
analysis and critique of Pinnock's work, this book examines a cluster of issues
surrounding the unevangelised and its implications for christology, soteriology
and the doctrine of revelation.
2002 / 1-84227-047-8 / xviii + 362pp

Scott Swain
God According to the Gospel
Biblical Narrative and the Identity of God in the Theology of Robert W. Jenson
Robert W. Jenson is one of the leading voices in contemporary Trinitarian theology. His boldest contribution in this area concerns his use of biblical narrative both to ground and explicate the Christian doctrine of God. *God According to the Gospel* critically examines Jenson's proposal and suggests an alternative way of reading the biblical portrayal of the triune God.
2006 / 1-84227-258-6 / approx. 180pp

Justyn Terry
The Justifying Judgement of God
A Reassessment of the Place of Judgement in the Saving Work of Christ
The argument of this book is that judgement, understood as the whole process of bringing justice, is the primary metaphor of atonement, with others, such as victory, redemption and sacrifice, subordinate to it. Judgement also provides the proper context for understanding penal substitution and the call to repentance, baptism, eucharist and holiness.
2005 / 1-84227-370-1 / approx. 274 pp

Graham Tomlin
The Power of the Cross
Theology and the Death of Christ in Paul, Luther and Pascal
This book explores the theology of the cross in St Paul, Luther and Pascal. It offers new perspectives on the theology of each, and some implications for the nature of power, apologetics, theology and church life in a postmodern context.
1999 / 0-85364-984-7 / xiv + 344pp

Adonis Vidu
Postliberal Theological Method
A Critical Study
The postliberal theology of Hans Frei, George Lindbeck, Ronald Thiemann, John Milbank and others is one of the more influential contemporary options. This book focuses on several aspects pertaining to its theological method, specifically its understanding of background, hermeneutics, epistemic justification, ontology, the nature of doctrine and, finally, Christological method.
2005 / 1-84227-395-7 / approx. 324pp

Graham J. Watts
Revelation and the Spirit
*A Comparative Study of the Relationship between the Doctrine of Revelation
and Pneumatology in the Theology of Eberhard Jüngel and of
Wolfhart Pannenberg*
The relationship between revelation and pneumatology is relatively unexplored.
This approach offers a fresh angle on two important twentieth century
theologians and raises pneumatological questions which are theologically crucial
and relevant to mission in a postmodern culture.
2005 / 1-84227-104-0 / xxii + 232pp

Nigel G. Wright
Disavowing Constantine
*Mission, Church and the Social Order in the Theologies of John Howard Yoder
and Jürgen Moltmann*
This book is a timely restatement of a radical theology of church and state in the
Anabaptist and Baptist tradition. Dr Wright constructs his argument in dialogue
and debate with Yoder and Moltmann, major contributors to a free church
perspective.
2000 / 0-85364-978-2 / xvi + 252pp

Paternoster:
thinking faith

Paternoster
9 Holdom Avenue,
Bletchley,
Milton Keynes MK1 1QR,
United Kingdom
Web: www.authenticmedia.co.uk/paternoster